(SHAKEEL ZUBAIR)
Wing Commander
Pakistan Air Force.

30 NOV, 2000

THE STORY OF THE
PAKISTAN
AIR FORCE

1988 – 1998

A BATTLE AGAINST ODDS

PAF BOOK CLUB

Directorate of Education

THE STORY OF THE
PAKISTAN
AIR FORCE

1988 – 1998

A BATTLE AGAINST ODDS

SHAHEEN
FOUNDATION

First published 2000

ISBN 969-8553-00-2

Produced by
Oxford University Press.
Printed by
Asian Packages (Pvt) Ltd., Karachi.
Published by
Shaheen Foundation.
13-L Commercial Area,
F7-2, Islamabad, Pakistan.

CONTENTS

In Tribute

To
the successive top leadership of
Pakistan's air arm, for steering this
committed fighting force through a
decade of unexpected challenges
and upheavals that demanded
exceptional competence and
courage to inspire and to draw forth
the very best from the men and
women who together make up the
Pakistan Air Force.

THEN AND NOW

On 13 April 1948, the Father of the Nation, while addressing a small band of enthusiastic airmen at the fledgling nation's Air Force Flying School, delivered the following historic message:

A country without a strong Air Force is at the mercy of any aggressor; Pakistan must build up her Air Force as quickly as possible. It must be an efficient air force, second to none.

The Quaid-i-Azam addressing the parade at Risalpur on 13 April 1948

Exactly forty-nine years later, Air Marshal (Rtd.) Asghar Khan who, as Officer Commanding, Royal Pakistan Air Force Flying Training School, had received the Quaid and heard his inspiring words, was speaking as Chief Guest at the Golden Jubilee Parade of the PAF Academy, Risalpur. He had this to say:

It goes to the credit of the Pakistan Air Force that it took the Quaid's words with a heroic spirit, and has since lived up to his expectations. The PAF is known today, as it was then, for its discipline and professional competence. It has acquitted itself with credit in both the wars in which it was called upon to participate. Remember: present conditions require you not only to be 'second to none' as the Quaid commanded you, but with the odds so heavily against you today, you must be far more competent than any possible adversary in the difficult and exacting field in which it is your privilege to serve. Pakistan must not be as the Quaid had said, 'at the mercy of any aggressor.'

Air Marshal (Retd.) Asghar Khan addressing the parade at
PAF Academy Risalpur on 13 April 1997

"The application of Air Power is now a profession of considerable complexity demanding technological mastery, a sense of command, structure, speed, fire, distance and impact in proportions quite different from those applicable on land and sea. Not greater, nor lesser, but different. It demands discrete professionalism which must not be subordinate to the primary interests of another service, that would lead directly to the subordination of air power itself to the detriment of all services."

AVM Tony Mason
Air Power,
A Centennial Appraisal
Brasseys, 1994

Foreword

The Story of the Pakistan Air Force (1988) adequately covered 40 years of existence of the Pakistan Air Force. The book was well received both at home and abroad for its broad outlook and objectivity. Lest the fog of time should thicken over events of intervening years, I thought it would be appropriate to record them before their possible recession to oblivion—and, of course, to provide much-needed continuity to the earlier work. That is how the idea of bringing out second volume of *The Story of the Pakistan Air Force*, covering the period 1988-1998, came to my mind. One would hesitate to call it history because of its limited canvas — and our close proximity to annals of the past one decade — to impart enough historical vision and perspective. Yet, the value of a book of this nature for future historians can hardly be disputed.

I would like to compliment the entire team of PAF History Project on fruition of their painstaking efforts over the last one and a half years. Writing about contemporary happenings is always a difficult proposition. Yet, what has turned out can be fairly described as an objective appraisal of available information within a limited span of time. I am sure this new volume would greatly interest all those who have closely followed PAF's progress over the years — those who don the PAF uniform, the personnel of sister-services, the PAF veterans and the wide spectrum of readers at large.

(PARVAIZ MEHDI QURESHI)
Air Chief Marshal
Chief of the Air Staff

29th May 2000

PREFACE

The Story of the PAF published in 1988 was the first authentic chronicle of the events of the Service. It covered a period of over forty years, tracing the beginnings of the nascent RPAF from the chaotic conditions at the time of Partition to the year 1987. When in July 1998, I was asked by the then Deputy Chief of the Air Staff (Trg.) if I was willing to update the previous book, I was both overwhelmed and apprehensive. Overwhelmed because I was being given the honour of writing about the Service with which I had spent most of my adult life, and apprehensive because it seemed a daunting task. It was explained to me that the Chief of the Air Staff was of the opinion that one did not have to wait for another four decades to get to know how the Service had progressed over the years. That is how the idea of this book emerged.

At the very outset it was agreed that the idea of updating the previous book was unworkable. Instead it was decided that a second volume covering the decade 1988-1998 be compiled. I realized at once that the decade was one of the most difficult ones that the PAF had had to face. The Afghan War was at its fiercest before winding down in 1989. The country was subjected to all kinds of sanctions and, out of all the Services, they affected the PAF the most. We set about the task assigned to us in right earnest. A team of officers from different branches, with supporting staff, was in position by about November 1998. Administrative support such as computers and other equipment was also arranged for the project which came to be known as 'Project PAF History'.

The team was given access to the relevant official documents and to the Air Staff at Air Headquarters. In response to a letter from the VCAS, the Commands, Bases and Units started sending us data which included all reports of work undertaken during the previous ten years. In between, the team members visited selected Bases and Units to obtain firsthand information from their respective records. Another valuable source of information was interviews held with the serving and retired officers. Those interviewed included four former Chiefs of the Air Staff, Air Chief Marshals Jamal, Hakimullah, Farooq Feroze and Abbas Khattak. The interviews were not limited to senior officers only. All those who had played a significant role in some form or the other were invited to relate their experiences. This was especially applicable to the participants in the Afghan War, an account of which had not been published before.

During the initial period of the Project, the major task was to organize and collate all the material that had been collected. The Project Team applied itself to this monumental task energetically and with utmost devotion, and the outcome is this book. We have tried to base our narrative on facts which came to light during our research, and have not allowed ourselves to be influenced by opinions expressed by anyone, irrespective of his position in the past or present hierarchy. We hope that readers will find the outcome of our efforts readable, absorbing, and a worthwhile addition to their library.

This book would have not seen the light of day but for the personal interest and encouragement of the Chief of the Air Staff, Air Chief Marshal Parvaiz Mehdi Qureshi. He monitored the progress of the book closely, and helped remove the organizational and administrative hurdles that came in our way. A great deal of credit goes to Air Vice Marshal Parvez Nawaz, the then DCAS (Trg.) who was deeply involved in the project from the very beginning, until he was assigned to the DP Division as DGDP. He ensured that the team was provided with the wherewithal to undertake this task. The Vice Chief of the Air Staff and the other PSOs readily extended any help that was needed. One must also record the manner in which the then Acting DCAS (Trg.) Air Commodore Abdul Ghaffar and the incumbent DCAS (Trg.) Air Vice Marshal Arshad Rashid Sethi, have provided unstinted support to the Project.

One could go on giving the names of all those who have helped us in accomplishing our task but the former CAS, Air Chief Marshal Jamal A. Khan, needs particular mention. He perused the draft with a fine tooth comb, and made corrections and suggestions that have immensely enhanced the quality of the text. There were others such as Air Commodore Shahzad Chaudhry, the PSO to CAS, and Group Captain Hali, DPR, whose suggestions were very relevant and were therefore incorporated in the book.

Finally, this book would not have materialized but for the tireless efforts of the members of our team, i.e., Air Commodore Zulqarnain, Group Captain Zia, Group Captain Talat, Wing Commander Satti and Squadron Leader Naeem. Even the most difficult circumstances never discouraged them and they continued to work day and night. The staff provided to the team also deserves special praise for the support they provided, despite several handicaps, usual in such undertakings. It was indeed a team effort.

May 2000   Air Marshal A. RASHID SHAIKH (Retd.)
                                                          Project PAF History

THE PAF
AT A GLANCE
(A comparison, 1988-1998)

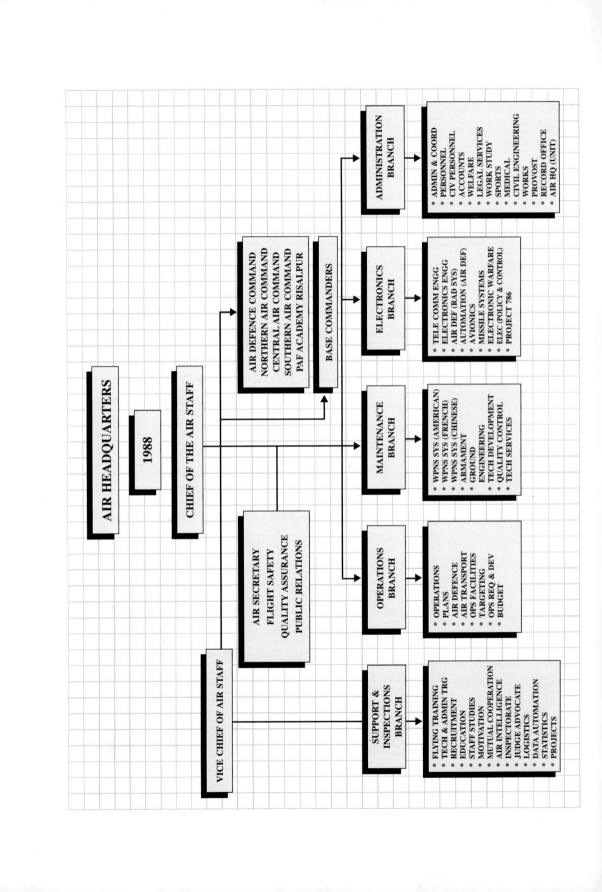

AIR HEADQUARTERS

1988

CHIEF OF THE AIR STAFF

VICE CHIEF OF AIR STAFF

AIR SECRETARY
FLIGHT SAFETY
QUALITY ASSURANCE
PUBLIC RELATIONS

AIR DEFENCE COMMAND
NORTHERN AIR COMMAND
CENTRAL AIR COMMAND
SOUTHERN AIR COMMAND
PAF ACADEMY RISALPUR

BASE COMMANDERS

ADMINISTRATION BRANCH

* ADMIN & COORD
* PERSONNEL
* CIV PERSONNEL
* ACCOUNTS
* WELFARE
* LEGAL SERVICES
* WORK STUDY
* SPORTS
* MEDICAL
* CIVIL ENGINEERING
* WORKS
* PROVOST
* RECORD OFFICE
* AIR HQ (UNIT)

ELECTRONICS BRANCH

* TELE COMM ENGG
* ELECTRONICS ENGG
* AIR DEF (RAD SYS)
* AUTOMATION (AIR DEF)
* AVIONICS
* MISSILE SYSTEMS
* ELECTRONIC WARFARE
* ELEC (POLICY & CONTROL)
* PROJECT 786

MAINTENANCE BRANCH

* WPNS SYS (AMERICAN)
* WPNS SYS (FRENCH)
* WPNS SYS (CHINESE)
* ARMAMENT
* GROUND ENGINEERING
* TECH DEVELOPMENT
* QUALITY CONTROL
* TECH SERVICES

OPERATIONS BRANCH

* OPERATIONS
* PLANS
* AIR DEFENCE
* AIR TRANSPORT
* OPS FACILITIES
* TARGETING
* OPS REQ & DEV
* BUDGET

SUPPORT & INSPECTIONS BRANCH

* FLYING TRAINING
* TECH & ADMIN TRG
* RECRUITMENT
* EDUCATION
* STAFF STUDIES
* MOTIVATION
* MUTUAL COOPERATION
* AIR INTELLIGENCE
* INSPECTORATE
* JUDGE ADVOCATE
* LOGISTICS
* DATA AUTOMATION
* STATISTICS
* PROJECTS

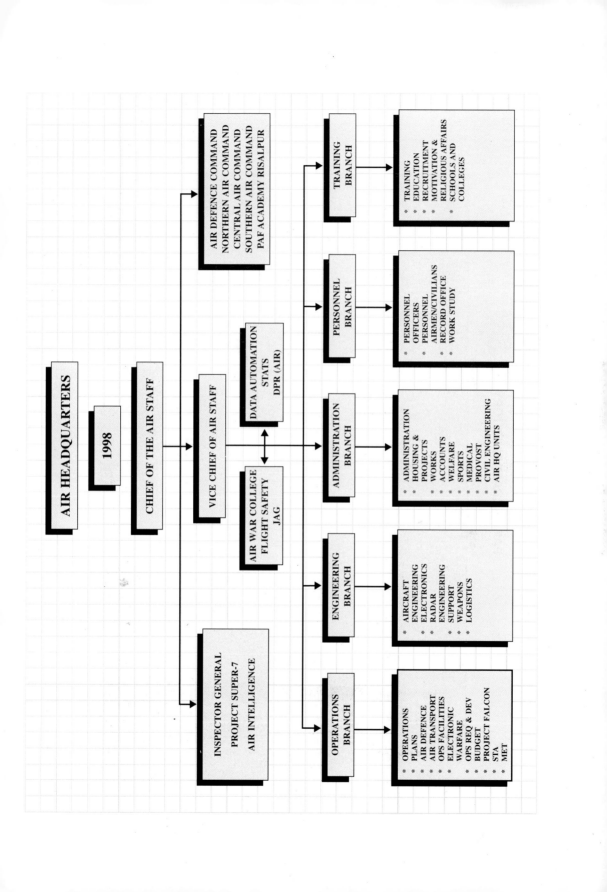

AIR HEADQUARTERS

1998

CHIEF OF THE AIR STAFF

INSPECTOR GENERAL
PROJECT SUPER-7
AIR INTELLIGENCE

VICE CHIEF OF AIR STAFF

AIR DEFENCE COMMAND
NORTHERN AIR COMMAND
CENTRAL AIR COMMAND
SOUTHERN AIR COMMAND
PAF ACADEMY RISALPUR

DATA AUTOMATION
STATS
DPR (AIR)

AIR WAR COLLEGE
FLIGHT SAFETY
JAG

OPERATIONS BRANCH

* OPERATIONS
* PLANS
* AIR DEFENCE
* AIR TRANSPORT
* OPS FACILITIES
* ELECTRONIC WARFARE
* OPS REQ & DEV
* BUDGET
* PROJECT FALCON
* STA
* MET

ENGINEERING BRANCH

* AIRCRAFT ENGINEERING
* ELECTRONICS
* RADAR ENGINEERING
* SUPPORT
* WEAPONS
* LOGISTICS

ADMINISTRATION BRANCH

* ADMINISTRATION
* HOUSING & PROJECTS
* WORKS
* ACCOUNTS
* WELFARE
* SPORTS
* MEDICAL
* PROVOST
* CIVIL ENGINEERING
* AIR HQ UNITS

PERSONNEL BRANCH

* PERSONNEL OFFICERS
* PERSONNEL AIRMEN/CIVILIANS
* RECORD OFFICE
* WORK STUDY

TRAINING BRANCH

* TRAINING
* EDUCATION
* RECRUITMENT
* MOTIVATION & RELIGIOUS AFFAIRS
* SCHOOLS AND COLLEGES

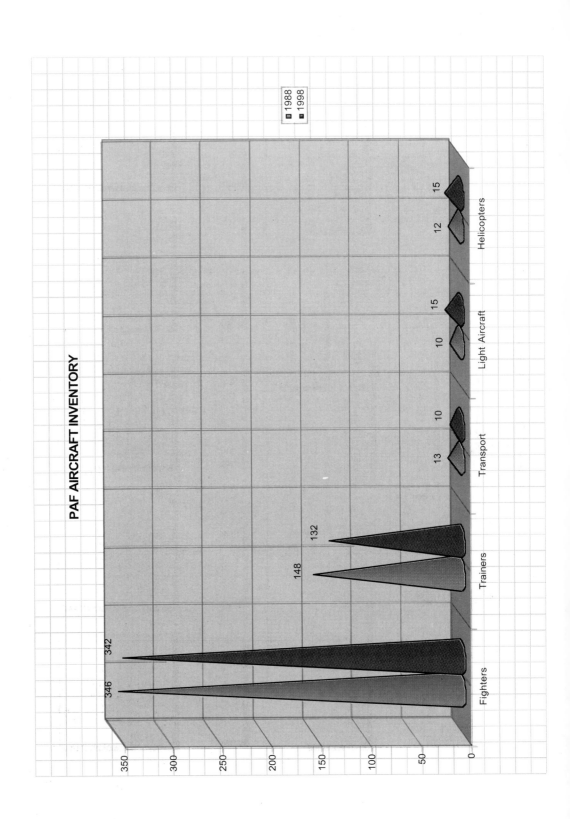

PAF AIRCRAFT INVENTORY

1988
1998

	Fighters	Trainers	Transport	Light Aircraft	Helicopters
1988	346	148	13	10	12
1998	342	132	10	15	15

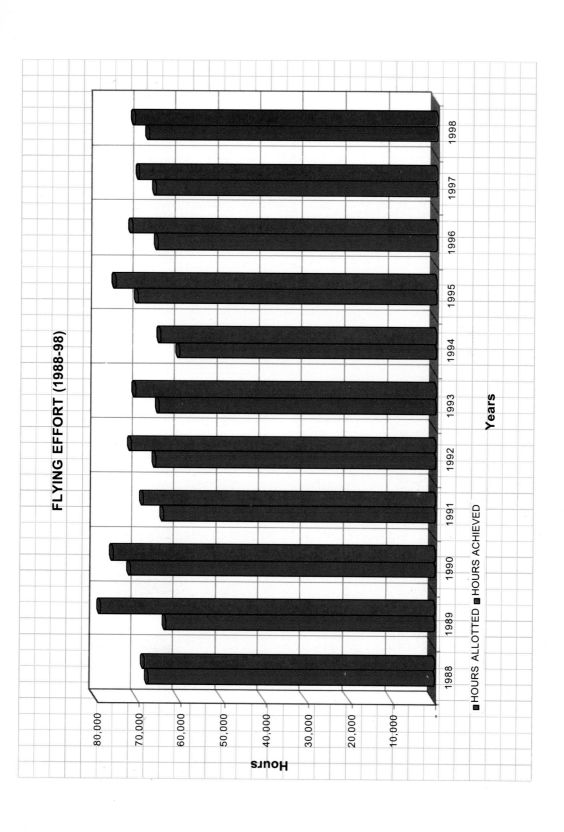

FLYING EFFORT (1988-98)

Hours

80,000
70,000
60,000
50,000
40,000
30,000
20,000
10,000

1988 1989 1990 1991 1992 1993 1994 1995 1996 1997 1998

Years

■ HOURS ALLOTTED ■ HOURS ACHIEVED

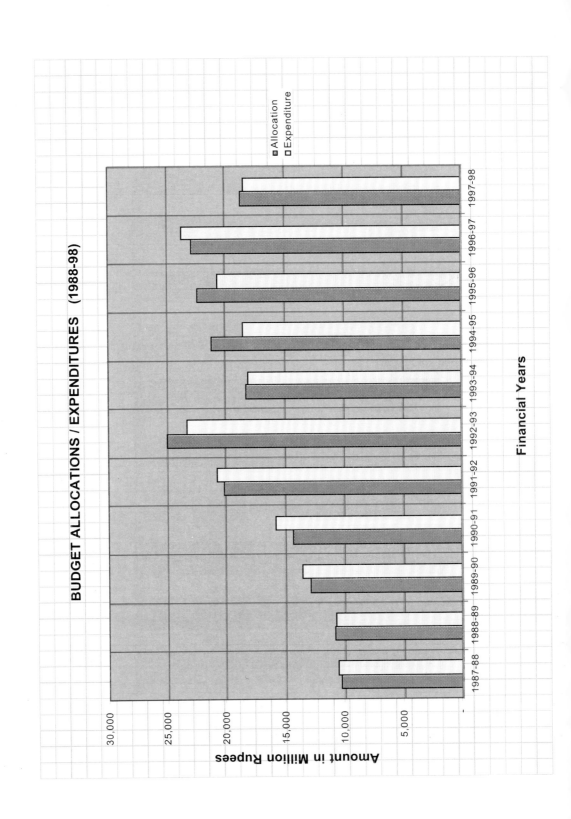

BUDGET ALLOCATIONS / EXPENDITURES (1988-98)

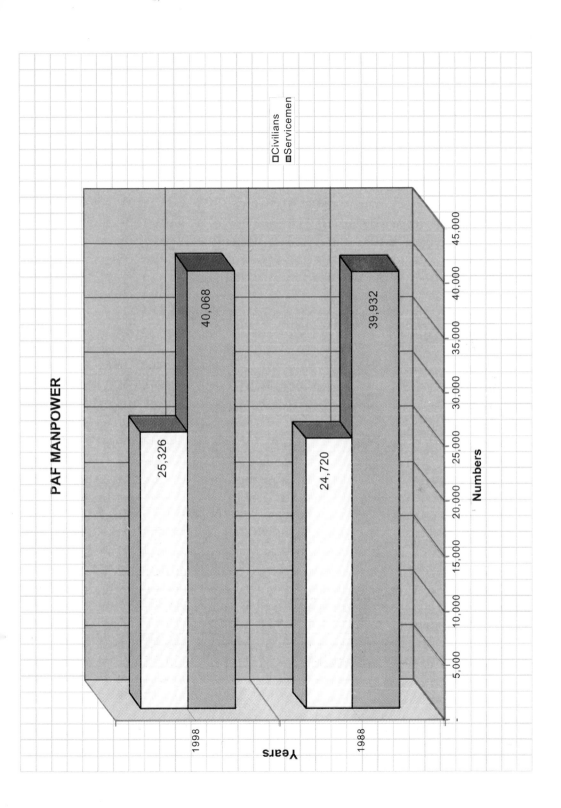

PAF MANPOWER

□Civilians
■Servicemen

Numbers

Years

1998

1988

40,068

25,326

39,932

24,720

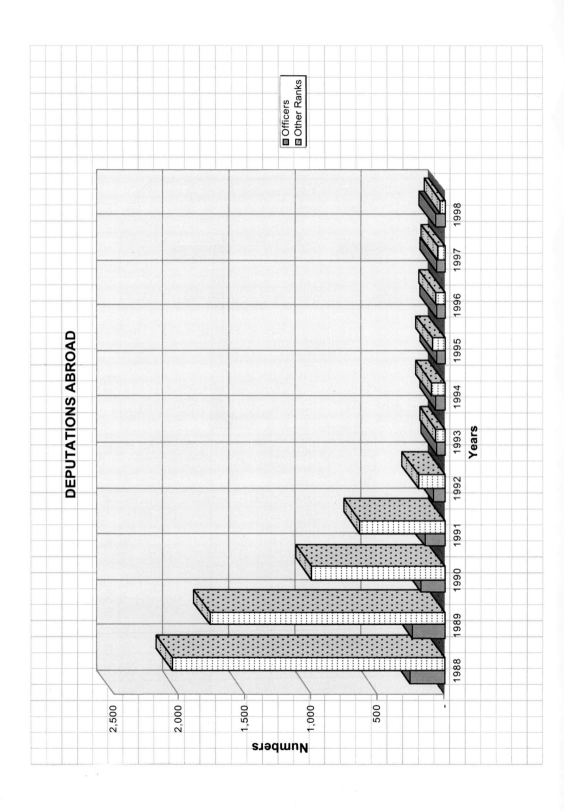

DEPUTATIONS ABROAD

Numbers

Years

Officers
Other Ranks

2,500
2,000
1,500
1,000
500
-

1988
1989
1990
1991
1992
1993
1994
1995
1996
1997
1998

AN
INVENTORY
OF PAF
AIRCRAFT
1998

Formation of F-16, F-7, A-5 and Mirage aircraft

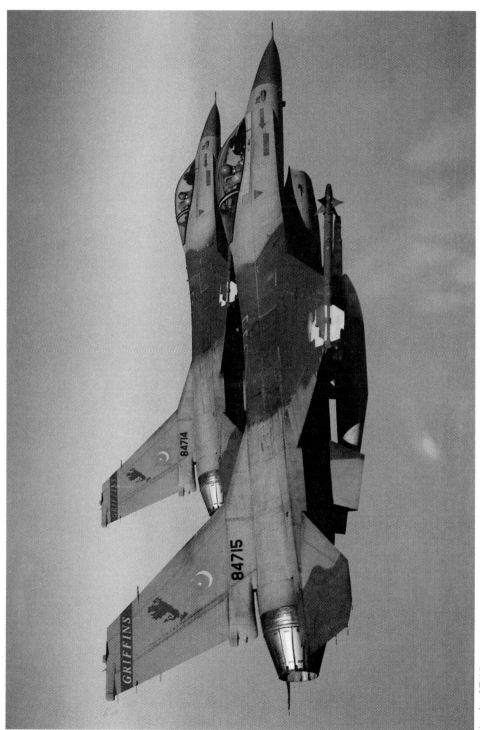

A pair of F-16s

A formation of F-7Ps

F-6

FT-5

K-8

T-37s flying over Islamabad

Boeing 707

C-130

Falcon DA-20

F-27 Foker

Y-12

Piper Seneca-II

Beach Baron

Cessna-172

Mushshaq

Allouette-III

تُندیِ بادِ مخالف سے نہ گھبرا اے عقاب

یہ تو چلتی ہے تجھے اُونچا اُڑانے کے لیے

1 THE CHEQUERED DECADE

Momentous Milestones

In the barren hills of Chagai in Balochistan, Pakistan tested its first group of nuclear devices on 28 May 1998. The events of that day, when Pakistan went overtly nuclear, would have a profound effect on the future course of events, not only in Pakistan but in the whole region and perhaps the rest of the world. There was a sea-change in the security scenario and strategists the world over were busy revising their theories and predictions. Pakistan was forced to abandon its nuclear ambiguity—for which it had had to suffer heavily for nearly two decades—because of the brazen manner in which India conducted its nuclear explosions on 11 and 13 May 1998 and then tried to intimidate Pakistan with its new found nuclear might. Despite persuasions and temptations of unlimited assistance from some of the mightiest in the world, Pakistan could not but respond to India's blatant display of naked power. The introduction of nuclear weapons in the region, specially in the context of India-Pakistan relations, would indeed entail drastic revisions in their respective strategies. How has the strategic balance been disturbed and what steps would be required to restore the equilibrium and at what cost? Questions such as these would no doubt be engaging the minds of those entrusted with the responsibilities for the security of the nation. The PAF has a vital stake in the new development and no doubt it will, as always, rise to the occasion. The fact of the matter is that the introduction of nuclear weapons in subcontinental politics will be a major factor in the formulation of strategies as we enter the new millennium, and a major landmark in the life of the nation.

A decade earlier, another fateful event had altered the course of Pakistan's history. On the afternoon of 17 August 1988, a PAF C-130 transport aircraft crashed, under clearly suspicious circumstances, soon after taking off from Bahawalpur. All thirty-one on board were killed, among them General Ziaul Haq, the President of Pakistan. Travelling back to Islamabad with the President were several senior military officers of Pakistan and the American Ambassador with his US Army Advisor. They had gone to the Bahawalpur Corps area earlier that day to witness a demonstration of the latest American M-1 tank being evaluated at that time by the Pakistan Army. The accident was a tragedy of great magnitude not only for the Air Force, which prided itself on its safety record, but also for the nation. The loss of so many important lives, including that of the head of the state, was bound to affect the destiny of the nation. General Zia's eleven-year rule had come to an end abruptly, and the nation had to make a new beginning. The PAF as a Service had to adapt itself to a new set of leaders and a new form of government. This transition was largely smooth because the PAF's professional orientation and its priorities were duly recognized by all the governments that came into power subsequently.

The C-130 crash attracted global attention owing to President Zia's decisive role in the Afghan War. The C-130s had been flying with a good safety record all over the world for over four decades, and certain features of this crash were very unusual. The PAF, through a high-powered investigation team, identified the most likely causes of the accident. Since the C-130 crash victims also included the US Ambassador and his Chief of the Office of Defence Representative in Pakistan (ODRP), additional teams of the US Government and the USAF carried out their own investigations and also exchanged information with the members of the PAF inquiry team. Although the actual cause remains shrouded in mystery, from all indications it appeared to be a case of sabotage engineered through some sophisticated means. This could have been facilitated by some laxity in security of the VIP aircraft by the agencies responsible for it. Whatever the cause, this tragic accident was a precursor of events in the decade that followed.

Pre-1988 Survey

In March 1988, Air Chief Marshal Hakimullah assumed command of the PAF. There were several events in the preceding years, when Air Chief Marshal Jamal A. Khan was at the helm of affairs, which were very significant and had their due impact on the Air Force in the subsequent years.

Since its very inception, the PAF had prided itself on the credo of its professionalism, single-minded devotion to the fulfilment of its assigned role in the defence of the country, and on nurturing the traditions of integrity of character, dedication to service, and selflessness. However, over the years, some of these values seemed to have eroded and the image of the Service was under threat of being besmeared. Of course, no organization, even a closely knit and highly disciplined body such as the Air Force, can be an island of all that is noble and desirable, when values and standards and ethics are on the slide in the rest of the country. It was bound to be affected, as it indeed was, although on a much smaller scale. Personal interests, inter-branch rivalry, influence peddling, misrepresentation of facts were some of the evils that seemed to be creeping into the Service in the eighties, which called for all out efforts to stem the rot. One of the first tasks undertaken by Air Chief Marshal Jamal was to highlight the

detrimental effects of this slide on the efficiency and effectiveness of the Service. Thus the publication of a PAF Doctrine, AFM Command 1, and its wide circulation within the Air Force, was meant to provide a permanent source of guidance for all those who don the PAF uniform.

The winter of 1986 witnessed an event that could have resulted in an India-Pakistan war but for the timely action taken by Pakistan. The Indian Army decided to conduct a large scale exercise, 'Brass Tacks.' This military exercise, conducted close to the Pakistan border in the south, has been termed as probably the largest to be held after the end of the Second World War. It was conducted while the Afghan War was at its fiercest, thus Pakistan requiring to cope with a two-front war situation. India's aim seemed to be to intimidate Pakistan politically, and to coerce it into submission with its military might. It was also surmised at that time that should any chinks appear in Pakistan's armour, India would seize the opportunity to go for a military solution. Pakistan saw through the game and through deft diplomatic moves, supported by appropriate military deployment, frustrated the Indian designs. Indians had to prematurely call off the exercise and redeploy in order to counter Pakistani counter moves. The PAF worked very closely with the Army and was stretched to the limit to deploy its assets on wartime footing without compromising its commitments on the Afghan border. It was a challenge that the Air Force met in concert with the other two Services to thwart India's aggressive designs.

In 1986, a major organizational shift, which was long overdue, became the subject of some ill informed criticism. The College of Aeronautical Engineering (CAE), which was established at PAF Base Korangi in the sixties, with USAF cooperation, and had built up a reputation for its academic excellence, was shifted to PAF Academy, Risalpur, which had long been the training institution for PAF pilots. A decision in principle to have the initial training for all its officer cadre at Risalpur had been taken in the 1970s, and the PAF had begun construction of a modern campus for the Academy in 1978. The campus was completed in 1986 and the CAE was moved to Risalpur. The new, university-like complex of facilities was meant to forge greater combat cohesion within the officer corps and to develop lasting comradeship amongst officers who had to work together in peace and war. It was also aimed at optimizing the limited Air Force resources. Unfortunately, this move was subjected to unwarranted criticism by some interested quarters who even tried to make political capital out of it. Timely action by the then Chief of the Air Staff to brief the President, the Prime Minister, and the others concerned in the hierarchy, helped to quell this mischief. Consequently, the CAE now functions as an integral component of the PAF Academy at Risalpur and the benefits of this change are visible in terms of greater understanding, better camaraderie and most importantly, significant contribution to operational effectiveness.

An event of significance during the period under review that merits special mention is the appointment of Air Marshal Azim Daudpota as the first and the only non-local commander of the Air Force of Zimbabwe (AFZ). It was in 1983 that the President of Zimbabwe, during a Non-Aligned summit, requested the late President Ziaul Haq for PAF assistance for his country's Air Force. He asked for an Air Marshal who could be appointed as the Commander of the Air Force of Zimbabwe. Air Marshal Daudpota (then AVM), was selected by the President for the special assignment and given the local rank of Air Marshal (He was subsequently confirmed in

Air Marshal Azim Daudpota as Commander AFZ

that rank). A team of officers and airmen was picked to assist him in his task of rebuilding the AFZ.

Air Marshal Daudpota's appointment as Commander of the Air Force of Zimbabwe was approved by that country's Parliament before he assumed command on 24 July 1983. During his tenure in Zimbabwe, Air Marshal Daudpota not only helped a demoralized and devastated AFZ to stand on its feet but also groomed a local, Air Marshal Jesiah Tungamirai, to take over when he left Zimbabwe in January 1986. On his departure, he was awarded the second highest medal, the Zimbabwe Order-of-Merit in the Class of Commander, by the President and Prime Minister of Zimbabwe, for his meritorious service as Commander AFZ.

PAF's Role in the Afghan War

The Soviet invasion of Afghanistan in 1979, and the fighting that raged for nearly a decade, posed manifold and complex problems for Pakistan. Most of all it posed a menacing security threat to the country, which had to be countered through both political and military means. Militarily, Pakistan had always been geared to face the threat to its eastern borders but had neither the infrastructure nor the wherewithal to simultaneously fight a two-front war. The Soviet Union and India were linked with each other through a 'Treaty of Friendship', signed in 1971 on the eve of Pakistan's dismemberment, and together they could land Pakistan in a nutcracker situation. During this period, the two countries coordinated their activities on several occasions to pressurize Pakistan not to support the Afghan cause. The political leadership had decided that acquiescing in Soviet occupation of Afghanistan would not only betray a neighbour but would also eliminate a buffer against Soviet advance in the area. Also, there was no guarantee against further Soviet expansionist designs threatening Pakistan's sovereignty.

Under these circumstances, the PAF and the Pakistan Army were called upon to use their assets to stem the tide on the western front and at the same time not reduce their vigil on the eastern border. The PAF had hardly any infrastructure to make it effective on the western border. It had only two airfields at Peshawar and Quetta. Its air defence assets, especially the low-looking radars, could not be effectively deployed due to the problems of terrain and logistics. The PAF also needed modern weapon systems to deal effectively with the kind of threat posed from across the border. The frequent air violations of Pakistan's airspace, to attack and harass Afghan refugees, built up pressure on the PAF to meet this threat. It was under these circumstances that the PAF had to bargain hard with the US Government to acquire the F-16 aircraft, and thereafter PAF's involvement became meaningful.

However, throughout the war, the PAF was required to operate under stringent Rules of Engagement (ROEs). Forbidden to fly in 'hot pursuit' across the border, the PAF aircraft were not allowed to shoot any aircraft unless the pilot was sure that the debris of the enemy aircraft would fall within Pakistan territory. Added to the complexity of the issue was the question of the detection of intruding aircraft who indulged in a hit-and-run type of air violations. The intermittent and short track lengths available to the ground radars made it very difficult to intercept these raids. Nevertheless, the PAF rose to the occasion and deployed mainly its F-16 force to the maximum limit. It had to fly daily Combat Air Patrols (CAPs)—best known as 'West-Cap'—at wartime rates along the Afghan border to deter or deny any penetrations by hostile aircraft targeting the Mujahideen. Despite many restrictions and limitations imposed due to political factors, the pilots and the ground controllers together managed to shoot down eight Soviet/Afghan aircraft, and there were many that were let off only because of the uncertainty about the debris falling on the Pakistan side of the border.

The timely induction of F-16s and the deployment of scarce air defence assets in some very inhospitable and difficult terrain enabled the PAF to effectively minimize the menace of air intrusions from across the border. The PAF repeatedly highlighted the urgent need for obtaining AWACS type aircraft and how this would add substantially to the PAF's interception capability. Despite these efforts, the US Government could not be persuaded to release this system. The PAF's commitment during the Afghan War was not without its detrimental effects. The intense CAP flying caused a war-like liquidation of spares and the type of flying (CAPs) hindered the squadrons' training capacity to produce new combat-ready pilots.

The PAF's role in the Afghan War and its operations in support of the other two Services, did not receive adequate recognition by the decision makers at that time and even less by the governments that followed. The heavy consumption of spares and the wear and tear of the equipment needed large doses of spares replenishment which was not provided for in the budget of subsequent years. Perhaps the PAF, keeping up its tradition of maintaining a low profile, also did not project its critical role, under the most difficult and unconventional circumstances, in bringing about the end of Soviet invasion in Afghanistan. Nor did it call attention to the cost it had to bear.

Pressler Strikes

With the winding down of the Afghan War and withdrawal of the Soviet forces from Afghanistan, the US interest in the region virtually evaporated. The main objective of US support to Pakistan and the Mujahideens was to compel the Soviet Union to vacate Afghanistan. During the ten years that the fighting raged in Afghanistan, the US Government had turned a blind eye to Pakistan's nuclear programme despite the passing of the Pakistan-specific Pressler Amendment by the Congress. Suddenly, it seems, the US President woke up to the reality that Pakistan's nuclear programme was weapons-oriented and that it attracted the punitive provisions of the Pressler Amendment. Pakistan, which had been living from year to year under the shadow of this infamous piece of US legislation, had hoped that the US President would continue to give it the waiver in return for all the sacrifices and help given by it in serving the US's global interest. But, once again, the point was driven home that a country's national interest reigns supreme, and that since giving a waiver no longer

served the US interest, it would not continue to do so.

The impact of the Pressler restrictions was damaging to Pakistan's defence potential in general, but its most severe effect was felt by the PAF. Just a year before, after a detailed review of force structure for the year 1991 and beyond, the PAF had arrived at the conclusion that a mix of F-16s, Mirages and F-7 (Chinese version of Mig-21) would serve its requirements for the next twenty years or so. Based on the review, the PAF had placed orders for seventy-one F-16 aircraft (eleven from the funds available from the old US-supported sales programme and sixty from its own funds). This contract was placed in jeopardy although Pakistan continued to pay its installments under the expectation that the US Government would soon relent and release aircraft that were contracted before the restrictions were imposed. Additionally, the Pressler enforcement suspended all transactions under the Foreign Military Sales (FMS) programme, and training assistance. The net result was that even the repairable items sent to the USA were withheld. The other weapon systems of US origin such as the C-130, T-37 and T-33 aircraft, the TPS-43 air defence radars, and the automated air defence system were affected. Nineteen T-37 aircraft obtained on lease were grounded. Luckily for the PAF, a few commercial channels remained open from which some badly needed spares could be obtained. The prices to be paid for such spares were three or four times higher, but the consolation was that the delivery period was cut down. Budgetary restraints also came in the way and all users had to strictly prioritize their purchase requirements.

Life after Pressler

Times of trouble bring out the best in people. So it was when the US Government turned off the tap. Initially, the PAF used that extra stock of spares that it had carefully built up to maintain the various US origin weapon systems. The main concern was to keep the F-16 fleet operational. At one stage the whole of the F-16 fleet had to be grounded due to engine related problems. But the challenge was immediately accepted and a programme of engine inspections and depot level work was initiated to recover the aircraft. 'Falcon-Up', a safety related F-16 upgrade programme, and other upgrades were undertaken by the PAF after obtaining the necessary accessories and spares through commercial sources. However, since commercial procurement was more expensive, budgetary restraint forced the Air Force to cut down its flying targets. Even then, the uphill task of keeping the PAF aircraft affected by Pressler, flying, was tackled spiritedly. Alternate sources of spares were identified and everyone, from the top to the lowest ranks, harnessed their wit and energies to overcome, to a great extent, the Pressler barrier. Spares support was available for the C-130 fleet through commercial sources, but again, to minimize expenditure, the flying target was reduced. In the case of T-37s also, the flying syllabus at the Academy was adjusted to reduce the utilization of T-37s, and T-33s, used for photo reconnaissance and target towing, were phased out in 1993. Keeping the six TPS-43 high-looking radars serviceable was a real challenge because any unserviceability would have meant gaps, which the air defence could not afford. The PAF also depended on US sources for spares for the air defence automation system, and their non-availability created many problems, which were overcome with a great deal of ingenuity.

Ever since the enforcement of the Pressler Amendment, the Pakistan Government had been hoping that, considering the unfair and the discriminatory nature of their restrictions,

the US Government would ease the sanctions. In fact, the Government continued to pay installments for the contracted F-16 aircraft until 1993, when it dawned on powers that be that the US was unlikely to ever release the F-16s. With a great deal of persuasion, the US Congress approved what is known as the 'Brown Amendment', which allowed the Pakistan Government to reclaim all the equipment, with the exception of the F-16s, which had been paid for before Pressler. The PAF seized the opportunity to retrieve spares worth approximately $100 million but forewent spares/equipment worth $65 million, which were meant for aircraft that were not released. The released spares helped the PAF to undertake essential upgrades to the F-16 fleet. Pakistan's entry into the nuclear club in May 1998 led to new US sanctions under the Glenn Amendment that closed all US sources and the PAF had once again to fall back on its own ingenuity to keep its aircraft flying.

Review of the Force Structure

The enforcement of the Pressler Amendment in October 1990 all but torpedoed the Force Structure Review of 1988, whereby the PAF had planned to induct an additional seventy-one F-16s and ninety-five F-7s. It would have provided a hi-tech element of 100 F-16s, in addition to the fleet of Mirages, and about 135 F-7s. This was an unexpected blow and the Air Force had to review its options quickly. It had an unexpected piece of good luck just before the Pressler restrictions were imposed. The Australians, who wanted to dispose off their Mirage III fleet, found a ready customer in the PAF. The aircraft, which were obtained at a bargain price, were considered to have outlived their useful life and, initially at least, were considered useful as back-up for spares for the existing PAF fleet. Once the aircraft, the accessories, jigs and fixtures were brought to Pakistan, it was realized that most of the aircraft could be recovered and that the accessories, jigs and fixtures that came along would considerably enhance PAF's repair capability. Mirage Rebuild Factory (MRF) Kamra was given the task, and it was able to recover forty-five aircraft. The PAF was still left with spares and equipment worth about US $500 million.

The Air Force had already planned to replace its Chinese F-6 fleet with the F-7s and the initial lot was already in the country in 1988. Subsequently, the second lot arrived and in 1992 the PAF decided to order another forty F-7s. The induction of F-7s was necessary not only to provide the PAF with a weapon system that would redress the numerical disparity with the enemy, but also to enable the pilots to keep in good fighting trim. The aircraft were upgraded to carry a wider range of weapons, Martin Baker seats, and avionics from Western sources. These forty aircraft, unlike the earlier lot, came with all the modifications and upgrades done at the factory in China.

It was obvious that the PAF would also have to depend on its old Mirage fleet, and the ones acquired from Australia, for the foreseeable future. Structural life extension of the Mirage III fleet was undertaken, and a programme for the modernization of the fleet with INS, HUD, AVTR, Chaff and Flare capabilities was completed at the Pakistan Aeronautical Complex at Kamra, while the installation of Griffo-M radar is nearing completion. Another important development in sustaining the numerical balance, especially with the likely phasing out of A-5 aircraft, was the decision to purchase ex-French Air Force Mirages. After surveying the available aircraft in many countries, the proposal of SAGEM, a French firm, to sell forty Mirages (thirty-four Mirage—single seat and six Mirage III—dual

seat) was accepted. The aircraft and engines were to be completely overhauled and modified with modern avionics before delivery, scheduled in the period 1997-98. Some unavoidable difficulties disturbed the delivery schedule, but the whole lot was expected by the end of the year 2000.

Another induction that strengthened the air defence was the acquisition of portable, short range, Mistral surface to air missiles (SAM) from France. During the summer of 1989, the Government decided to make funds available to make up very dire deficiencies of the three services in view of mounting tension on the borders with India. The funds had to be utilized before the end of the financial year (30 June). The Army and the Navy were able to get the major share because the Air Force realized that nothing could be procured off the shelf within the stipulated time frame. The PAF was aware that their limited inventory of the Crotale missile system was not only getting old but was also inadequate for all its needs. Under these circumstances, the then CAS, Air Chief Marshal Hakimullah, made a bid to induct the Mistral system and was successful in getting a first installment of these missiles from the PAF's own budget which was subsequently adjusted by the Government. Additional lots were bought later. Mistral provided the much needed defence against air threat to the Forward Operating Bases (FOBs) and the Main Operating Bases (MOBs) as well as other VPs. Night vision devices have been provided to those operating the Mistral so that the system is also effective at night. Whether the PAF should have opted to buy the Mistral SAM system or something else when the funds were made available, has been the subject of some criticism. But in the final analysis, it seems that the option exercised was the best and has gone a long way in enhancing the PAF's air defence capability. The Pakistan

Navy also acquired this system subsequently. Recently, the PAF has added the indigenously produced 'Anza' shoulder-fired-missile system to protect the forward located air defence assets.

The Elusive Hi-Tech Option

The Force Structure Review of 1988 had envisaged a fleet of 100 F-16s that would have taken care of the hi-tech requirement well into the twenty-first century. The Pressler restrictions enforced in October 1990 completely changed the scenario, and the plans went overboard. The F-7s with avionics upgrade and the additional Mirages from Australia, together with the forty ex-French Air Force Mirages acquired through SAGEM company and their upgradation met, to a great extent, the PAF's needs for a medium-tech weapons platform in the short term. But without a hi-tech component, the PAF lacked the edge that it had hoped to maintain against the much larger force of the adversary.

The options available were not many. There was the French Mirage 2000 which the PAF had evaluated in the early 1980s. When the F-16s were made available by the US Government, primarily because of the Soviet intervention in Afghanistan, the PAF's interest in the Mirage 2000 waned. Some optimists in both the Foreign Office and the PAF thought that the Pressler intervention was a temporary phase, and deft diplomacy and pressure from the US industry would result in early lifting of the embargo. The PAF leadership thought it prudent to start looking for an alternative. The Mirage 2000 seemed a natural option to be explored. However, it appeared to be still in the developmental stage, especially with regard to avionics on board. The situation changed substantially when PAF teams evaluated the Mirage 2000-V in 1993-94 and found that

the performance of the aircraft had been considerably enhanced. Also, it had an avionics package that was as good, if not better, than that of the F-16.

The PAF did not wish to commit itself to the Mirage 2000-V without looking at other alternatives. The Russian SU-27 and the Swedish Gripen were strong contenders. There were a number of middlemen peddling the SU-27 and other Russian aircraft from the former Soviet Union republics. But the PAF was wary of acquiring anything that did not have the stamp of approval from Moscow because ultimately the maintenance of the aircraft depended on sources within Russia. The available options were evaluated in the countries of the former Eastern Bloc but the problem of Russian approval remained. Ultimately, the PAF was invited to evaluate the aircraft in Russia itself and the team found that the performance of the SU-27/SU-30 met its requirements. Despite a nod from the various echelons of the Russian hierarchy, political approval from the top was not forthcoming. The Swedish Gripen could have also fitted the bill but because it had several components of US origin, including the engine, it had to be ruled out.

The Mirage 2000-V was left as the only realistic option that fulfilled the PAF's operational requirements. The then Prime Minister was able to persuade the French Government to agree to the sale of forty aircraft. The price tag was $4 billion for the whole package, which appeared exorbitant although the government was willing to allocate resources for the deal. The PAF needed funds to the tune of nearly $715 million for other critical deficiencies such as the upgrading of the air defence network etc. and thought that it could negotiate with the French to reduce the per unit cost of aircraft and use the balance for making up those other deficiencies. The PAF at that time was also in the process of evaluating an avionics package from Western sources for the joint Pak-China Super-7 aircraft and thought that by installing such a package on the Mirage 2000-V and marrying it to the BVR missile, the unit cost of the aircraft could be considerably reduced. At the insistence of the air staff, the French, initially reluctant, carried out a study and finally came up with the 'solution' that if the PAF bought a certain number of the original Mirage 2000-V, they would consider offering to the PAF a lower-priced 'Mirage 2000 Light', as it was then called. The PAF, in the meanwhile, had continued its study of the aircraft configuration that would best suit its needs and of all the other supporting equipment that would be needed to operate the system.

While all this was going on—the PAF's study and its efforts to reduce the overall cost of the package and the then Government's keenness to clinch the deal for $4 billion at the earliest—a controversy raged in the Press and in some interested circles, about the choice of Mirage 2000-V as the best and most viable hi-tech weapon system for the PAF. It was apparent that the PAF was the innocent victim of political wranglings and of vested interests keen to make a quick buck in the bargain. As things turned out, there was a change in the government, and the deal never came through. The PAF was left high and dry without a hi-tech element in its inventory.

Looking at the Future

The induction of the Chinese F-7 and the Australian and ex-French Air Force Mirages with their upgrades, met the PAF's operational requirements of a medium-technology inventory component in the short term. But looking beyond the year 2005, the PAF needed something that would meet its needs for a weapon system of this category for some twenty years. The PAF wanted aircraft that should not only have the operational configuration of its choice but that were also free from any threat of embargoes. Another important criterion was that the aeronautical industry of Pakistan should be actively involved in its manufacture. That is how the idea of the Super-7 was born.

The Chinese first approached the PAF in 1992 for the design, development, and co-production of the Super-7. After detailed evaluation of the proposal and discussions with the Chinese, the Government approved the PAF recommendation for co-development and co-production in October 1994. The Super-7 was to be a multi-role, lightweight day/night fighter which could be configured for air superiority and/or ground attack roles. The airframe was to be of Chinese design and the engine RD-93 reconfigured from the Russian RD-33. The avionics suite and the weapons package of the PAF Super-7 was to be of Western origin. A formal agreement in principle between the PAF and the Chinese was signed in October 1995. This allowed the two sides to work out the multifarious details that go into a venture of this kind. An MoU was signed between the two governments in February 1998 and a formal contract in June 1999. It would be about five years before the first batch of the tested aircraft would be available and hopefully would enable the PAF to phase out its fleet of Mirages, F-7s and A-5s.

Engineering Challenges

The decade under review saw the PAF pass through some of the most critical periods in its history. The enforcement of the draconian Pakistan-specific Pressler Amendment and its impact on the operational capabilities of the PAF, the induction of the Chinese F-7s, the Australian Mirages, the K-8, and the

Mistral were some of the challenges that the PAF was called upon to face. It had to undertake tasks that had always been done abroad, build facilities through unconventional means and improvisation to meet the exacting criteria of performance and safety requirements, and generally keep the aircraft flying. This was a challenge that the PAF engineers faced and met with great success. It was possible for them to do so because the new breed of engineers and technicians had been trained to very exacting and contemporary standards in institutions that had also kept pace with the advances in technology. Airmen's training in technical trades was drastically revised to enable them to handle the latest technological developments. Training on computers was included as a compulsory part of the syllabus. Similarly, the College of Aeronautical Engineering (CAE) was equipped with a modern computer laboratory to allow it to be used for a variety of purposes such as teaching, experiments, and Research and Development (R&D). The curricula were upgraded and some new courses incorporating the latest in the field of aerospace and avionics engineering were included. Split level Master of Science programmes were introduced at the CAE in collaboration with the National University of Sciences and Technology (NUST) to allow a greater number of qualified officers to get their education from recognized foreign universities.

Partly because the PAF had come of age and its engineering skills had matured, and partly due to the compulsion of circumstances such as the Pressler restrictions, the PAF was able to successfully undertake tasks that would have been impossible in the past. Avionics upgrade on the F-7, A-5 III, and Mirages, F-16 factory level tasks such as 'OCU' and 'Falcon-Up', F-100 engine upgrade, F-7 engine overhaul, C-130 PDM, Alouette overhaul, T-37 structural life enhancement programme, Crotale 4000 overhaul, and similar major engineering achievements were features of the last decade. A major role was played by Pakistan Aeronautical Complex (PAC), Kamra in many of these achievements. The various factories established at PAC were expanded and modernized to undertake projects such as the recovery of the Australian Mirages, and the co-production of K-8 aircraft with China, production of Super Mushshak, overhaul of F-100 engines of F-16 etc. It is also a feather in the cap of PAC that the Mirage Rebuild Factory (MRF) was the first among the defence establishments in Pakistan to qualify for the ISO-9000 certification. The remaining factories achieved the same soon after.

The landmark decision, taken in 1990, to amalgamate the various specialities in the Maintenance Branch into one common Engineering Branch, may or may not have contributed to the remarkable achievements of PAF engineers in the last decade. But it certainly created a big upheaval. The leadership at that time felt that the majority of activities in the engineering field were such that they needed no specialization. Only when advanced repair or overhaul or R&D were involved, specialization would come into play. It was felt that any graduate, whether in aerospace or avionics engineering, could perform the maintenance activities at the base level with some cross training. Another important reason, the one that probably outweighed all the other justifications, was the inter-branch rivalry, which was damaging to the overall interests of the Air Force. Based on the recommendations of a Committee that was appointed to go into the whole issue, the then CAS issued orders on 1 March 1990 to merge all the technical branches (excluding Data Automation) into a unified Engineering branch. There was a lot of nervousness amongst the affected officers, but soon matters settled down. Practical difficulties cropped up during the implementation and there were some other uncalled for deviations from the road map recommended by the Committee. These needed to be catered to. The experience of the last eight to nine years, since the decision was taken, has helped to settle most matters. It has been appreciated that specialization is appropriate at junior levels and real integration is more practical in the ranks of Group Captain and above, and further, that Logistics should continue as a separate entity within the Engineering-Branch and that CAE qualified engineers should not be wasted against these vacancies. The main advantage of the amalgamation of engineering sub-branches is that there has been a definite improvement in maintenance management. Inter-branch rivalry has been reduced to a great extent, which has contributed to the overall health of the Service.

Decision Making at the Top

The demise of General Zia in 1988 saw a radical change in decision making at the top level in so far as the defence forces were concerned. General Zia could be faulted for many reasons during the decade that he wielded power, but not for failing to follow an enlightened policy in defence decision making. It was because of his military background and the nature of his appointment perhaps, that the armed forces functioned as a well-knit team during his tenure. Visualizing an integrated military strategy, he called regular meetings of the Joint Chiefs of Staff Committee (JCSC) and the Defence Committee of the Cabinet (DCC) until 1985, and made himself available even when not required to be present. He listened at length to the points of view of the Services Chiefs and gave due weightage to their arguments. He was particularly sensitive to the requirements of the smaller services and was able to resolve competing demands amicably. When pitted against the might of the Soviet-Afghan threat on the western border, he was careful that the Army and the Air Force operations remained consistent with Pakistan's Afghanistan policy objectives.

With the coming in of the political governments in 1988, there was a change in not only the style of governance but also in the management of affairs of defence and security. There were nine changes in the government during the period, five of them were regular and four were interim. Naturally, national security decision making received a back seat during frequent changes in the government. The DCC met fairly regularly under the PPP government but security issues did not receive the priority that they required. It seemed that the government was more concerned with procurement of weapons on the basis of specific sources and at pre-designated costs. There were also allegations of influence peddling and kickbacks, which marred the atmosphere. During the PML government, the DCC met infrequently and most decisions on national security issues seemed to be taken in isolation or in direct consultation with various Services Chiefs, mostly the Army Chief.

The JCSC, however, continued to meet quite frequently and there was good interaction between the three Services. Unfortunately, JS Headquarters no longer had the authority that was needed to make it an effective body. The Army assumed the dominant role and had a virtual veto on all decisions. Even the authority granted to the JCSC in its charter was not always observed, such as in postings of officers to the inter-Services organizations e.g. NDC, ISPR and even to JS Headquarters itself. Besides, continued political instability in the country during the period required frequent Army interventions mostly at the behest of the heads of state or governments in power at that time. This made the position of the Army more dominant and, though a good deal of cordiality existed between the highest echelons of the three Services, the Air Force and the Navy came to play second fiddle. The decade also saw a continuing decline in the economic health of the country and the availability of funds for any new induction or upgrades in the Services decreased almost in proportion to the increase in sophisticated weaponry acquisitions by India. In such an environment, the allocations of funds became *ad hoc* and although both the Army and the Navy recognized the critical needs of the Air Force, when the question of actual allocations came up, the PAF seldom succeeded in getting its due. The imposition of the Pressler embargo had hit the Air Force the hardest because it was deprived of the hi-tech edge of F-16s that it had ordered in large numbers. Besides, the air defence ground environment (ADGE) had become old and needed immediate improvement. At one stage $4 billion for purchase of forty Mirage 2000-V had been negotiated by the government with France, and the PAF was keen to acquire the weapon system though at a lower cost. The PAF wanted to negotiate a reduction in the price tag and the interest payments so that about $750 million could be saved to upgrade the ADGE. The acquisition of Mirage 2000-V, in the meanwhile, became a controversial issue and was subjected to adverse comments alleging incorrect choice of system, strain on the economy, and involvement of kickbacks. When change in the government followed, both the interim and the subsequent Muslim League governments found that the state of the country's economy was such that it could

not afford the acquisition. Thus the PAF was once again left empty handed without a high-tech weapon system. The fact that the Air Force operates in a medium that stretches over both land and sea; and that neither the Army nor the Navy can operate freely unless the skies are safe, seems to have been ignored when it came to distributing the funds available for defence.

The Legacy Lives On

The PAF has maintained its professional image throughout its existence. Officers and men of the Force are proud inheritors of a legacy of warriors who have left a permanent imprint on history. So it was in the decade that has just passed. There were no large-scale wars as such. The PAF's involvement in the Afghan war was of a different nature. It was more of a covert unconventional war, a war restricted by very difficult Rules of Engagement (ROEs). Still, the PAF lived up to its reputation by not only bringing down several Soviet/Afghan intruders but deterring them from frequent violations of the border. The Air Force also responded with prompt deployment when threatened by the Indian exercise 'Brass Tacks', or when providing cover to the country's nuclear installations. Realistic training and exercises have helped the PAF to maintain a qualitative edge over its adversary, which is one of its primary strengths.

There have been ups and downs for the Service during the decade. Its finest hour was when it distinguished itself in the Afghan war, but its low came when the Pressler restrictions frustrated the PAF's future plans and also forced it to cut down on its operational training. Nevertheless, since human ingenuity is at its best in situations of pressure, the PAF engineers rose to the occasion and performed tasks that had seemed impossible. The high command succeeded in restricting the damage caused by the Pressler restrictions, and in keeping the fighting force in good trim. The frustration of the PAF at the denial of a hi-tech combat aircraft notwithstanding, the Force was in good form as far as its professional expertise was concerned, and would remain at peak readiness whenever called into action.

Looking back at the decade under review, one can say that it was one of the most difficult decades since the fledgling Royal Pakistan Air Force came into being at the time of independence. But spurred on by its proud heritage, it retained its reputation as a compact, efficient, and hard hitting force. The proud legacy is carried on.

'Little minds are tamed and subdued by misfortune, but great minds rise above it'
Washington Irving

2 THE PAF IN THE AFGHAN WAR

An Overview

When the Soviet Union invaded Afghanistan in 1979, after having exercised restraint for nearly a century, Pakistan was sandwiched between two hostile states. The two-front situation, with India in the east and the Russian forces in the west, was a grave challenge to Pakistan's security. The coordinated moves by the Soviet-Indian axis under the Indo-Soviet treaty of 1971 continued to jeopardize Pakistan's security. The threat gained significance with large-scale aggressive deployment of the Indian Army and Air Force. The Soviet fleet, along with the Indian Navy, regularly held power projection exercises off the coast of Karachi. There was a quantum jump in the violations of the Pakistan airspace by Russo-Afghan aircraft. The Soviets started bombing the Afghan refugee camps in Pakistan, killing a large number of civilians. At times, Pakistani villages were also targeted. In June 1980, the Soviet Union became a direct neighbour of Pakistan when the Afghan puppet ruler Babrak Karmal ceded the Wakhan strip.

Some Western countries saw the occupation of Afghanistan as the Soviet Union's final move southward to fulfil her longstanding ambition of reaching the warm waters of the Indian Ocean. In the process, Pakistan became a front-line state almost overnight. The Mujahideen, supported by Western military and economic aid, led the resistance to the Soviet expansionism. The war continued for ten years at an enormous cost to Afghanistan in terms of human lives and suffering. By 1985, the Afghan war seemed to be reaching a critical phase. The Mujahideen, who had acquired modern weapons and gained experience in guerrilla tactics, were bristling with confidence. The Soviets, on the other hand, were determined to block supplies coming from across the border and warned Pakistan against assisting the rebels. Air and ground violations took place all along the western border. Pakistan's leadership had no choice but to confront the Soviets, in order to safeguard the country's frontiers. In view of the nature of violations and the serious handicap in the employment of ground forces, and the difficult terrain, the PAF had to play a major role.

Throughout this period, Mujahideen rebels continued to harass military forces of the occupying power as well as the Afghan regime that it was supporting, and there is little doubt that both sides sustained heavy casualties. In Pakistan, the impact of the 1979-89 Afghan war was almost equally far-reaching. The country was flooded by hordes of refugees anxious to escape the conflict. This provoked border violations by Soviet and Afghan aircraft that intruded into Pakistan on 'search and destroy' missions.

For the PAF, in particular, this was a real dilemma, since it was directly responsible for safeguarding the national airspace, at a time when it was not at war but was also far from being at peace. Nowhere was the pressure felt more keenly than in Peshawar, which merited the status of being a 'front-line' base for much of the decade by virtue of its proximity to the Afghan border. The fighter squadrons based at Peshawar remained at various states of readiness throughout the ten years in question. 1983 marked a turning point, with the arrival of the F-16s in Pakistan. Based in Sargodha, these aircraft took on the main brunt of the operations. Their distance from the western border, however, reduced their patrolling time. The PAF, therefore, was compelled to start operations in September 1986 from Kamra, which provided a jump platform closer to Afghanistan, and greatly improved the reaction time for the PAF.

Pakistan's political and military leadership rose to the challenge. The decision to resist Soviet military aggression at all costs was one of the boldest policy decisions taken at the national forum. The far-sightedness behind this decision will certainly be acknowledged by posterity. However, the revised land strategy in general, and air strategy in particular, were dictated by the constraints of policies set forth by the political leadership. The factor that eased the situation for Pakistan was the commonality of perceptions between Pakistan and the USA. This convergence of national interests motivated the United States to offer military sales to Pakistan.

By 1989, the fierce Mujahideen opposition had caused the Soviet forces to become exhausted with their fruitless, decade-long campaign. The Soviet invasion was finally reversed, and the Soviet Union had to vacate Afghanistan in utter despair. Before their withdrawal, the demoralized Soviet Army had lost 14,000 soldiers and spent some $7 billion on the war. It had killed about 1.3 million Afghans, made five million of them refugees, destroyed 60 per cent of all their villages and laid waste 70 per cent of all agricultural land in Afghanistan. The intensity and brutality of attacks in 1986-87 signified the superpower's frustration at its failure to overcome the Afghan resistance. This led the increasingly chagrined Soviet military to employ chemical weapons and lay extensive minefields (estimated by the UN to number 6200) in which many Afghan civilians lost their lives. From early 1987, the Soviet Union had become actively involved in the Geneva negotiations, partly in order to change her image, but at the same time she continued her relentless operations against the Mujahideen groups, both in Afghanistan and Pakistan.

From a historical perspective, the Afghan war had a unique feature. For the first time, Soviet air power was used in operations against a Third World air force. The employment of air power by the Soviets was limited to hit and run raids against undefended and exposed targets in the border belt. It nevertheless established sufficient contact between the two air forces, with sporadic engagements taking place from time to time. These skirmishes occurred over inhospitable terrain, which added further significance to the whole conflict.

The month of September 1988 saw an increase in intensity in the war in Afghanistan. By then the Soviet Army was making last ditch efforts to sustain itself in Afghanistan. Tension on the Pak-Afghan border increased. The frustrated Afghan regime, supported by the Soviets, increased provocative violations of Pakistan's air space. The Russo-Afghan aircraft grew bolder, and increased their attacks on civilian population in border areas to pressurize the Pakistani government into giving up its Afghan policy.

Strategically, the Vietnam war was a defeat for the US; and it was a humiliating and costly experience. The Afghan war was a far bigger catastrophe for the USSR. The air effort rates generated by the Russo-Afghan Air Forces must not have been less than those generated by the Americans in Vietnam; the quantum of air effort and the losses incurred have not been documented. Nevertheless, the losses were colossal enough to jeopardize the entire war effort of the USSR, forcing her to retreat. The economic implications of the war were so severe that the giant empire eventually collapsed.

Political Factors

After the imposition of martial law in Pakistan in 1977, the attitude of the Western democracies had become rather lukewarm. This attitude was completely transformed from 1980 onwards. With Pakistan's struggle against Soviet expansionism, both political and financial support started flowing in more freely. Financial aid was necessary for the sustenance of millions of refugees. Large quantities of light weapons were also funnelled to the Mujahideen through Pakistan. The security policy of Pakistan had two objectives: first, to exert a sustained pressure on the Soviet Union to withdraw from Afghanistan; and second, to defend her security while making all efforts to avoid open confrontation with the super power.

There were approximately 340 Refugee Tented Villages (RTVs), set up along a 1,000-mile segment of the Durand Line. The population of the RTVs rose to four million Afghans. The result was the ever increasing tribal feuds as well as disruption of the socio-economic life of the original inhabitants of the affected area. The fragile infrastructure i.e. roads, grazing lands, and water sources, suffered greatly because of over use. For the illegal trafficking of arms and narcotics spawned by wartime laxity on its border, Pakistan had to pay a very high price and still continues to be affected by its adverse effects.

Military Factors

Prior to 1979, Pakistan had never given much consideration to a threat from its western border. Therefore, within the limited resources available, the entire focus of Pakistani defence planners had been on investing in the infrastructure along the eastern border. There were a number of air strips available in the area but none of them were jet-capable. The Pakistan Army had kept a token presence in some of the British cantonments to concentrate on some sensitive spots along the Durand Line. The infrastructure in terms of roads, tele-communications, fuel, and munitions' storage was virtually nonexistent.

Following the Russian invasion of Afghanistan, the threat from India was also intensified in a coordinated manner. Pakistan was quick to condemn the Soviet aggression in Afghanistan, and her support to Mujahideen fighting against the Russian troops was an open secret. Soon Pakistan became the target of serious military threats on both its flanks. India tried to increase the pressure by large scale offensive deployments of her Army and Air Force along the eastern border. Besides, both Soviet and Indian navies frequently held exercises not far from the Karachi coast. In response to this, the Government of Pakistan (GOP) formulated a political and military policy that remained stable and unchanged until the withdrawal of Soviet forces in early 1989. In accordance with the GOP's military policy, the joint and single-service plans of the Pakistan Army and the PAF were reviewed and suitably amended. While doing so, the possibility of a two-front war was taken into account. The plan that emerged hinged on keeping a high state of preparedness, and maintaining an east-west balance of forces until such time that quick deployment and redeployments between the two sectors became necessary.

The command and control of the PAF units involved in the Afghan war was especially problematic. Two to three Air Commands had to interact to launch an operational sortie. The concerned AOCs had to coordinate closely with their Army counterparts on the hot lines throughout the war. The heaviest of all demands made on the PAF was the daily and year-round Combat Air Patrols (CAPs) that had to be flown at 'wartime rates'. The purpose of these CAPs was to deter the air violations by the Russo-Afghan aircraft that would frequently attack the Mujahideen. A number of PAF squadrons were involved in those CAPs along the western border. The implications of this unavoidable operational activity were two-fold. Firstly, the affected squadrons had to curtail the tempo of their peacetime continuation training for different roles and training of fresh pilots; secondly, the intensive flying on CAP missions consumed spares at enormous rates without a corresponding contribution towards training. Therefore, during the war, the squadrons' ability to produce new combat-ready aircrew was retarded.

Another significant factor was the frustration of PAF fighter pilots due to strict Rules of Engagements (ROEs), which were decided by Pakistan's political leadership because of obvious sensitivities. The fighter pilots had to scramble from their bases in the event of an impending air violation or to fly combat air patrol for long hours. At times they picked up contact with the enemy aircraft and yet were not allowed to chase them across or close to the Durand Line. A fleeting encounter with the enemy would soon lead to utter despair when the enemy aircraft, after dropping their ordnance on Mujahideen camps, would cross over leisurely to the other side. This adversely affected the squadron pilots' spirits. Day and night they were engaged in what they thought was a largely fruitless activity, severely constrained as it was by the ROEs.

Pakistan's Afghan policy earned the animosity of the USSR, but strong support from the international community strengthened the resolve of its leaders. The GOP did examine all options, including some less risky ones, but keeping the track record of the Soviet Union and the national interests of Pakistan in view, finally decided to adopt the only viable course open to it. To some critics at home, Pakistan's stand appeared to be quite perilous, but the fact was that Pakistan had acted primarily to protect its own national interests.

President Carter made an offer of assistance to Pakistan, which was rightly turned down by President Zia, who called it 'peanuts.' Carter had been weakened by various crises at home and abroad and was later succeeded by the more aggressive President Ronald Reagan. The new president offered Pakistan large multi-year economic and military sales packages. As Pakistan wanted a 'no strings' relationship, it turned down a US request to participate in the planning and conduct of operations. Instead, it accepted military hardware against cash payments.

The US wanted Pakistan to buy only that equipment which it could employ within a short time frame. As such, the US Department of Defence pressed Pakistan to purchase F-5Es and/or ground attack A-10s which could be made operational in a shorter time frame. However, the PAF, keeping the overall regional scenario in mind, continued to insist on the F-16s. Eventually, the Americans agreed to sell the F-16s to Pakistan but refused to clear the AIM-9L missiles, precision guided munitions, and the chosen electronic warfare equipment. The PAF successfully challenged the US plea that the sale of such equipment might jeopardize the security of its NATO allies. Ultimately, these thorny issues were settled and Pakistani pilots were converted on to the F-16s in record time, and the first lot of Fighting Falcons flown by PAF pilots arrived in Pakistan in early 1983. The US equipment was selected primarily because of its high quality and cost effectiveness. It also gave Pakistan the highest possible degree of credible defence. The Americans bargained hard, but Pakistan did not compromise and in the end obtained the equipment it wanted.

From the middle of 1986 onwards, the 'Westcaps' began to pay off, resulting in the shooting down of a number of enemy aircraft. On one occasion, unfortunately, an F-16 Leader shot down his own No. 2 in a manner that was hard to understand. Certain units which were deployed in the east were re-deployed to the west. When the threat from India increased, the units were again shifted to the eastern border. This massive logistical exercise was achievable only because the forces remained flexible in coping with the threat of war on two fronts, simultaneously.

In the spring of 1987, the Army and the PAF jointly developed a new SAM-AAA deployment plan to improve the defence of the border areas. The plan included both short and long term measures involving the reallocation of some existing surface-to-air assets and the acquisition of new weapon systems. After it was approved by the JCSC, the plan was cleared for implementation by the DCC in April 1987.

National Security Decision Making

In the meetings of the Defence Committee of the Cabinet (DCC) and the Joint Chiefs of Staff Committee (JCSC), as well as many informal meetings of the national leadership, doubts were expressed about the management of conflicting policies of confrontation and provocation avoidance—it was like walking on a tight rope. However, based on reliable military and diplomatic intelligence, a consensus emerged that the existing policy was winning and the Soviets were seriously contemplating withdrawal of forces from Afghanistan. Despite considerable situational stresses, Pakistani political leadership remained committed to the two-track policy. The special ROEs laid down for the PAF and the Pakistan Army were important extensions of this policy.

The DCC met once in two months and the JCSC every month. Additional emergency sessions of these bodies were, however, held depending on the gravity of the situation. General Zia presided over most of the meetings and remained the head of the decision making structure throughout the Afghan war. Prime Minister Junejo was deeply perturbed over the increasing number of air violations and bombings resulting in the killing of a large number of civilians. Things became very serious when four Russo-Afghan helicopter gunships flew over Parachinar and randomly attacked people and properties. The media and the National Assembly took up this issue and Pakistan's Afghan policy came under sharp criticism. What the public did not know was the inadequacy of the existing air defence system in the mountainous terrain. It was not possible to install a linked network of the Low Looking Radars (LLRs) in that area. The solution to the problem lay in the immediate induction of three AWACS E-3 Sentries, which could provide the necessary early warning of low flying incoming raids. Also proposed by the then CAS was the induction of a limited number of balloon borne radars. To tackle the low flying intruders, the induction of Stinger SAMs was also recommended. In 1985 and early 1986, the air violations had increased to such an extent that PAF was forced to airlift some loaned AIM-9L missiles on an emergency basis from the US stocks.

Pakistan's structure and process of decision-making was well-established and institutionalized by the late seventies and was effectively used throughout the Afghan war. Despite his unusual powers and authority, President Zia always called JCSC and DCC meetings to discuss and decide all national security issues. The JCSC had been in existence for over a decade, and had come of age. Its members were aware of the serious deficiencies in the country's higher defence organization that had been highlighted during the last two India-Pakistan wars. Besides, the senior staff of the three Services had learnt to be more accommodative to the inter-Services needs. The cooperation among the three Services and the ministry of defence was at its best as compared to any other time in the history of Pakistan.

The Limitations of Air Defence

A major handicap for the PAF during the Afghan war was the lack of early warning due to the absence of an air defence infrastructure. The rough terrain, high mountains, and absence of vital communications aggravated the problem. The PAF eventually managed to create a modest early warning network by positioning some low-looking radars in inaccessible areas. Additionally, Mobile Observer Units (MOUs) were strategically placed throughout the 1,400-km long belt to provide a reasonably accurate surveillance of Pakistan's western border. It is a tribute to the courage and tenacity of the officers and men of the PAF's air defence system, who, while supporting these deployments, endured extremely uncomfortable and harsh living conditions, and performed admirably in adverse weather conditions.

In a fairly short duration, the PAF was able to create a reasonably effective air defence network. However, there were two major limitations. First, because of the extended length of the border and the limited ability of the PAF's radar network to look inside Afghanistan, air defence was handicapped in reacting quickly to an incoming threat. The PAF was compelled to offset this disadvantage by flying extensive CAPs. Consequently, many valuable flying hours were committed to CAPs and the results, as is normal in such circumstances,

were not commensurate with the effort spent. An airborne early warning platform, if available, would have increased the radar coverage and reduced the PAF's reaction time. The second limitation stemmed from the difficult-to-implement ROEs. These rules usually permitted only a single slashing attack while ensuring that the debris fell positively inside Pakistani territory. Air defence fighters were committed only in the event of an actual ingress, and this tended to delay the reaction time of PAF fighters giving ample time to the enemy aircraft to complete their missions. The moment the enemy intruders noted that the PAF aircraft had been committed, they would turn around and exit. A number of kills were missed due to late committal and the requirement to ensure that debris fell inside Pakistani territory. When visual contact with an enemy could not be converted into a kill, this naturally bred frustration amongst the pilots.

The entire PAF air defence system was designed to cater for only the eastern contingency. The operational and vital support equipment had, therefore, been selected keeping in view the generally flat eastern terrain. Regardless of the threat from the west, the PAF could not afford to lower its guard on the eastern border, due to the hostile posture of the eastern neighbour who was also an ally of Soviet Union and a sympathizer of the puppet Afghan government for obvious reasons.

Despite these serious challenges, the PAF adopted certain measures to develop a viable Air Defence Ground Environment (ADGE) in vital areas of interest. As an initial step, few MOUs were deployed. Due to the inhospitable terrain, they could not be spread in an effective manner. The Control and Reporting Centre (CRC) located at Mianwali was, therefore, tasked to look after the air defence of the western border. However the controller/pilot team concept was not initially

41

well established because of the distance between the fighter bases and the CRC.

The Shooting War

During the Afghan war in which nine fighter squadrons of the PAF took part actively, the PAF logged 10939 sorties entailing 13275:40 hours. A total of 2476 enemy air violations were recorded involving 7,589 enemy aircraft. During these violations, and as a result of the bombings that were carried out, 418 civilians lost their lives while 877 received injuries. Eight enemy aircraft were shot down by six different pilots, all belonging to the F-16 squadrons. Flight Lieutenant Khalid Mahmood of 14 Squadron was the top scorer with three kills. Besides, there were a large number of enemy aircraft that defected or were forced to land in Pakistan. There were also several near engagements and missed opportunities. (See chapter 9 for details.)

Being the only air superiority squadron in the north at that time, 15 Air Superiority Squadron was one of the first to be tasked for Air Defence Alert (ADA) duties following the Soviet invasion of Afghanistan in December 1979. As many as 6+2 and 8+2 F-6 aircraft were put on ADA duties. Similarly, from 1980 onwards, 23 Squadron located at Samungli was as engaged in air defence duties as 15 Squadron. On 1 March 1980, a Russian IL-26 violated Pakistani air space and came as far as Risalpur. Two F-6s from 11 Squadron, Chaklala, scrambled to challenge the intruder. The formation intercepted the bandit and fired a warning burst. The IL-26 turned back towards the border and its pilot started transmitting radio calls for help. Following this, six Mig-23s appeared in three different formations. Two F-6s were scrambled but were ordered not to take any offensive action; therefore, no engagement took place. But this certainly was an indication of things to come.

During 1985, there were occasional incursions by Afghan aircraft but the situation was not serious. The MOUs thinly deployed on the western border reported these violations. The Army received Stinger SAMs in 1985 and deployed them near the border at Kharlachi (Parachinar), Topsar (Landikotal), and some other areas. The Peshawar-based Corps Commander of that time, Lieutenant General Aslam Beg, had claimed that the Army would be the first to shoot down an Afghan aircraft, a feat the PAF had been unable to achieve till then. The beginning of 1986 saw growing and repeated violations of Pakistani air space with a heavy loss of life and property among the Afghan refugees, particularly in the Parachinar sector. In the second week of May 1986, the violations intensified. On 17 May 1986, 483 CRC vectored a pair of F-16s on a dawn CAP towards two intruding enemy aircraft. During a brief engagement, two Su-22s were shot down. The Army and FC were contacted and requested to locate both the wreckage and if possible the pilots, if they had bailed out. The Army located the wreckage, but as predicted, the tribesmen were in the process of loading the wreckage onto a tractor. It was brought to the FC Officers' Mess at Parachinar. Everyone was excited about the first kill. Pakistani and foreign journalists were brought to Parachinar and shown parts of the aircraft that consisted of two elevators, vertical stabiliser and after burner nozzle. The PAF was able to claim the first 'kill' after all.

Soon the Afghans were violating Pakistani airspace from Arandu in the North to Wana in the South. Only a pair of fighters was available to confront them. The government directive was to thwart the enemy without cross-border manoeuvres. This was a difficult directive to implement. The ROEs were reviewed and the concept of 'Slashing Attack' was formulated. The aim was to make a single high speed pass to shoot an enemy aircraft and then to extricate quickly so that minimum time was spent in the combat area.

In an incident during 1987, four Afghan aircraft intruded as deep as Shabqadar (near Charsadda). Two F-6s on ADA from Peshawar were scrambled. One aircraft aborted. The controller, abiding by the ROEs, did not commit his other fighter. An opportunity to score a kill was thus missed.

Air violations by a number of Afghan/ Soviet aircraft were reported by the MOUs at midnight between 2-3 August 1988. By the time the radars were switched on, the intruding aircraft were exiting. They were carrying out night attacks on Mujahideen camps well within Pakistan. In a calculated move, a night CAP was mounted the next day and radars remained on. The MOUs remained on high alert. The enemy aircraft appeared, as anticipated, and one was shot down by an F-16. The pilot was captured.

How Tactics Evolved through the War

The PAF received its first twelve F-16s by August 1983 and the additional F-16s were thereafter delivered in batches of 2-4, and the numbers built up slowly to come up to the full strength of the first squadron only by August 1984. So the first approximately two years were spent in training as many pilots as possible to build up a number that matched the very large pilot requirement of the first 3-shift, 24-hour fighter of the PAF. Simultaneously, the squadron was also assimilating a complex weapon system and building up the individual experience of its pilots. New munitions were being received at the same time and pilots were training for high skills on each. Thus the pilots' operational envelope on the F-16s kept expanding well after the initiation of the

Afghan-related air operations. But the squadron had to develop the combat tactics in step with the progressively higher skill levels that the pilots were gaining in stages.

Basic Skill on the Aircraft
Other than the effort expended on the CAP missions, 150 additional hours per month were flown for training. This meant extensive flying, as well as some strenuous efforts by planners, pilots, maintenance crews, and logistic supports. All came through with meeting or exceeding the targets assigned to them and they did it with an unblemished safety record. Each individual became a thorough professional, and even those few who did not make the grade did try very hard. All were a source of pride for the squadron commanders and the Air Force.

Development of Tactics During Operations
Despite their limited experience on the aircraft, the pilots were trained to fight under a set of stringent ROE. A very careful geometric definition of their combat profiles was worked out to effect the engagements and aerial kills under the ROE discipline. Specific air combat training sessions then followed in the ROE-dictated scenarios and different batches of pilots were taken through the demanding schedule over the next four years, and all this was achieved without a single mishap. Whenever mistakes were made, special corrective action was immediately taken to pull everyone back into the highly professional fold.

Exercise Peak CAP
A continual research effort was maintained to analyse the changes in the pattern of operations followed by the Soviet/Afghan

air units to get a better understanding of the enemy and to develop the optimum tactics to deal with him. A major tactical effort in this process was when the 'Exercise Peak CAP' was planned and launched under the direction of Air HQ. Peak CAP was meant to adapt the F-16's combat tactics very specifically to the changes occurring across the border in the enemy's tactical flying and formation patterns. Two core groups of the PAF's best controllers and pilots were selected and given short but intensive training in the newly developed intercept geometries, tactics, and SOPs that were calculated to maximize successful engagements. These groups were then used to train other less experienced crews. Some special, and necessarily complicated, tactical profiles were also developed and practised by the core pilot-controller groups, for randomly launching these special missions during peak threat periods. Simplicity too was a requirement built into most of these newer tactics. Peak CAP thus represented the development and confident execution by the pilot-controller teams of more effective and flexible attack profiles that made ROE-abidance simpler and surer. PAF has every reason to be proud of such ingenuity and initiatives of its operational units.

Coping With Mig-29 and BVR Threats

The PAF—and specifically the F-16 pilots— were on occasion up against elements of a superpower's air force. Newer technology and tactics were continually entering the arena. The introduction of the Elint type aircraft by the Soviets had posed a new problem, and the squadrons promptly introduced new counter-tactics and safeguards, without compromising their mission effectiveness. The PAF thus passed through several phases of tactics evolution

that were in step with each increase in the quality of the threat it was facing. In the meantime came the dramatic news that a true BVR missile was soon to be introduced by the Soviets in the war zone with some Soviet Mig-29s. Although the pilots were never to engage this type of aircraft in combat, following an immediate operator-level research initiative, the PAF's first-ever anti-BVR tactics were introduced. The efficacy of these tactics was soon recognized by the Combat Commanders School (CCS). The CCS adopted them for its F-16 courses and subsequently for use in most fighter squadrons as well.

Successful Encounters

Some of the successful encounters during the Afghan war need to be recounted in some detail because these constitute the PAF's only live combat experience since the 1971 war, to date. The war also provided an opportunity to all the combat elements such as the pilots, the air defence controllers, and the maintenance crew to test their endurance, assets, and skills.

Qadri Opens the Account for the PAF

a. Pilot	Squadron Leader Hameed Qadri (Leader)
	Squadron Leader Mohammed Yousaf (No. 2)
b. Controller	(Late) Flying Officer Arshad
c. Date	17 May 1986
d. Aircraft Shot	Two Su-22
e. Area	Near Parachinar

Squadron Leader Hameed Qadri beside the wing of the SU-22 that he shot down on 17 May 1988

Leader Hameed Qadri checked the area on his radar from 0-40,000 feet up to 60 NM. He verified that two intruders had violated Pakistani airspace by 5 NM southwest of Parachinar.

When the two enemy aircraft started heading towards Parachinar at more than 500 knots, the controller asked the formation to accelerate to combat speed. Sensing a possible encounter, the leader asked his wingman to carry out the necessary checks, including cooling of AIM-9L and switching off the anti-collision beacon and navigation lights. Watching the enemy at height, the formation also descended to a minimum safe altitude of 10,000 feet. As the bandits were continuing to turn to an easterly heading, Squadron Leader Qadri checked if any other enemy formation was in the vicinity. He did not see any other aircraft on his radarscope. The controller also confirmed that the other pair had exited towards the south.

The Leader asked his No. 2 to offset himself to the right to sandwich the enemy aircraft flying in wingman formation. Normal drill and pre-briefed tactics required an almost simultaneous approach to fire AIM-9L missiles on the two aircraft. The Leader also ensured that he had the Airborne Interception (AI) lock on the southerly intruder and his No. 2 on the northerly one. He also broke the protective glass of the tank-jettisoning button and punched the two wing drop tanks. Around 6 NM, he moved his head from the REO (AI scope) to Head-up Display (HUD) and attempted to pick up the speck that would have been the bandit in the TD (target designator) box in the HUD field-of-view. He visually picked up both the enemy fighters. Closing in, he uncaged the AIM-9L and the rasping sound in his headset confirmed that the seeker head of the missile on the left outermost rail had acquired the infrared (IR) signature of the bandit. He did not, however, get the flashing

Starting from February 1986, No. 9 Squadron had been providing sweeps at various CAP stations on the western border along with other PAF squadrons. The Russo-Afghan Air Forces had been operating close to the border with different types of aircraft ranging from Hind helicopters to Su-25, Su-22, Mig-21, and Mig-23 aircraft. They were by then violating the Pak-Afghan border with increasing frequency. The situation was tense and many close encounters had already taken place without successful results.

A formation of F-16s on a CAP mission was required to be on station before the first light, east of Parachinar. The formation took off in pre-dawn darkness and reached Hangu—their CAP station. The radar controller, Flying Officer Arshad, reported four Afghan aircraft violating the Pak-Afghan border by 4-5 nautical miles (NM). Squadron indication of the missile diamond. The pass had become almost dead head-on and made the whole interception geometry highly time-compressed. He fired his first missile after receiving the first flashing of the diamond at a range of 12.2 NM. While it was still dark underneath, the Parachinar valley lit up from the flash and the trailing plume of the Sidewinder missile. The bandit, who was recognized as an Su-22, pulled away; he was not hurt. Qadri also saw the Sidewinder self-destroying, miles away. After crossing the bandits, Qadri made a hard left climbing turn with 7.5g. After a 180 degree turn, he saw both the Su-22s turning level and No. 2 at his 7 o'clock position. From here onwards Qadri narrates the account of his first kill:

I watched my No. 2 cross to my right side and called visual as well as tally. I called 'engaged' and quickly locked one of the Sukhois. I got all parameters right on one of them, uncaged the missile seeker head and fired my second AIM-9L missile. With a plume of fire and smoke, the missile from the right rail raced in a wide semicircle to the right. Taking tremendous lead, it soon reversed towards the target in a series of corrections and exploded on impact with the turning Su-22.

Qadri then looked back to clear his tail. He continued to keep the second aircraft in his sight and asked No. 2 to keep his tail clear. This is how he scored the second kill:

I fumbled with my switchology while attempting to select AIM-9L on Stores Management System and hands-on-throttle-and-stick (HOTAS). The silhouette of the first aircraft was visible. The other aircraft was in a left turn. His radius of turn and my energy state gave me confidence that I could easily achieve kill parameters both with missile and guns. During the turn, I found myself hitting the fringes of the AIM-9P missile. I pulled a high yo-yo as I was in a totally offensive position. My target was now in a nose-down

and heading towards Afghan territory. After apexing, I quickly rolled back and fired a three-second burst on the exiting Su-22. I stopped firing when a trail of smoke and flash from his aircraft confirmed a lethal kill. Through a split 'S', I headed east of Parachinar.

Immediately after landing, the leader's video cassette was watched by the base authorities and later by the concerned staff of Air Headquarters. All of them commended the pilot and the controller on duty, for doing a good job. Squadron Leader Hameed Qadri did an outstanding job of engaging the targets, maintaining excellent situation awareness, and remaining extremely cool in trying conditions. He could have easily extricated himself after shooting down the first Su-22. Displaying aggression and boldness, he pursued and shot down another Su-22 with guns at closer ranges. The PAF awarded the Sitara-i-Basalat to Squadron Leader Hameed Qadri.

Shooting Down a Ferret

a. Pilots   Wing Commander Razzaq (Leader)

Squadron Leader Sikander Hayat (No. 2)

b. Controller   Squadron Leader Pervaiz Ali Khan

c. Date   30 March 1987

d. Aircraft Shot   An-26

e. Area   Near Miranshah

Wing Commander Abdul Razzaq and his No. 2, Squadron Leader Sikander Hayat were vectored towards two slow speed intruders that the controller visualized to be electronic

Wg. Cdr. Abdul Razzak (now Air Cdre.) shot down one AN-26 believed to be an ECM aircraft, on 30 May 1987

intelligence (ELINT) aircraft heading towards a radar position at Parachinar. He had no hesitation in the existing wartime conditions, to permit the F-16s to shoot down the military transport aircraft, which though unarmed, was violating Pakistan air space. Wing Commander Razzaq recalls the encounter in the following words:

The vector given by the controller started the flow of adrenaline. All the preparatory actions were over in less than 30 seconds. The bandits (two of them) were reported close to Parachinar; another 30-40 miles had to be covered. Soon the controller reported that now only one bandit was violating the border. The second had turned away. When I brought the target into the TD box at 3-4 NM, I realized that it was a slow moving, larger aircraft. I asked for permission to shoot, which was quickly given. With an overtake rate of well over 200 knots and a low IR signature; the minimum range cue was lying close to 4,000 feet. Effectively, I had no more than a 1.5

second firing window available. Everything worked as conceived and with the press of the button, the missile was on its way. As I was breaking off, I saw the missile impact the target. No. 2 also released his missile, which also impacted the target. The enemy aircraft crashed on the snow-clad mountains below.

Badar Shoots Down an Su-22

a. Pilots   Squadron Leader Badar-ul-Islam (Leader)

Squadron Leader Khalid Pervaiz Marwat (No. 2)

b. Controller   Squadron Leader Saif-ur-Rahman

c. Date   16 April 1987

d. Aircraft Shot Su-22

e. Area   Near Thal

47

Squadron Leader Badar-ul-Islam shot down one SU-22 near Thal on 16 April 1987

This formation took-off at 0630 hours and headed towards the CAP area near Thal. After three or four orbits, the radar reported some activity well within the Pakistani border and vectored the formation towards the intruders. The leader quickly got his No. 2 in shooter cover position and the two headed west in full burners. The leader picked up four blips on his radarscope, which was confirmed by the radar controller. At a distance of about 7 NM, the leader visually picked them up. Since it was early morning, with the sun behind him, the leader could clearly see all the four shining aircraft. He narrates the story of this kill in these words:

Although faster, we were also climbing and had to chase the targets for a little while before they came into missile range. During the chase, I asked my No. 2 to keep an eye on the other two aircraft that we had previously seen. The moment I got a flash on the missile reticle, I fired my first AIM-9L missile. It was a unique experience. I had never fired a missile before.

As the missile left the rail, it caused a slight yaw. I kept looking at the missile in some awe, but then lost it and started to look towards the target. In a couple of seconds, there was a big red flash around the aircraft that I was targeting. It started to spiral towards the ground in a left-hand turn. I locked on to the next aircraft and fired the second missile. The controller informed us that we were getting close to the border and that we should break off and head back. As soon as my second missile left its rail, I broke left and asked my No. 2 to do the same. During the process I looked over the canopy railing and saw another big flash in the area where my second target was. I dived down and headed towards Bannu and started to look for my No. 2 and returned to base.

Squadron Leader Badar-ul-Islam claimed to have shot down two aircraft, in his post mission report. However, after examining all the evidence the PAF awarded him only one kill. Nevertheless, he did an outstanding job of remaining cool and skilful during the intercept.

Painting by Hussaini depicting the encounter of 4 August 1988

Shooting Down the First Soviet Aircraft

a. Pilot   Squadron Leader
                     Athar Bokhari

b. Controller   Squadron Leader
                     Taufeeq Raja

c. Date   4 August 1988

d. Aircraft Shot   Su-25

e. Area   10 NM West of
                     Miranshah (Boya)

In those days, in addition to the scrambles that had then become routine, two or three pairs of F-16s would fly CAPs in the west on a regular basis. On this day, a scramble was ordered half an hour before sunset. As the No. 2 of the detailed formation was not yet fully night current, the leader decided to go alone. On the initial vector, he was at full throttle. As the violating aircraft had turned back, he was asked near Hangu to fly at normal speed and to set up a race course CAP pattern north of Bannu at 10,000 feet. The next fifty minutes were uneventful as he kept flying at 120/300 degrees. By this time, it was dark. Then came the opportunity for a kill, so narrated by the pilot:

> I was vectored on a heading of 300 degrees, and the controller reported the target 30 degree left, 15 NM. I turned left and called contact. The GCI controller clearly told me to go ahead and shoot the target. I achieved a head-on IR lock on one aircraft at 7 NM flying high. He started to turn right at 6.5 NM, putting me on at 3.5 NM. I engaged burners and closed to less than 2.5 NM from the target before the desired launch zone (DLZ) started to flash. As all the parameters were met, I fired the missile and saw it go towards the target in the TD box on the HUD. I next saw a ball of fire in the TD box. I broke left to 120 degrees, descended to 5,000 feet, and dispensed chaff and flares. On looking back at the 8 o'clock position, I saw 4-5 flares at about 3-4 NM and mistook them initially for missiles. It all but stopped my heartbeat but my controller reassured me that there were no other aircraft in the vicinity. I then took a safe passage home.

The wreckage of the shot down aircraft was located, but not the pilot. The tribal people caught him the next evening and handed him over to the authorities. His name was Colonel Alexander Rutskoi who later became the Vice President of the Russian Federation. Both the pilot and the controller displayed calm professional competence in shooting down the first Soviet-piloted Su-25 aircraft at night. It was an excellent example of pilot-controller teamwork.

Squadron Leader Athar Bokhari (now Group Captain) shot down one SU-25 near Miranshah on 4 August 1988

A reconstructed AIM 9L Missile that was used to intercept Soviet-Afghan air raids

Shooting Down Two Mig-23 Aircraft

a. Pilots   Flight Lieutenant
Khalid Mehmood (Leader)

Squadron Leader
Anwar Hussain (No. 2)

b. Controller   Squadron Leader
Irfan-ul-Haq

c. Date   12 September 1988

d. Aircraft shot Two Mig-23s

e. Area   South of Chitral
(Nawagai)

This formation took-off from Minhas (Kamra) air base at 0606 hours after a detailed mission briefing. The formation set up CAP in Nawagai area at 10,000 feet AGL as directed by the GCI controller. At about 0640 hours, the controller vectored the formation to a northwesterly heading for two enemy aircraft that were heading east. No. 2 picked up the intruders flying at 34,000 feet on his AI. Meanwhile, the targets had turned away and started flying parallel to the border in a northerly direction.

The GCI quickly repositioned the formation for four other potential intruders that were heading east. At 18 NM, the leader picked up one blip followed by five more blips within a second. No. 2 also had AI lock on these targets. However, the GCI radar was reporting only five blips. The enemy aircraft appeared in two distinct formations on the scope. There were four aircraft in the first formation and two in the trailing one. The leader locked on the last bogey in the first formation and took necessary tactical actions. The F-16s were flying at 10,000 feet while the intruders were flying at 34-36,000 feet. The F-16s initiated a climb.

They were closing in fast towards the enemy at rates higher than 1,000 knots. The radar controller was continuously updating on the rapidly changing aerial situation. The rear section of two enemy aircraft was flying faster than the front one and had come quite close to the leading section. Vital seconds were passing quickly. The leader rechecked his electronic sensors (ALR-69) to confirm that no enemy aircraft had locked onto his formation. At the same time, with the help of HUD TD Box, the leader quickly picked up the enemy aircraft visually at 7 NM and announced it on the radio. The leading section of the enemy was flying in a right extended echelon with a distance of about 4,000 feet between each aircraft. The rear section was also in the same formation and was positioned to their left side. All six aircraft were Mig-23s, camouflaged in khaki colour.

The leader closed in and at a distance of about 7 NM, the computer had started flashing the DLZ symbol on the HUD, confirming that the enemy was within his AIM-9L missile range. However, the other two conditions i.e. the IR tone and missile seeker head being locked on the target were not met. This was probably because the enemy had brought the throttle back as a part of his counter tactics to the IR missiles. The leader was closing in fast and he made three attempts to lock the missile seeker head-on with the enemy aircraft but all without success. Luckily, in the fourth attempt, when less than 2 NM from the enemy aircraft, his AIM-9L seeker head locked the bogey and he got solid audio tone that further confirmed that he could fire his missile. In the words of Khalid:

At 1.7 NM, I launched my first missile. My aircraft shuddered as the missile left the aircraft, upsetting me for a while. This was my first experience of firing a missile. I saw my missile taking a lead for its target while I started looking for other enemy aircraft. I had made an oblique, left to right, low to high, conversion attack on the enemy at 130-140 degrees aspect angle. After firing the first missile, I reversed my bank to clear my belly from any unnoticed enemy threat. At this time, I was 1-2 NM behind all the enemy aircraft, which is an ideal position for shooting down a bandit. The leading section was exactly in front of me, whereas the trailing section was 11 o'clock just a few thousand feet ahead. I had rejected lock from my first target and switched over to Missile Override ACM 20 x 20 radar mode for auto lock on the enemy aircraft. This action would also select AIM-9P missiles that were more suitable for firing under the new set of conditions. I chose the third aircraft of the leading formation as my second prey; the No. 2 and leader could become my subsequent targets. When my Sidewinder-P missile left the aircraft rail, I saw it navigating towards the target. I quickly took aim for the next target.

While Khalid was busy doing this, the GCI controller announced that two enemy aircraft were behind him. He immediately turned around to face the new threat but found nothing. A mistake had been made; the radar controller had given him a wrong break due to false clutter on his scope. Khalid's next target had meanwhile flown out of his weapon ranges and was heading for his own territory. Chasing the enemy was out of the question because of tactical considerations and strict instructions to avoid violating the Afghan air space. Khalid decided to exit in a safe tactical manner.

After the mission, the Base authorities as well as squadron pilots saw the video repeatedly. Everyone was convinced that Khalid had achieved the kills; however, the wreckage was not found and nothing was heard on the subject for a few days. Meanwhile, a team of American experts analysed the recording and commented that in all probability, missiles had hit the target. Later, Inspector General Frontier Corps (IGFC) visited the squadron about seven weeks later. Since the combat area fell under his jurisdiction, he had organized the search and recovery of the wreckage. The search party had reported that one aircraft had fallen on the Pakistani side of the border while the second debris had drifted into the territory controlled by the Afghan troops. The Afghan forces had mined the area to curb Mujahideen movements; therefore, the recovery of the wreckage was not possible. As explosions above 30,000 feet caused the wreckage to be scattered over a large area, and due to the risk of mine explosions, only one missile pylon of the downed enemy aircraft was recovered and presented to the IGFC by the search party.

Hat Trick for Khalid

a. Pilots   Squadron Leader Ehtsham Zakaria (Leader)

Flight Lieutenant Khalid Mehmood (No. 2)

b. Controller   Squadron Leader Saif ur Rahman

c. Date   3 November 1988

d. Aircraft Shot   Su-22

e. Area   West of Thal

Squadron Leader Khalid's third and PAF's last confirmed victory came during the course of a CAP mission near Kohat. On this occasion, Khalid was flying as No. 2 in a two-ship formation of F-16s. The encounter opened with Khalid and his leader at 10,000 feet when they were informed by GCI that six unidentified hostile aircraft (bogeys) were heading towards the border. A subsequent message confirmed that three of them had violated Pakistani airspace while the other three stayed right on the border line.

On a heading of 280 degrees, the two F-16s moved to engage; the lead quickly informed GCI that he had radar contact. Khalid obtained a lock on the No. 2 aircraft, which was flying on the southern side of the formation. They continued to close the gap but at a distance of 8 NM, Nos. 2 and 3 of the enemy formation executed a 180 degree turn that very quickly allowed them to regain the security of the Afghanistan airspace. For some reason, the leading Afghan fighter kept coming in and at a range of 7 NM, the F-16 lead pilot obtained a visual contact, with Khalid following suit moments later. At this time both F-16s were still at 10,000 feet while the bandit, an Su-22, was some 7,000 feet higher. Both F-16s then initiated a gradual climb as the Su-22 began turning to depart, the enemy pilot having been warned by his GCI of the presence of the two F-16s. His tardiness in heading for safety was to prove fateful. The leader elected to press home his attack, but the Su-22 pilot then showed good tactical sense by turning to face the threat. This prevented the first F-16 from launching a missile. Besides, the leader had experienced some difficulty with his Sidewinder, which may have prevented him from engaging the target. In choosing to evade the threat posed by the leading F-16, the Su-22 pilot placed himself at the risk of attack by Khalid, who wasted no time in making a hard right turn into the Su-22 and launched an AIM-9L from a range of 2.7 NM in a head-on pass. While all this was going on, the lead F-16 began manoeuvring into a position which would enable him to engage the Su-22 with gunfire from a 6 o'clock position. He still had some way to go when Khalid's Sidewinder struck home. Smoke and flying panels issued from the damaged fighter, which continued flying about 10 NM inside Pakistan.

Khalid realized very quickly that the Su-22 was damaged. He waited a few more seconds before launching another AIM-9L at an aspect angle of about 150-160 degrees. The missile had barely left the rail when the enemy pilot ejected. This missile also scored a direct hit, causing the Su-22 to break in two and to head earthwards in flaming debris. The entire incident was observed from the ground by personnel of the Pakistan Army and by Pathan tribesmen. The wreckage of the Afghan Su-22 fell 10 NM from Thal on the bank of river Kurram.

Maj. Gen. Ghazi-ud-din Rana presenting a Kalashnikov rifle to Flight Lieutenant Khalid Mahmood

Pakistan's Militia forces in the area apprehended Captain Abdul Hashim, the pilot of the ill-fated fighter.

A tribal chief in the Kohat area contacted Air Headquarters (Air HQ) and expressed the wishes of his people to present arms to the pilot who had shot down the Afghan aircraft. Following the directive of the CAS, the Base Commander Kohat arranged a special function, to commemorate the occasion. Most of the civilian and military dignitaries of Kohat, some senior PAF officers from Air HQ and many tribal chiefs were invited. In the ceremony, Khalid was presented a pen-pistol (on which his name was engraved as Pilot Officer Ababeel), a stiletto, two scabbards of Klashnikov rifle and some bullets for the pistol. Besides, a copy of the Holy Quran, wrapped in the national flag,

placed in traditional coloured hand-woven 'Changairs', was also presented to Khalid. It was according to him, quite a touching moment.

For the PAF, that was just about it, although Khalid was to enjoy a further moment of excitement when flying solo during a hot, night scramble mission in an F-16B on 31 January 1989. On that occasion, he was directed to investigate a border violation near Bannu and he headed towards the area at 10,000 feet under GCI control. Repeated attempts at obtaining an IR lock on the enemy contact (which was down at 2,000 feet and which was suspected to be on a bombing raid) failed to meet with success. As Khalid moved closer under GCI control, the aircraft put its light on and was revealed to be an An-24. Displaying outstanding airmanship, Khalid let it go. He pulled up and began flying above it, advising GCI that the An-24 was probably planning to defect. Ultimately, the transport aircraft made a landing approach over the River Kuram (a dried-up riverbed), apparently because the pilot believed it to be a paved runway. Moments after touching down, the An-24 struck a palm tree and cartwheeled before being engulfed in a massive explosion, followed by numerous secondary detonations of the ammunition it was carrying.

Near Engagements/ Missed Opportunities

The First Encounter

a. Pilot   Flight Lieutenant Anwar Hussain (Leader)

         Flying Officer Amjad Bashir (No. 2)

b. Controller   Flight Lieutenant Zahid Bangash

c. Date   11 February 1986

d. Area   Parachinar

The wing of an SU-25 aircraft shot down by the PAF

A formation of two F-6s took-off for a CAP mission, and once over the station, started to hold at 15,000 feet. Within a few minutes the controller saw two blips on the radarscope almost touching the border from the northeast of Parachinar. He immediately vectored the CAP towards the targets. The leader called 'tally' (visual contact) and manoeuvred to engage. Two more aircraft appeared on the radarscope. The leader was informed immediately, and again he called 'tally'. The bogeys had already violated the border and were now turning back. The CAP aircraft were happily placed behind them at 3 NM. The bogeys were maintaining speed close to Mach 1 and soon re-entered their own territory. The controller, therefore, asked the leader to turn back. The leader said that he could get them and he was going for them. Saying this, he crossed the Pak-Afghan border. The controller kept urging him to disengage but the leader did not reply. Suddenly, four more aircraft appeared on the radarscope heading towards the F-6s. The controller passed their position to the leader who called 'tally' with four Mig-23s. Now there were eight enemy aircraft against two F-6s. The leader now realized that he was heavily outnumbered; he turned about, hit the deck, and returned to the Base.

The First Near-Engagement (F-16s versus Afghan Su-25s)

a. Pilots   Group Captain
                 Shahid Kamal (Leader)

                 Squadron Leader
                 Rahat Mujeeb (No. 2)

                 Squadron Leader
                 Khalid Chaudhry (No. 3)

b. Controller   Squadron Leader Saif ur
                 Rehman

c. Date   12 April 1986

d. Area   Near Parachinar

The formation took-off early in the morning and proceeded towards Parachinar as briefed. The controller was vigilant and reported enemy aircraft close to the border. The formation checked fuel and switches on a call from the leader and cooled the AIM-9Ls. At about 20 NM short of Parachinar, the formation noticed two blips close to each other heading into Pakistan territory. The leader locked the enemy fighter and announced that he was engaged (i.e. committed into attack). The formation raced on at combat speeds on a westerly heading. The enemy fighters were sampled and before long, the leader fired his first missile on the enemy aircraft. The formation turned about with the leader still in front; the mutual cover more effective, but no missile impact was seen.

The controller again turned the formation around and reported enemy fighters still in our territory, apparently unhurt and unaware of the PAF pilots' intentions. The leader again locked the Afghan aircraft while No. 2 and 3 maintained formation and mutual support 3-4 miles behind. On closing in, the leader again found the target within missile range and fired another missile and missed the target again. After this, the leader handed over the lead to Khalid Chaudhry and fell back in battle formation with No. 2. After a couple of turns, the new leader spotted two Su-25s flying in simple wingman formation. He got a quick lock-on and after meeting all the parameters, fired the missile, which headed for the enemy and thereafter turned right into the sun. The formation then turned towards easterly heading.

Group Captain Shahid's film revealed that he had valid locks on both the occasions. However, he had fired both the missiles at the outer DLZ missile ranges against receding targets that were powered by engines without reheat (the Su-25s do not have afterburners). Since these aircraft were flying at cruising speeds, they radiated very little IR energy at the outer limits of AIM-9L DLZ. Khalid's failure to hit the target could not be analysed because his aircraft was equipped with a history recorder instead of an airborne video tape recorder (AVTR).

A Lost Opportunity

a. Pilots   Squadron Leader
                 Rao Qamar Suleman
                 (Leader)

                 Flight Lieutenant
                 Nawaz (No. 2)

b. Controller   Squadron Leader
                 Saif-ur-Rehman

c. Date   14 May 1986

d. Area   Near Parachinar

A formation of two Mirages of 18 Tactical Attack (TA) Squadron took-off from Kamra at 1100 hours to mount a CAP southeast of Parachinar at 15,000 feet. The controller informed the formation about a number of

56

slow flying targets coming towards the border. After an abortive attempt to pick up contact, the formation descended to 3,000 feet and flying at 550 knots, picked up tally with six Mi-24 Hind gunship helicopters at 3-4 NM range. The gunships were flying at 7-8,000 feet. The leader decided to engage the front helicopter and asked his No. 2 to take the last helicopter. He put the sight on the helicopter and got an immediate radar lock-on. However, there was no missile lock-on. At 1.4 km range, the pilot went to rapid air-to-air gun mode. At around 900 meters from the target, he pressed the trigger but the guns did not fire. The leader broke off and No. 2 closed in to his target. He pressed the trigger at a range of 8-9,000 meters but the guns did not fire. Thus, he also broke off. The formation landed back safely.

In the post-flight, the gun circuit breaker of the leader's aircraft was found to have popped out because of an electrical short-circuiting in the gun pack. No. 2's gun had not fired because, while selecting the switches to Hot (armed), he had not removed the gun trigger latch. Thus, a golden opportunity to kill two gunship helicopters was lost because of bad luck on the part of the leader and lack of experience on the part of No. 2.

The Near Engagement of F-16 Aircraft with Mig-23s

a. Pilots	Squadron Leader Hameed Qadri (Leader)
	Squadron Leader Yousaf (No. 2)
b. Controller	Squadron Leader Shahzada
c. Date	19 June 1986
d. Area	Quetta

The Afghan Air Force had increased its air activity north of the Samungli area during the third week of June 1986. No. 9 Squadron was tasked to send a CAP mission to northwest of Ziarat to check enemy activity. As per mission briefing, the border was not to be approached closer than 30 NM in the Quetta-Chaman sector and committal was to be avoided unless specifically ordered by the controller.

The formation was asked by the controller to climb to 30,000 feet and set up a CAP station 50 NM north of Quetta. After 40 minutes of CAP, the controller committed it against a formation of two intruders violating Pakistani airspace. The leader correctly abandoned the attack at 20 NM and turned back. However, the controller again committed the formation to the same bandits that were positively violating the border now on a different heading. The leader, while maintaining AI contact, took all the required tactical actions. He then closed in on the two Mig-23s flying in wingman formation. When all the parameters were right, the leader tried to shoot the bandits, first with the AIM-9L and later with AIM-9P. Unfortunately, due to a technical fault, the left drop tank had failed to jettison. This malfunction inhibited firing of missiles from all hard points. Since the missiles could not be fired, an opportunity to score a kill was lost. Without trying the option of using guns, the leader invited his No. 2 to have a go at the bandits. No. 2 reported that he had a valid IR lock but the range was slightly more. Therefore, a few more seconds were required to close in for a valid shot. In view of the ROE for this specific mission, the leader asked his No. 2 to break off and both the aircraft disengaged as instructed.

Rules of Engagement (ROEs)

Ever since the occupation of Afghanistan by the Soviet forces, the PAF was confronted with the delicate issue of how far it should go in engaging hostile aircraft. General instructions were issued from time to time but the ROEs for the PAF fighter-interceptors, based on the Government's overall policy, were formally issued on 8 February 1986 for the first time. From this date to September 1988, those ROEs were revised four times. In other words, on an average, a new amendment came after every eight months.

According to the initial ROEs, CAP aircraft were to be committed only after the intruder had entered the border and flown towards the interior for one minute. After committal, only a single slashing attack was permitted. It was mandatory that the debris of the downed aircraft should fall within Pakistani territory. A missile attack was to be preferred and a pair of missiles was to be fired against a single target. An intruder attacking the border posts could be intercepted only when it was at least 1 NM inside the border. In such a situation, interceptors were to be vectored preferably along the general borderline.

According to the ROEs revised and issued in March 1987, CAP aircraft were to be committed only when the intruder had entered the border and penetrated 5 NM into Pak territory. The engagement with the enemy aircraft was confined to within 5 NM inside the Pakistan border; debris must still fall within Pakistan territory. However, after committal, if a kill was imminent, the pursuit could be continued up to the border. Hot pursuit across the Durand line was not permitted. The limitation of single slashing attack still held.

According to the rules issued in May 1987, only F-16s were to be employed for CAPs. In case of non-availability of F-16s, F-6/A-5 could be launched but they could be committed only when the intruder had penetrated 15 NM or more inside Pakistan territory and Pakistani interceptors were not outnumbered by more than a 1:2 ratio. However, F-16 aircraft on CAP could be committed after the intruder had entered the border and flown towards the interior for 5 NM/1 minute, whichever occurred earlier.

The ROEs issued in September 1988, were more aggressive in nature and they gave greater freedom to the pilots. According to those rules, a target aircraft was to be declared hostile if it came closer than 5 NM from the Pakistan border and its track behaviour indicated that the aircraft was likely to violate Pakistan's airspace. After committal, the decision to continue or to break off was to be made by the pilots. Moreover, in case of violations, pilots were to make positive efforts to shoot down all or most of the aircraft. Their actions were to be bold and aggressive but tempered by their best professional judgement.

It is important to remember that the ROEs had to be subordinated to the political dictates of the situation. The GOP did not wish to escalate the Afghan conflict under any circumstances. Doing anything else would have been strategically counter-productive. So the rationale behind the ROEs was deterrence, to keep the cross border violations to a minimum, and to shoot down any intruding Russo-Afghan aircraft whenever possible. Since most of the Afghan refugees had settled close to the Pak-Afghan border, the Soviets saw the tented camps as training and launching bases for the Mujahideen. The three most convenient overland routes to Afghanistan led from Landikotal, Parachinar, and Miranshah. Thus, the areas close to these population centres became regular bombing targets for the Soviet/Afghan fighters and armed helicopters. These raids often spilled into

Pakistan. Whereas the urgent need to put an end to these blatant violations was duly recognized, there were many limitations. Firstly, the intruders would fly parallel to the border and bomb their targets by violating only a couple of miles thereby giving an impossibly short reaction time for any effective interception. Secondly, to avoid escalating the war, the PAF fighters were denied the freedom of hot pursuit, and shooting down an enemy aircraft was still allowed only if the pilot could ensure that the debris would fall inside the Pakistan territory. Thirdly, engaging with a negative force ratio and in the enemy territory was simply forbidden by the ROEs.

The Role of Air Defence

The CRC located in the Mianwali area was hooked up to a combination of MPDR-45 and MPDR-90 low-looking radars at various locations through several radio relays. The ADGE comprising of MPDRs and MOUs was created in two areas i.e. the Miranshah-Peshawar axis and the Quetta area respectively. The air defence assets also included one SAM flight, which was deployed in the Miranshah area for a short duration. The sub-control center at Samungli was upgraded to Sector Operation Centre (HQ Wessec), exclusively for the Quetta area. The northernmost radar was deployed in the Laram area, while the sensors close to border were deployed in the Landi Kotal and the Khojak areas.

The MPDRs and MOUs remained deployed at their sites for over a decade and provided sustained operations in some of the toughest field conditions. They operated from dawn to dusk on optimum antenna tilt to enable detection at medium and high altitudes. The watch hours for some of the sensors were gradually increased to round-the-clock mode. In the Quetta area, all the radars operated on independent mode and reported to the SOC. The radars in Norsec were hooked up to a CRC. However, weapon controllers also manned each of these radars to allow independent operations whenever required. Thus, the overall manning level remained extremely low. Besides being undermanned, they were also short of system experts. Initially, F-6s from Peshawar and Samungli provided periodic CAPs in their respective areas. Their primary role was to deter the enemy by showing their presence. There were specific instructions to limit engagements. More frequent CAPs were mounted as the number of violations increased. With the arrival of F-16s, the number of CAPs in Norsec area was enhanced to allow the availability of a pair every alternate hour. The night CAPs were also mounted simultaneously. The air defence units controlled the patrolling aircraft closely and precisely near the border areas. The ROEs required prior permission of the regional air commands (available on hot lines) for committal.

The Afghan air violations remained restricted to the border areas. Their targets were the refugee camps along the border. Thus, the CAPs present in the area could not be committed against hit-and-run attacks even when engagement possibilities by hot pursuit existed. In the post-1985 period, the air violations started to become increasingly violent. The ROEs were changed and the committal clearance came more freely. As a result, there were a number of engagements resulting in shooting down of enemy aircraft. Keeping in mind the enemy air activity, a continuous effort was made to improve the ADGE. In one example, a radar was re-deployed on top of a hill. The mule track leading to the top was developed with the help of the Army and the radar was shifted to the new site. The performance of the radar improved dramatically and it adequately

Commanding Officer with controllers at the site of the Mashlak Radar

covered the gaps between the Cherat and Parachinar radars. Later, when the Afghan activity shifted to the Dir and Warsak area, another challenging hilltop site was selected near the Laram area, and an MPDR-90 was deployed there to provide cover to the Chitral area.

Initially, all the sensors were on operational watch from dawn to dusk. Later, they were put on half-hour standby. The communication links, however, had to be maintained round-the-clock. Certain power generators, too, had to be run continuously. Some CRCs had night time standby crews at the sites. In the beginning, two CAP stations were selected i.e. one between Hangu and Kohat and the other slightly east of Peshawar. Later the CAPs were anchored,

depending upon the situation. Night ADA was committed, as the situation demanded. The ADA effort was shared between Kamra and Sargodha air bases.

In the normal mode, the CRCs could receive the back-told tracks up to 100 NM around the centre of the map in use. With the change-over to wide-area automation, numerous centres were prepared to look after the entire air space of Pakistan. CRC in Mianwali area was using the map that had Attock as its centre and could get a high-level back-told picture up to Parachinar only. This was a serious limitation as the high-level and low-level radar pick up could not be integrated, particularly when an engagement was developing. The CRC requirement was to have Kohat as the map centre so that the high-level pick up across the border could be displayed on the scope and the controller could accordingly update the fighters. It was not possible to divert the attention of the controller towards the high-level air situation while he was busy controlling an engagement. This problem was referred to all the relevant agencies like CADAM, 108 AED etc. The cost quoted by the manufacturers for developing Kohat as the map centre was not only very high but also required six to eight months. While these efforts were going on, the controllers at the CRC, through trial and error, managed to develop a command instruction to the computer to shift the map to any place of their choice without any expensive modification. This proved very effective and a systematic methodology was worked out to employ this system in all the CRCs. When Hangu was selected as the map centre, the operations became easier to handle. High-level air surveillance information was used to the PAF's advantage, and on several occasions, it helped to ascertain the exact number of aircraft in a formation.

In keeping with the ROEs issued by the NAC, the controllers were required to ensure that the ratio between adversaries and PAF fighters never exceeded 2:1. On numerous occasions the Afghan aircraft, while approaching the border, flew tight formations. The radar would generally show only two blips indicating two aircraft. Close to or on the border they usually turned out to be four or more aircraft. The CRC display is synthetic while the MPDRs indicate the likely strength of aircraft in a formation as raw radar picture. The controllers were deployed at key MPDRs that helped overcome this serious limitation and provided standby cover in a situation where a CRC was not available. Besides, the controllers were also responsible for ensuring that the debris of the downed aircraft fell

inside Pakistan. The situation proved tricky for those aircraft which were operating very close to the border. They normally violated the border by 1-2 NM before turning back. The controllers on the other hand had to announce committal in code words at distance of not less than 15 NM from the adversaries.

The duty staff of the higher echelons monitoring the progress of an interception (SOC, NAC) tended to micro-manage the units controlling the missions, thereby restricting their freedom of action. Consequently, the superiority of the available weapon system was not often fully exploited.

The personnel of MOUs and sensors in the Norsec area were rotated periodically; the personnel in the Wessec remained at their location for a minimum period of one year. For boarding and lodging, the majority of the units made temporary arrangements on a self-help basis. Water, fuel, and rations were supplied on mule backs at certain sites and during winters, ice had to be melted at some of the sites for washing and drinking. At most of the locations, the movement of personnel remained restricted for security reasons. They generally remained cut-off from their families for the duration of their deployment. At some sites, the men and officers shared common lodging and boarding facilities. The mobile air defence units were not structured to function in remote areas for prolonged durations. A number of the units had to move out at short notice and without adequate preparation. The officers who were commanding units thus remained occupied, making provisions for better living and working conditions for their men throughout their tenure in office. Their determination and perseverance paid off, as at no stage was the morale and courage of their men found wanting.

In the Quetta area, the approach road to the Khojak radar site was mined. A 3-ton transport carrying the controller for the duty ran over one of the three mines. Except for minor damage to the transport luckily there were no other injuries or loss of life.

For reasons of security, the MOUs in the tribal belt were co-located with FC personnel in their posts. In one incident, the local tribesmen kidnapped the personnel of one MOU (three men and one jeep) while they were moving to their post in the Kohat-Miranshah area. The Political Agent, Miranshah recovered them only after paying ransom.

There is a hill behind the Thal airfield which is an old landing strip. The Army was installing a radio relay system on top of this hill, and was also making a road. The Army was requested to widen the road so that an MPDR could be deployed on top of the hill. Close to Taimoor Garh, there is another hill in the Dir area, which is nearly 7,000 feet high. A road was built leading to the hill, with the help of the NWFP government. From the top of the hill, one could see across the Afghan border all the way into the Paka Khan area across the hills and the Lowari Pass.

The Policy Compulsions of the Afghan War

It seems necessary here again to set straight some misconceptions regarding the PAF's role and performance in the Afghan war. The prevalent reality, which has been repeatedly brushed aside by those who remain dissatisfied with the 1:8 exchange achieved by the PAF in the Afghan war, is that both the PAF and the Pakistan Army were required to adhere to a policy of avoiding escalation laid down by the Government.

This policy was adopted after much debate at the levels of the DCC and the JCSC, and all the three air chiefs of the time fully acquiesced in it. The specific components of the policy were, that:

a. Pakistan was not trying to win the war for the Afghani people. Pakistan was, however, determined to provide several kinds of moral, material and diplomatic support to the Afghan resistance, but while doing so it was required to avoid a direct or escalated involvement in the war.

b. Pakistan's real threat was from India. That threat had increased during the Afghan war due to the Soviet pressure on India to assume real and credible threatening postures against Pakistan. Exercise Brass Tacks was one example. Several experts from the US Departments of State and Defence had, for the first time, accepted that there was a serious threat to Pakistan from India.

c. All the critically needed modernizations that were taking place in the Pakistan Army, Navy and Air Force were to be preserved for defence against India.

d. The PAF was under orders to use all the means it could, to avert an intensified air war directly with the Soviet air power. That was a distinct possibility and if it had materialized, Pakistan's Afghan war policy would have suffered a serious setback.

e. A dramatically demonstrated inferiority of the AAF at the hands of the PAF in unrestrained air engagements could have triggered the Soviet Union to escalate the air war in a face-saving reaction. Such an escalation, maintained even for a few days, would have been disastrous for Pakistan's security, and for national interest.

f. On the other hand, since the Pakistani armed forces were being given access to some top-of-the-line US military equipment, in recognition of their status as allies, it was necessary to make use of such equipment in support of the Afghan war. Only then could the political leaders in America and Europe justify the sale clearances for the sophisticated weapon systems that Pakistan was receiving.

*. The Air Force ROEs were carefully formulated in the context of the aforementioned security compulsions and national objectives. The ROEs were neither designed nor suitable for the maximization of the PAF's aerial kills in the Afghan war. Anticipating the under-standable frustration that the ROEs would generate amongst the pilots and controllers who were involved in the Westcap operations, frequent indoc-trination briefings at the level of the squadron and unit commanders were held. The more senior among these unit commanders were periodically briefed by the Chief of the Air Staff—and more frequently by the VCAS, the two AOCs and the DCAS (O)—to keep them updated on developments in the national policy on the Afghan war.

Analysis

The Afghan war was not a war in the classical sense. Firstly, the PAF was engaged in purely defensive air operations. Secondly, the overriding political consideration was that the PAF involvement should be kept to the minimum. Pakistan did not wish to escalate this conflict. From this point of view, it was a frustrating experience for the PAF. The Afghan Air Force and the Russian aircraft were frequently bombing border targets within Pakistani territory. The PAF could not really retaliate to prevent them from such action.

During this war, the limited resources of the PAF were stretched to their limits. The aircraft maintenance remained under great pressure. The F-16s were loaded and unloaded a number of times in a 24-hour span for training and operational missions. The endurance of the aircrew was tested to the extreme limit. In the beginning, the F-16 pilots came early in the morning, flew a CAP mission, and then flew a sortie with trainee pilots before having a late lunch. They returned at night for ADA duties. It was always long hours, odd flying times, and a tiring schedule. Night training and currency had to be maintained. A pilot had to be scheduled keeping in mind his fatigue level and mental state. Similarly, for engineering officers and technicians, double shifts had to be shared. The personnel were super-charged and they worked well beyond their normal endurance. It was a proud performance made possible through unflinching dedication and commitment. Their performance mirrored the best of the PAF's enduring traditions of excellence. The PAF—and especially the F-16 crews—emerged from this long trial as disciplined and mature professionals deriving the maximum benefit from their extended exposure to warlike conditions. What they gained in terms of rich experience of combat and endurance, they imparted to their younger charges in the years that followed. Their determination to excel, not merely succeed, has been their gift to the PAF.

The lack of intelligence about the adversary's mode and concept of operations forced the PAF to prepare and brief their combatants for all possible contingencies. While that may be a safe mode of operations, it was not the most effective way from the combat point of view. The excessively cautious attitude of the combatants put them in a defensive frame of mind, compelling them to miss several opportunities of making a kill.

For a brief period, the concept of delivering a 'single slashing attack' was adopted by the PAF. This meant the execution of a single firing pass on an adversary, at a high speed, to ensure minimum exposure time for its own interceptors in a combat zone that was often characterized by the presence of multiple hostile aircraft. The slashing attack was a difficult tactic to apply in all situations, but was chosen for its consistency with the national policy objectives. In due course, other attack profiles (including the zoom attack) and other tactics were tested, and those considered suitable were developed for each type of fighter assigned to Westcap duties.

The ROEs took into account the constraints of the radar-masking terrain and the minimal ADGE. The Pak-Afghan border spans the rugged Hindukush mountains, so that one's precise location with reference to the Durand Line can be difficult to interpret visually. This forced the PAF pilots to rely largely on the ground radars to keep them from violating the border-related ROEs. Typical was the case of an F-16 pilot who had been ideally positioned behind an enemy aircraft with all the attack parameters right, his missile locked and ready to fire with the push of a button, when the diligent (and very unhappy) pilot elected to turn back because he thought the wreckage would fall on the Afghan side of the border. To meet the limitations of ROEs, a single slashing attack well inside our own area was the only option allowed. For the fighter pilots, flying top of the line combat aircraft and confident of producing kills if allowed to fight freely, the ROEs restrictions were simply anathema. The field commanders, while catering for the national policy, devised suitable tactics to tackle the situation under the given circumstances. The average duration of a Westcap was one hour and forty minutes. Each CAP mission involved a cat and mouse game with the enemy. The moment F-16s were vectored towards the enemy, the intruders would withdraw to the safety of the Afghan air space only to return a few minutes later. The restrictions of ROEs often caused frustration and strain on the pilots.

They had to watch the enemy; plan their intercept geometry; and when in firing ranges, abandon the attack to avoid entering Afghanistan. It was normal to arm the missiles for the final firing, once or twice during each mission. The adrenaline would flow and the pulse rate would increase in preparation for action that would mostly not occur. For fighter pilots flying F-16s, this was an actual shooting war—an undeclared combat involving a handful of people; for the rest it was life as usual.

In April 1987, catastrophe struck from a most unexpected quarter. While leading a Westcap of two F-16s near the border, a very experienced F-16 pilot was guiding his No. 2 through a manoeuvre while preparing to engage some Afghan intruders reported in the vicinity. In this stressful situation, the leader picked up his own wingman on his radar scope and mistakenly identifying the blip as one of the enemy intruders, shot down the wingman. Fortunately, the No. 2 was not killed, and ejecting safely he was soon rescued. But the impossible had happened and it rightly came under severe criticism at all levels. For some time thereafter, a certain degree of over-cautiousness was inevitably imposed on the tactical freedom normally exercised by both pilots and ground radar controllers. At the crucial stages of committal, vital decisions were at times delayed because the controllers were seeking permission or clarification from higher headquarters. Such were the effects of the un-warlike Afghan war.

Once the number of F-16s and pilots trained on them began to increase, the PAF resorted to employing these aircraft mostly for Westcaps, partly releasing some squadrons for other tasks. In this war, the enemy always had the initiative and the PAF was perforce operating in a reactive role. It was seen repeatedly that Russo-Afghan fighters approached the Pak-Afghan border only when they were sure that no Westcaps were nearby. The F-16s were the best fighters to employ against the intrusions because only this aircraft had a long on-station time, a deep-look AI radar, and a number of superior air-to-air weapons.

The PAF was constrained by the geopolitical situation, the terrain, the lack of airborne early warning, the absence of beyond-visual-range (BVR) missiles and, above all, the highly restrictive ROEs. Therefore, the enormous air effort generated by the PAF was never expected by its leadership to achieve the large number of aerial kills that would surely have been attainable without these constraints. The young and aggressive PAF pilots had to be treated with empathy, and repeatedly briefed on this point, in order to keep their frustration levels within tolerable limits.

The contribution of the air defence elements during the air operations on the western border, was truly significant. The professional competence and dedication of the air defence controllers were strong links in the chain that formed a well-knit and effective team, and contributed towards several kills. The teamwork of pilots and controllers was subjected to an acid test and both came out with flying colours. The performance of the engineering officers and technicians was, in the highest PAF traditions, simply superb.

Impact of the F-16 on the Afghan War

The initial response to increasing Soviet/Afghan incursions into the Pakistani airspace was to use the conventional air defence effort. However, the PAF was neither equipped to effect a viable response nor were the Soviets deterred from frequent border violations. The entry of the F-16 weapon system into the Afghan war, in 1983 and

onwards, changed the scenario—there would be no more free rides into Pakistan's airspace. The PAF was kept engaged in this undeclared war for the next five to six years. Only the participating aircrew of this weapon system knew the rigours they had to go through in terms of long day and night CAPs, occasional shoot-outs, and understood the high premium on showing restraint and displaying remarkable discipline and thorough professionalism.

The F-16 operations in the Afghan war had their own share of initial problems. As the training and induction of the aircraft progressed rapidly, the PAF F-16 fleet was undergoing a number of upgrades and additions. This hampered the achievement of optimum level of performance from the aircrew. Thus the initial group of pilots who had been trained in the USA, when brought back to the system for a second time around, found themselves unfamiliar with a weapon system that had changed its capability remarkably during the intervening period. For example, the induction of AIM-9L and the upgraded Radar were sufficient to make any relative old timer irrelevant to the operational employment of the aircraft. The fact that the F-16 aircraft still fared well in the Afghan war scenario goes to the credit of those pilots and supervisors, who had to apply their background knowledge of operational employment to prepare a team of pilots capable of taking on threats from Russo-Afghan aircraft.

A select group of pilots received their initial training on the F-16 in the USA. For obvious reasons this training was limited to the basics of aircraft employment only, and restricted to the then flying Block-10 aircraft. As those pilots honed their personal skills in their first year, they rightly concentrated on the basics. They were made increasingly aware of the precious resource placed under them and the necessity of avoiding all risk by not exploring capabilities beyond what had been taught to them during their initial training. Therefore, for a long time, the initial orientation of training on the F-16 aircraft did not go beyond the basic and trusted level of employment and remained confined to base level competence in air combat. To be fair to those pilots, the F-16 of those days was very much a single target track, close combat aircraft. But then the various interactions of the many aids to help develop a complete situation awareness were rarely researched. This was done in later years with similar resources, notwithstanding the advantage of experience that the latter entrants to the system were able to develop.

The new set of supervisors who succeeded the pioneers was not encumbered with the highly standardized training regimes of the latter. Air superiority was extended beyond the known orthodox situations; employment began appearing as the more dominating factor in the applicable training exercises; Air-to-Air firing practice was initiated to impart greater confidence and awareness to the aircrew. Similarly, Air-to-Ground exercises were undertaken and delivery of all types of weapons from the F-16 practised. At the same time the Afghan operations continued unabated and just as the confidence of the F-16 pilots grew with better and more focussed training, their performance improved in the Afghan air operations.

Meanwhile, the number of aircraft had also grown since the initial days of their induction in the PAF. The initial model brought into the country underwent a series of upgrades in equipment and avionics that materially affected the performance and capability of the basic aircraft. These changes were as follows:

a. The basic Block-15 Radar was upgraded to Block-15S level. This meant a capability enhancement with far-reaching

effects. A 'Single Target Track' capability on the Radar was now added with a 'Search while Track' capability, popularly known as the SAM mode. A pilot now locked onto a single target did not necessarily have to be blind to other threats; he could see other targets and read them. His situation awareness thus improved exponentially. This, however, also meant that new tactics needed to be evolved, where this increased information could be effectively used.

b. AIM-9L got inducted in the PAF; this was a major capability enhancement. The PAF was not used to front quarter weapons, and needed to practically relearn the essentials of tactical weapon employment. The weapon needed an essential drill of actions before the launch, breaking from the earlier practice of 'See and Fire' that was prevalent with the AIM-9P. It thus became a matter of intense discipline to follow all the requirements before a weapon could be launched. What added to the problem was the initial non-availability of any training rounds, precluding any 'hands on' practice of the aircrew. As was obvious, AIM-9L employment needed dedicated practice before any aircrew could be declared operational for tactical employment of the weapon. When the training rounds were received, they were only four; two each were handed over to the operational Squadrons. The fresh inductees on the F-16 system were still getting their initial training dedicated to AIM-9P tactics and training. The responsibility for training these pilots on the AIM-9L, therefore, again shifted to the operational squadrons, which were by then still in the learning curve. Inadequate training resources further compounded the difficulties.

c. Another essential input towards development of complete situation awareness comes from the Radar Warning Receiver (RWR). While the practical aspects of this integration have stayed constant, the periodic upgrades of the ALR-69 continued over the years and required a constant reappraisal of the tactical use of this additional information.

What began in 1985 as a tentative introduction of the F-16 in Afghan operations, only two years after the induction of the aircraft on the PAF inventory, was realized in the form of a mature and a more reliable force which came into being in 1989. The statistical evidence of the success of the aircraft over the Afghan and Soviet assets in Afghanistan in terms of a highly beneficial kill ratio, was yet another proof of the enhanced capability of the F-16 over the contemporary fighters. Failures of a tactical nature, and those of decision making at the tactical level, were personal and could be attributed to the process of a learning curve of the F-16 aircrew. Some initial errors in the training concept were rectified through introduction of refined training processes more in line with PAF's own doctrine. Development of viable tactics, and research based upon known enemy behaviour helped institute a training process that was relevant to the actual, prevailing circumstances. This bore fruit in terms of sound tactical application. The beneficial consequences of these measures, moreover, were evident in the form of highly proficient pilot-controller teams that undertook various successful missions. An additional benefit was the much improved general awareness of the entire F-16 community about tactical application in complex scenarios. In a prolonged and uncertain war, which was undertaken with some strict political and tactical considerations, the performance of the relatively young group of F-16 pilots needs to be acknowledged. They went through intense battle pressures in every mission; for them, each mission was 'Hot', regardless of whether or not it materialized as such. Almost every mission had 'Hot' vectors; if they did not result in engagements, that was due to the stringent ROEs.

The F-16 system benefited immensely from this experience; a tradition of realistic training developed, and all activities are now targeted with the ultimate objective of being useful in a real war scenario. In the long run, this F-16 culture was picked up by the rest of the Air Force.

The Effort Expended on CAPS

There is unfortunately a mistaken impression that the CAP effort during the Afghan war was non-productive. Nothing could be further from the truth. All air forces fly a vast range of missions in war and the CAPs among them are not expected to eventuate into an engagement every time. But each CAP mission remains a combat mission in every way. In the words of Air Commodore Shahzad Chaudhry who commanded 9 Squadron from July 1987 to December 1988,

I feel that the negative impression has been the result of our experience of the Eastcaps. Our eastern CAPs were no doubt dead serious, devoted as they were to providing cover to our nuclear installations. But in actual execution they were mostly yawn-stifling exercises. We knew we were flying them primarily as over-insurance to prevent an improbable but nevertheless impermissible-at-any-cost threat from materializing. But during Eastcaps we also knew that ready to shoot as we were, with virtually no ROEs holding us back, our controllers and pilots had never actually engaged with that threat. The east and west CAPs were thus poles apart in both their objectives and execution.

The Impact of CAP Effort on Normal Training in the F-16 Squadron

The CAP effort did not preclude normal training. As stated earlier, the need for continuous training was imperative in the F-16 squadrons, not only to enhance the skill levels and experience of the already inducted pilots but also to cater for the new pilots who were regularly streaming in. Air HQ had budgeted for the extra training effort and just to give time to the squadrons for it, the Westcap missions were assigned to different F-16 squadrons in turn. But even when an F-16 unit was on its operational cycle, almost 50 per cent of the available flying hours were used for training. A squadron on operational cycle always had the freedom to generate on its own, additional hours for flying training. To take on both activities simultaneously meant a lot of extra work and exertion, but every squadron commander felt happy to do it because it qualified and kept proficient nearly all his pilots, in both surface attack and air superiority roles. It was during such maximum performance periods that truly exceptional dedication and commitment to excellence characterized the F-16 crews and their supporting personnel.

The Engagements

Engagements on the western border can be classified according to two identifiable eras. There was the initial involvement, from May 1985 to early 1986. During this period, the extent of involvement, and the ROEs had not yet been clearly formulated, and the initial engagements were thus based on the briefing given to the participants. The Soviet tactics were still undeveloped and basically focussed on bombing the Mujahideen assembly areas. They obviously thought little of PAF's capability to disrupt their mission. The second era of PAF's engagements could be described as better planned and better executed; this began somewhere in early 1987 and lasted until February 1989. These eras were interspersed with relative periods of calm when the Soviet incursions ceased altogether, but the PAF activity continued unabated.

There Should Have Been More Kills

Many of those who had the opportunity to sit through some of the mission briefings and debriefings in the F-16 squadrons, and thus were able to gauge the professional dedication and aggressiveness of the F-16 pilots, would reject outright the underlying insinuations of those who were disappointed that there were not 'more kills'. The then squadron commanders of F-16 squadrons claim confidently that there was no overcautiousness on their part, nor were the ROEs ever allowed to inhibit a bolder exploitation of their combat environment. That environment might appear fairly benign to an outsider. However, during the war, the combat crew worked on the basis of intelligence briefs provided to them by Air HQ who, in addition to their sources within Afghanistan, also obtained for them all that the American Department of Defence and the CIA were willing to provide. 'Keeping those briefs in mind, it would have been foolish on our part to assume the Afghan air environment to be fairly benign', recalled one squadron commander.

There was of course the usual 'butterflies effect' when some inexperienced pilots and controllers were placed in a combat situation, the first few times, but with experience this was soon overcome, as was evidenced by their rapidly improved performance curve. No engagement ever suffered because of this natural phenomenon, and all CAP missions were executed in a highly professional manner. The PAF pilots and controllers remained dedicated to achieving maximum success without violating the operational policy which had been laid down.

A Russian Colonel Confesses

Some years after the Soviet forces evacuated Afghanistan, an ex-squadron commander of an F-16 squadron came across a Russian colonel in a Western capital. The latter had been the squadron commander of a Soviet Air Force bomber squadron that had been deployed to fly combat missions against ground targets both in Afghanistan and Pakistan. He recounted some details of his missions into our border areas and the impact of the F-16s on his squadron's operations. He confided that the presence of the F-16 CAPs weighed heavily on the minds of his pilots. They were, therefore, inclined to make very high level and supersonic bombing runs near the Pakistani border, not caring much about achieving accuracy, only concerned with exiting the area at the earliest opportunity. Such a pattern of operations had been noted by the PAF controllers also, and now its reason was revealed. The PAF had also noted the poor bombing accuracy of the enemy aircraft.

Some Lessons Learnt

During the Afghan war, the PAF learnt some new and valuable lessons, besides relearning some old ones. The PAF as a fighting force learnt to operate and fight in a low intensity but protracted conflict, within some self-imposed and strict rules of engagement. This was an invaluable experience to a new generation of pilots who had not seen action before this war. The experience of this war was quite reassuring for the PAF, for its personnel showed tremendous devotion and dedication. The leadership at all levels proved its mettle. Some weaknesses were, however, also exposed and rectified.

The need for real time intelligence was highlighted as a pre-requisite for cost effective employment of air power.

The non-availability of BVR missiles, poor ADGE, and lack of airfield infra-structure along the western border emerged as major weaknesses in the PAF's force structure.

Air defence weapons like shoulder mounted SAMs, radar controlled SAMs, and radar-controlled guns would have been more effective in the Afghan war environment, but their numbers were meagre. If they were to be backed up by good low-level and air-to-air surveillance systems, the cost would have been very high. Therefore, better survivability assets and better surveillance and intelligence systems would be indispensable if the PAF were to fight a similar war again.

The significance of the lesson that air power is most effective in the offensive role was brought home.

The Depletion of PAF Resources and the Unsuccessful Efforts to Replenish Funding

During the Afghan conflict, that lasted for almost ten years, the PAF had to generate a tremendous flying effort spearheaded by the F-16 fleet. The chart below elucidates the number of sorties/hours flown by various squadrons during the war. The PAF had gone through an experience in which it was subjected to a substantially heavy commitment *vis-à-vis* the other two Services, which did not experience the kind of wear and tear that the PAF had to go through. Most people are not aware of this. For the PAF this was virtually a secret war, subjecting the air force assets to a great deal of stress. The government did not publicly acknowledge the contributions of the Air Force and the rigours the PAF was exposed to. The PAF, as usual, avoided the glare of publicity.

SORTIES/HOURS FLOWN DURING THE AFGHAN WAR

SQUADRON	SORTIES	HOURS
9 SQN	2,221	3,701:40
14 SQN	1,825	2,585:20
11 SQN	346	8,96:15
15 SQN	2,521	2,142:10
26 SQN	2,479	2,394:25
5 SQN	108	141:30
23 SQN	737	563:50
17 SQN	628	824:05
18 SQN	20	27:25
TOTAL	**10,939**	**13,275:40**

After their induction in 1983, the F-16s achieved 7,182 hours in about six years. This huge flying effort caused significant wear and tear on the fleet. During the last year of the Afghan war, their performance reached its peak, and about 85 per cent of the entire F-16 missions were being flown as CAP missions during day and night, mainly on the western border. Out of those missions, as many as 90 per cent were deployed on the western border and the rest were assigned to the defence of Pakistan's nuclear installations. Each aircraft was flying as many as thirty to thirty-five sorties per month, subjecting the aircraft engines, airframe, and the logistic system to great stress.

Pakistan had, meanwhile, ordered additional F-16s, and for several years continued to make payments against the signed contract. However, in October 1990, when the Pressler Amendment was invoked, the PAF had to come to terms with reality. The impact of the Pressler restrictions and how the PAF minimized its damaging effect, have been discussed in the next chapter. This new development immediately created a gap that jeopardized all the planned modernization of the Force structure. Additionally, thanks to the Pressler Law, the induction of an alternate high-tech aircraft was to become a constant worry for the PAF leadership during the years that followed.

3 MAINTAINING FORCE EQUILIBRIUM— THE UPHILL TASK

The New Inductions

The post-Afghanistan war period, according to Air Marshal Aliuddin, was the most difficult time in the PAF's history. It was a period of extreme resource constraint. Almost all the traditional sources that had helped the PAF to maintain a qualitative edge in terms of equipment, management, and organization, were of Western origin. The strengths of the PAF had been its training standards and its interaction with some of the leading Western air forces, especially the RAF and the USAF. After the war, Pakistan lost her strategic importance for the West. The traditional sources dried up and grave problems followed.

The natural life span of any weapon system is twenty-five to thirty years. Although the flight safety record of the PAF had been impressive during the previous decade, it had not yet achieved the ideal near-zero accident rate. On an average, eight to ten aircraft are lost each year because of the type and intensity of flying that the PAF undertakes. On account of attrition and retirements alone, the PAF has to induct, on the average, about twenty-two aircraft per year just to maintain the numbers in its fleet. It is a figure that stuns most people— something not visible in a cursory review. In the past, the PAF had been managing to preserve numbers. The F-6s were inducted in large numbers and thereafter some additional Mirages were added to sustain the fleet. While the F-16 force was gradually building up in the early 1980s and the PAF was short on numbers, the A-5s were procured to keep the overall strength from depleting.

In the post-Afghan war period, with the Western sources drying up, the biggest dilemma for the PAF was how to maintain and sustain the numbers. The induction of a hi-tech aircraft was one part of its crisis; the sheer sustenance of the fleet was another. Most of the Western powers were ready to sell new submarines, tanks, surface-to-air guided weapons, and self-propelled artillery for the Army, and Pakistan purchased a substantial number of these from the Western sources. But the PAF was effectively denied access to any hi-tech aircraft because, as the argument went, that would have brought about a qualitative change in the capabilities of the Pakistan armed forces. Even for the sustenance of the fleet in terms of sheer numbers, the options were limited. Adding more F-6s to the fleet was ruled out. The PAF chose the F-7 instead, which is marginally better than the F-6 in capabilities like range, endurance, and relative sophistication of its weapon systems, etc. Additionally, some used or retired Mirages in the form of spares that could be acquired at a reasonable price from the market, could then be overhauled, refurbished and put to use. Apart from these options, some other aircraft of similar capabilities might have been available, like the Mirage F-1 from the French suppliers.

It made sense to the PAF leadership to stick to aircraft types that were already flying with the PAF. Owing to the already available infrastructure, these could be integrated into the existing mainstream with relative ease. This is what the PAF did. At a very low cost, the Australian package that gave forty-five additional Mirages, was contracted; something which could not be envisaged when the deal was made. The PAF also received in the bargain, spares worth $500 million, which the PAF was able to consume or put in its stores. Innovations such as these kept the PAF going. But such interim measures caused the PAF to gradually lose the qualitative edge that it had earlier enjoyed in the region.

During that difficult decade, while the sustenance of the fleet was the most pressing problem and the acquisition of a hi-tech aircraft had been stalled for some time, the PAF did not sit idle. It decided to upgrade its older aircraft with low cost avionics systems over which it could exercise control, and also to upgrade some weapons on these aircraft to enhance their capability. The cost of a state-of-the-art modern fighter/bomber aircraft or something close to it, would have been to the tune of $35 to 60 million per unit. A comparable capability could, however, be acquired by upgrading some of the PAF's existing aircraft in terms of radar performance, weapon delivery, accuracy, and nav-attack systems that could be managed within around $3 million per aircraft. Equipping an older, less capable aircraft would have been an inefficient solution. So the PAF went for the upgrades like the ROSE (Retrofit of Strike Element), which gave the old Mirages very good nav-attack, weapon delivery, and other capabilities.

The Griffo radar development programme is now nearing completion after some unavoidable delays. The two versions of the Griffo radar (Griffo-7 and Griffo-M) have been reasonably successful and have significantly enhanced the aircraft combat capability. The Griffo-M, which would be equivalent to or slightly better than the existing APG-66 of the F-16 radar, would give the PAF additional night capability. The PAF also inducted weapon systems, some indigenously, and others through resources such as the Air Weapon Complex. So,

whereas the PAF did not have access to high technology and support from the West, and despite some limitations in the systems available from elsewhere, it did acquire whatever was possible. An acceptable level of combat capability, readiness, and deterrence was maintained throughout. Besides, there were other, smaller programmes during this period. The Air Force went for Mistral and Anza—surface-to-air missiles and terminal defence systems. The ageing French surface-to-air missile system was in need of an upgrade, and so a major programme was undertaken. The Air Force thus kept its older weapon systems aircraft from becoming obsolete. Chaff and Flares dispensers, radar warning receivers, and laser automates for more accurate weapon deliveries were all added to the old aircraft to increase their capability. What could not be improved was the performance of the aircraft from the engine and airframe points of view.

Sometime in the near future, if the PAF could acquire a genuine hi-tech aircraft that could see it through the next twenty to thirty years—in the class of the Mirage-2000, F-16s, Grippen, etc.—then similar upgrades might be possible to keep the PAF abreast with any new air threats as well.

The Complexity of Modernization Programmes

Several studies were conducted by the PAF between 1984 and 1986 to determine the best replacement option for the F-6 aircraft. From the very outset it was clear to the PAF that the country's financial resources would not permit the acquisition and operation of the latest Western aircraft in large numbers. Therefore, the PAF considered an unconventional option: updating an existing and proven aircraft by incorporating in it equally proven high technology, off-the-shelf components, from amongst the best available. This programme called 'Project Saber-II' envisaged modifying the existing Chinese F-7 (Mig-21) airframe with a modern American engine, radar, radio, IFF, and weapons. The new aircraft was to be assembled from kits supplied by China, USA, and from those manufactured at Pakistan Aeronautical Complex, Kamra. The expected delivery time of this aircraft was estimated to be ten years. After separate exhaustive discussions with the Chinese and potential American participants in the programme, the concept was found promising, workable, and economically attractive. On the basis of these initial conclusions, a feasibility study was ordered at a cost of $2.5 million, in which PAF engineers participated with their Chinese and American counterparts. Clearances were obtained from the governments of China and the United States.

In January 1987, Grumman Aerospace Corporation was awarded a contract to carry out a concept definition study of Sabre-II. Grumman conducted the study in cooperation with Chinese and PAF engineers, and it was completed in August. According to this study, the cost of the Saber-II would exceed the price of an 'austere' model F-16 that had been offered for $13 million per aircraft. The projected performance of the Saber-II was inferior to that of the F-16 in terms of manoeuvrability, payload, and radii of action. Another aspect highlighted by the study was that the projected service life of the Sabre-II could be increased from 2,400 to 3,000 hours compared to 8,000 hours for the F-16. Additionally, the Sabre-II would need to qualify for carrying optional equipment like Forward Looking Infra Red Pods, Laser Designator Pods, and various air-to-air and air-to-surface missiles like Sparrow (BVR), Penguin (Anti-Shipping), and HARM (Anti Radiation) Missiles. All these would have entailed additional costs.

Project Saber-II, apart from providing a replacement of F-6 at an affordable cost, also envisaged a transfer of technology to Pakistan and the participation of PAC Kamra in the assembly of the aircraft leading to its eventual manufacture. While the concept was technically feasible, it remained a high-risk project with a production cost exceeding the target cost of about $8 million as specified in the Air Staff Requirements. Therefore, the viability of Saber-II was indicated to be doubtful by the study, on the grounds of cost and development risks. The project was effectively killed by the breakdown in US/Chinese relations following the incident in Tiananmen Square.

Concurrently with the Sabre-II project, the Air Staff studied and developed another replacement option, of acquiring a mix of 113 F-16s (at a unit cost of $13 million) and fifty-five readily deliverable Chinese F-7M. The proposed F-16 was to be an 'austere' model, achieved by introducing some operationally acceptable de-sophistication. The significance of the F-16 (113) was that it would enable the PAF to be assured of nine full strength squadrons of F-16s for the next twenty years. Similarly, fifty-five F-7Ms were considered enough to maintain two full strength squadrons for twenty years. Air Headquarters found that this option offered the best combat power with the least risk, and required the shortest delivery period. For a timely response in the face of changes in both the quantum and accelerated timing of the Indian military threat, the PAF found that the only appropriate course was to avail of this option (113 F-16s and fifty-five F-7s). These were the preferred options of the PAF leadership in 1986.

The adoption of this option included, as a first step, 'off-the-shelf,' immediate acquisition of twenty Chinese F-7M fighters at a cost of about $4 million per aircraft. However limited the operational capability of the F-7M, it provided the most inexpensive element and urgent means of preventing the PAF's force degradation and forestalling serious vulnerabilities in the years 1988 and beyond. The main idea behind this acquisition was to prevent rapid loss of capability while the PAF's F-6s were winding down towards the end of their life. They were beginning to show their age, despite a programme of upgrades, and their natural replacement was the successor of the F-6 in Chinese service, the F-7.

The immediate acquisition of twenty F-7Ms had also the merit of enabling the PAF to build up a large pool of pilots and technicians trained on this type, which, although based on an old Soviet design, could with reasonable effect, impede advancing enemy forces and provide air cover in an emergency. Familiarity with the F-7M could thus give the PAF a standing capability of inducting a large number of F-7Ms from China in a heavy attrition war or a longer than expected war, or indeed in any situation of severe crisis. The very large reservoir of F-7Ms in China could, in these circumstances, prove to be a vital source for bolstering Pakistan's stamina in resisting aggression to the maximum extent.

Another factor favouring the F-7M acquisition was that if financial or political constraints made it impossible to rapidly acquire 113 or even a lesser number of F-16s, the F-7M would provide the most affordable interim capability until a suitable alternative to the F-16 could be found.

The PAF's need for the replacement of the F-6s, for Operational Conversion training of new pilots (i.e. training of young academy graduate pilots to their first fighter), was of paramount importance. The F-7M seemed to be an attractive option at a very reasonable cost, for this role.

The Programme Cost (cost of aircraft plus initial equipment and spares) for the acquisition of one squadron of F-7M (twenty aircraft) was about $80 million. This cost included the initial package of spares for two years and all tools, testers and special purpose equipment to support this aircraft up to the intermediate level of maintenance. The existing F-6 facilities with F-7M testers and support equipment were considered sufficient to support operational and maintenance activities related to the operation of the new aircraft. No upgradation of facilities was contemplated.

The Chinese manufacturers (CATIC) were requested to provide some planning and budgetary estimates for the F-7M. As expected, they made even their initial offer quite attractive, both in terms of the required investment and the long-term repayment schedules.

Force Structure Review
During most of 1988, a Force Structure Review was in progress at the Air Headquarters. It was necessitated by the likely exit of the F-6 fleet from the Service and also because the existing fleet of Mirages was rather small. The PAF wanted to decide on its force structure for the year 1991 and beyond. At that time, after extensive deliberations, and after having examined all the available data on all the available options, including F-16s and Mirage-2000s, there emerged a consensus among the Air Staff that the PAF should opt for more F-16s if the US Government agreed. The PAF teams also evaluated Mirage-2000 E at that time. It was also decided that F-6s should be gradually replaced with F-7s. In 1988, the PAF was operating 332 fighter aircraft of which 179 were F-6s that had been inducted during 1965-70. These aircraft were approaching the end of their operational life and it was

forecast that by 1995, most F-6s would have to be replaced. Accordingly a development plan was proposed, which recognized that F-6s could not be replaced by expensive aircraft like F-16s. A mix of low and high cost/performance aircraft was proposed. This plan was approved by the government in 1989 and subsequently, contracts were signed for ninety-five F-7s and seventy-one F-16s. This development plan increased the number of F-7s from fifty-five to ninety-five.

The PAF decided to opt for the F-16s over one or two less attractive options that were available. At this stage, Iqbal Akhund, who was Advisor to the government at that time, wrote a letter to the PAF, probably at the behest of the Prime Minister, expressing his concern that the PAF was being extensively influenced by American interests. He urged the PAF to aim for diversification and, therefore, consider the Mirage-2000 aircraft, which had remained, off and on, an examined option. The PAF responded to this advice by telling the government that it had selected the F-16s on merit. It rationalized the entire process, by calling attention to the infrastructure that had already been set up and also to the higher costs involved in acquiring a different type of hi-tech aircraft.

In the implementation of the Force Structure Review-1988, the PAF was guided by the strategy evolved by Air Chief Marshal Hakim of going from smaller to bigger programmes. At that time, FMS-2, the US military sales programme, was also available to the PAF. Out of its share, which was close to about $260 million, the PAF managed to convince the Pentagon in December 1988, and signed for eleven replacement F-16s and 360 AIM-9 missiles. Ijlal Haider Zaidi, the then Defence Secretary, had promised to provide $200 million every year for five or six years to purchase any number of aircraft the PAF could get.

The Induction of the F-7P

The F-7M was first evaluated by the PAF in early 1987. The evaluation included both air-to-air as well as air-to-ground performance. For that purpose, two aircraft were ferried to Pakistan and trials conducted at Peshawar and Masroor.

The PAF's F-7P 'Skybolt' is a variant of the F-7M 'Airguard', which was improved for export to customers familiar with Western aircraft. The two-piece canopy of the F-7M and F-7P has greater bird strike resistance and comes with a GEC Avionics Head Up Display and weapons aiming computer plus other new avionics. Two extra underwing hard points are provided among a range of other improvements. Of these, the most significant for the PAF's Skybolt are the Martin Baker 10L zero-zero ejection seat and the provision for up to four AIM-9L Sidewinders. A radar warning receiver (RWR) was also to be fitted in all the aircraft.

The F-7P's 13,450-lb thrust, WP-7N engine gives it a thrust-to-weight ratio similar to that of the heavier Mig-21 Bs, but its lighter airframe provides a wing loading claimed to be even lower than the F-16's. This makes the F-7P an excellent fighter in an environment where the IAF's front line inventory includes more than three hundred Mig-21s.

The PAF had an interest in the Mig-21 because of its good performance and reliability, as reported by many PAF pilots who had flown the aircraft while on exchange tours with the Arab air forces. One of these pilots, Flight Lieutenant Sattar Alvi, had shot down an Israeli Mirage III with a K-13 air-to-air missile while flying a Syrian Mig-21 in 1971. Pakistan ordered twenty F-7Ps and four FT-7 two-seat trainers. They were delivered to 20 Squadron in November 1988.

Further consignments of F-7Ps came in lots of sixty in 1988-89, fifteen FT-7s in 1990-92, and forty F-7Ps in 1993. The induction of extra numbers was necessitated by the enforcement of the Pressler Amendment as a result of which the F-16s, ordered and paid for, had not been released. At that time there was no other immediate way to redress the numerical deficiency. With the 135 aircraft received, six squadrons as well as a squadron of Combat Commanders School were equipped. All F-7Ps were ferried from China to Pakistan by the PAF pilots.

The then existing Sky Ranger 7M GEC Marconi radar had several operational limitations, so the PAF floated tenders to all the companies working on the GEC avionics in South Africa and Italy for developing a combat mode, small, very economical, but effective radar for the PAF's F-7 aircraft. The Italian FIAT Company was selected out of many of the most reputed radar developing companies, as its offer was very economical and very sound. Also, they could do it in the time frame that suited the PAF. Therefore, the contract was given to FIAT to design and develop this radar for meeting the PAF's operational requirements without making huge investments into major aircraft modification, particularly in the nose section of the aircraft. The contract, for 100 radars to be co-produced by FIAT and KARF (Kamra Radar Factory) at PAC Kamra, was signed in June 1993. After co-production, the same facility was to be converted into depot level maintenance for this radar.

The last batch of forty F-7s was inducted in 1993 under a cost-effective contract. The package, including aircraft engines, spares, support equipment, and all the aircraft, came fully modified and upgraded. In the bargain, PAF got the best AVTR, which is better than that of the F-16, the Martin Baker seat, modern radios, RWR, and chaff and flare capability conforming to the specifications spelled out by the PAF. CATIC was also asked to bring their own missile to Pakistan

for tests and trials. With these attractive provisions, the contract was signed for $223 million as against $160 million earmarked by the government for the purpose. Whereas arranging the additional funds was problematic, the provision for the modifications was kept in the contract so that after receiving the equipment within one or two years, the payment schedule could be spread over ten years or so.

All the aircraft were received within one year of signing the contract. This contract was quite unprecedented because the forty aircraft came fully modified and fully operational while enough funds remained available in the contract for other elements. For example, one hundred AVTRs were to be bought from GEC through CATIC, to upgrade the PAF's existing fleet of A-5s and F-7s. More radios and sixty IFF/SIF sets were also to be bought through the same contract. About $30 million in the contract were earmarked for the development of about 200 RWRs and chaff and flare units locally. The 200 RWRs and chaff and flares units were co-developed, co-produced, and co-assembled in Pakistan. This contract made a major contribution towards the operational readiness of the PAF, apart from boosting Pakistan's local manufacturing capacity and the transfer of technology.

In order to support the F-7 fleet, an overhauling facility had to be established in Pakistan. This facility was quite expensive even in China. The PAF decided to set up this facility at Faisal where most of the engines were overhauled. The available engine test bed was meant for F-6 and not for F-7 aircraft. This posed a unique problem during the engine test runs, when the deflector at the rear of the exhaust tunnel was repeatedly breaking up. The CATIC team came to Pakistan thrice but could only suggest the installation of an independent test bed for the F-7 engine. The matter was discussed at the Air Headquarters level and it was decided to design and manufacture the deflectors locally. The cost came to one tenth of what was quoted by CATIC. The job was completed in three months and the test bed has been functioning satisfactorily ever since—a tribute to the creativity of our engineers.

Australian Mirages

On 24 April 1990, the Australian Defence Minister announced the sale of fifty used Mirage fighters and spares to Pakistan for A$36 million. This was reported by the electronic media in their news bulletin the same evening without any comment on the deal. The news published in the *Sydney Morning Herald* the next morning revealed that the federal government was selling fifty Mirage fighters to Pakistan despite concern among the ministers and senior officials that this could be politically embarrassing for Australia, as the Indian government was, true to its usual form, sure to raise a hue and cry over the proposed sale.

The Indian High Commissioner issued a statement the same evening saying, 'The sale will not contribute to stabilization of the situation in South Asia which is the stated aim of Australian policy towards the region.' The aircraft had a lethal potential, the statement added, and it was particularly unfortunate that the sale should take place at a time when tensions in the subcontinent were high on account of the Pakistani instigation and assistance to terrorist elements in Jammu and Kashmir. The sale could hardly send a message of restraint to Pakistan. The High Commissioner next chose to speak to the Australian TV and Radio channels to capitalize on the opportunity to malign Pakistan and link the sale to the Kashmir crisis. In the course of his interviews, he tried to portray Pakistan as

the mastermind behind the freedom movement in Kashmir, alleging that Pakistan was running about forty training camps where young Kashmiri militants were being trained for terrorist activities. He expressed the view that the sale of Mirages to Pakistan would put Pakistan at an advantage *vis-à-vis* India. He falsely claimed that the disputed state of Kashmir was an integral part of India and that the people of Kashmir had already exercised their will to join India.

This generated a debate in the Australian media about the timing of the sale and its possible repercussions. The media enlisted the views of the government, opposition leaders, and defence analysts. A Foreign Affairs spokesman said, 'The Indian government had been kept fully informed of the negotiations by the Australian High Commissioner in New Delhi as well as through the Canberra mission. Both India and Pakistan had been told that the contract would be reviewed if there was any outbreak of hostilities between the two countries. We can understand Indian concern but we have at all times kept them informed. The aircraft were sold by tender after being advertised worldwide in a purely commercial exercise.' The Australian Prime Minister also said that in case hostilities broke out, the sale could be reviewed.

The Australian opposition leaders and some intellectual circles also objected to the timing of the sale, saying that Australia should not be seen as promoting the conflict in South Asia and that the sale should not be allowed to jeopardize Australian efforts to improve relations with India.

Almost all the defence analysts interviewed by the Press and the electronic media, were unanimous in their view that the sale would not affect the balance of power between Pakistan and India as the latter already enjoyed military superiority over Pakistan. The Pakistan Embassy in

Canberra also took timely and effective action to counter the Indian propaganda. The Australian government stood firm, and the deal went through. The Australian Press played a constructive role throughout the controversy.

A Pakistani team was sent to Australia to inspect the aircraft. All these planes had been protected from corrosion in three different hangars, on the edge of the Woomera rocket range in South Australia. Originally purchased at A$11 million each when new, the Mirages remained in service from the early 1960s until November 1987, when they began to be mothballed and replaced by F-18s. The package, apart from fifty Mirage aircraft, consisted of aircraft engines, drop tanks, ground support equipment, and manufacturing raw material and spares. After Pakistan decided to avail of this attractive opportunity, Air Chief Marshal Hakimullah formed a project team on 12 April 1990 to oversee and manage the entire process of induction of these aircraft into the PAF. The contract was signed on 15 April 1990 for A$27 million, with the payment spread over a seven year period at an average rate of A$3.5 million a year. The PAF budget had to share 50 per cent of the cost of this acquisition, with the rest coming from government sources. It was a remarkable success story.

The consignment was transported from Australia to Pakistan on a Pakistan Navy vessel. From the Karachi harbour to PAF Base Masroor, the entire load was conveyed on trailers specially hired from civil sources. Parking places for the aircraft, and hangars to house the bulky containers were made available at the Base. Then came the evaluation and inspection of the aircraft, stores, and equipment, as well as the modification status and history of lifed components. PAF Base Masroor was initially selected to recover these Mirages. However,

it was later realized that the facilities at Masroor were not adequate; therefore, the whole programme was shifted to Kamra in January 1991.

The aircraft were dismantled and transported in C-130s to PAC Kamra, where according to the directive of the CAS, the aircraft were systematically inspected and serviced at the Mirage Rebuild Factory (MRF). Inspections at the MRF revealed that all the Mirages did not require a complete overhaul. A new 2P+ inspection was devised, which extended the life of the aeroplanes before reaching the General Overhaul (GOH) stage. Those already nearing the GOH stage were put through this inspection. For this purpose, the MRF had to operate six docks and work on a two-shift basis for an early recovery of the aircraft. Any additional manpower required by PAC Kamra to complete the manning requirements of the second shift was provided by the PAF. The Ministry of Defence provided extra funds required for this recovery effort.

A team of engineering officers from the PAF and PAC was formed to carry out a comparative analysis of the maintenance concepts followed by the PAF and the Royal Australian Air Force (RAAF) for Mirage Weapon System. A comprehensive report was thus put up for streamlining and standardizing the maintenance practices in the PAF. It was initially decided that out of the fifty aircraft, twenty would be recovered. The Air Staff decided to get the remaining aircraft repaired by buying the parts required for replacement. The aircraft wings had limited life. By fitting used wings on those aircraft, which were available for sale in France, South Africa and other countries, the PAF could recover as many as forty-five aircraft. The Air Staff decided to exercise this option and a target was set for the recovery of forty-five aircraft. Both the options i.e. modifying the existing wings or eplacing them with used wings, were studied. Finally, the PAF managed to procure fourteen wings in 1992 at a very low price.

To operate these aircraft after recovery was quite a risk. Therefore, a lot of maintenance and quality assurance processes had to be introduced to make sure that the first aircraft to be flown satisfied the pilots. Both the French and Australian components were studied at the Component Wing, MRF Kamra, and the life of each component was fixed in a manner that was both economical and safe for the PAF.

The second major problem faced by the PAF was the recovery of engines that had been grounded about five years before. It was, therefore, decided to carry out a major inspection on these engines at Sargodha and Masroor. After the engines passed the initial test, they were sent to Kamra, which had the advanced test bed facility to check the operation of the components as well. During this process, about 20 per cent of the engines were rejected.

Out of a total of forty-five aircraft recovered, thirty-three were given the 2P⁺ inspection, which is a lower level inspection than the General Overhaul; and the remaining twelve aircraft underwent General Overhaul. All thirty-three aircraft were upgraded with the standard avionics package and later improved with additional upgradations. The avionics upgrade project named 'Retrofit of Strike Element' (ROSE) was conceived in 1992 and commenced effectually from April 1995. The avionics package included Inertial Navigation System, Head Up Display, Airborne Video Tape Recording System, and self-protection systems like RWR, Chaff and Flares. A modern airborne radar, the Griffo-M was also retrofitted. Foreign companies that manufacture this radar were asked to make competitive presentations. After a thorough scrutiny, the Griffo-M radar was found to be the most cost effective, and a feasible option. When the Americans released 360 AIM-9L missiles under the Brown Amendment, it was decided that the Mirages being upgraded and equipped with the Griffo-M radar must also be made capable of carrying the AIM-9L missiles. The hardware modification of this project had been completed, but its software was under development. The SAGEM company, which was carrying out the upgradation of Mirages, had developed their own FLIR Pod. They needed to carry out the proto-typing of this equipment on an aircraft, free of cost, so that if found fit, the PAF could buy them. FLIR modification on these aircraft was also in progress.

Out of a total of fifty Mirage aircraft received from Australia, PAC Kamra ultimately recovered forty-five. Out of eight dual models, seven were recovered and allotted to 5 Squadron. Out of the forty-two single-seat Mirages, thirty-two aircraft with the ROSE configuration, were allotted to 7 and CCS (Mirage) Squadrons. Four aircraft belonging to Photo Reconnaissance category and an additional aircraft were recovered and allotted to 5 Squadron. One aircraft had crashed prior to ROSE modification. The remaining five aircraft were found beyond recovery and were reduced to spares.

The Pressler Amendment

The military sales programme of the US government was being channeled through the Foreign Military Sales (FMS) organization's Peace Gate Programmes under which the PAF had acquired its F-16s. In October 1990, the US Government (USG) imposed Pressler restrictions on Pakistan and suspended all military assistance, sale, or transfer of military equipment or technology through the FMS. Also suspended was all training assistance under the International Military Education

Training (IMET) Programme. However, the commercial channels remained open but were three to five times more expensive as compared to FMS.

The PAF's FMS-1 Programme consisted of four major contracts signed for the induction and support of F-16s. These contracts were named Peace Gate-I, II, III, and IV. PG-I dealt with the initial purchase of six F-16s and their follow-on support at a cost of $156.20 million. PG-II covered the sale of an additional thirty-four F-16s and their follow-on support, at a cost of $1.085 billion. PG-III related to the induction of eleven F-16 aircraft to be provided by the USA to compensate for resources expended during the Afghan war. The value of this contract was $205.49 million, and it was to be funded by the US Government credits under the FMS-2. The PG-IV programme was related to the induction of sixty F-16s and their subsequent follow-on support. It was valued at $1.406 billion. These aircraft were to be delivered to Pakistan from March 1993 to February 1997. Pakistan had paid $658 million under PG-IV. Further payment was stopped when delivery of F-16s became highly doubtful.

First, there was the iniquity of the USG refusing to honour the contract by not delivering the paid for F-16s. Then came the outrage over the refusal even to return to Pakistan the accumulated sum of nearly $670 million (it was returned—piecemeal—after many years of procrastination). Finally, there was the ludicrous situation wherein because the undelivered F-16s that had been sitting on the tarmacs in the US were Pakistani property, the PAF was asked to pay parking charges. In the words of the well-known Pakistani journalist Maleeha Lodhi, Pakistan had indeed the distinction of being 'America's most sanctioned friend.'

The Effects of Pressler Restrictions

Under the Pressler Amendment, the US President was required to certify annually that Pakistan did not possess a nuclear device, before any aid could be released to Pakistan. In October 1990, President Bush did not issue the certificate, therefore, all assistance and/or sale of military equipment and technology to Pakistan was stopped. Consequently, the FMS programme and action on new or pending LOAs (Letters of Offer and Acceptance) was suspended. Any FMS—financed commercial contracts—were also disallowed and all material and repairables held by US companies were confiscated. To add insult to injury, storage charges were also levied against the held-up material stored in the US depots! Besides, new lease agreements, security assistance teams and IMET relationship were all disallowed. However, CETS (Contractor Engineering Technical Services) and CFOS (Contract Follow on Support) were allowed to continue.

In the aftermath of these restrictions, the USG established a Material Utilization Control Office (MUCO) for the stocktaking of all the withheld PAF assets in the US. Those assets included all spares and equipment ready for shipment or on order with different firms (on completion of production). These assets were stored by MUCO at various locations in the USA.

In order to absorb the shock of the Pressler restrictions, extensive studies were conducted by the PAF to work out alternate courses of action for ensuring continued maintenance support to the F-16 fleet. The damaging effects of Pressler started showing after the end of 1991, when the reserves in the depot started dwindling and the PAF managers of this project had to determine what to buy and from where. Earlier, this was done by the F-16 Programme Management at Utah, USA, who were nning this programme for all the users of the F-16, worldwide. But now the entire burden had to be borne by the PAF. The -16 Project in Pakistan had to determine nd monitor the failure rate of various omponents, cater for their pipeline-time, and anticipate the requirement of funds for their replenishment etc. They had to decide what to buy, how to buy, and also what the ze of the required stock should be. Initially, he PAF had a year's stock that was radually built up according to the directives f the Air Staff. Commercial contracts were nade with US-based Original Equipment Manufacturers (OEMs) for spares as well as echnical support. Similar contracts were rawn up with some European sources of upply and repair, in an attempt to economize n the cost through competition between lifferent foreign firms.

Originally set up in 1982, the PAF's Project Falcon (F-16) grew into the only lepartment in the PAF that provided one-vindow operations. It looks after virtually everything required for the F-16, i.e. udgeting, contracting, ground and flight afety modifications, pilot's training (to some extent), procurement of new equipment, etc. t has turned out to be a wonderful experiment because in a one-window operation, a single unit is totally responsible or the entire system. The Chief Project Director Falcon was always given complete reedom, and he delivered the goods. He nade the decisions himself on what and how o procure and when to contract, etc. in conformity with the budget that he was llocated.

The Brown Amendment

The Brown Amendment was passed in February 1996 but the US Department of Defence delayed its implementation till May 1996. This resulted in the release of all the spares and equipment held in MUCO, to the PAF. However, the release of the F-16 aircraft was not approved under this amendment. Therefore, only the equipment purchased before October 1990 was released. CETs and CFOS contracts were renewed. However, the storage charges were not waived. Besides, the Report of Discrepancy (ROD) was accepted only for wrong billing and defects, pre-inspection was not allowed, items with expired shelf life were not replaced, and all assets were required to be transported to Pakistan by 31 August 1996.

The PAF was quick to realize that the equipment and accessories that were meant to support the withheld aircraft were now of no relevance. Therefore, a study was carried out to determine the utility of spares and equipment released under the Brown Amendment. A series of meetings were held with USAF to resolve the issue. Consequently, spares and equipment worth $65 million were identified as expendable for the PAF's requirement, and were marked for possible diversion by USG. The assets identified by the PAF were retrieved in the quickest possible time through air or sea. The value of the total stores received under this amendment was approximately $100 million.

At the time of the final settlement, the total cash received by the GOP, in two installments, from 1996-98, was $509 million ($184 million and $325 million). The second installment of $325 million also included some left over amount from PG-III. Besides, Pakistan received goods worth about $140 million.

Upgrade Activity

With the release of withheld assets, the PAF embarked upon two major upgrades on its F-16 fleet related to obsolescence and aircraft structural integrity, namely 220E/OCU and Falcon-Up. These upgrades would have ensured uninterrupted maintenance support to the fleet while simultaneously obviating the possibility of aircraft structure related Class III 'A' (major) mishaps. Falcon-Up modification was contracted commercially with LMTAS (Lockheed Martin Tactical Aircraft Systems), whereas 220E/OCU modifications were being executed and supported under CFOS through the FMS Programme.

The Glenn Act

In the aftermath of the May 1998 nuclear tests by Pakistan, the USG imposed fresh sanctions, *vide* the Glenn Amendment, that terminated all sales of defence articles and services to Pakistan. This resulted in the US State Department cancelling all licenses and other commitments such as pending procurement orders. All parts sent to USA for repair or overhaul were withheld at the repair sources. All Technical Orders and Publications support, and technical support for Falcon-Up, were terminated. With the discontinuation of Foreign Military Sales, in-country Engineering Technical Services provided by Lockheed and Pratt and Whitney, FMS funded CFOS, all USAF controlled technical and safety related publications, spare support released under the Brown Amendment, and technical and spare support for OCU/220E, were all terminated.

The imposition of US sanctions forced the PAF yet again to suspend ongoing OCU/220E upgrades and to support and operate a mixed bag fleet. Additionally, the technical assistance being provided for Falcon-Up modification was also terminated. However, the PAF decided to continue this modification independently and by 1998 had successfully completed modification on two aircraft. It goes to the credit of the PAF engineers and technicians that the second

aircraft was modified without Lockheed assistance. The work on the third aircraft was in progress at PAF Base Sargodha through indigenous effort. The PAF lived up to its traditions, its performance soaring under the pressure. In difficult times, engineering initiatives and improvisations are at their best in the PAF.

In order to cushion the effects of the Glenn Amendment, Project Falcon conducted two exhaustive critical studies in July and October 1998. Measures taken to ensure the viability and operational status of the F-16 fleet in the light of these sanctions were as follows:

a. Stocktaking of all available spares and support equipment was accomplished to anticipate shortfall of spares. All ongoing upgrade activities except Falcon-Up were suspended. Besides, all FOB kits were retained at PAF Base, Sargodha.

b. Alternate sources of repair/supply in the international market were identified for procurement of deficient spares, to increase the number of modified aircraft for better supportability of a mixed fleet.

c. In-country Engineering Technical Services (ETS) were established to provide technical support to field units in consonance with CFOS provided ETS support.

d. Concrete steps were taken to enhance indigenous repair capability.

The Impact on other Weapon Systems
C-130: When the Glenn sanctions came, the PAF had twelve C-130s that provided peacetime mobility and wartime logistic support to the combat squadrons. The transport fleet also meets the essential needs of the Pakistan Army and Navy, and provides a portion of the PAF's EW capability. The embargo also affected this

fleet adversely. Although the C-130 support capability was commercially available worldwide, it was very expensive and time consuming. Out of the various repairables held in the US, 145 belonged to this fleet. Due to the suspension of delivery of the purchased engine test stand, the C-130 fleet was experiencing difficulty in that area. All this had adversely affected the serviceability of the fleet. Maintained largely through commercial sources, the annual flying target of the C-130s had to be reduced somewhat.

T-37: Ever since its inception, the PAF Academy's Basic Flying Training (BFT) Wing has been flying T-37 aircraft. This had been smooth sailing until the Pressler Amendment came into effect and the T-37s ran short of spares. The PAF's T-37 fleet included nineteen T-37 aircraft leased from the USAF. After the expiry of the lease agreement in February 1994, these aircraft were withdrawn from active service, and since then they have been awaiting further disposal by the USG. The aircraft are parked in hangars, and are periodically inspected by the US officials. The life expiry of T-37's ejection seat actuators (CAD/PAD items) forced the PAF to fly the aircraft on extensions. Similarly, a large number of engines falling due for overhaul, adversely affected aircraft availability. The commercial solution to these problems was five times more expensive as compared to the FMS. Therefore, the target of T-37 fleet was reduced and the flying syllabus was readjusted. The training of Qualified Flying Instructors (QFI's) on T-37 aircraft in the FIS was also stopped and only MFI-17s were used for the purpose. The QFIs, who were subsequently posted to the BFT Wing, have to undergo a short refresher course on T-37 aircraft before they are deployed on instructional duties.

T-33: Prior to the enforcement of the Pressler Amendment, the PAF was operating eighteen T-33 aircraft that used to undertake peacetime photo reconnaissance and to tow aerial targets for air-to-air gunnery. Due to expensive or limited spares support, their operational cost became increasingly prohibitive. Regular cannibalization reduced the number of available aircraft. Ultimately, the aircraft were phased out from the Service on 30 June 1993.

TPS-43 Radars: Six of these air defence radars remained continually in use to provide high-level coverage over Pakistan. The system became the main victim of US sanctions. There was no spare radar and the failure of any radar meant vulnerable gaps in the air defence system of the PAF.

Air Defence Automation System: The automated air defence network of US origin gives the PAF the edge in this field, in the region. Limited spares support led to cannibalization, and this reduced the availability of the system.

Miscellaneous Effects: Most of the aircraft in the PAF inventory are equipped with US avionics and communication equipment. The communication equipment in the ATCs, ground radars, and Mobile Observer Units is also of US origin. Moreover, most of PAF's ground equipment, workshop equipment, calibration and reference standards, and weapons are also of US origin. A halt in the release of their spares warranted the use of commercial channels. This option was cost intensive and the associated delays reduced the availability of the systems/equipment.

Minimizing the Damaging Effects of the Pressler Amendment

In the post-embargo scenario, the PAF leadership was confronted with many challenges. The first consideration was to preserve the existing fleet; the second, to see that the disparity of numbers *vis-à-vis* the enemy did not assume dangerous proportions; and the third, to make serious endeavours to look for hi-tech aircraft in the world market, that would prove a suitable alternative to the F-16. The PAF applied its best talents in various fields to deal with each of these serious challenges.

In 1991, when the enforcement of the Pressler Amendment had started to show its damaging effects, the F-16 fleet was hit by engine-related problems, and all the aircraft were grounded. The engine inspections and depot level work were initiated at PAF Base Sargodha to recover the aircraft. Project Falcon had to overcome many odds in order to get the F-16 engines back on the line. Out of thirty-two aircraft, ten were recovered the same year; however, it took two years to recover the entire fleet. With the backdrop of the Pressler restrictions, this was no mean achievement. In the words of the then CPD Falcon, Air Commodore Tanveer (now an Air Vice Marshal):

> We took up this challenge. I think it was a good thing that happened to us as we started to learn how to carry out business ourselves. Once we got into it, the typical thing was contracting because contracting by the Government of Pakistan through the Ministry of Defence and others was a very trying thing. I had to learn how to get through with them (DGDP/FA etc) and how to convince them. On the eve of my leaving the Project, the F-16 fleet was in a better shape than it had ever been during the FMS days. The then CAS, PAF had stated in one of the Air Board meetings that despite the Pressler, we were in a better shape as far as the serviceability,

reliability, spares' storage, etc were concerned. We had gone to commercial sources and we were spending hot cash. In return, we were able to urge the suppliers to give us the spares expeditiously because they were now getting money directly from us. So we could exert a lot of influence on the US suppliers and even on the Lockheed Company. They were far more responsive to us as compared to their FMS customers. We started seeing what all was required and how much of it we really needed. We were building our stocks for difficult times. We are still flying and surviving. We have a lot of war reserves with us. We have not compromised on our serviceability, reliability and our operational capabilities. When we, for the first time, came under sanctions, I think it became a challenge for our flyers, engineers and others. We all had to adapt very quickly. We were disconnected and even the information regarding flight safety matters was not available to us. We had to fight our way through the American system to get our combat units going.

Falcon-Up, which was an upgrade programme of F-16s, was prohibited under the Pressler Amendment. However, the PAF managed to obtain it by convincing the Americans that the programme was a safety-related one, and did not enhance capability. The Project team also learnt how to manage money most efficiently. Earlier, the Americans used to manage the entire programme including the FMS funding. There was a lot of money that was recovered by the PAF out of this system. The Pressler Amendment did not prohibit sales from commercial sources and that was the only window open to the PAF. But anything falling into the sphere of upgrades did not get through. In some cases the F-16 configuration had changed and the weapon system had advanced to the next configuration, thereby making the PAF system obsolete. The USG would decline to repair the PAF equipment on this ground. Project Falcon had at times argued successfully with the USG that refusing a capability would mean the stoppage of work in the system operated by the PAF, and that was not the aim of Pressler. The Project managed to convince the Americans on some of the things like OCU (Operational Capability Upgrade) and Falcon Upgrade programme. The USG was also refusing to sell items for the F-16 ejection seats (CAT-I), produced exclusively by the US Navy for the entire world. The PAF had to fight for these CAT-1 items for two years, and ultimately permission was granted for the orders to be placed with the US Navy through General Dynamics. A private firm in USA was contacted to procure some other denied munitions, on a commercial basis. In those days Wing Commander Javed Sabir was stationed in the US, and he proved to be the key person in tracking the sources for the munitions that the PAF needed. The PAF also managed to get things done through Ireland, Belgium, England and, in some cases, from France, in order to counteract the embargo on the various items. Initially, the flying effort was reduced, and in 1991 it dropped to almost zero for a time because the fleet was grounded. It rose again to an optimum level, but was kept well below the levels achieved during the Afghan war, when the PAF was logging 300-400 hours per squadron, per month. The limiting factor was the financing, and the GOP allocated only a specific amount in foreign exchange. That amount ranged between $8-10 million and sometimes up to $15 million, depending upon the PAF's commitments. Some funds were also generated out of the FMS funds held by the USG, though mostly to build up stocks. A portion of the amount thus recovered was diverted to Project Plus, the upgrading of the F-16 computer hardware.

In 1991, when the flying went down to zero, the focus shifted to recovering the F-16s. Questions were also raised at this time about the utility of the F-16 squadron at Minhas Air Base where it was deployed essentially for the Afghan war. The issue was, therefore, debated at Air Headquarters and it was decided to aggregate the F-16 assets and the support equipment at one place for maximum economy, but without compromising operational mobility. The extra ground support equipment was also moved and placed as war reserve. Prior to the nuclear tests by Pakistan, one F-16 Squadron was deployed within six hours after the move order was issued.

In order to maintain the numbers in the fleet, the PAF inducted additional F-7 aircraft. Simultaneously, the PAF also launched two major programmes. The first was to upgrade and overhaul the Mirage fleet whatever its number, and the second, to upgrade as many other aircraft as possible to improve the fleet performance. The upgradation of other aircraft types was also initiated. This included the Structural Life Extension Programme (SLEP) for T-37s, and the provision of a better air-to-air radar for the F-7 (Griffo-7), which was about to go into production. The upgradation of radar on the A-5 aircraft was not considered necessary because its service with the PAF was coming to an end; however, RWR, Chaff and Flares were added to it. The Mirage-Vs which were already equipped with nav-attack systems, were subjected to similar upgrades. The PAF also decided to put the existing Mirage-III fleet through structural life enhancement, avionics upgrade, and RWR. Later the Griffo-M radar was also added. The avionics upgrade on the Mirage fleet is complete and the prototyping of the Griffo-M radar was expected to be completed in the near future.

Throughout this period of extraordinary adversity and sanctions, all the senior and younger staff members at the Air Headquarters worked in high gear. Reviews were held each month, each quarter, and on a six monthly basis while revising PAF's Force Structure Programme. Keeping in mind the availability of funds and many other constraints, alternative sources were tapped and availed. One such option was the purchase of used and discarded Mirage aircraft available in several countries. That was how the forty odd Mirages from France were contracted. The details of this project have been narrated elsewhere in the book.

In order to sustain the fleet in the long term PAF went to work on the Super-7 programme which, broadly speaking, envisages the replacement of multiple types of aircraft like Mirages, A-5s, F-6s, and F-7s in a phased manner, over the next ten to fifteen years. It will be a low cost solution but the avionics and the weapons packages would be acquired much in the same manner that the PAF adopted for the ROSE programme from Western sources. These specific packages would give a reasonable capability to the PAF in medium techno-logies over the next fifteen to twenty years. In addition to maintaining a certain minimum number of aircraft in the PAF through the Super-7 programme, the requirement for some hi-tech aircraft of superior capability would still remain. These would be needed in order to give the Air Force a technological advantage, or at least a technological equivalence, with the regional powers. In the post-cold war period the PAF has been denied access to hi-tech aircraft on two accounts: firstly, the capability has been purposely withheld by the Western powers in view of Pakistan's nuclear programme, secondly, the increased political pressure on the diplomatic front was such that Pakistan did not seem to be looked on with favour by any of her traditional Western suppliers, including the French. Within the internal

defence establishment, the PAF had come under criticism for not being able to decide what it wanted from the government. Such a perception was manifestly unfair. There had been only three realistic options, namely the Mirage-2000-V, SU-30, and the SU-27. The factors of dependable availability, relevance, and affordability of the three weapon systems always emerged as the main consideration in most of the studies carried out by the PAF. To complicate the question further, the events of the past few years show that the Swedish Grippen and the Russian SU-30/ SU-27 aircraft were not really dependably available to the PAF because of Pakistan's adverse diplomatic environment. The only feasible option had been the Mirage-2000-V but that too remained mostly mired in controversy due to the political leaders' propensity to taint each defence acquisition with corrupt practices.

The Induction of the Mistral Missile

The period after the 1971 India-Pakistan war witnessed rapid advancements in the field of strike aircraft and their weapon delivery systems. Similarly, more effective ground-to-air weapon systems for targeting aircraft also entered wide usage. Visualizing the need to effectively counter the existing aerial threat, the PAF decided to procure a weapon system of low cost but with a high kill probability, which could meet the requirements of the early twenty-first century. The 'Mistral' missiles were finally procured in 1991 for this purpose.

The inherent flexibility of deployment/ employment of this system enables the user to deploy it in FEBA (Forward Edge of Battle Area) or for point defence or in-depth VPs. It is a fire and forget, portable, short-range, surface-to-air weapon. The missile is equipped with a highly sensitive infrared homing head, which can intercept high or low speed aircraft and anti-ship missiles. With a maximum speed of Mach 2.4, the missile has an effective range of 4.5 kilometres (head on). It is an all weather weapon system.

Prior to the induction of the Mistral weapon system, the PAF had been equipped with Crotale SAMs, since 1976. However, due to the limited number of squadrons on its inventory, the PAF's capability remained restricted to the defence of a few Main Operating Bases (MOBs) and Forward Operating Bases (FOBs). In the beginning of 1991, the role of two of the MOU squadrons was changed after the re-equipment of these squadrons with the Mistral weapon system. Due to its relatively low cost, a sufficient number of Mistrals was procured, which could provide adequate defence for all the MOBs and FOBs. Since 1991, both the squadrons have participated in almost all the major PAF exercises, like 'High Mark', 'Saffron Bandit', 'Bedaar', 'Shendur' etc. Also, the participation of the Mistrals in inter-Services exercises like 'Shamsher-e-Behr', 'Sea-Spark', 'Sea Lion', and 'Blue Dolphin' proved their effectiveness. The results in these exercises were quite encouraging and well above the expectations of the PAF.

The induction of Mistrals meant a substantial enhancement in the effectiveness of terminal defences. It is an extremely useful missile that has enhanced the PAF's capability, both by day and partially by night, while using night vision devices. To increase its effectiveness further, the PAF has also incorporated Terminal Weapon Control Centre (TWCC). TWCC is deployed now on all PAF Bases whereby information to Mistrals, Crotales etc, and operations at each VP are now coordinated in a smooth and effective manner. Combined with TWCC, the Mistral has enhanced the defence of VPs against attacking aircraft very effectively.

The Induction of Anza

The induction of the Anza Weapon System in the PAF was prompted by myriad factors. First, the performance of shoulder mounted portable missiles in the Afghan war against slow speed threat had proved to be quite impressive. Second, the Gulf War strategy of creating a blind corridor by knocking off the peripheral air defence sensors by Apache gunship, underlined the need for equipping such sensors with defensive weapons. Third, the expansion of air defence assets and their possible wartime deployment close to the border increased their vulnerability in a manner similar to the Gulf War scenario. These factors supported the acquisition of additional SAM defences for the PAF air defence assets. Hence, the PAF decided to induct the indigenous Anza MK-1 missiles in May 1994. Subsequently, a radar squadron was re-designated as the Anza SAM Squadron, and its role and task were revised accordingly.

The Anza SAM is locally produced at the KRL and is in use for air defence of forward radars against helicopter or other aerial attack. At present, the Anza is not night capable but this capability can be acquired by providing night vision devices to the operators. It is not a very hi-tech system, but with this capability, the short range threat from a helicopter to forward deployed radars can be effectively countered. The Anza Weapon System has completed one cycle of induction and has strengthened the PAF's air defence a great deal.

The system was used for live firing in May 1998. The proof test of the system achieved much higher results, surpassing its theoretical kill probability. The system also participated in exercises 'Shendur' and 'Vigilance'. The versatility of the system was proved beyond doubt.

Live Mistral Missile fired by No. 242 Squadron at Sonmiani range on 25 April 1998, heading towards the target

The Induction of Crotale 4000

In order to augment the capability of the existing Crotale-2000 weapon system, one squadron comprising two flights of Crotale-4000 (advanced version of Crotale-2000) was inducted in the PAF in 1985. A new squadron was formed on *ad hoc* basis; however, equipment and manpower remained pooled up with the existing squadrons of Crotale-2000. In 1996, the *ad hoc* establishment of this squadron was converted into permanent establishment.

Since its induction, the squadron has been deployed at designated sites for the defence of vital installations and is providing round the clock capability. The Crotale-4000 is definitely an inventory upgrade. It is a good system and has given the PAF an additional capability over the Crotale-2000. Although the main parameters of the Crotale-4000 are similar to those of the 2000 series, some additional facilities in the new system give it an edge over the earlier Crotales.

A new feature of the Crotale-4000 was its ability to operate without a cable link through IVRDL (Inter-Vehicle Remote Data Link) improving the range between the Acquisition and Firing Units to 3.5 kilometres. Additionally, TV tracking mode facility in the FU (Firing Unit) made tracking possible even with the tracking radar switched off in a jamming environment. The maintenance of electronic and electro-mechanical parts is also more efficient in the new Crotale.

The Induction of K-8

The Karakorum-8 (K-8) aircraft is a joint venture of the Pakistan Aeronautical Complex (PAC) Kamra, and China Aero-technology Import and Export Corporation (CATIC). The K-8 project commenced in 1983 when the replacement of the T-37 basic trainer fleet was contemplated for the first time. In 1984, the PAC negotiated with CATIC to co-design and co-develop a basic jet trainer aircraft. For this purpose, the L-8 aircraft was selected and renamed Karakorum-8. An agreement was finalized and signed in 1986. Another four years were consumed in establishing the design and performance parameters of the aircraft that satisfied the Chinese and the PAF requirements. The first prototype K-8 flew in November 1990. Test flights of the aircraft were conducted from January 1991 to May 1992, to verify its performance parameters. After it had completed the test flights successfully, the production of a small batch of the aircraft was launched in May 1992. The joint sales and marketing agreement was signed in April 1993, and a contract to purchase a batch of six aircraft for PAF was signed in April 1994.

A full description of the roles that could be gradually assigned to the K-8 aircraft in the PAF was to be determined after the completion of the evaluation phase. Keeping the task in view, a dedicated K-8 Evaluation Flight was established at the PAF Academy, Risalpur in October 1994. The Flight was tasked to evaluate and check the suitability of the aircraft for both basic flying training and fighter conversion training. A batch of eight qualified flying instructors along with the newly appointed officer commanding the K-8 flight, were sent to China for their initial training on K-8 aircraft.

Six K-8 aircraft were ferried from China to Pakistan in November 1994. The Prime Minister of Pakistan and the then CAS, Air Chief Marshal Abbas Khattak, formally handed over those aircraft to the K-8 Evaluation Flight at the PAF Academy. On that occasion, Wing Commander Waqar A. Nasir, the test pilot PAC Kamra, stole the show by performing some superb maneuvres in a solo aerobatic display in the K-8.

After the aircrafts' arrival in Pakistan, the evaluation phase of the K-8 commenced in

The former Prime Minister of Pakistan, Mohtarma Benazir Bhutto inspecting the K-8 aircraft at its induction ceremony, PAF Academy, Risalpur, 25 January 1995

November 1994, and was completed in February 1996. During this period, the aircraft went through a comprehensive evaluation process involving more than 1,200 hours of flying, during which it was tested for all the flying phases in the typical basic flying training syllabus. After having successfully completed this evaluation, the aircraft was considered fit for pilots' training. To utilize the aircraft more effectively and to carry out further evaluation, a flying instructor course was conducted on the K-8 aircraft. Six pilots with reasonable flying experience were detailed to undergo the course in April 1996. These officers successfully completed the course, and later joined the K-8 Evaluation Team.

After the induction of the K-8 aircraft, the Flight was tasked not only to continue further evaluation of the aircraft but also to prepare its operational publications, according to PAF standards. The Flight worked day and night and finally compiled the aircraft Dash-1, Checklist, Patter Book, Local/Operating Procedures, and Pilots' Guide Book.

The evaluation and improvement of the K-8 did not stop. The Flight continued to monitor the aircraft performance closely, and based on the Base Line Configuration (BLC) and flight safety standards, recommended a number of modifications. All these modifications were accomplished with the help of the AMF at Kamra. The Flight also carried out armament trials on the K-8 at PAF Base Minhas, from 9 December 1996 to 1 January 1997, and achieved excellent results.

The Flight was then asked to start basic flying training of cadet pilots on the K-8. A batch of ten Aviation Cadets from

101 GD (P) Course was inducted for this purpose on 1 October 1996, and all of them successfully graduated on 22 November 1997. A second batch of ten Aviation Cadets from 103 GD (P) started the course on 1 December 1997 and finished on 22 October 1998. One student pilot from this course had to be taken off flying training on medical grounds. It is interesting history that from the second batch, Aviation Cadet Tabarak Hussain became the first student pilot to receive the Best Pilot Trophy as well as the Sword of Honour. At present, the K-8 Flight is training eight Aviation Cadets of the 104 GD (P) Course.

Due to a glut of training aircraft in the world market, the K-8 has so far not attracted international sales. A joint Pak-China marketing campaign was recently established. Potential sales are being explored in Myanmar, some African countries, and the Middle East. It is hoped that the programme will gather momentum in due course of time, because the K-8 is superior in many respects to competing trainers from other countries.

The Induction of Y-12

The Y-12 is a non-pressurized, twin-engine, general-purpose aircraft of Chinese origin. Various versions of the Y-12 aircraft include passenger, VIP, cargo, parachute jumping, maritime surveillance, geological survey, tree seed spreading, and aerial photography etc. By 1995, eighty-one Y-12 aircraft were operational in seventeen countries around the world.

The first Y-12 aircraft was handed over to the PAF for trial and evaluation on 15 May 1993. The aircraft was evaluated for passenger and VIP communication, and was found suitable for PAF's requirements. The second Y-12 aircraft was acquired by the PAF and both were formally inducted

in the PAF and handed over to 41 LCA Squadron in December 1996. Both Y-12s are in eleven-seat configuration and are equipped with modern navigation and communication equipment of US origin. The Y-12 aircraft is also equipped with an effective air conditioning system and a weather radar with a colour display making it an all weather aircraft.

More Mirages
Background
In the second half of 1992, the PAF had a genuine concern over the gap that would be created by the phasing out of the A-5s in 1997. After considering various courses, the purchase and re-lifing of some used Mirages seemed a practical option. The sources included Belgium, Spain, France, Zaire and Lebanon. In 1995, the planners at Air Headquarters established an operational requirement for at least fifty such aircraft. On the directive of the CAS, the feasibility of a package of forty Mirages was validated and the case for allocation of funds was taken up. The government released the necessary funds.

In order to reliably assess the physical condition of these Mirages, a PAF team visited Spain, France, and Lebanon, while the Air Attache in Paris was asked to inspect the Belgian aircraft. During their visits, the team inspected seventy-one Mirages and submitted their report. Similarly, the Defence and Technical Attache in Paris inspected twenty-five aircraft from SABCA, Belgium.

On 25 May 1995, after a post-visit presentation to the Air Board, the Chief of the Air Staff approved the formation of a Project Team to manage all aspects related to a cost effective induction of about forty Mirages in the PAF fleet. These aircraft were to be of a single variant, capable of a surface attack role, not exceeding a total cost of $120 million, and were to form two viable and homogeneous fighter squadrons, fully supportable within the PAF maintenance resources and infrastructure.

Obtaining Proposals

The project team sought proposals for the intended purchase of Mirages from all the potential vendors, and simultaneously launched a market study. The PAF's own overhauling experiences in Kamra were kept in view to work out the expected costs of each aircraft and the related package. During a visit to France in 1995, the Project Team was pleasantly surprised to learn that forty Mirage-Vs and about forty Mirage-IIIs of the French Air Force were available for sale at quite a reasonable price. The French Mirage-V suited the PAF requirement because of its longer range and additional payload. Later, through various coordination meetings in Pakistan, the PAF and AIRCO worked out a detailed proposal which included the required statement of work. Representatives from the French DGA and the French Air Force accompanied the AIRCO team, to demonstrate their full support to the PAF-AIRCO agreements and obligations.

The SAGEM Proposal

SAGEM (Societe D'Avionics de Generales Electricite et de Mechanique) is a French company that has Defence and Security Division as one of its main branches. In this division, SAGEM specializes in three specific categories, i.e. inertial navigation, electro-optic equipment, and system integration. In project ROSE, the PAF was already acquiring thirty-six Mirages upgraded by SAGEM through their inertial navigation and system integration

departments. In August 1995, SAGEM combined their upgrade skills with the potential sales opportunity, and proposed to the PAF a package deal of forty Mirages at a quoted cost of $150 million.

As the SAGEM proposal became more and more attractive and feasible, the PAF negotiated a further reduction in costs so that they actually fell into its feasibility regime. Through numerous discussions, SAGEM came up with a revised proposal of $124 million in November 1995. According to this proposal, the package was to consist of thirty-four Mirage-Vs (single-seat) and six Mirage-IIIs (dual-seat) of the French Air Force, making a total of forty fully overhauled aircraft. Out of the forty aircraft, twenty Mirage-Vs (single-seat) would be modernized to the ROSE-II standards (ROSE-II modification was the same as ROSE-I except that Griffo-M Radar was replaced with FLIR). The engines installed on the aircraft would have a minimum life of four years and 300 hours. The package would also include the required ground handling equipment/ground support equipment, alternate mission equipment, and line replaceable units. Besides, the kits for RWR, CFD and GPS would be installed on all the aircraft.

Keeping in view the overall SAGEM package *vis-à-vis* the quoted prices, the offer appeared quite viable to the PAF. According to a conservative estimate, the cost of this package should have been at least $146 million. On 27 December 1995, the PAF gave the go ahead, and the contract for the forty Mirages was finally signed on 1 February 1996 for a total amount of $118 million.

This deal had become somewhat controversial mainly due to misreporting in the Press. The PAF preferred to have the necessary modifications done in France because PAC Kamra was, during that time frame, already busy overhauling the PAF's

Mirages. Accepting any additional work would have unnecessarily delayed the delivery of the French Mirages to the PAF without making any difference in cost.

SAGEM encountered problems on purchase of spares which they needed for the timely and efficient running of their work. Thus the programme suffered delays during most of 1997 and 1998. However, the company managed to get the first batch ready by September 1998, when PAF pilots ferried across eight Mirages on 22 September 1998. The remaining aircraft were still in the process of being handed over to the PAF, when the text of this volume was completed.

The Search for a Hi-tech Aircraft

The enforcement of the Pressler Law by the USG energized the PAF to look for non-American hi-tech aircraft. Starting from the end of 1990, to 1993, the PAF completed several evaluations of almost all the aircraft available in the market at that time. The first was the British Tornado, which was rejected as it was very expensive and did not meet the PAF's requirements. Then the evaluation of the Mirage-2000 E was also carried out. In the meanwhile, a lot of middlemen started approaching the PAF, offering the sale of Russian combat aircraft. They comprised locals, as well as foreigners from different parts of the globe. One of the serious offers came from Poland. The PAF leadership, however, used this offer only to evaluate the Mig-29 and SU-27. By appearing to negotiate with the PAF, the Russians were probably manipulating the Indians, as demonstrated by the IAF entering into a hurried contract with Russia for SU-30s, without getting enough data on the aircraft. The direct Russian response to Pakistan throughout this period remained highly discouraging, and this was clearly due to political reasons.

Mig-29 and SU-27

In January 1991, the Pakistan Army expressed its interest in procuring Soviet military hardware. Later in the year, the PAF too wished to evaluate some Russian fighter aircraft for possible purchase. Until that time, Moscow had considered Pakistan as a hostile country and had placed it on the prohibited list for the sale of arms. Therefore, any sale of arms by Russia to Pakistan was simply out of the question. However, after the disintegration of the Soviet Union, privatization of its economy, and Russia's declaration that it would have a balanced approach in its relations with India and Pakistan, there was hope that the Russian Federation might be willing to sell military hardware to Pakistan. Efforts were initiated at an appropriate level to understand the Soviet system and thus approach the right channels. On 19 June 1991, a written request was made to the Ministry of Defence of USSR that Pakistan was interested in procuring Russian military hardware. In August 1991, a similar approach was made to the Soviet Embassy in Islamabad.

During a meeting with the Prime Minister of Pakistan on 21 December 1991, the visiting Vice President Alexander Rutskoi of Russia stated that his country was keen to engage in military cooperation with Pakistan. According to him, Russia would respond readily to Pakistan's request for a whole range of military equipment, including front line aircraft. The PAF was urged to explore the prospects of purchasing sophisticated aircraft like the SU-27 and the Mig-29. During a meeting between the Russian Vice President, the COAS, and the CAS, it was decided that a list of equipment of interest to the Pakistani armed forces would be handed over to the Russian Vice President and this was done on 3 January 1992. The Prime Minister in his letter dated 13 January 1992, directed the Foreign and Defence Ministries and the CAS to take immediate steps to initiate a dialogue with Moscow, and if necessary, send a high level combined Services delegation to Russia for talks to explore the purchase of aircraft and other military equipment. On 19 March 1992, in a Letter of Intent addressed to the President of the Russian State Commercial Company, the PAF indicated its interest in evaluating Russian front line aircraft with the associated weapons and specialist equipment as well as air defence systems and surface-to-air missiles.

In March 1992, Mr. Sintsov from the Russian Concern of Defence Industry visited Pakistan on the invitation of Air Headquarters. He was also given an opportunity to visit the GHQ. On his return from Pakistan, he submitted a detailed report to various agencies, including the KGB, in which military sales to Pakistan were supported. In April 1992, the Russian parliament reconsidered its arms sales policy. Pakistan was removed from the prohibited list and placed in the second list of countries with regard to whom balanced decisions could be taken after deliberation. At this stage, efforts were initiated through official channels to enable a PAF delegation to visit Russia. In 1992, the Russian government decided that preliminary negotiation could take place; however, the final contracting would be subject to political agreement between the leadership of the two countries. On 29 September 1992, Russian authorities informed the Pakistan Ambassador, Mr. Akram Zaki, that political clearance on behalf of Russia had been given for the commencement of Pakistani-Russian military cooperation for which the Joint Services delegation could start working.

Meanwhile, in response to an invitation from the Polish defence minister to the CAS, a PAF team was sent to Poland in April 1992 to evaluate the Mig-29, SU-27, and air defence systems along with available weaponry. The team, headed by Air Commodore Mushaf Ali Mir (now Air Vice Marshal), started its preliminary work and soon discovered that the SU-27 was not available in Poland. During their stay, the team faced certain constraints like the apparently conflicting objectives on the two sides, the language barrier, lack of adequate opportunity for flight evaluation, non-availability of certain information, etc. The team recommended that since evaluation of such equipment was not possible in user countries, an in-depth evaluation should be conducted at the source i.e. in Russia for the Mig-29 and the SU-27. Apparently, the aircraft offered for sale were far below the PAF expectations. However, the PAF continued to use this approach to evaluate the SU-27 aircraft. After a lot of persuasion, the Russians agreed to come to Poland for discussions, but no other, more direct route was offered to the PAF at that time.

During its second visit to Poland, the PAF team attempted to persuade the Russians to provide all the data on the SU-27 and the Mig-29. They were told that the PAF would like to evaluate the flying capabilities of the aircraft, to which they were not agreeable. Later on, they relented and a third team visited Russia in October 1993 through Poland, and thoroughly evaluated both the Mig-29 and the SU-27. Both the aircraft were unacceptable to the PAF in the configuration that they were being offered. The team, however, recommended that the Mig-29-M, if offered, was a better choice for the PAF. The SU-30, a modified version of the SU-27 came into the market at a later stage.

A six-member delegation led by the Additional Secretary of Defence had already visited Moscow from 11 to 21 October 1992, at the invitation of the Russian Ministry of

Foreign Economic Relations. This was the first delegation of its kind and as such, its aims and objectives were essentially exploratory in nature. However, the delegation achieved more than the mere exploration of the possibility of military collaboration between the two countries. Signing of the Protocol of Understanding between Spetsvneshtekhnica and the Pakistan delegation during this visit was a major breakthrough towards bilateral military cooperation. Various weapon systems pertinent to all military Services of Pakistan were evaluated for a possible purchase contract in the near future. The SU-27 and the Mig-29 were test flown.

While the visit opened up avenues for further deliberations on arms purchases from Russia, political clearance from the Russian Government remained a key pre-requisite. A large military package deal was likely to secure early political approval in favour of Pakistan. It was also learnt that powerful heads of commercial concerns would also exercise sufficient pressure on the Russian government to accord the political clearance. Revisions in the Russian foreign policy for more balanced relations with India and Pakistan were considered to be favourable constituents for Pakistan. India, however, continued to exercise sufficient influence in Russian political circles to thwart any major military deal with Pakistan.

In October 1993, the Russians conveyed their interest in arranging a demonstration of the SU-27 in Pakistan after the Dubai Show. But this never materialized for reasons unknown to the PAF. Subsequently, a two-member team from SOKOL—the manufacturer of the Mig-29UB—visited Air Headquarters in November 1993, and offered to sell the Mig-29 aircraft. The team also offered to bring in a Mig-29 to Pakistan for in-country evaluation. This offer also did not materialize.

On 17 December 1993, the Pakistani Ambassador in Moscow had a meeting with the Chief of the Russian External Intelligence Service, Mr. Primakov, to discuss defence cooperation with Russia. Mr. Primakov was very forthright and categorical in saying that Pakistan was not serious in the purchase; rather, it intended to use the negotiations as political leverage against the USA and to drive a wedge between Russia-India relations. He said that Russia was serious in selling defence equipment, but that Pakistan should indicate specific orders backed by financial guarantees.

A Russian delegation led by Mr. Alexander V. Temerko visited Pakistan's Defence Production Division on 23 December 1993. During their visit, the team leader stated that the time was ripe for Pakistan and Russia to initiate a dialogue for exploring the possibilities of defence collaboration. Mr. Alexander stated that the Russian government had appointed a Commission headed by him to discuss and negotiate arms sales to Pakistan. However, he emphasized that defence collaboration, which included sale of defence equipment to Pakistan, would be subject to political clearance by the Russian Government. He communicated that the Russian Ministry of Defence had considered the possibility of supply of T-72 tanks, Kilo Class Submarines, and anti-aircraft systems to Pakistan at this stage. While responding to a question, the Russian leader stated that the sale of equipment used for defensive purposes had a better chance for clearance by the Russian Government than the equipment that could be used for offensive purposes. Accordingly, the Mig-29 aircraft had a better chance than the SU-27 which fell into the offensive category. The requirement of defence equipment for Pakistan was conveyed on 10 November 1993 in a Letter of Intent addressed to the Ministry of Defence of the Russian Federation.

A meeting took place between the Chief of the Air Staff and the Ambassador of the Russian Federation at Air Headquarters, on 27 December 1993. During the meeting, the Ambassador expressed the hope that the resumption of military cooperation with Pakistan would increase stability in the region. He was of the view that it was a logical decision and Moscow should take it. However, he added, that it would take time and effort to change public opinion in the two countries. He opined that at the government level, Russia was convinced about Pakistan's sincerity in resolving outstanding issues between the two countries.

In his letter to the Prime Minister on 28 July 1994, the CAS asked the government to guard against any Russian proposal of piecemeal sale. The PAF's prime interest in the Russian option was focused on the acquisition of a hi-tech aircraft—a consideration that must remain at the top of the negotiation list. Simultaneously, among the hi-tech aircraft, the SU-27 should be the first choice, the Mig-29 being the second or an additional option. The PAF would make a final choice after a thorough evaluation of these aircraft in Russia or in Pakistan.

A meeting was held at Air Headquarters between the visiting Russian delegation and the Air Staff on 13 December 1994, to discuss the possible sale of the SU-27 and other Russian defence equipment to Pakistan. During the meeting, whole range of issues, including political clearance by the Russian government, operational and technical details, maintenance and logistic support, training, weapons, delivery schedules, and the costs involved, were discussed. In the end, the team leader also proposed that the PAF should seriously consider purchasing a flying command post and a compatible ground based air defence system.

From November 1994 to Novembe 1997, Air Chief Marshal Abbas Khattak wa the CAS, PAF. This period, according to him, had been very exacting, as the PAI had to adjust itself to the styles o governance of three different government in the three year period. During the same time, two Army Chiefs also left office. A a result, the PAF's restructuring plan tha had been on hold since 1990 continued to suffer from delay and indecision. The re equipment of the PAF, especially with a hi tech combat aircraft, was very important The CAS wrote to the government tellin them about the prevailing situation. He also met the Prime Minister, pleaded his case and explained the necessity of exploring al options. There were several offers from Ukraine, Russia and Belarus that needed to be thoroughly examined. He also urged the Prime Minister to visit Russia as soon as possible to further explore the option of purchasing Russian hardware, which was relatively inexpensive.

On 20 January 1995, Pakistan's High Commission in New Delhi, while quoting a news item in the *Pioneer*, datelined Washington, stated that the Indian Government had informed the US administration and Congress that Russia had given assurances that the SU-27 aircraft would not be sold to Pakistan. Meanwhile, another offer was made to the PAF by Belarus to sell them thirty SU-27 aircraft, but once again Moscow's political clearance was neither promised nor given.

On 28 October 1997, the Pakistan embassy in Moscow informed Air Headquarters that the Russian government had taken a political decision not to sell military equipment to Pakistan. That was the end of the story as far as the attempted induction of Russian aircraft in the PAF was concerned. The Indian lobby had won!

The Induction of JAS (Grippen)

A three member SAAB team gave a presentation on the JAS-39 aircraft at Air Headquarters on 8 August 1994. During the presentation, the characteristics, performance, and avionics of the aircraft were discussed in detail. The aircraft appeared to be an attractive option for $25 million a piece. It consisted of 60 per cent Swedish, 20 per cent European, and 20 per cent American components. From the PAF's perspective, further progress on the matter was subject to the guarantees with regard to the US made equipment used in the aircraft. Earlier, Air Chief Marshal Abbas Khattak had paid a visit to Sweden where he talked to the concerned people about the PAF's interest in the aircraft. All those present in that meeting, including the Swedish Air Chief, were excited about the potential of Pak-Swedish cooperation. They agreed to initiate the necessary process to obtain the American clearance. Later, Air Chief Marshal Abbas Khattak also met the American Air Chief in Belgium during an air show and sought USAF support. The American Air Chief in turn promised to take up the issue with the US Secretary of State.

The Swedish ministry for foreign affairs thereafter received a request from the SAAB aircraft company in which they informed the ministry that Pakistan was keen to purchase the JAS-39 Grippen aircraft. SAAB's request was not processed because Sweden had indirectly approached the concerned authorities in the USG regarding the possibility of purchase of aircraft by countries where restrictions such as the Pressler Amendment were in force. The Americans were very categorical in their reply in stating that Sweden could not sell the aircraft to a country affected by the Pressler Amendment. This eliminated the Grippen from Pakistan's list of feasible choices.

The Induction of Mirage-2000

The acquisition of the Mirage-2000 was studied for the first time, alongside F-16, as a possible replacement for the obsolete F-86 and ageing F-6 aircraft, in 1981. After preliminary briefings and analyses at the Air Headquarters, a team of specialists from the PAF visited France in March 1981 on the invitation of the French government, to carry out a detailed evaluation of the Mirage-2000. During this evaluation, the performance of its air-to-air radar was found to be inferior to that of the F-16. The radar had only a limited capability for detecting aircraft flying at low altitudes. The manufacturers were expected to overcome this limitation by 1984-85. Besides, the ECM capability was also limited. The average cost per aircraft was quoted as $22 million. The slight gain in technology was costing the PAF about $8-10 million more than the estimated outlay on the F-16, whereas its performance was no better, if not inferior to that of the F-16. That is why the PAF opted for F-16s rather than Mirage-2000s in 1981.

The second evaluation of the Mirage-2000, carried out by a PAF team in 1985, revealed that the radar continued to have only a marginal capability against low flying aircraft. A solution was expected around 1987 when a new radar (RDM) would be fitted in the aircraft. Since the first evaluation by the PAF, the Mirage-2000 had qualified to carry the Super-530D medium-range, and Magic-II short-range air-to-air missiles. The medium-range S-530D missile was of special interest to the PAF. However, due to the reported industrial problems and delays, production schedules of missiles could not be made available to the PAF team and, therefore, an important aspect of evaluation remained in some doubt.

The third evaluation was carried out in January 1987. It was the time when the Force Structure Programme was being reviewed at

Air Headquarters. The PAF had by then evaluated almost every aircraft to form an opinion (by 1988) as to what force structure was suitable for the PAF. It was again because of the preferred F-16 that the Mirage-2000 aircraft was rejected. In February 1992 again, the Mirage-2000 E was evaluated and rejected mainly for two reasons. It did not provide the technological jump that the PAF was looking for, and the number offered was too small, i.e. only twenty, at an extremely high cost. At that stage, the PAF decided to opt for the Super-7, used Mirages, F-7s, etc, and the necessary upgrades. The French, meanwhile, found that this (Mirage-2000 E) aircraft would not be saleable unless its air-to-air performance was improved and made comparable with the rival fighters.

After the imposition of the Pressler restrictions on Pakistan in 1990, the PAF initially remained optimistic that the Americans would eventually change their mind. There existed a false perception among the PAF leadership that their traditional ally could not simply leave PAF in the lurch. Around 1992, the PAF once again started contemplating the acquisition of twenty to forty Mirage-2000s. But by then, the French were not very keen to sell the aircraft to Pakistan with its full capabilities. The French position was centred around four issues. Firstly, it was Pakistan's alleged involvement in Kashmir and its stance *vis-à-vis* India (thanks to a strong Indian lobby). Secondly, Pakistan's nuclear programme was a major irritant. Thirdly, the French thought that Pakistan was using the Mirage-2000 as a ploy for the Americans to release the F-16s. Fourthly, the French considered Pakistan a doubtful customer because of its economic difficulties.

Seventy-one F-16s under PG-IV were to be delivered to Pakistan during the period 1993-95. When the delivery of F-16s became increasingly doubtful, fresh efforts were launched to acquire a new aircraft of similar capability. The Mirage 2000-V was offered to the PAF for re-evaluation during 1992-93. On re-evaluation, it was assessed that this model had, for the first time, incorporated the technological jump that the PAF had been looking for in the past.

In the months between February and October 1994, the PAF showed a keen interest in acquiring this aircraft. Two evaluations were carried out—one by Air Commodore Zahid Anis, and the second by Air Commodore Najib and Air Commodore Qazi Javed. (All of them are now Air Marshals). The aircraft was found to more than match the performance of the F-16, both in terms of type of weapons and the avionics that it carried.

In July 1995, the Air Staff held extensive deliberations and agreed that the Mirage-2000-V met the performance criteria set by it. The Chief of the Air Staff, M. Abbas Khattak sent a letter to the Government of Pakistan (PM Benazir Bhutto), conveying the PAF recommendation to acquire Mirage-2000-V for PAF, as it fully met its requirements. The government gave the go ahead signal and in August 1995, Air Vice Marshal Mushaf Ali Mir was made the Chief Project Director of this Project. An independent team comprising top professionals from various branches of the PAF was formed to assist in carrying out the technical evaluation, in anticipation of the system's induction.

The package offered by the French was obviously not based on the PAF's operational requirement *vis-à-vis* its operational deployment in a future war against the enemy. Therefore, the project team conducted a thorough evaluation of the aircraft to learn more about its deficiencies, so that the French government could be asked to remove them in order to make it fully mission worthy. The quoted cost at that time for a package of thirty to thirty-two aircraft, along with the required weapons and complete 'O' and 'I' level back shops, was about $3 billion. This figure remained to be negotiated downward. The mode of payment was linked with the delivery schedule. This meant that 20 per cent of the payment was to be made at the time of signing the contract, another 20 per cent after twelve months and, twelve months later, i.e. from T0 (Time Zero) plus twenty-four months, another 20 per cent of the payment would have to be made. So, within two years, Pakistan was supposed to pay 60 per cent of $3 billion. The remaining 40 per cent, timed with the delivery schedule of each and every item, were to be paid in six months. The Government of Pakistan could not pledge such a large amount because the total delivery period for all the items was a maximum of five years. Starting from the signing of the contract until the end of five years, the GOP was supposed to have made the full payment of $3 billion. The French Government was asked to offer a credit line, so that the deliveries could be initiated in the projected time frame but the payment could be spread over a longer period. This financial arrangement added another billion dollars to the cost which shot up to $4.1 billion, to be paid back within ten to twelve years. Although the DCC had approved this project for $4.1 billion to be funded in ten to twelve years, the yearly disbursement allocation by GOP did not fully match the French yearly financial proposal. All efforts were in hand to bring down the credit cost so that the total cost of the project and the amount of the GOP funds could match, but the deal was called off before these steps could be taken.

The PAF continued to press for the technical package it had carefully decided upon. This meant that firstly, the initial induction cost should be as low as possible. Secondly, in quantitative terms, the package should meet our invoiced operational requirement. Also, the PAF insisted that the French company should be persuaded to set up a local manufacturing element, back shops, and depot level facilities, in order to reduce the life cycle cost of this aircraft. The PAF had to fight against the typical French tactics calculated to justify an exorbitant pricing policy. This was not a small task; it took the Project Team almost a year. However, when the package was finalized, nobody from the GOP's side was ready to negotiate the cost. It was only the PAF who was doing it, because it was trying to obtain the best terms as well as reduce the cost of the credit line. Then, in a sudden move, the President of Pakistan dismissed Prime Minister Bhutto's government on 5 November 1996. The interim government that followed was of the view that the treasury did not have the necessary funds to support the contracts, even with the availability of the French credit line. This view was taken despite the fact that both the DCC and the MOD had earlier approved the funds for the purpose.

Some elements in the Pakistani media (inspired perhaps by vested interests) also did not support the purchase of the Mirage 2000 because of the deliberately distorted projection of this programme. It was frequently quoted as a 100-million dollar fighter whereas the actual cost was $40-45 million, depending on the optional equipment desired by the buyer. The spares support and the missile package (both costly groups of necessary items for the aircraft) were often added to the aircraft cost to make it seem exorbitant. The cost of the Mirage was not compared with that of the other aircraft using the same yardstick. While the quoted purchase price of a rival fighter was given in terms of its 'fly away' cost (aircraft only, without spares and weapons), this figure was dishonestly compared with the 'programme' cost (aircraft, spares, weapons, and equipment) of the Mirage. It was a clear case of comparing oranges with apples but the PAF could do little except to issue some periodic clarifications that naturally went unnoticed. The interest on the loan was also being mixed up with the 'programme' cost of the Mirage, further distorting reality. As far as the professional judgement of the PAF was concerned, the Mirage 2000 V remained and (barring fighters of US origin which almost always give the best value for money), still remains the best choice to fulfil the need for a hi-tech element that can maintain a reasonable balance against the enemy's air power.

On the whole, the government had been alive to the urgency of making up the PAF's deficiency—caused by the non-delivery of the F-16s. However, during some formal meetings, it became clear that the government was powerless to enforce its decision. And on the occasions when it did— as during the 1993-1996 period when the Prime Minister herself supported the Mirage purchase—the project unfortunately became tainted and controversial at the hands of the opposition parties in the parliament. Pakistan's fluctuating economy also played its part, as did the vested interests of those who did not wish such a large package to go to the Air Force, forgetting that nearly $700 million were refundable to Pakistan from the USG on account of the reneged F-16 contract. A very large induction involving some $2-4 billion spread over a ten to fifteen year period just for the PAF, obviously also imperilled the future acquisition plans and the sustainability of the other Services. Consequently, inter-Services wrangling over the allocation of budgets from a relatively shrunk basket became a serious problem to resolve. If funds were given to meet the induction of the Mirage into the Air Force, this surely would have been seen as being done at the cost of similar modernization plans of the two sister Services. Therefore, in the overall national context, the government had no alternative but to seek a fresh prioritization of the Services' demands. It now mattered little that the PAF was in fact not making a fresh demand but desperately seeking to offset the effects of the reneged F-16 contract in which money had already been invested several years earlier, with the support of all three Services. The Air Force leadership felt eventually that the two sister Services had begun finally to appreciate the unique circumstances under which the PAF had been made the victim of American foreign policy. They are now fully supportive of the PAF's needs even though the fulfilment of these might mean some sacrifices on their own part.

The Super-7

The requirement of a new medium-tech combat aircraft for the PAF was dictated by the need to replace its ageing medium-tech fleet of F-6s, F-7s, A-5s and Mirages, which would be progressively retiring during the first decade of the next century. In anticipation of this reality, the PAF had been looking for a suitable replacement fighter that could be afforded in large numbers and could match the performance of the aircraft on the enemy's inventory.

In February 1992, the China Aero-Technology Import and Export Corporation (CATIC) invited the the PAF to invest in the Super-7 programme in return for full participation in the design and development phase with exclusive co-production rights of up to 59 per cent of the Super-7 airframe. The development cost of the Super-7 airframe was estimated to be $150 million, which was to be equally shared by both sides. The PAF evaluated and scrutinized the proposal, and in July 1994 requested formal approval of the programme from the DCC, as it would meet both its operational and technical requirements. The programme also offered a rare opportunity to stimulate the aviation industry in Pakistan.

The DCC's approval in principle for the co-development and co-production of the Super-7 aircraft with China was granted on 12 October 1994. Subsequently, a Programme Management Office (PMO), headed by a Chief Project Director (CPD) was established in early February 1995 at the Rear Air Headquarters, Peshawar. On 9 February 1995, the Prime Minister visited Air Headquarters where she was given a presentation on the Super-7 Project. She verbally approved the formation of a Super-7 Board of Directors with the CAS as its Chairman and eight members representing the Ministry of Defence and the PAF. The formation of the Board was formally notified on 15 February 1995.

The Super-7 was planned to be a multi-role light-weight day/night fighter. It would be able to attack ground targets and ships, and engage enemy aircraft at considerable range. The Chengdu Aircraft Design Institute (CADI) would develop its airframe with some help from the Mikoyan Design Bureau of Russia. It would be equipped with a Russian engine; the same as that of the Russian Mig-29 (RD-33), which had been reconfigured for installation in the Super-7 and designated RD-93. However, a very important aspect of a fighter aircraft's combat capability is governed by the quality of its avionics suite and the weapons that it carries. The PAF's Super-7 would carry a European avionics suite, which would include a multimode Pulse Doppler Radar, a mission computer, INS, multi-function displays, etc. The weapons package would include a variety of conventional weapons, guided weapons, and a potent SRAAM and active MRAAM. The Chinese designation

for their version of the aircraft is FC-1. The FC-1 represented basically the same airframe as the Pakistani version but it would have indigenous avionics and weapons, besides some small differences in aircraft systems and equipment.

A considerable number of PAF engineers and pilots were expected to participate in the development phase with the Chinese design team and the vendors of Western avionics and weapons. A team of pilots and engineers would be specially trained to participate in the flight test phase.

The PMO team made its first visit to China in April 1995 to evaluate the work done on the programme. On its return it made recommendations to the Air Board in areas where improvements in the operational capability of the Super-7 were required. Lengthy discussions between the two sides on the PAF's Air Staff Requirement (ASR) during July/August and again in October, at Air Headquarters, with frequent participation by the Chief of the Air Staff culminated in the agreement, which was formally signed on 14 October 1995.

The ASR laid down that in order to achieve performance goals and standardization, the avionics package and weapons for the Super-7 would be of Western origin. The PMO Super-7, in coordination with the airframe designers, had to define the avionics package. Vendors were asked to submit proposals, and a feasibility study for integrating the avionics package was carried out. Besides the selection of the equipment, the statement of work along with the cost evaluation and the contractual negotiations continued among the three parties from 1995 to 1998.

A significant milestone of the programme was the signing of the MoU between the governments of Pakistan and China during the visit of the Prime Minister to China in February 1998. The two sides agreed to jointly develop the aircraft, and subsequently induct it in their air forces. The PAF and CATIC have worked closely on the Super-7 contract. The contract between the two countries was finally signed during the Prime Minister's visit to China in June 1999.

The first flight of the Super-7 prototype is expected within three years. The flight testing of the aircraft would be spread over a period of about two years. This would be followed by the production of a small batch and later, serial production.

The Super-7 is vital for the PAF as it is expected to fulfil about 70 per cent of its operational requirements. At a critical time when the PAF was without better options, the Project Super-7 was given a great deal of impetus. Even while the GOP was constrained by limited resources, the PAF pressed hard for this collaborative venture to kick off.

Earlier, the then CAS had unsuccessfully attempted to involve Turkey and the UAE in a cooperative venture like the Super-7. The Turks were fully committed to their F-16 programme, and the UAE preferred to pick things off the shelf. The Chinese believed in affordable options and weapons to defeat the enemy. They had contended that putting the avionics on Super-7 would be the PAF's responsibility. However, Air Chief Marshal M. Abbas Khattak had taken a strategic stand and finally convinced the Chinese to collaborate with the PAF in the avionics venture also. According to him, 'the nuclear blast may have given us some respite, but it is a fact that the PAF has faced a very difficult and traumatic period during the last ten years'.

The PAF in the Inter-Services Scenario

During the last decade, the PAF was receiving its due share of the defence budget for day-to-day running of the Force and there had not been any serious problems. However, there were serious constraints as regards new measures and additional inductions. After the induction of the F-16s in 1983, and of a batch of F-7s that were received in between, the Air Force had not been able to induct any major weapon system, radars or upgrades, communications, etc, because the necessary funds were not being made available at the national level. Only a few large defence investments had been made, like submarines and frigates for the Pakistan Navy, and modern tanks for the Army. Due to the stalled F-16 contract, the PAF was still waiting for its turn to be given a major allocation. Unfortunately, when it comes to the acquisition of aircraft systems for the Air Force, the funds involved are much higher than those required by the other Forces for similar modernizations. To quote an example, even in the US, an average of 40 to 45 per cent of the defence budget goes to the Air Force while the Army and the Navy share the rest. The reason is that the aircraft, systems, piecemeal systems, etc., cost that much more. Therefore, the dilemma is that in the event of fresh acquisitions of some hi-tech aircraft or radar systems by the PAF, its share of the pie seems much larger than that of the other two Services.

After the creation of the JCSC in 1976, the three Services became far more cohesive by sitting down together and deciding things in a spirit of give and take. Decisions became more consensual and therefore, were able to vastly improve the scope and effectiveness of joint operations. The JSHQ, over which there had been numerous debates, has turned out to be a fine institution, and despite some of its shortcomings, has proven its worth. Regardless of who heads it and what decisions are taken there, the three Chiefs and their representatives can sit together and discuss virtually every issue on a monthly asis, and then make recommendations to the government or take time to resolve their occasional disagreements. Pakistan seems to be, on this account, perhaps better as compared to other regional countries. Today there is a far better understanding of each other's requirements and better interaction both at the level of JSHQ and also in terms of cooperation among the three Services. Commanders meet quite often and keep each other informed of their plans. More often than not, in a situation where one Service participates, it invites the other two as observers in order to get their views and advice where necessary. Despite a few problems that occur periodically, there are very good reasons for the JCSC to continue. The way it is running right now, the Army feels that the body can be most effective only if the Army Chief is also the concurrent Chairman, JCSC. If he holds only the office of the Chief of the Army Staff, and some other officer from the Army becomes the Chairman, the latter's effectiveness is considerably diminished. The CJCSC does not command troops and he does not have control over the senior leadership. In the Higher Defence Organization (HDO) of Pakistan, the Army certainly wields the preeminent power and traditionally its interaction with the Government is much more than that of the other Services. It is called in to assist civil power and even at the provincial level, it is the Army which is called upon to help the civil administration. But does this mean that the Army should have an upper hand in making all decisions on Inter-Service matters? There are divergent views about this question.

According to Air Chief Marshal Jamal, during his tenure as CAS, there existed a great deal of harmony and goodwill between the Services Commanders and the JSHQs. General Zia's influence was very important as he had a way of putting things in such a manner that the interest of all the Services merged into the greater national interest. It resulted in the smooth running of the whole structure.

Similarly, Air Chief Marshal Hakimullah, recalled that the Inter-Services relations in his time were also good. General Aslam Beg, the COAS and Admiral Yastoor-ul-Haq, the Chief of the Naval Staff, were very understanding. The CAS was quite frank in projecting the role and limitations of the PAF to his counterparts so that there were no false hopes or illusions. The Ministry of Defence under the then Defence Secretary was very understanding and helpful. All the participants in the JCSC understood the needs of each other's Services.

Air Chief Marshal Farooq F. Khan, during his tenure as the CAS, claimed that he had very good relations with all the governments. According to him, until 1997, the Army used to share all strategic decisions with the PAF while keeping a harmonious control on JSHQ.

Contrary to the views of some of the retired Air Chiefs given above, there is another side of the picture painted by other important personalities who were interviewed on this subject. One such view was that the last decade saw an increasing political intervention in military affairs especially in so far as the procurement process was concerned. At times this also seemed to reflect the interplay of vested interests. The last ten years also characterized the Pakistan Army's continued assertive and dominant role throughout, in matters of national importance and those related to defence matters, to the exclusion of the other two Services. The Army continued to play the role of the most powerful member of the HDO, and the other two Services had to contend with this scenario in managing a whole range of problems, from the very minor Service and inter-Services issues to the weightiest ones at the Joint Services level.

One of the Chiefs of Air Staff interviewed, felt that the problem of the lack of understanding between the three Services could only be effectively tackled by a higher degree of commitment by the higher echelons—commanders and so on. He thought that the effort for promoting understanding and cooperation had to be a constant struggle. It had to be sustained by a continuous effort. According to Air Chief Marshal Jamal, President Zia, during his eleven years of rule, understood the whole system and used to be even-handed with the three Services. In his era, there was equality and the government ministers as well as the HDO members at the helm of affairs understood the needs of each Service. The Chiefs of the Services were free to approach the President and to explain their needs, and they could be assured of getting their fair share. One retired CAS recalled that the politicians usually succumbed to the Army. The Army also did not extend an equitable treatment to the other Services. They invariably managed to get everything they asked for. The other two Services, including the Air Force, found it exceedingly hard to convince a politician or a bureaucrat to give them their due share. In comparison, during Zia's era there was equality and understanding, and one did not have to offer explanations.

According to some of the serving officers who were interviewed, there is now a visible lack of interaction and cooperation among the three Services, which is a gap that the JSHQ should have bridged during the last ten years or so. But as the designation itself makes clear, the Joint Staff are not Joint Operations, as they do staff work and not operations-related work. As such, there has to be an organization, which should help in improving both command and control and the interaction amongst the three Services. From the PAF's point of view, the key problem is air space management in a war scenario. It is one of the weakest areas whether it is over the sea or over land whether it is with the Navy or with the Army. In spite of a lot of lip service, cooperation interaction and interfacing relating to air space management remain the weak areas even in the new millennium.

There has been a lot of individual effort at the tactical levels, to improve inter-Services cooperation and understanding by holding seminars and exercises. This contribution has largely come from individual initiative, and has earned greater cooperation between the lower echelons. However, at the strategic level, such interactions are far from ideal. At the joint Services level, the three Services should always be talking about joint operations, and that should be the hallmark of joint planning in the country's defence. Not a single piece of equipment should be acquired unless all three Services agree to buy it. The Southern Air Command is perhaps one formation, which could be presented as a model for inter-Services cooperation. Successive Air Officers Commanding in the South have tried their best and participated wholeheartedly in the exercises of both the Services at various levels. But there are certain deficiencies that the Air Force and Navy have been attempting to remove for a very long time but with little success. The acquisition of surveillance radars for the coverage of the entire Makran coast, whether it is to be done by balloon borne radars, surface radars or by AEW, is a real issue. Unless it is addressed, the PAF's efforts may prove to be wasteful and uneconomical during war. The provision of a force multiplier like AEW, on the other hand, would indeed enable optimum use of assets and thus cut down unnecessary air effort on CAPs.

4 OPERATIONAL PREPAREDNESS— THE CUTTING EDGE

Operational preparedness is the ultimate objective of any dynamic air force. In order to meet a threat from any quarter, the PAF keeps itself in a high state of readiness. This capability of instant and effective reaction is dependent upon factors like manning position, command over and knowledge of equipment, and the capability of optimizing it. Intertwined with these important factors is the essential need for the preservation and judicious utilization of costly hardware. The history of warfare has proved beyond any doubt that the human factor is the most important ingredient in determining the outcome of war. Nevertheless, the role of technology in the modern day world cannot be overlooked.

After the 1971 war, the serious deficiencies in manpower were redressed through a crash training programme. While the search for better equipment is always an ongoing process, the PAF has been quite conscious of its limitations and therefore, has strived hard through a rigorous training programme to offset some of the disadvantages in relation to the threat it is likely to face. Whereas the PAF is a small air force—almost one third the size of the Indian Air Force, its operational doctrine has to be of a reactive nature. It is committed to responding to the enemy's offensive plans. It will not have the luxury of choosing its own ambit of tactical air operations. That is why the mission of the PAF is very explicit in stating that its primary and all-encompassing function is the air defence of Pakistan; any other functions are subsidiary in nature. The existing operational training that is undertaken in the squadrons is in conformity with the demands of the mission and operational doctrine of the PAF. The induction of various weapon systems is also undertaken to ensure that the PAF remains capable of fulfilling the expectations as specified by the government.

The PAF's operational squadrons could be optimized for air defence, surface attack, and/or multi-role functions with a combination of air defence, surface attack, maritime operations or photo reconnaissance dependent upon the weapon system held with the unit. Depending on the role, wartime roles are notified that are complete in all respects. Squadron commanders are briefed to fully understand not only the wartime roles but also the engineering and manpower requirements of their squadrons. Having understood the wartime roles, a squadron commander makes it a point to visit the Forward Operating Bases (FOBs), which depending on the unit's role, would be the wartime locations of the squadron.

Operational training in the PAF squadrons focuses on role orientation, optimization, and a high degree of realism in a well-defined operational training programme. Air Headquarters issues a three-yearly operational training programme to enable the field commanders to plan their own training schedules. This training programme is designed to ensure the highest state of war preparedness of all the combat squadrons. During the past decade, the PAF conducted a wide variety of exercises and programmes to train and evaluate its combat elements in preparation for their wartime roles.

Exercise 'Wide Awake'

Exercise 'Wide Awake' has been conducted by fighter squadrons for the past several years, with an aim to improve and test the ability of bases and fighter squadrons to react to operational requirements at short notice in peacetime. Based on the past experience of this exercise, the procedures and assessment criteria were reviewed in 1997. The review was designed to bring the exercise in close conformity with the war role of various squadrons and to make the assessment in line with the policy governing the Assessment of Combat Efficiency of the Squadrons (ACES).

The regional air commands task all the operational squadrons under their command for exercise 'Wide Awake' once in every six months. A squadron, which does not conduct this exercise during a particular half for some reason, is tasked twice in the subsequent half so as to complete the quota of these exercises for the calendar year. The OCUs (Operational Conversion Units) and the CCS (Combat Commanders School) are tasked only during the slack period between the courses, if deemed appropriate. An additional exercise could also be tasked by the Inspector General's Branch during the annual visit to bases.

The tasking orders for the exercise are issued not more than fifteen hours before the first TOT specified by a regional air command. This warning is invariably given after working hours. All serviceable aircraft of an operational squadron, including ADA aircraft, are to be flown in the exercise. The aircraft are fully loaded as for operational missions. All formations are required to approach the designated range at 250 feet AGL after a low level run of at least 70 NM. The rules governing the exercise, and the armament to be carried are specified. The squadron then raises a post-exercise report, including armament results, within ten days.

past experience, the rules governing this exercise were modified in 1996 to bring the latter in consonance with the wartime role of the various squadrons. The frequency of this exercise is the same as that of Wide Awake, i.e. once in every six months. The tasking is done by the regional air commands. The completion of two such exercises for each combat squadron is mandatory. The OCUs and squadrons of the CCS are tasked only during the slack period between the courses. The half-yearly requirement is not applicable to these squadrons. This exercise is conducted under the command and control of the squadron commander with the base commander exercising overall supervision through the OC Flying Wing.

The flying effort required of a squadron varies according to its role and the type of aircraft. F-16 and Mirage squadrons have as their task a night component also. A day prior to the exercise, tail numbers of the participating aircraft are required to be passed to the regional air commands by the squadron. Once selected, aircraft cannot be changed during the exercise. Similarly, names of participating aircrew are to be forwarded to the respective commands a day prior to the commencement of the exercise. Aircraft and aircrew rotation for exercise Flat Out, forms part of the ACES evaluation for maintenance efficiency and combat training, respectively.

The exercise is conducted on two consecutive days. The exercise hours are calculated from the first take-off till the last landing. The type, number, minimum duration for different missions, and the configuration for various aircraft and squadrons are all specified in the relevant orders.

Exercise 'Flat Out'

The aim of this exercise has been to train for surge operations in war. Because of the induction of new aircraft and in the light of

Dissimilar Air Combat Training (DACT)

DACT Camps have been regularly scheduled in the PAF to provide tactically realistic learning environments for the training of pilots and air defence controllers. They are held twice a year at the level of regional air commands. The methodology adopted has varied from time to time. The variations were governed by the performance of the aircraft taking part in the exercise, weapons simulated by them, and the different wartime scenarios for which this training was designed. The overall objectives of this training, however, have always remained in harmony with the PAF's concept of operations. These objectives are to practice the 'pilot-controller team' concept; to familiarize pilots with employment potential of dissimilar aircraft; to enable controllers to handle aircraft in multiple bogey and close controlled scenarios; to validate the evolved game plans, and to give practice to both pilots and controllers to operate under ECM environment.

The DACT Camps are always preceded by a comprehensive preparation involving both academics and flying phases. In the academic phase, in-house lectures and discussions are conducted to provide a baseline for a sound theoretic formulation of tactics, which can be later put to the test in the air. In the flying phase, a gradual buildup is planned in order to provide the experience and confidence required for handling more demanding exercises. The preparatory phase also promotes teamwork and mutual understanding among the participating units. Mainly two types of scenarios are practised in the DACT Camps, i.e., conventional versus conventional aircraft and conventional versus modern high-tech aircraft that are equipped with airborne intercept radar and beyond visual range missiles. Electronic Counter Measures (ECMs) are also integrated in the DACT Camps to make the missions more demanding and realistic.

As the major role of the PAF in any future conflict would be air defence, therefore, the training given is focussed on air defence, and the DACT Camps provide an excellent opportunity for role-orientated training of pilots and air defence controllers.

Exercise 'Saffron Bandit'

In order to keep the PAF's fighting elements at the peak of their efficiency, the Combat Commanders School was vested with the responsibility of conducting annual visits to all the fighter squadrons to enhance their combat awareness and for the purpose of assessing their combat efficiency. Later, Air Headquarters instituted Squadron Combat Upgradation Programme (SCUP), which started in June 1990. Two fighter squadrons and a number of CCS pilots and air defence weapon controllers participated in each cycle, which lasted for a month. Four such cycles were conducted, and they concluded in October 1990. In order to further consolidate the professional architecture of the PAF, a new exercise, 'Saffron Bandit' was launched in September 1992. This exercise was conceived and anointed by the then DCAS (O), Air Vice Marshal Shafique Hyder. Air Commodore Najib Akhtar, and Air Commodore Zahid Anis, along with the operations staff at Air HQ, did the necessary spadework to put it into action.

The exercise runs concurrently with the other planned events and is aimed at providing a realistic environment to the PAF aircrew to apply the basic skills acquired through the training syllabi of every fighter squadron. The syllabi are in line with the specified role for the respective weapon systems. The objectives of this command level exercise are quite broad-based. The exercise includes role-oriented, applied training to the pilots in near-realistic scenarios and effective training of operational controllers in the planned phases of combat flying. This approach not only aims to achieve standardization of tactics/

Mistral Missile operators in action at Thal during Exercise Saffron Bandit–92

tactical procedures, and up-gradation of tactics, but also generates applied thinking to varying scenarios in the exercise.

Saffron Bandit is designed on the building block concept. It progressively increases in complexity, and various elements are added with every mission to provide a complete threat scenario towards the final stages of the programme. The assets are employed in offence versus defence set up with the respective weapon systems taking up their prescribed role. Some of the missions are planned to culminate with actual weapon deliveries against tactical targets at the live firing range.

The exercise is chalked out in an area around the PAF's tactical training range. All targets are selected within a specified area. A bomb line is demarcated as a boundary between the offensive and the defensive areas of employment. The altitude of operation in the specified area extends from low level to 20,000 ft AMSL. The range has been developed with more realistic structures such as a concrete bridge, a 'SAM' site, and

a command and control center. An airfield close by is yet another target used for practising mass raids.

All the targets are set up with an array of surface-to-air threats to provide practice to the missile crews, and for the pilots to use skills in weapon delivery and attack planning. Some other targets within the radar lit up areas like bridges, railway stations, and stretches of roads and railway lines are selected as targets for some missions.

The threats employed against attacking targets vary with every mission. In the initial phases of interdiction attack, the AAA and SAM are simulated so as to enable the aircrew to cope with simpler employment considerations. In the subsequent missions the defences are in the form of low level radar, with only a limited track length and a pair of interceptors. The subsequent missions entail an integrated defence system involving AAA, Mistral, Crotale, Low Level Radars with progressively increasing track length and pairs of interceptors increasing from one to three towards the last mission. ECM/ESM support is provided by DA-20 aircraft and the types of mission include both offensive as well as defensive counter air operations.

A syllabus of ten sorties per operational pilot is prescribed for the offensive squadrons while those operating in the defensive role are able to fly thirteen sorties per pilot. Details on every mission in terms of the target, defences, threats, attack and weapon options etc. are all pre-decided. This is also the case with formation sizes and supporting elements. A progressive analysis of all operations culminating in comprehensive debriefs for the participating squadrons is finally put upto the Air Staff after the exercise. The data available from these exercises enables the PAF to validate the current tactics and standardize the PAF doctrine for most aspects of applied air power. An elaborate organizational structure has been put in place to plan, conduct, and monitor these exercises.

Saffron Bandit exercises have proved to be extremely useful. They have helped upgrade the operational efficiency of PAF squadrons and their standardization. This is a non-assessed exercise, which is overseen by the Combat Commanders School. It evokes keen and enthusiastic participation among both pilots and controllers. At the end of each exercise, the CCS carries out a detailed analysis in order to identify strong and weak areas *vis-a-vis* operational readiness at the field level. This exercise was conducted in 1992, 1994, and 1997.

'High Mark' Exercises

By periodically testing all assets of the PAF at the same time in a warlike situation, the exercise series called 'High Mark' gives the participants a good understanding of how they will fly and fight under challenging environments. When all the units of the PAF are deployed simultaneously at numerous locations, there are no days or nights. The personnel manning the squadron are made to live and operate in exactly the environment that they would face during an

The former Prime Minister of Pakistan, Mohtarma Benazir Bhutto being briefed at PAF Base Sargodha on 7 December 1989

actual war. 'High Mark' also gives tremendous initiative to the young commanders in the field who are asked to look after their own assets and to act independently. It is important to cultivate in a young commander the ability to handle highly dynamic situations. It is equally important to test all the systems, not only flying, logistics, readiness, and weapons, but also the working of the operations branch in simulated wartime conditions. These exercises include various aspects like administration, deployments, the C-130 support, management of air defence elements, and even other logistic chains like the railway, etc. These exercises have paid dividends over the years, as the squadrons learnt to deploy in the shortest possible time, often surpassing the redeployment standards laid down by the planners at the Air Headquarters. The 'Operational Readiness Inspection' (ORI) during these exercises has also proved very useful. During the last decade, High Mark exercises were held during 1989, 1993, and 1995.

'High Mark-89' and 'Zarb-e-Momin'

Exercise 'High Mark-89' was held from 14 November to 23 December 1989. The aim of this exercise was to create a realistic operational environment for the full range of air operations and to employ all participating units in their war roles and to identify weaknesses affecting mission accomplishment. With the overall directive in mind, the exercise was structured in a manner which ensured that besides achieving the desired aim, maximum air support was made available for the Pakistan Army's major exercise, 'Zarb-e-Momin'.

The exercise was conducted on a two-force concept. The AOC, NAC commanded Blueland Air Force (BAF) from his battle headquarters located at Chaklala, while the AOC, CAC commanded Foxland Air Force (FAF) from his battle headquarters at Sargodha. The exercise was conducted in three stages. Counter air operations (CAO) including DACT were designated as Stage-I, weapons delivery as Stage-II, and land support operations as Stage-III. The

The former President of Pakistan, Mr. Ghulam Ishaq Khan and Air Chief Marshal Hakimullah during the Exercise High Mark–89

respective force commanders were given the freedom to plan and exercise their allocated assets in Stages-I and III of the exercise. Stage-II was controlled from the COC (Command Operations Centre). The overall battle scenario was portrayed as that of Exercise 'Zarb-e-Momin' and accordingly the air assets were divided to suit the requirements of the exercise.

The exercise commenced with the declaration of Phase-I on 14 November 1989. Phase-II was declared on 22 November 1989. The movement of squadrons took place according to the schedule. A total of 1,083 fighter sorties were flown during the deployment and Phase-II operations. Phase-III was declared on 30 November 1989. This phase lasted till 22 December when the exercise was concluded and units re-deployed to their peacetime locations. A total of 5,236 sorties were flown by both the air forces (BAF and FAF).

Conduct of Operations

The counter air operations phase was spread over five days. During the first two days, the BAF was largely on the defensive. The next two days, the FAF was on the defensive and on the fifth day, both attacked each other's VPs and defended their own. An important feature of CAO was the employment of electronic warfare assets. This was the first exercise where DA-20 along with ESM and ECM equipment was used. The major lesson was that EW equipment required frequent testing and also that its operational employment was required to be integrated with the overall air plan.

At the end of the CAO phase, with a day's gap for change of configuration, three days were devoted to DACT, which was controlled by the COC. Over 800 sorties were planned but only half of them could be achieved due to bad weather. A night ground

defence exercise was conducted at Sargodha. A group of 105 SSG troops and fourteen PAF commandos raided the base defended by 842 personnel, consisting of GCs, Provost, MODC, and technicians. An RRR exercise was carried out at Rafiqui. This exercise pointed to some deficiencies in the equipment, material, and more importantly, in trained manpower. Balloon barrages were deployed at Sargodha and Rafiqui without encountering any difficulty.

The Contributions of the PAF in Exercise 'Zarb-e-Momin'

It was during the exercise Zarb-e-Momin-89 that the Air-Land warfare concept was tried out for the first time on a very large scale. Plans were integrated at both the headquarters and field formations level. The Northern Air Command (NAC) and corresponding Corps (8B and 18B) interacted in order to understand each other's requirements at the strategic and tactical levels before finalizing the air support plans.

The BAF headquartered at COC Chaklala, operated from four airfields. Air Defence radar assets were allocated under the control of Northsec at ADOC Chaklala, working under the overall command of AOC NAC. At the conceptual stage, it was agreed by the BAF and Blue Army (BA) Commanders that air support for land operations should be provided only at the crucial stages of land battle, such as, in a riposte. As the BA plans crystallized for such a riposte, the BAF organized its air defence radar coverage to provide surveillance over the BA assembly areas and subsequent battle-zones.

The BAF fighters provided air cover over the assembly areas to obtain a favourable air situation from R+3 onwards. Photo reconnaissance missions to collect information on the enemy disposition were flown earlier. From 'R' Day the air action started at full scale. BA's surge requirement, contrary to the earlier plans, changed considerably from R+1/R+2 onwards. Therefore, BAF operations were stretched over eleven days, providing a high sortie production rate. Despite some difficulties and persistently bad weather during the early hours of the day, the BAF achieved 962 sorties of air support in all forms against a planned target of 1,324 sorties.

Air defence operations in Zarb-e-Momin provided for the first time an insight into the problems of providing air cover to a moving battlefield. BAF demonstrated practically that the ADGE could be kept in step with the changing bomb-line through redeployment of radars in the combat zone. Before the commencement of Zarb-e-Momin, the BAF ADGE was shifted and radar units were re-deployed in order to illuminate the entire land battle area in accordance with the battle plans of Blue Army. These deployments were coordinated with the Army's advance. Radar re-deployments were carried out with the progress of the land battle. A total of 221 sorties were flown by the BAF, intercepting 420 FAF aircraft. The FAF generated 354 raids, of which 207 were intercepted.

Large-scale and moving air space management in these integrated Army/Air Force operations was undertaken for the first time. A total of 1,384 Army aviation aircraft were handled. The existing concept was largely validated. However, some difficulties were faced concerning the indiscriminate use of the radar facility by the operators, radio discipline, etc. Besides, it was realized that there should be an efficient console at the CRC to monitor the activities of the Army Aviation aircraft.

Interdiction

The BAF planned a total of 124 sorties of interdiction and achieved 117 sorties. These included deep interdiction of enemy bridges, with F-16s carrying LGB/ATLIS. The PAF umpires repeatedly awarded destruction of bridges from R-3 onwards, but the Army Control Headquarters withheld the award to suit the battle design. Night interdiction was conducted by Mirages.

Of the 563 sorties planned for armed reconnaissance, 299 sorties were achieved. Those were pre-planned against expected targets indicated by the Army intelligence and against opportunity targets in specified areas or line features such as communication arteries. The efficacy of Battlefield Air Interdiction (BAI) is entirely dependent on acquiring advance knowledge of target systems, their location, and type. This is one area that should have received greater attention.

Close Support

Out of 412 sorties planned for close support, 324 sorties were achieved. Post-exercise analysis revealed certain problems related to poor radio contact with the FACs, non-availability of updated maps, navigation problems related to the improper selection of Contact Point (CP), and lastly, delays in mission tasking, leaving insufficient time for mission planning.

Tactical Air Transport Support

Tactical Air Transport Support was provided to the Army for para-drops and air supply. A total of eleven C-130 sorties were provided. These missions involved detailed co-ordination of Director Air Transport (DAT), Tactical Air Support Centre (TASC) and Special Services Group (SSG). All the missions were flown successfully.

Photo Reconnaissance

The Photo-Reconnaissance activity was directly controlled by the COC. A total of three

LORAP sorties were tasked, out of which two were flown to obtain enemy field deployment intelligence prior to the outbreak of hostilities. Seven Panoramic photo missions were planned and six achieved during the operations.

Claims/Awards, Stage-III

During this stage, 796 ground attack claims were made of which 761 were awarded, giving a success rate of 95 per cent. Targets included bridges, tanks, armour vehicles, transports/convoys, troop concentrations, logistic installations, railway stations, trains, rail/road junctions, landing pads/airfields, aircraft on the ground, and radar sites. Cumulative air-to-air claims of escort and air defence missions amounted to 535 enemy aircraft. Against those, 515 kills and twenty-four damages were awarded.

Lessons Derived

Exercise 'Zarb-e-Momin-1989' provided a rare opportunity for the PAF to participate in a field exercise involving an Army field headquarters consisting of multiple corps. Active involvement of the PAF and the Pakistan Army formations in strategic and tactical planning was very productive in creating a mutual understanding of each other's capabilities, limitations, and concepts.

An important lesson of this exercise was that the requirement of planning and committing air effort in support of Army operations is a task fraught with complications. The planned commitment of air support becomes totally irrelevant to the actual requirements during operations as the battle unfolds. However, the close support procedures, integration of Army Air Defence assets with the PAF, and tactical reconnaissance with real time information on targets, emerged as the issues that needed to be tackled at the inter-Services level. Since then a lot of water has flown under the bridge!

'High Mark–93'

Exercise 'High Mark-93', based on a single force concept, was held from 16 October to 16 November 1993. All the operational flying units including 22 OCU, participated. The remaining training squadrons continued with their normal tasks. An elaborate umpiring organization was set up under the overall supervision of the IG's Branch to evaluate the activities generated during the exercise.

The aim of the exercise was to create an environment in which air operations could be conducted to provide realistic and role-oriented operational training to combat aircrew, fighter controllers, and other personnel of the PAF. The specific objectives of that exercise were: firstly, to familiarize all the personnel with their wartime role; secondly, to assess the functioning of the Command and Control system, and finally, to create a simulated Air-Land battle scenario in coordination with the Pakistan Army.

In order to achieve these aims and objectives, the exercise was divided into different stages to avoid simultaneous execution of all types of missions thus facilitating the validation of specific existing concepts. Stage-I was designated for counter air operations, Stage-II for battlefield support operations, and Stage-III for tactical weapon delivery. The governing guidelines for the first two stages were an eastward orientation of the defence, near realistic air defence effort and ADGE, and operations in two geographically separated battle zones. The third phase was programmed for delivering ordnance through a tactical approach on the Thal Range, on a pattern similar to exercise 'Wide Awake'.

During Stage-I of the exercise that lasted for four days, the attacking force generated 738 CAO sorties. Another sixty-seven sorties of airfield strikes were flown during Stage-II. Thus a total of 805 CAO missions were flown during the exercise, which constituted

TWCC Crew in action during Exercise High Mark–93 at No. 242 Sqn

156 raids. The raiders claimed 1,873 bombs, out of which 1,512 bombs were awarded, thereby giving a target-kill-rate of 80.72 per cent. Exercise High Mark-93 was yet another milestone for the PAF and proved to be a success in achieving the desired aims and objectives.

'High Mark-95'

Exercise 'High Mark-95' was conducted in September/October 1995. A total of 3,650 sorties were flown, of which 3,400 sorties were exercise sorties and the remaining were for Functional Check Flight (FCF), ferry etc. Ten FOBs/MOBs were activated for the purpose and the participating units included nineteen operational squadrons and sixteen air defence units. The aim of the exercise was to create an operational environment in which the full range of air operations could be conducted, to enhance the training of PAF's combat crew and support elements.

The exercise was a major operational activity, involving the fighting elements from nearly the whole of the PAF. Spearheaded by the Operations Branch, the exercise was vigorously supported by air defence, engineering, and all other arms of the PAF. Some formations of the Pakistan Army and the Pakistan Navy also took part. During the exercise, all PAF assets and fighting elements were moved to their wartime locations. The PAF's transport fleet shuttled extensively between the main operational bases and the forward operational bases, transporting the necessary paraphernalia and support manpower. All combat aircraft of the PAF, including F-16s, Mirages, F-7s, A-5s, and F-6s, participated in the exercise. While this large scale activity had a tremendous training value for the PAF as a whole, it also provided the Operations Branch with an opportunity to validate its concepts.

The air defence element of the PAF participated in the exercise 'High Mark-95'

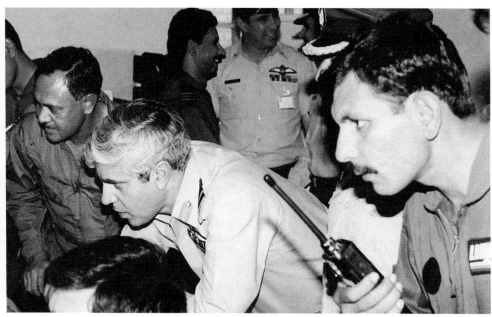
Air Chief Marshal Muhammad Abbas Khattak visiting No. 249 Sqn during Exercise High Mark–95 at PAF Base Farid

with its usual vigour. Most of the air defence assets were deployed in the field at their designated operational sites. The exercise provided an opportunity to the battle staff to conduct air defence operations in a realistic battle environment. Various doctrines and new concepts were practised and validated in the real combat scenario. Additionally, certain contingencies were also exercised that included quick redeployment of assets and conduct of operations in degraded mode.

The efforts of the Engineering Branch of the PAF also bore fruitful results. The exercise was accomplished successfully by maintaining an extremely high rate of serviceability and reliability. During this exercise, the Electronics Branch provided a high serviceability rate to the PAF communication network. The COC was connected in a secure tactical speech network with the regional commands and the MOBs/FOBs participating in the exercise. The arrangement was tried for the first time and was found to be highly

effective. Three CRCs with twenty-one associated sensors were deployed for the exercise, in the South and Centre Sectors.

In order to evaluate the performance of different elements in the exercise, the PAF's Inspector General's Branch was mandated as an independent body, to undertake umpiring functions. To meet this complex task, an umpiring organization was established to closely monitor and report on all aspects of operations, engineering, air defence, and administration activities, with special emphasis on exercise planning, concept of employment, and resource management. The activation of the FOBs, being one of the main objectives of the exercise, also came under close scrutiny. A group of specialist officers constituting an umpiring team were positioned at each MOB/FOB. The team reported on various aspects of the exercise to the Chief Umpire's organization at the COC as well as at the umpires of the regional commands. To ensure that all umpires

115

understood the processes of umpiring, monitoring, and reporting, and their individual duties and responsibilities, detailed umpiring instructions were issued and an extensive briefing session was conducted by the IG's Branch.

The directorate of Data Automation was tasked to provide a management and information system for the exercise, utilizing System-36. This system had previously been used in similar exercises since High Mark-86 for transmitting tasking orders and receiving after-mission reports. However, its scope in High Mark-95 was considerably enhanced. A computer network was established to interconnect the COC, RACs (Regional Air Commands), MOBs, and FOBs, down to the squadrons and ADA huts. Besides, a number of field and command contingencies were planned and practised.

The highlight of the exercise was the visits to the exercise area by the top hierarchy of the country, including the Prime Minister, the Defence Minister, the Chairman Joint Chiefs of Staff Committee, the Chief of the Army Staff, and senior military and civil officers who were briefed on the exercise operations. The Minister of Defence, senior military officers, and other dignitaries separately visited the operational area of the exercise in the central and southern sectors of Pakistan. They also witnessed aerial combat which included mass raids on the airfields and retaliatory measures adopted by the air and ground defence forces.

Project 'OPSNET'

During Exercise High Mark-95, a need for improved management of operational information was strongly felt at the Air Headquarters. Realizing the pace of development in the field of information technology, the Air Staff granted the approval for a PC-based solution in January 1996. Later, to accomplish the task, a five-member team was nominated and the project was baptized 'OPSNET'.

The aim of this project was to replace the then existing obsolescent operational information system with a secure, computerized network, which could present accurate and real-time operational information with the ability to provide instant analysis as and when required. The scope of the project included setting up a computer network in a client-server environment, to manage operational information for providing decision-making support to the Operations Branch. To achieve the desired objectives, the project team was assigned a three-dimensional task in May 1996: To define the users' requirements and supervise the application development; to establish wide area network using DEFCOM media and its trials; to train the users and the technical staff, and to compile the system documentation.

The proposed system was designed to assist the users at the field level to maintain a log of their flying activity. At Air Headquarters, it would generate data for the daily morning brief of the Operations Branch, a weekly picture of combat squadrons, quarterly air staff presentation, and an annual audit of each squadron's cyclic training by the Directorate of Operations.

Mid-course in July 1996, the project team was also tasked to develop a separate application for the Inter-Squadron Armament Competition. Despite the limited time, resources, and expertise then available to the team, 'Bulls-Eye 96' software received appreciation from the CCS staff conducting the exercise, the air staff, and all other participants. This additional commitment gave a lot of confidence to the project team, as its designing, development, and implementations were solely their own effort.

To establish a basic infrastructure for the wide area network, all the combat squadrons at major operational bases were to be connected initially to the Air Headquarters. The project was to be accomplished in three phases. In the first phase, a network between two combat squadrons and the Air Headquarters was planned for the trials. In the second phase, the network was to extend to all the combat units at the major operational bases. In the third phase, the network was to expand to FOB level for the Air Headquarters to exercise command and control of the COC and the training units as well.

By December 1997, the second phase of the project was implemented. As per the initial plan, the project had to install the system at the PAF Academy, Mianwali and Chaklala, after which all the FOBs were to be included into the network. Accordingly, the software module for training units had to be developed earlier than the wartime or COC module. Later, the project was asked to extend the network to the FOB level, prior to its extension to training units. Therefore, the project developed the application for the COC earlier than planned. This module would be utilized in the next command level exercise. After the exercise, the software would be evaluated and subsequently the training units would be connected to the network.

The OPSNET system provides sufficient security to prevent any violation against system integrity by an unauthorized intruder. For authorized users of the system at present, the system is embedded with a number of security measures.

Inter-Squadron Armament Competition—1989

Armament Competitions are a regular feature of the PAF and are designed to hone and test the skills of its operational crew. During the past decade, an inter-squadron armament

competition was held at PAF Base Masroor from 4 March 1989 to 21 March 1989. Fire Power Demonstration followed the armament competition and was held on 25 March. The multi-role F-16 squadrons of the PAF bagged all honours in the competition. Air Chief Marshal Hakimullah, Chief of the Air Staff, presided over the prize distribution ceremony held at the Masroor Air Base.

Squadron Leader Gul Abbas Mela of the 'Arrows' lifted the trophy for the best individual performance. He was declared the PAF's Sher Afgan-89. The second and third best marksmen were Wing Commander Avais and Squadron Leader Khalil, respectively. All of these top performance trophies were won by the multi-role squadrons, which speaks highly of the F-16 weapon system.

No. 17 Air Superiority Squadron outclassed the remaining squadrons flying the weapon systems not equipped with the inertial navigation system. Speaking on the occasion, Air Chief Marshal Hakimullah said that the competition was a major test not only of the efficiency of the aircraft and effectiveness of their weapon systems, but also of the prowess, alertness, and professional skill of the pilots and maintenance crews. He congratulated all the participants and organizers of the competition for maintaining a high performance profile over an extended period of time and achieving outstanding results.

Fire Power Demonstration—1989

On 25 March 1989, a massive firepower demonstration was staged by different types of strike aircraft of the PAF at the Sonmiani firing range on the Balochistan coast. Scores of F-16, Mirage, A-5 and F-6 aircraft unleashed thousands of bombs, missiles, rockets, and other munitions. The President of Pakistan, the Prime Minister, and high ranking civil and military officers witnessed the demonstration. The demonstration started with the veteran T-33 trainers, towing the Pakistan flag and the PAF ensign behind them. This was followed by a low level run of F-16s, shattering the sound barrier as they pulled up in a steep climb. Another formation of F-16s flew in with their 20-mm guns, firing thousands of rounds into pre-designated targets.

The battle-tested F-6 then fired its 30-mm machine-gun rounds. The fighters later fired their 68-mm rockets in salvos of seven each. The Mirage, which had been in service with the PAF for over two decades, then boomed into attack with its cluster bombs. Delivering this area denial weapon from a very low level, it sprayed 147 bomblets in every CB unit it dropped. The A-5 then entered the demonstration with a napalm attack at very low altitude. This was followed by a low level attack by high speed Mirages armed with Durandal anti-runway bombs. The bombs penetrated into the runway strip laid out for the demonstration and exploded below its surface with shattering effect.

The climax of the demonstration came with the firing of highly modernized anti-tank missiles and laser guided bombs by F-16 aircraft. They also fired TV guided Maverick anti-tank missiles against dummy tanks, which blew into fragments as the 'fire and forget' missiles hit the targets. Next, the F-16s attacked a bridge, which was knocked out by laser-guided bombs fired from a stand-off range.

The A-5s thundered in again, releasing retarded delivery bombs, followed closely by a flight of F-16s which also released a similar payload. Salvos of glide bombs delivered by F-16s, in dive, was the last item in the demonstration It was a thrilling display of the capabilities of the PAF and what it can do when called upon to perform its assigned role.

Inter-Squadron Armament Competition—1996

The Inter-Squadron Armament Competition (ISAC-96) was held at PAF Base Masroor from 10 October to 29 October 1996. The competition was held after a gap of seven years and its objectives focused on providing the operational elements an opportunity to display their marksmanship skills in competitive environments. The competition also provided an arena to enable the participating personnel to share their experiences and technical know-how, and for evaluating the performance of different weapon systems of the PAF in armament delivery.

Nearly all the fighter squadrons of the PAF took part in this event. The Combat Commanders' School was tasked by Air Headquarters to conduct the competition with the AOC, SAC exercising overall command and control of all the activities. The stipulated competition disciplines included strafing, level bombing, rocketry, dive-bombing, and air-to-air firing on towed banner targets.

For ease of planning and expeditious conduct of the competition, participating squadrons were divided into two groups and the competition into two phases. During Phase-1, the first group undertook air-to-ground exercises while the second group conducted air-to-air banner firing. During Phase-II, the exercises for the groups were reversed. Fifty-six participants flew a total of 667 sorties. Squadron Leader Asim Zaheer of 9 Squadron was declared the 'Sher Afgan'. Wing Commander Imran Amin of the same squadron followed closely. Besides four F-16 pilots, five pilots from the Mirage weapon system and one pilot from the F-7 weapon system were placed within the top ten positions. Air Chief Marshal Muhammad Abbas Khattak, the then Chief of the Air Staff, awarded the trophies and certificates of excellence in different weapon system categories at the concluding ceremony.

Firing of Air-to-Air Missiles—1998
One of the major objectives of the PAF was achieved in April 1998 when, for the first time in its history, air-to-air missiles were fired from all PAF aircraft. Earlier, the PAF had not been able to carry out firing of these missiles against a drone or a heat emitting projectile. It was done piecemeal on one aircraft at a time, which was not very satisfactory. However, during this demonstration, all air-to-air missiles on the inventory of the PAF were successfully fired from A-5, F-7, F-6, FT-6, Mirage, and F-16 aircraft. All surface to air-missiles, of the IR-homing type, including the Crotale, were also fired on drones and on projectiles. The results were quite encouraging. It was reassuring for the PAF that the whole system was working; the missiles, their storage etc. were in good shape. It was a new exercise that had tremendous training value for the pilots, technicians, engineers, and air defence weapon controllers. It reinforced the confidence of the air force in a vital category on combat munitions.

Air Defence Exercises
To improve its operational efficiency by enhancing its combat preparedness, the PAF has always been steadfast in providing realistic practical training to its aircrew and weapon controllers. This round-the-year training activity under which various day/ night air defence exercises are planned and conducted in each sector's area of responsibility, is an important event. Being the highest air defence echelon of the PAF, the Air Defence Command monitors and controls each exercise closely, and then draws up lessons to remove the short-

comings. While specifying the aim and objectives of an exercise, the role and task of the unit/squadron participating in the exercise is given due consideration. Each exercise is made more difficult in its later stage, enabling aircrew/weapon controllers to handle war-like situations. From 1988 to 1998, a total of 113 routine air defence exercises and three major exercises like Zarb-e-Momin and the High Mark series were conducted.

During High Mark-89 and Zarb-e-Momin exercises, the PAF accomplished its tasks by generating more than five thousand sorties, which is twice the effort generated by the PAF during the India-Pakistan war of 1971. For better inter-Services coordination, a number of joint PAF/Naval exercises namely, the 'Sea Lion', 'Blue Dolphin' and 'Sea Hawk' series were also conducted during the last decade.

Multi-National Exercises
A series of exercises, code-named 'Inspired Alert', were conducted in collaboration with the US Navy (USN). They were held twice in 1994 and 1997, and once each in 1995 and 1996. The aim of the exercises was to provide realistic training environments to the aircrew and combat controllers. The exercises invariably included DACT, surface attack, ASV (Anti-Surface-Vessels) missions, and mass raids against harbours.

In 1994, USN F-18s were deployed at PAF Base Masroor. In the subsequent exercises, however, they operated from the carrier itself. Planning sessions for this exercise were held jointly at Masroor Air Base in which representatives of the Operations Branch, HQ ADC, HQ SOUSEC, officers commanding of participating squadrons and the USN were present. A comprehensive ground and flying training programme was chalked out for the PAF

Two American officers with a Pakistani colleague during Inspired Alert–96

the PAF to plan a coordinated deep-sea strike against an actual aircraft carrier and its task force. The DACT phase enabled the PAF pilots as well as controllers to devise and practise dissimilar air combat tactics to counter aircraft equipped with AI and all aspect missiles. The USN has also been extending invitations to PAF aircrew to visit the carrier. Debriefs of these exercises were normally held on board the carrier. The Admiral of the Fleet along with the Air Wing Commanders and USN squadron commanders attended the debriefs, while the AOC SAC, Base Commander, and OC Flying, Masroor represented the PAF side.

Surveillance Targeting and Analysis (STA)

In the mid-eighties, the PAF had plans to induct new reconnaissance cameras, IRLS (Infra Red Line Scan), and ELINT Falcon DA-20 aircraft. Additionally, the LORAP (Long Range Aerial Photography) capability was to undergo an upgrade for improved performance. Given these sensors, the volume of work in coordinating, controlling, and analysing the missions of subject platforms was estimated to increase manifold. The existing organization was inadequate to meet the increased task and it was feared that the information gained by these additional sensors might not be utilized fully due to the lack of a dedicated workforce. There was a need for sifting, collating, and analysing information gathered from different sensors and the surveillance agencies before dissemination to operational units. The experience gained in induction of new weapon systems like F-16 and A-5 in the same time period also suggested that a dedicated team should be made responsible for the DA-20 aircraft.

pilots prior to these exercises. In the DACT phase of each exercise, depending on the weather, roughly 50-100 sorties were flown against US carrier based F-14s, F-18s, and EA-6. For this purpose, a TPS-43 radar was made available to the PAF aircrew while an MPDR-90 served as a backup.

USN fighter formations carried out live deliveries over the Sonmiani Range, and the PAF was invited to carry out simulated mass raids against the carrier task force. After each exercise, the missions flown were analyzed to identify the strengths and weaknesses in the tactics and procedures.

The exercises provided an opportunity to the PAF aircrew and radar controllers to compare their performance and validate their game plans and tactics against an adversary equipped with AI (Air Intercept) radar. The ASV missions provided a rare opportunity to

The Chief of the Air Staff, therefore, directed in October 1985 that a Sub-Directorate of Surveillance, Targeting and Analysis (STA) was to be set up within the

Missile R-440 in flight fired from a firing unit at Sonmiani—May 1998

Operations sub-branch under ACAS (Ops). The CAS directed that the sub-directorate be formed initially as a project team, to oversee the induction of the Falcon DA-20 aircraft expected to arrive in 1986. After completing the induction process of the aircraft, the composition of the project team was to be altered and upgraded to a sub-directorate. The Photo/Optical section of the Directorate of STA was to be established along with the project team to start its work on LORAP photography that had already been carried out. Simultaneously, during the project induction phase, ground work and evaluation of equipment for the sub-directorate and for the information storage library was also to start. The objectives of the new sub-directorate were to coordinate the efficient utilization of available surveillance resources, to analyse the data so collected, and to prepare and disseminate targeting and operational intelligence information within the PAF. The sub-directorate was established in November 1985 to perform its assigned role and task within the Directorate of Operations.

Apart from planning and arranging photo missions on a regular basis, the directorate ensures tactical utilization of COMINT data by the fighter squadrons and hence enhancement of their awareness of enemy air operations. It also arranges regular meetings of the EW Policy Committee. Bi-monthly operational intelligence reports are prepared and submitted to the Air Staff. All operational activities and serviceability states of 24 EW Squadron are monitored, directed and controlled by the Directorate. Besides, special tasks studies or analyses are carried out from time to time.

Assessment of Combat Efficiency of Squadrons (ACES)

The System of ACES was incorporated in 1984-85 for the first time in the form of an AFL (Air Force Letter). The AFL is revised every year till it becomes an AFO (Air Force Order). A major revision was done under the chairmanship of the Director of Operations in 1989 when the ACES concept was reviewed and given a totally different perspective; even the disciplines in the ACES trophy were revised. This was done for the first time not on a policy dictated by Air Headquarters, but with the help of the field commanders. The squadron commanders, the officers commanding wings etc., were all called and there was a detailed discussion on a comprehensive agenda. The system was implemented after achieving a consensus among all the field commanders.

All operational squadrons, including the CCS squadrons and the OCUs, are evaluated and categorized at least once a year. Although one categorization per year is normally planned, Air Headquarters can order a second evaluation of a unit if a noticeable degradation in a squadron's performance is observed. The state of preparedness of the combat squadrons is evaluated and categorized by an ACES team. This team evaluates the performance of the squadron for the preceding year. Each unit's awareness and preparedness for its wartime role, its combat flying training, and weapon system maintenance are the major evaluation areas.

During its visit to a Base, the ACES team evaluates all the squadrons on that Base. The assessment criteria for the three disciplines of the ACES categorization are issued in order to standardize the procedure for the evaluation of combat squadrons by the ACES team. The general principle embodied in the stipulated procedure is to assess the success of a squadron in using its available assets and resources to achieve its peacetime and wartime roles. While an objective approach is ideal for standardization, the complexity of the job makes it essential that a degree of subjective assessment be made in areas that are not amenable to an objective evaluation. The ACES team evaluates the combat readiness of each squadron. These assessment criteria are reviewed from time to time.

The ACES team ascertains the unit's awareness and preparedness for the war role through a war preparedness quiz, a check of war flight plans, briefing for an operational mission, and by ordering exercises Wide Awake, Flat Out, and the Weapon Loading Exercise. All operational pilots of the Base are given a collective quiz to assess their knowledge of the performance of enemy aircraft, munitions, advanced aircraft radars, surface to air missiles, and air defence measures, etc.

Each squadron's performance in exercises Wide Awake and Flat Out, held during the period of assessment, is evaluated. 50 per cent of the marks are allocated to the generation of the required effort in the stipulated time, and 50 per cent to the results achieved in each exercise. Every squadron is also given an operational task of loading a stipulated number of aircraft with given weapons. The performance is closely monitored and the squadron is penalized for each major and minor safety violation observed.

The ACES team verifies the accomplishment of the cyclic training programme from the unit's record through spot checks of authorization and logbooks. The squadron's score depends upon a number of factors like training programme accomplished, number of pilots instrument-rated and/or night current in the period under review. The ACES team also checks the armament scores and aerial combat cine (or video) results for the period under review. However, armament scores in exercises Flat Out and Wide Awake are not included in this assessment. The pilots of the squadron are also given a quiz from the weapon system Dash-I and checklist. Similarly, the ACES

team evaluates a squadron in other disciplines like weapon system maintenance, survival equipment status, airborne armament equipment status, avionics equipment state, and serviceability/reliability. Additionally, training performance and skill level, equipment of logistic resources, Quality Assurance Programme (QAP), and documentation are the areas that are thoroughly looked into.

Trophies are awarded to the Best Squadron in Awareness and Preparedness for War Role—War Readiness Trophy, Best in Combat Flying Training—Combat Flying Training Trophy, Best Squadron in Weapon System Maintenance—Maintenance Efficiency Trophy, and Overall the Best Combat Ready Squadron—Best Combat Ready Squadron Trophy.

Air Defence Excellence Competition (ADEX)

To improve the operational efficiency and to enhance combat preparedness of the air defence units, a scheme of systematic evaluation has been instituted. The aim of this evaluation is to bring about standardization and improve operational readiness through a healthy sense of competition among the air defence units. This evaluation, instituted in February 1993, resulted in the award of the Air Defence Excellence Trophy (ADET) to the best unit. The activity was renamed the Air Defence Excellence Competition (ADEX) in October 1996, which conveys appropriately the core theme of the evaluation process.

The Inspector General's Branch annually evaluates the performance of the designated air defence units in three disciplines, namely, operational activities and preparedness for wartime role, combat training activities, and weapon system maintenance. The air defence units are equipped with an assortment of equipment, which though used for similar tasks, are significantly different in operability and maintenance requirements. As such, for the ADEX competition, the units that are more or less compatible have been classified into different groups.

The unit's assessment for a calendar year is conducted through the systematic checking of relevant records and reports, and validated through tests in practical and theoretical proficiency. In order to become eligible for the 'ADEX' competition, all Sector Operational Centres and GCI units have to perform an operational task for at least six months or participate in two or more air defence exercises during the period under evaluation. The SAM squadrons have to be either operationally deployed for a total period of sixty days, or should have participated in two or more air defence exercises. For the MOUs, 50 per cent of the unit has to remain deployed for a period of sixty days, or must have participated in two or more air defence exercises during the period under evaluation. A unit that becomes ineligible is penalized in the points allocated to it. These points are also deducted from the parent sector's net score for the award of the trophy. HQ ADC, however, may grant exemption to a unit, if deemed appropriate, and recommend its participation in the ADEX competition.

The ADEX programme for a year commences during the second half of the year and continues till March in the following year. Each unit is evaluated once in a year; however, if a unit achieves a below average score, it may be re-evaluated within three months. A unit's evaluation is to be conducted piecemeal, if required, and also during field deployments. The IG's branch must provide a seventy-two hour warning for ADEX to the candidate unit. A minimum of 70 to 80 per cent of the unit's personnel are to be available on duty during ADEX. To bring about the maximum possible uniformity and standardization in the process of evaluation, the system has been based on clearly established principles and criteria. The assessment criteria for AD units encompasses three major disciplines: operational preparedness, training activities and weapon system maintenance.

An order of merit has been defined for the best performance in each group. A minimum of 'C' grade is essential for the award of trophies. The Outstanding Performance Trophy is awarded to the best unit in each group. Among the SOCs, the Air Defence Excellence Trophy is awarded to a sector based on the performance of the SOC itself as well as the participating AD units under its control. As a token of recognition, HQ ADC may allot special radio call signs to the SOC and GCI units achieving the top positions in ADEX during the year.

Compatible air defence units have been grouped together for the purpose of the competition. Each group is to compete for a trophy in its speciality. The various ADEX trophies awarded to the AD units are the Best CRC or its equivalent unit, the Best Unit in the Tactical Radar Group, the Best SAM Squadron, the Best Unit in the Composite Group, the Best MOU Squadron and the Best Sector.

Flight Safety

The accident rate of the PAF in 1950 was twenty-six per 10,000 hours. However, within the next fourteen years, it dropped to a single digit. But while the accidents reduced, the cost of aircraft steadily increased. The postmortem of each accident confirmed the existence of a fatal combination: the failure to anticipate the hazards to flight safety and the failure to prepare the PAF personnel and their environment to combat those hazards. The

'AF leadership has, over the years, ndeavoured with a high degree of success, o instill in the minds of air and ground crew he need to focus on the requirements of their nission. That is how a number of precious ives and costly aircraft were saved. Anticipation and preparation are the keys to ombat the peacetime foe, namely the voidable mishap. It is certainly not a oincidence that for successful wartime operations, the same pre-requisites of eadiness apply. Neither operational ompetence nor flight safety can be at their peak without also being at their peak eadiness.

The PAF is a relatively small tactical air orce, faced with an adversary many times ts size. Therefore, maintaining a high state of readiness is strategically essential for it. The PAF follows a vibrant and dynamic safety programme. It is proactive in nature and focuses on man, machine, and media. Out of these, 'man' being the lynchpin receives the closest attention. In a developing country like Pakistan, the nation has to make profound sacrifices to equip its military forces with the necessary wherewithal to thwart the designs of the aggressor. Therefore, it is a moral duty to guard the precious assets zealously. In this context, the role of flight safety is of paramount importance. The PAF has to concertedly endeavour to protect its resources from loss or damage. Like any other modern air force, the PAF follows a progressive and comprehensive flight safety programme. In view of the economic constraints, it has become all the more imperative to take meticulous care of the weapon systems and strictly abide by the highest standards of safety.

Flight Safety and operational readiness are inseparable; they complement each other. Safety lies in preparedness, which is the most reliable insurance against accidents. Every accident averted through preparation and every occurrence pre-empted, signify the material addition of an aircraft to the nation's fighting potential. It follows that in quintessence, flight safety is one of the best force multipliers. It is through safety that each person amongst the rank and file contributes to the operational preparedness of the PAF. The commitment to excellence and vigilance enables this organization to achieve its safety goals and accomplish its missions.

The Tools

Flight Safety has two main tools at its disposal, namely, Accident Prevention and Accident Investigation. The former encompasses creating safety consciousness among the personnel, a host of preventive measures such as clearly laid down procedures and techniques for all kind of operational and maintenance activity, and the creation of environments conducive to safe operations. On each Base, monthly flight safety, ground safety, and quality assurance meetings are held in which all the associated air and ground crews participate freely. An Annual Flight Safety Review, chaired by the CAS, is regularly held for in-depth stocktaking of all issues pertaining to flight safety. A flight safety 'Newsletter' containing valuable articles and first person accounts is issued at regular intervals.

Accident Investigation Board (AIB)

The PAF's Accident Investigation Board-I and II, located at Islamabad and Masroor respectively, are entrusted with the task of conducting investigations into major accidents. Some of the members of these teams are trained abroad and they represent both operational as well as engineering branches. During the last decade, AIB-I and II conducted sixteen and forty-four major inquiries respectively.

Institute of Air Safety

The Institute of Air Safety was established on 27 March 1984. The aim was to promote flight safety by training selected personnel as flight safety experts, who could evolve, enforce, and manage dynamic and aggressive flight safety programmes within the PAF. The decision to establish this institute has paid rich dividends in that it has been able to effectively influence the flight safety programmes of the PAF. To date, the Institute of Air Safety has conducted twenty-four Flight Safety Officers, twelve Aircraft Accident Investigation, thirteen Safety Programme Management, fifteen Technical Investigation, nineteen Ground Safety Officers, and two Quality Assurance courses. In these courses, 1,403 students were trained, comprising 986 from the PAF, 252 from the sister Services, thirty from civil organizations and 135 from the defence forces of friendly countries.

The Institute is equipped with the unique facility of a 'Crash Laboratory', which makes it the only one of its kind in the region. The Institute is affiliated with the University of Karachi for the award of postgraduate diploma for the graduating Flight Safety Officers.

The Quality Assurance Programme

The Quality Assurance Programme (QAP) was introduced in 1984 at PAF Base Sargodha on F-16 aircraft at the Organizational and Intermediate (O & I) levels of maintenance. This programme was based on the USAF concept of 'Combat Oriented Maintenance Operation' (COMO) and was amended to suit the PAF's peculiar

environment. The experts from General Dynamics at Sargodha imparted initial training to selected personnel who then assumed the task of conducting this training programme that continued till late 1986. During this period, about fifty officers and 350 technicians were trained and thus a pool of trained manpower was created for the expansion of the QA programme to other weapon systems and bases.

Recognizing the benefits of the QA programme and with the availability of trained manpower, it was decided to expand the programme to the other weapon systems. Consequently, QA Squadrons were established on the nine flying Bases on the pattern of the programme at Sargodha. This expansion of the QA programme necessitated the presence of a central policy-making and guidance agency. In 1987, the Directorate of Quality Assurance was formed under ACAS (FS) to look after such matters. The directorate also prepared the Quality Assurance Manual AFM-74.

Due to the apparent similarity of inspections by the IG's Branch and the Directorate of Quality Assurance, it was decided to merge the two. This arrangement did not work because the QAP turned into an inspection-oriented agency against its concept of being 'user friendly' and was, therefore, shifted back from IG's Branch to ACAS (FS) in 1997. At that stage, a revitalization of QAP was initiated to make it a user friendly programme, and efforts were made for the enhancement of personnel awareness regarding the QAP through lectures, visits, and formal/informal talks. During that process, a number of policy matters were resolved. The syllabi for the QA courses for both officers and men were revised. A new QA course (which included the introduction to ISO-9000) for officers was introduced at the Institute of Air Safety. The Quality Assurance Manual was once gain revised to make it more realistic and comprehensive.

In 1997, keeping in mind the recognition of Quality Management Systems worldwide, the CAS directed that the programme be extended to the engineering/logistic and air defence depots. The initial training to officers/airmen was imparted by the directorate, and new QA squadrons were set up at Lahore, Malir, Faisal and Sakesar. The squadrons at some other Bases were enlarged to take up the additional task.

New Measures

In order to give further impetus to flight safety efforts, some of the measures introduced lately include: the establishment of a Human Factor Research and Advisory Cell, a campaign to reduce Bird Hazard related occurrences, orientation towards accident prevention in calculating awards for flight safety trophies, and a simplified system of award of green endorsement. In addition, a lot of new literature on flight safety-related issues is being prepared and distributed.

Flight Safety Trophies

The PAF Bases vie for different flight safety trophies. These trophies represent the contest at the Base as well as squadron level, and were named for the first time in April 1994. These are the Rahim Khan Inter-Base Flight Safety Trophy, the Turowicz Inter-Base Maintenance Efficiency Trophy, the Sarfraz Rafiqui Inter-Squadron Flight Safety Trophy (Fighter Squadrons), the Iqbal Ahmed Inter-Squadron Flight Safety Trophy (Transport Squadrons) and the FS Hussain Trophy for the Best FSO of the year.

Showing The Flag

A well-orchestrated air display is no doubt a heart-warming spectacle. The PAF continued to stage two kinds of displays during the last decade i.e. mass fly-past during the Pakistan Day Parade on 23 March each year, and exclusive Air Force displays comprising aerobatics, formation flying and fire power demonstration. The cult of showmanship, which was the hallmark of the PAF in the past, is on the decline, perhaps due to greater professionalism and cost consciousness.

Flypast participants of No. 9 Squadron, 1997

During the last decade, the PAF continued to stage fly-pasts, with a varying number of aircraft, during the Pakistan Day Parade each year. The CAS in an F-16 has invariably led the fly-past. His aircraft usually approaches at low altitude, pulls up steeply in front of the dais followed by vertical rolls that continue till the aircraft disappears from sight. This is followed by formations of various aircraft on the inventory of the PAF. In the past, the fly-past was at times followed by the solo aerobatics of an F-16 and a K-8, and formation aerobatics by T-37's which were flown by the PAF Academy's aerobatics team, 'Sherdils'. This has been recently discontinued for economy and other reasons.

Yaum-e-Fizaia (7 September) is a day that is eagerly awaited by the general public. On that day, thousands of people flock to the PAF Bases that are opened to the public. At these venues, they are able to see the aircraft put on static display. Throughout the day, different types of aircraft appear overhead to carry out manoeuvres at fixed times, that enthrall the public.

A special feature of the Air Force Day is the ceremony for change of guards at the Mazar of the Quaid-e-Azam in Karachi. Aviation Cadets from the PAF Academy, Risalpur assume guard duties at the Mazar. The Air Force Bases of Chaklala, Lahore, Peshawar, Sargodha, Mianwali, Multan, Masroor, Rafiqui, Risalpur, Minhas, Samungli, and Risalewala are opened to the general public on that day.

The PAF fighter, training, and transport aircraft, including the F-16, the F-7P, the A-5, the F-6, the C-130, the FT-5, and the T-37, present impressive flying displays at the Bases. These displays attract the attention of a large number of people who turn up to watch them. Selected PAF retired officers have continued to be invited as chief guests to inaugurate the day-long Air Force Day celebrations.

Turkish F-16 Show

As an expression of solidarity and goodwill towards the PAF, four F-16s from the Turkish Air Force (TAF) flew to Pakistan to participate in the Golden Jubilee Celebration of the PAF in September 1997. On 2 September 1997, the Turkish aircraft entered the Pakistan air space South of Omara, and were escorted to PAF Masroor from where they departed for Sargodha.

The air display at PAF Base Chaklala was planned on 7 September 1997 at 1000 hours. The President of Pakistan was the chief guest on the occasion. The air display comprised the F-6 Flag aircraft, fly-past 'Vic' comprising twelve aircraft (four A-5s, four Mirages and four F-7s), fly-past by Turkish F-16s, aerobatics display by 'Sherdils', 'bomb burst' by four F-16s, and solo F-16 aerobatics. Major Ibrahim Jan led the formation of Turkish F-16s from 181 Fighter Squadron, which flew past at a speed of around 500 miles per hour. The Turkish pilots performed a tactical pitch out and landed one after another.

After taxiing back, the Turkish aircraft switched off and lined up in front of an F-16 aircraft where they were introduced to the President of Pakistan. Pakistani and Turkish flags along with different multi-coloured flags were placed at suitable locations behind the parked aircraft. The President presented gifts to the Turkish pilots and also had a photograph taken with them to mark the occasion.

Commenting on the fraternal relations between Pakistan and Turkey, Major Ibrahim, the leader of the Turkish team said, 'It is a pleasure to have performed a show in Pakistan. Pakistanis are more like brothers than friends and the relations between the

Red Arrows over Islamabad

two countries will continue to flourish and expand.'

Air Show at F-9 Park Islamabad

As an expression of solidarity, the Red Arrows—the aerobatic team of the RAF—paid a fraternal visit to Pakistan on the occasion of the Golden Jubilee celebrations on 24 November 1997. Originally formed in 1965, the team was currently composed of nine Hawk aircraft. Squadron Leader Simon Meade led the team. Although it was a working day, people flocked to the F-9 Park, Islamabad, in large numbers. The President of Pakistan, Farooq Ahmad Khan Leghari, the CAS, Air Chief Marshal Parvaiz Mehdi Qureshi and several other civil and military officers witnessed the show.

The classic Diamond-9 formation over the Margala Hills was an interesting sight. Emitting coloured smoke, the Red Arrows manoeuvred the aircraft in the air, fascinating the crowd with their professional excellence. The most interesting manoeuvre by the Red Arrows was the creation of a huge red heart with the smoke emitted from the aircraft. The last manoeuvre was Vixen Break, performed by the formation by splitting upwards and outwards.

At the same display, fifty Mushshaq trainers of the PAF flew past making the figure 50, symbolizing the completion of fifty years of Pakistan. The 'Sherdils' of the PAF Academy Risalpur also performed aerobatics in T-37 aircraft, which was followed by a 'bomb burst' by four Mirages at an altitude of five hundred feet. An F-16 aircraft also performed solo aerobatics.

The Story of 'Sherdils'

Squadron Leader Bahar-ul-Haq (later Air Vice Marshal) who was an instructor at the

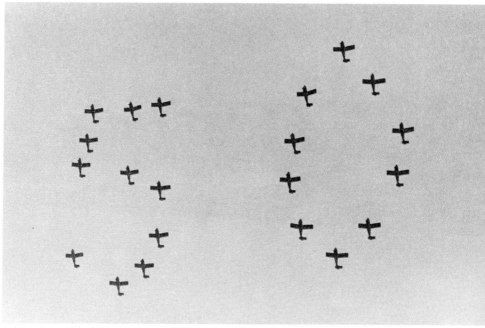

A formation of Mushshaq aircraft led by Group Captain Zafar Iqbal Mir over Islamabad, commemorating the Golden Jubilee of the PAF

RAF College, Cranwell, UK in the early seventies, had been a member of the College Aerobatics Team. On his return to Pakistan, he conceived the idea of raising a similar aerobatics team at the PAF Academy, Risalpur. It was decided that the aerobatics team should perform aerobatics on graduation parades to demonstrate the professional skill of the flying instructors.

The first four-shipper was formed in August 1972. It flew on 17 August for the first time, followed by several trials and rehearsals. The team was finally constituted under the leadership of Wing Commander Imtiaz Bhatti, SJ, and the Officer Commanding Flying Wing at that time. The performance of the team won instant acclaim, and it became the star performer on occasions when air displays and firepower demonstrations were organized in honour of dignitaries, heads of states and military delegations, from time to time.

The type of formation and sequence of manoeuvres of the team have remained unchanged since its inception: line astern to box formation during a loop, then cloverleaf, steep turn, barrel roll in box and finally the breathtaking bomb-burst. Those who have watched the eight-minute spectacle will agree that the performance of the team is simply superb. The team flew for the first time as 'Sherdils' on 19 September 1974.

To add vividness to the aircraft display, the participating T-37s were painted all red. However, maintenance of the red-painted aircraft without the costly polyurethane coating became a problem. The team had to revert to the standard Academy paint scheme i.e. day-glow orange nose, wing tips and tail. In 1980, the academy inducted six ex-USAF T-37s. They were polyurethane treated all white. To give them an impressive look, red streaks were superimposed on the all-white background.

130

With this colourful new appearance, and with the coloured smoke already in use, the Sherdils' manoeuvres were now more attractive. The Sherdil Aerobatics became a regular feature on all graduation parades as well as on the Pakistan Day parade at Rawalpindi-Islamabad. The team also performed at various places in the country on Yaum-e-Fizaya and on some other occasions.

The academy had to disband the Sherdils in the wake of the Pressler restrictions. The aerobatics display on graduation parades at the Academy was revived from June 1996. It was an exciting part of the Combined Graduation Parade of 99 GD (P) and 44 CAE courses held on 6 June 1996. The Sherdils once again won the hearts of the spectators.

Aerobatics by K-8

25 January 1995 marked another milestone for the PAF on the road to self-reliance in the field of sophisticated state-of-the-art hardware. On that day, the then Prime Minister handed over the first K-8 documents to the Officer Commanding, Basic Training Wing of the PAF Academy, Risalpur at an impressive parade. The Air Officer Commanding, PAF Academy, AVM Hameed A. Malik in his brief overview of the K-8 project called it a fine blend of eastern and western technologies.

Group Captain Waqar then took up the PAF's first K-8 for an impressive air display that demonstrated the operational versatility and manoeuvrability of the aircraft. He flew the K-8 through a variety of sharp turns and continuous rolls to prove, besides his own unerring command of the machine, the operational soundness and capability of the machine itself. He performed steep left-and-right hand turns, vertical climb and roll, rapid continuous rolls, low inverted pass at 500 feet, and so on, to the great excitement of the onlookers. According to some eyewitnesses, the Group Captain's demonstration was a treat to watch. Being the test pilot of the Pakistan Aeronautical Complex, Kamra, Group Captain Waqar also had the opportunity to perform aerobatics on

Gp Capt. Waqar A. Nasir test pilot of PAC Kamra, in the cockpit of a K-8

the K-8 aircraft at several international air shows such as at Singapore in 1992 and 1996, in Thailand in 1993, at Dubai in 1993 and in Bangladesh in 1992.

Defence of Strategic Installations

After the Israeli attack on Iraqi nuclear installations, there were apprehensions that Pakistan could be the next such target. As far back as in 1982, the CAS, PAF had issued a directive and tasked AOC Air Defence Command to take suitable measures for the air defence of the nuclear facilities at Kahuta, and to earmark additional resources. An Operations Room was immediately readied for proper monitoring of the air defence situation specific to this task. At the same time, a study of the ground defence of Kahuta was carried out and a series of new measures were introduced. A special contingency plan was issued on 10 July 1982. In the event of a pre-emptive strike by the enemy against Pakistan's vital installations, plans were worked out in detail, including those for retaliatory strikes. A series of exercises are periodically held to keep a continuous check on the operational readiness of all units earmarked for participation in this contingency. From March 1985, initially F-6s, and later A-5s and Mirages, were assigned in rotation to carry out ADA from Chaklala. These efforts were subsequently reinforced by the availability of F-16s for night ADA. During the period of the Afghan war, CAP missions by F-16s to defend the strategic installations were an additional task of the F-16 force. CAPs were launched whenever necessary—at times they were flown non-stop for twenty-four hours.

During 1985-86, there were occasions when actual scrambles for this contingency were ordered and initial actions for retaliatory strikes against the enemy targets were also undertaken. In late June 1986, the DCC met to consider a response to an unexpected and very strongly worded threat against Pakistan's nuclear facilities from the Soviet Union. The note, delivered personally to President Ziaul Haq by the Soviet Ambassador, had declared that since Pakistan's nuclear programme was military in nature, it posed a direct threat to the Soviet Union, from the south. Also, since the USSR considered Pakistan to be following a dangerous course (i.e. its Afghanistan policy), it would accordingly 'have to take retaliatory steps'. The Foreign Minister, who was then already in Washington, had immediately seen the Secretary of State and the American Vice President, and both had been spontaneously supportive. Within three days, President Reagan had written to President Zia assuring him of the USG's unwavering support and to inform him that he had personally asked the Soviet leadership to desist from making such threats against Pakistan. While the USG's prompt response in the crisis was reassuring, the DCC regarded the ultimatum most seriously, and held a long discussion of the various motivations and implications of the Soviet demarche. The possible routes and profiles of a Soviet attack on Kahuta from the West-Northwest—with or without Indian collusion, were considered. The defensive measures already in place for Kahuta's defence and those that could be immediately added were also deliberated upon.

During 1986-87, intelligence from friendly sources reported collusion between the Soviet Union, India and Israel, and the likelihood of a strike against Pakistan's nuclear facility at Kahuta. Attacks from the north, northwest and even the western sector (these areas were totally unprotected in terms of early warning) were a cause of extreme concern. However, PAF's air defence network did an outstanding job of deploying of radars, MOUs and missiles.

132

Prior to the nuclear tests in May 1998 by Pakistan, 9, 11 and 7 Squadrons were moved to Shahbaz and Samungli for air defence duties. These squadrons were given a couple of hours of warning time to move to the new locations. Besides, 23 Squadron was also deployed at Sukkur for ADA duties and 17 Squadron carried out CAPs. 6 Squadron conveyed the necessary load of men and material to Quetta and to all other bases where squadrons were redeployed. The squadron moves were completed in record time and the fighter jets roared in the skies, keeping vigil, while the last minute actions for the nuclear tests were underway. Similarly, 14 Squadron was moved to Chaklala in record time, for the defence of the Kahuta area.

Air Defence Ground Environment (ADGE)

No. 454 Crotale Squadron was amongst the first air defence units that deployed one of its flights for the defence of the Kahuta area, as early as in 1979. Later, in October 1982, the squadron was shifted from Sargodha to Chaklala and entrusted with the sole responsibility of providing defence to the national VP on a round-the-clock basis. In the mid-eighties, one flight of another Crotale squadron was shifted to Chaklala and was deployed to augment the defence of the area. Again in 1991, 451 Crotale Squadron was shifted from Peshawar to Chaklala, and its equipment and manpower was pooled into 454 Squadron. In 1985, two flights of Crotale 4000 (advanced version of Crotale 2000) were inducted in PAF with the *ad hoc* establishment of a new squadron. They were deployed at their designated sites in June 1985 for the defence of Kahuta. In 1982, the PAF acquired a long range SAM system from China known as Red Flag-II which was capable of intercepting targets

flying up to 80,000 feet. The system was renamed 'Black Arrow', and both of its squadrons were deployed in the area and made operational on 26 October 1983. Since then, the squadrons have provided round-the-clock operations in a high state of readiness.

To further augment the defence of Kahuta, five firing stations of the short-range Mistral surface-to-air missiles were deployed at the designated sites in October 1998. These missiles complement the longer ranges of other SAMs deployed in this sensitive area, very effectively.

To provide an effective low-level surveillance cover to the area, one CRC along with its full complement of radars, was made operational at PAF Chaklala in November 1985. The radar sites of the CRC are mostly located in difficult, hilly terrain. Under adverse conditions of weather and terrain, the CRC has been able to maintain its equipment efficiently and to provide administrative support to its personnel round the year. The unit personnel have always been fully prepared to take on the toughest of field deployments and to withstand the severest of weather encountered in the northern areas of the country.

During exercise 'Bedar' in May 1998, the CRC deployed the MPDR-90P radar in the Azad Kashmir area at a height of over 9,000 feet. Considering the heavy bulk of specialist vehicles negotiating the steep gradients in the terrain, the deployment and retrieval of the radar in itself was a big achievement by the CRC.

To counter any high-level threat emanating from the west or south west, a TPS-43G high-level radar was deployed in the Quetta area in October 1982. Ever since its deployment, the radar has been used extensively to provide surveillance on all high-level flying within its coverage. While practising for the defence of the Kahuta area under various contingencies, all forward

CAPs were controlled by the controllers of this radar.

Taking into account the hilly terrain of the northern area, which does not offer good low-level performance to the air defence system, the PAF decided to deploy a number of additional MOUs on its eastern border, in June 1981. Four different MOU squadrons have so far deployed their MOUs in multiple belts along the Line of Control, to cater for any low-level threat which the radars may not pick up due to the limitations of line of sight. To make MOU reports more effective with reduced reaction time, a mini RRF was established near Kahuta in 1985, on a permanent basis.

Another important aspect of the defence of Kahuta was the deployment of balloons in the area. Initially, Headquarters Air Defence Command tasked 6012 Balloon Barrage Flight of PAF Sargodha for this purpose. However, in view of the large area of responsibility, a new unit namely 6016 Balloon Barrage Squadron was raised in December 1986. Since its establishment, the squadron has performed round the clock operations as part of passive defence for the national VP. The unit is capable of deploying more than fifty mobile balloons at one time.

Ever ready

For the PAF pilots and controllers, there is not much difference between war and peacetime. They are subjected to heavy duty throughout their active careers. Exercises Wide Awake, Flat out and DACT Camps are held once in six months. During these exercises, the ability to react to operational requirements, to launch surge operations and the tactics of dissimilar combat are continually improved. Saffron Bandit, which takes place after every two to three years, focuses on the tactical delivery of weapons in accordance with the flight plans of various weapon systems. Similarly, a High Mark exercise that is also held after two to three years, gives a taste of a war situation to the entire Air Force. It tests all the systems, like administration, logistics, deployment and transport support, etc. Inter-Service exercises promote inter-Service cooperation, which is vital in modern warfare. Armament competitions, firepower demonstrations and live missile firing give confidence to the pilots, engineers, air defence controllers, and therefore to the PAF, that the system is working well.

All these exercises are independently assessed. The entire machinery of the PAF is geared to keep the PAF fit to take up any challenge that may arise. The PAF always fulfils its commitments, whether it is trans-frontier routine photography, ESM/ECM, defence of strategic installations, or any national contingency. When the civilian population of Pakistan is asleep at night, the dedicated pilots on ADA, and the air defence controllers, are awake, monitoring their sensors and ready to swing into action at the slightest violation of Pakistan's air space. Operational preparedness coupled with an impressive flight safety record are the real strengths of the PAF.

5 KEEPING THE MACHINES FLYING— ADAPTATION AND INNOVATION

Research and development are the parents of technology, and over the centuries they have proved to be very active and fertile. Today, technology has no limits—it is now making its way into the secrets of far away galaxies. Almost each and every living soul in this planet is beholden to technology in its present configuration and utility. It has become the need of all individuals, all organizations and all countries of the world. The PAF, since its inception, has been very receptive to its application in various forms. The decade of 1988-98 is a period when the PAF had to rely on the genius of its personnel to cope with very exacting situations. Thanks to their efforts, the PAF has managed to carry out a lot of impossible repairs and precise upgradations, and it has a number of creative innovations to its credit in various types of air and ground equipment. This course of sustained achievements and development is still emphasized in the PAF training institutions and there is no option but to continue it in the future. Besides economic benefits, technological advancement holds great promise for the Air Force in the new millennium, as the PAF is certain to be called upon to make new contributions to national security.

The Engineering Branch in the PAF has undergone major changes and improvements during the last decade and this has helped achieve great progress in engineering activities. New maintenance concepts and facilities have been introduced and the training systems have been revamped. These have brought about an improvement in maintenance practices, and the availability of spares has become smooth and faster. The adoption of more direct communication means has sharply reduced the frequent delays in maintenance, and that in turn has resulted in higher states of readiness. The use of computers in day-to-day maintenance has also raised the PAF's responsiveness and it has enabled the Engineering Branch to achieve a higher degree of professional competence.

Maintenance Management—New Dimensions

Since 1956, the USAF AFM 66-1 was being used in the PAF as a guideline for maintenance management. Meanwhile, the PAF inventory of equipment and weapon systems continued to change, and engineering activities underwent numerous organizational changes. New procedures were introduced and existing procedures were modified or replaced to meet the ever-changing requirements. In addition, the induction of the F-16 brought its own maintenance reporting, documentation, and working methodology. As such, it was decided to revise the existing AFM 66-1. The task was taken up in January 1997 and the revised edition of the manual was approved by the CAS on 2 July 1997. In its present form, the AFM 66-1 encompasses the maintenance management system that is in line with the PAF's work ethics and suits its environment.

The practice of having a Chief Technical Officer (CTO) was started after the induction of the F-16 system. Despite the fact that the CTO played a vital role in the F-16 system maintenance management, the addition meant running two parallel functions of maintenance management at PAF Base Sargodha, which did not exist at any other Base. To standardize the maintenance management functions at all Bases, the CTO concept was abolished in June 1990, and the entire set-up was brought under one maintenance manager, the OC Engineering Wing, thus standardizing the organization. This management approach, while leaving the F-16 system maintenance functions unaffected, helped in extending the F-16 system procedures and staff functions to all other weapon systems. This has greatly improved the maintenance management of all other systems. After validating the benefits gained by the reorganization at PAF Base Sargodha, the Air Staff directed the implementation of the same concept at all other Bases. Thus PAF Base Sargodha became a model Base and helped all other Bases to expand the F-16 system maintenance function and concept to the other weapon systems.

In 1987, Air Chief Marshal Jamal A. Khan, the then CAS, issued a directive to form a project team for the PAF Logistics Update System (PLUS) called the 'Project PLUS Team', in order to introduce the Online Transaction Processing (OLTP) based Automated Logistics Management System (ALMS). This concept was modelled on the F-16 logistics system that was inducted in the PAF in 1982. During the last decade, the proliferation of personal computers (PCs), the awareness amongst personnel about the power of computers, and the establishment of the first on-line real-time data processing computer network, referred to as the ALMS network, ushered in a new era in which computers became an important part of the functional set-up of each Base and unit. The ALMS computer network was installed and commissioned in 1991, and command-wise on-line computing facilities were made available to both supply and maintenance specialists. A subsequent milestone was the consolidation and purification of data relating to spares, and the on-line visibility of assets

provided to all authorized echelons of the PAF. A major facility was the introduction of the Data Processing Services concept wherein geographically dispersed, but authorized users were offered the data processing facility, and could access the common database. All maintenance and supply transactions were accomplished on computer terminals, and management reports were available at user premises for analysis and decision making.

In the past, a variety of work cards and job guides were in use for the maintenance of different types of weapon systems. The decision to standardize these documents for various weapon systems was taken at Air Headquarters, and the Directorate of Engineering Services was tasked to improve and rationalize the work cards and job guides used for inspection/maintenance and servicing of various weapon systems. The task was implemented through a Publication Cell established at RAHQ Peshawar in December 1993. The modified work cards were designed so as to reduce their number (using the concept of universal applicability), and to make them user friendly by introducing graphics and simplified instructions. Modified work cards have been produced for the F-7P, the Mirage, the A-5, the FT-5, the K-8, and the SF-25C Glider. All the work cards and job guides have been laminated for preservation and ease of use.

Education and Training: A Necessity Duly Accentuated

In the 1980s, there were a number of rapid technological advances in the field of computers, and both hardware and software were being upgraded rapidly. This change in technology introduced new computers and new software around the globe. The PAF also upgraded its computer hardware to keep abreast of the technological advancement.

Appropriate training was imparted to assimilate and operate the new hardware.

By then, the PAF had established a long-term and frequent-cycle requirement of training, and had decided to establish in-house training facilities. In 1986, the Computer Training Centre (CTC) was established on an *ad hoc* basis, with the task of monitoring the various computer training programmes and providing a basic level of training to the PAF personnel.

In the mid-eighties, when personal computers (PCs) became popular, in-expensive, and effective, the PAF decided to use them for office management. This caused the training load on PCs to become intensive and the CTC was tasked to expand its training capacity on PCs.

In September 1998, the status of the CTC was enhanced to Computer Training School (CTS), and it was established on an *ad hoc* basis at RAHQ (Badaber). The role and tasks of the CTS are to train the PAF personnel in computer proficiency, to provide an expert opinion on computer-related issues, and to evaluate/categorize the latest hardware/software technological advancements in the computer field. The CTS is also tasked to conduct professional training for newly commissioned officers and cadets of the Maintenance Data Automation (MDA) Branch. Refresher courses are organized whenever required. There are two types of courses for officers from other branches: the familiarization course on computer usage for office automation; and the executive course for managers that aims to educate middle and top management in making effective use of computers in automation and management decision-making.

The airmen's training consists of different courses. Data Processing (DP) assistants undergo a General Operation Course, and some of them are selected for the hardware maintenance course. The Office Automation Course is specifically designed for all other airmen and civilians. The objective of this course is to make the best use of computers in office automation.

The overall objective of the training imparted at the CTS is to enhance operational efficiency, to make the best use of available resources in the PAF through computer usage, and to stay in touch with the latest advances in information technology (IT).

In 1997, the CAS, Air Chief Marshal Parvaiz Mehdi Qureshi, appointed an IT and Communication Committee to study the comprehensive information technology requirements of PAF and to propose an eight-year plan for providing a viable Decision Support System based on the PAF Intranet. The committee spent one year examining the various options and consolidating various user requirements. It then prepared an eight-year implementation plan. The core of the plan was based on setting up a Wide Area Network (WAN) using the DEFCOM optical fibre as the communication media. It has been proposed that the Directorate of Data Automation be renamed the Directorate of Information Technology (DIT), and be headed by an Assistant Chief of Staff (IT). It is envisioned that in the next five to six years a responsive Decision Support System would be available, which would use an array of computers integrated by a strong data network.

Upgrading Training Facilities at the CAE
The College of Aeronautical Engineering (CAE) embarked on a post-graduate programme with the commencement of its first MS course, (MS-1) in September 1997. The National University of Sciences and Technology (NUST)-sponsored, split MS programme affords an opportunity to the PAF officers to pursue post-graduate studies in specific areas of avionics and aerospace

disciplines towards an MS degree from reputable foreign universities such as Michigan State University (USA), Iowa State University (USA), or New South Wales University (Australia). Under the programme, students of MS courses complete specified course work at the CAE and may qualify (depending on their academic performance during the MS course) to complete their MS thesis/research abroad. The split programme is of immense benefit to the PAF, as it will not only ensure a continuity of postgraduate qualified engineering officers but will also play a decisive role in the present age of specialization for the promotion of a culture of indigenization and self-reliance in the PAF.

To keep pace with the innovative advances made in teaching techniques, engineering design, and simulation methods, a need was felt for a modern computer laboratory at the CAE. To this end, the project of modernizing the computer laboratory was started in 1995, using the expertise available in the faculty. The hardware was purchased from the local market and assembled at the college. A variety of engineering designs and simulation packages were installed and subsequently used as classroom teaching aids, laboratory experiment platform and research and development tools. The computers were hooked up with the Local Area Network (LAN) that facilitated shared usage of resources (hardware, software and technical information etc.) among faculty members and students. Of late, another project focusing on the establishment of a computer laboratory in the cadets' mess has been taken up in order to provide a computing facility close to the living quarters of the aviation cadets. The facility will be available round the clock, and will overcome the inconvenience of having to make trips to the computer laboratory housed in the distant academic blocks.

For a meaningful research and development activity, access to resource-rich technical archives, and the ongoing research around the world, is of vital importance. Therefore, an Internet access facility was made available at the CAE in June 1997, to be used by the faculty as well as all graduate students. It was made available to the undergraduates too, within some limits. It has proved to be of valuable assistance in academic work and in research and development projects.

The CAE also has a number of laboratories with modern and sophisticated equipment. These play a vital role in training and research activities. In the recent past, some notable improvements have been made such as:

a. Installation of a data acquisition system on the subsonic wind tunnel in 1995. Now the complete process is controlled through a computer.

b. Acquisition of stress analysis data system (System-5000) for the structural laboratory in November 1996. This system is capable of reading data in both static and dynamic loading conditions and it can be viewed on a computer screen in real time.

c. Establishment of the computerized, numerically controlled machine laboratory with an adequate number of personal computers (PCs). These computers are linked with the CNC machines through local area network, and enable simultaneous use of the machines by multiple users.

In order to remain in step with the ongoing technological advancements taking place in the field of aviation engineering, the students at CAE are kept abreast of the latest curricula, by updating the different syllabi from time to time. Besides such upgrades,

The supersonic wind tunnel at the CAE being linked with the new data acquisition system

some new courses have been introduced in order to provide broad based knowledge to the students:

a. The introduction of a Computational Fluid Dynamics course at the MS level, in March 1998.

b. A full semester course on Computer Aided Design (CAD) has been taught since July 1994. The updated version of the software AUTOCAD is used for this purpose.

c. Since November 1998, the latest textbook on Aircraft Design has been included in the curriculum. Additionally, computer-based aircraft design coaching and analysis software, RDS, is used to make the conceptual aircraft design more meaningful to the students.

The future plan for enhancing training facilities at CAE includes establishing the Computational Numerical Analysis laboratory where 3-D analyses of various real life engineering problems in the fields of structures, fluid mechanics, and thermal problems—both static and dynamic—could be performed. Additionally, the plan for setting up the Composite Material Laboratory is also in hand.

Striving for Self-Reliance

I have ever held it as a maxim never to do that through another which it was possible for me to execute myself.

—Montesquieu

After the Pressler amendment and the Foreign Military Sales (FMS) embargo in 1990, the cost of spares shot up to several times in comparison to what it had been. As a result, the PAF had to identify alternative sources from which to buy its requirements, and to initiate the process of indigenization through research and development and reverse engineering. A number of units successfully consolidated their efforts in this direction and developed local facilities that

139

kept the air force assets serviceable and in a state of readiness. Many sources in the civil sector were explored, and to beat the cost factor of expensive electronic components, alternative commercial part numbers were identified for the customized components with the help of data books and parts master software packages.

The repair of avionics equipment had been frequently problematic, owing to the inadequacy of in-country repair facilities in this field. Several types of equipment had to be sent abroad and it was uneconomical both in terms of time and money. To address this issue, a Self-Reliance Cell (SRC) was established in 1996 at 107 AED. The cell is equipped with generic troubleshooting testers and state-of-the-art soldering and de-soldering tools. In order to facilitate trial repairs, a database comprising technical details of electronics components is also available at the SRC. Repair work at the cell involves functional testing of individual components of a faulty module. After the fault has been diagnosed, unserviceable components are replaced with serviceable ones. After the replacement of faulty components, the module is given a functional check and then declared serviceable. The isolation of faults using generic testing of components requires good troubleshooting skills and a sound background knowledge of the working of electronic components. Therefore, manpower at the cell is given extensive initial training to undertake such challenging tasks.

Since its inception, the SRC has repaired more than 1,600 items and thus saved the equivalent of Rs 288 million in valuable foreign exchange. Moreover, the repair cycle time has been reduced considerably, thus ensuring better availability of critical avionics systems.

During the mid-1990s, the PAF made a comprehensive upgrade action plan that included the installation of a radar warning receiver (RWR), chaff and flare dispenser (CFD), and ARS-134 radio on its entire fleet of F-7P, A-5, and Mirage aircraft. For this purpose, a dedicated team of engineering specialists from 107 AED, 102 AED, and CTDU was formed. Maintenance support was sought from the PEC, PIA, and Kamra Avionics and Radar Factory (KARF). The team was placed under the Officer, Modification Project who was responsible to ACAS (Elects.) for the accomplishment of the task. Until the end of 1998, this team had successfully conducted prototype modifications on A-5 and F-7P aircraft, for RWR and CFD.

During exercise 'Zarb-e-Momin' in December 1989, an F-16 aircraft met with an accident during take-off roll at Sargodha when its left main landing gear collapsed. The aircraft sustained considerable structural damage and remained out of commission for eight months. A team of two engineers and six technicians from the F-16 phase hangar worked dedicatedly alongside the General Dynamics technical representative to carry out structural repairs. In doing so, the PAF team not only saved valuable foreign exchange that would have been spent had a larger sized repair team been contracted through General Dynamics, but also gained valuable experience on F-16 structural repair that was eventually to serve the PAF well in the years to come. The aircraft was eventually recovered in August 1990.

Another major structural repair effort was made in January 1991 when another F-16 aircraft suffered extensive damage as it went off the runway during a dead stick landing. The repair effort involved the replacement of some major bulkheads and frames, that the PAF had never carried out before. Even though PAF Base Sargodha was not equipped to accomplish any major depot level tasks, the dedication and resourcefulness with which the PAF team accomplished this repair in collaboration with the General Dynamics repair representative, was exemplary. The aircraft was finally recovered in June 1993.

A safety modification of the leading edge flap rotary actuators (LEFRA) was overdue on the F-16 fleet for some time. It had not been carried out due to the non-availability of FMS technical logistics support following the Pressler restrictions. The alternative commercial channels for acquiring technical support for this modification were an expensive option. The PAF, therefore, decided to start this safety modification without seeking any outside technical expertise. The confidence that PAF had in its own technical expertise was well placed, because between April 1994 and December 1996, a total of thirty-two aircraft were modified by a dedicated team of twenty-two members. All the aircraft cleared their test flights (FCF) on the very first sortie. This was the first major depot-level maintenance that the PAF undertook on the F-16 structure.

Several other indigenous efforts were initiated during the period 1992-98 to overcome difficulties encountered due to the Pressler restrictions, and to ease off general budgetary constraints. Several individuals stood out as outstanding technicians on account of the efforts they put in to establish shop-testing facilities that not only improved the safety and availability of aircraft, but also saved a considerable amount of foreign exchange that would have been spent in getting the components repaired abroad. About seventeen testers were manufactured locally at PAF Base Sargodha alone, to test some of the most critical and frequently required spares. All these efforts saved approximately $400,000. In this connection, it would be quite appropriate to recall the special contributions made by Chief Warrant Officer Muhammad Amin of the F-16

Electrical Shop, who was one of the many technicians who helped in the successful completion of most of these programmes. His commendable efforts inspired many others to achieve higher levels of professionalism.

Research and Development

Imagination is more important than knowledge.

–Albert Einstein

It goes without saying that future wars will be won by air forces with superior avionics and electronic warfare systems. The past decade has witnessed a tremendous increase in the employment of Electronic Warfare (EW) in the modern day battlefield. Recent conflicts have established the decisive nature of EW for mission success. The field of EW is very dynamic, constantly demanding innovative countermeasures for each electronic measure taken by the adversary. This demands extensive R&D to study the enemy's capability and to prevent its effective use in the entire electromagnetic spectrum.

No. 606 R&D Wing is involved in the useful exploitation of the RF induction and the development of various viable systems in this domain. Some of the major work areas involve securing communications and radars against EW threats, and providing electronic and intelligence support to the PAF's airborne and ground-based systems.

In the area of deceptive jamming, No. 606 R&D Wing has contributed extensively. This complements the already existing EW support measures. The Wing has also established a depot level EW repair facility comprising state-of-the-art automatic test stations.

Communication security is another area where this unit has inducted certain add-ons to existing radios. These devices protect sensitive air and ground communications. Several upgrades have added to the operational effectiveness of EW-supported systems. This wing has not only been involved in extending technical support in the induction of new EW equipment, but was also responsible for the indigenous development of sensitive software. This wing has been actively involved in the maintenance and upgradation of COMINT equipment being accessed by different PAF users.

The Wing is additionally responsible for the Emitter Database Management (EDM) flights in the PAF. These flights are responsible for collecting hostile ELINT data as well as programming activity consistent with the latest intelligence information. It has also developed various indigenous systems to cope with the ever-changing requirements in the field of EW. These systems have increased the EW capability of the PAF.

Once an operational EW system has been created, it is also essential that it is put to effective use. This involves inculcating ubiquitous knowledge among the front line operators both on the system and at the conceptual level. No. 606 R&D Wing, apart from performing operational R&D on various EW systems, is also involved in the training of personnel in the operational and theoretical aspects of electronic warfare. The unit conducts regular training courses at various levels to increase EW awareness in the PAF.

In order to carry out research and development in the fields of infra-red and electro-optics in electronic warfare, the Special Task Group (STG) was established in 1976 at Badaber, Peshawar. Since then, the STG has successfully contributed not only in the assigned role and task, but also in the field of general airborne electronics.

The initial R&D efforts of the STG were triggered by a need for night vision capability for the PAF aircraft. Since then, the STG has successfully completed a number of such projects for various aircraft. Employment of advanced image processing and digital signal processing techniques have enabled it to develop state-of-the-art IR systems.

Operationally-oriented work in the field of airborne surveillance and reconnaissance systems was also initiated at STG. Instead of photographic film, digital imaging and data storage techniques were employed, allowing higher image resolutions at greater distances with minimum loss of detail. Later on, the STG also started work in the field of laser ranging, and the systems developed are now operational. Similarly, the STG has also developed several maintenance testers for existing avionics and EW systems. It is also developing expertise in the field of avionics data bus employed in modern aircraft. The capability to develop remote terminals and to install new systems on aircraft has been achieved. Avionics test rigs and avionics simulators have also been developed by using the avionics bus backbone.

The existing air defence automation system has been in use for the last fifteen years. To ensure its optimum performance, No. 118 Software Engineering Depot (SED) has been carrying out modifications and debugging in the automation system software which is huge in size and complexity. In terms of software modification tasks, 118 SED has completed eighty-two tasks at ADOC/SOCs/OCCs, conducted a number of software feasibility studies, and completed numerous projects using its own expertise and resources. This has not only enhanced our capabilities but has also led to huge savings.

CAE Supports R&D Efforts

Most of the faculty members at the CAE have MS and Ph.D. degrees in their fields of specialty. Their expertise is put to full use in solving engineering problems related to the PAF in particular and the nation in general. Besides the efforts put in by the faculty members, the final term students also undertake projects, some of which are later developed further. Some of the notable R&D efforts by the CAE are described in the text that follows.

A project of the Thermal Imaging System was undertaken in 1994 for concept evaluation and the implementation of different scanning techniques and display systems. The funds were provided by the Ministry of Science and Technology (MOST) through NUST. A laboratory model is ready and procurement of latest IR detectors is in hand for a field model of the system.

In 1995, the CAE undertook the project of designing and developing a Chaff and Flare Dispensing (CFD) system. The designing involved the development of three sub-assemblies: a control unit, a programmer and a sequencer switch. The CAE successfully developed the design concept of enhanced CFD and named it GT-1P. After the completion of the design work and laboratory model, the circuit diagram and the hardware were given to the Air Weapon Complex for prototyping and production.

A log periodic antenna for communication jamming has been designed, fabricated and tested at the CAE. The performance is comparable to the original antenna for a jammer system. The designed antenna satisfied the operational requirements and has been handed over to 606 R&D Wing for further development. Additionally, a portable, robust, conical discone antenna has also been designed, fabricated, and tested. It

Major-General Muhammad Ali Qudah, Chief of the Air Staff, Royal Jordanian Air Force, being briefed during his visit to the PAF Academy, Risalpur on 10 January 1995 about an avionics project made by an under training cadet

will be useful for the VHF-UHF communication intelligence system or radio sets.

An improved version of the Integrated Radio Control Panel for ARC 164/ARS 134 has been developed to increase the number of preset channels from twenty to ninety-nine. The smaller size would enable the accommodation of both this and the radio control panel of ARS-134 in the existing physical console.

The Mirage aircraft initially acquired by the PAF in the late 1960s were equipped with an inertial navigation system (INAS). In view of the high unserviceability rate and the inability of its manufacturer to further support its magnetic core memories, the PAF started working to replace them. A project was completed successfully at the CAE in 1998 using non-volatile RAM, and air trials are awaited.

Unit IV of the FM 200 radio equipment is a two-stage amplifier. The tuning of the unit had been a problem area for the PAF. A faculty member of the CAE was given the task of studying the system, developing maintenance algorithm, and training manpower to establish the repair facilities at 107 AED. The maintenance procedures were developed, the technicians were trained, and out of four unserviceable units, two have already been recovered.

The K-8 aircraft encountered a couple of canopy shattering occurrences at 25,000 feet. A complete structural and thermal analysis of the canopy was carried out at CAE, using the finite element method. The areas of high stress were identified for addressing the problem.

The project of developing a Logistics Forecasting System was undertaken with the aim of modelling a forecasting system on the basis of consumption of different aircraft components. The system is able to determine how much to order at a time, when to reorder and at what level, and it can calculate how much there should be in the pipeline and the reserve stock.

A study was conducted at the CAE to determine the effect of change in an aircraft's wing geometry on its aerodynamic characteristics. The purpose was to derive equations of a general twisted wing planform and convert these equations into a computer code. The developed code is capable of calculating the aerodynamic characteristics of a general wing and helps in determining the effects of change in wing geometry on these characteristics.

A comprehensive computer programme was developed at the CAE for performance estimation and stability evaluation of a Super Mushshaq, if converted into a four-seater aircraft. The code is fairly general and can evaluate performance parameters such as climb, endurance, range, turn, and propeller performance for any other aircraft of the type.

The manual computation method for an aircraft symmetry check, besides being laborious and time consuming, is prone to calculation mistakes. A software package has been developed at the CAE for the Mirage aircraft, that helps to obtain final results with the click of a button. A user-friendly interface enables the user to go through the steps without needing to know how the calculations are performed.

The fan assembly of the TFE 731 engine, installed in K-8 aircraft, has thirty blades. In case of damage, it is possible to either repair or replace the damaged blades, subject to certain limitations specified by the manufacturers. However, if the number of blades requiring replacement is large, such limitations put serious practical constraints on the choice of blades. This problem is modelled as a non-linear integer pro-gramming problem and a computer code is developed for automatic selection of blades.

The sets of blades chosen in this manner are guaranteed to cause minimal vibration problems. This concept is being extended for use on the WP-7 engines of F-7P aircraft, for selection of compressor and turbine blades requiring replacements.

Engineering Symposiums

The Directorate of Engineering Services has so far arranged two major engineering symposiums under the guidance of DCAS (Engg.). The first was held on 23 and 24 February 1997. It covered cyber warfare and other current issues of the PAF. The second in the series was held on 30 March 1998 in the Air HQ auditorium. The Chief of Air Staff, PSOs, and all senior engineering officers attended the symposium. The theme of this symposium was 'Indigenization—the Road to Self-Reliance'.

In his introductory speech, the DCAS (Engg.) highlighted the importance of self-reliance and briefly touched upon the various difficulties being experienced by the self-reliance programme of the PAF. The speech was followed by a review of the progress made, following the recommendations put forward during the Engineering Symposium-1997. On the issue of cyber warfare, it was pointed out that a high level committee, headed by DCAS (P), had been formed to develop a comprehensive strategy for the PAF, on information technology and security against cyber warfare. The committee has had several meetings and implemented various measures towards evolving a final strategy against cyber threats. With respect to the second part of Engineering Symposium-1997, (which was related to the key issues of maintenance and logistics management), progress was reported on issues such as re-engineering of maintenance management, quality concept in the PAF, re-vitalization of the OJT programme, and establishment of FTDs for all weapon systems.

The proceedings started with a mention of the self-reliance programme in relation to the past achievements, present status, and future plans of the PAF. It was recommended that the PAF should formulate an indigenization policy that should clearly lay down the short and long term goals of the self-reliance programme. Later, a number of participants made presentations on the various aspects of self-reliance in the PAF. Discussion about topics such as K-8 production, indigenization potential of Super-7, efforts through DGMP and Motor Vehicle Research and Development Establishment (MVRDE), and futuristic view of indigenous production at PAC constituted the major theme of the proceedings.

A lively question and answer session followed the presentations. Some important points, such as the extent of the indigenization effort that should be made by the PAF, the amount of financial resources that can be made available for indigenization, the career progression of officers involved in R&D work, and the career of officers and men at PAC Kamra, were discussed during this session.

Air Vice Marshal Niaz Hussain, DCAS (Engg.), summed up the proceedings in his closing address by highlighting the important issues raised by each speaker. He stressed the need to have a concrete policy on the indigenization programme.

In his closing address, the Chief of Air Staff appreciated the efforts of the Engineering Branch in general, and of the speakers in particular, for making the symposium a success. He was happy to note the progress made on the issues raised during the Engineering Symposium-1997 and urged that the critical issues raised during the present symposium be worked upon in the same spirit.

145

The Seventh National Aeronautical Conference

The survival of a nation in today's hi-tech world demands self-sufficiency in technologies that are critical to its defence. The establishment of an aeronautical industry is one of the major elements in the development of integrated national defence capabilities. The PAF has been on the forefront in contributing to this national objective.

The establishment of the College of Aeronautical Engineering (CAE), the Pakistan Aeronautical Complex (PAC), and the Air Weapons Complex (AWC); the co-production of K-8 aircraft, aircraft design centre for Super-7 aircraft, and other small R&D units are steps forward in providing the necessary infrastructure to support technological growth. In this context, the Seventh International Aeronautical Conference was jointly organized by the PAF College of Aeronautical Engineering and the Pakistan Division of the Royal Aeronautical Society (UK) in March 1995. Air Chief Marshal M. Abbas Khattak, Chief of the Air Staff, inaugurated the conference. A number of valuable papers, both by local and international speakers, were presented at the conference.

Facilities Developed and Projects Accomplished

The PAF, being a dynamic force, has inducted state-of-the-art equipment to develop an infrastructure that can meet maintenance requirements, thus allowing the Air Force to contribute effectively to national defence. During the last decade, the PAF has developed some unique and vital facilities that have not only helped to combat the embargoes and sanctions but also kept its fleet in a high state of readiness. The PAF's engineers and technicians have rightly earned praise for displaying professionalism in establishing in-house facilities that have both effectively neutralized many of the effects of embargoes and at the same time saved valuable foreign exchange.

Upgrading the Falcons

The F-16 Upgrade Cell was established in January 1997 to carry out factory level tasks on the F-16 fleet, namely 'Operational Capabilities Upgrade' (OCU) and a structural integrity programme called 'Falcon-Up'. Falcon-Up is an extensive, hard core upgrade that involves the elimination of structural problems endangering flight safety. It is accomplished through the dismantling of complete aircraft, replacement of bulkheads, longhorns, and thousands of new hardware items; and the use of hi-tech NDI techniques and cold working processes. On the other hand, the OCU is an extensive avionics system reliability enhancement programme involving major circuitry modifications, and the installation of new and modified components like combined altitude radar altimeter, ring laser INU, etc. It also includes the installation of the upgraded 220E version of the engine. As such, the OCU involves ten different Engineering Change Proposals (ECPs) comprising fifty different TCTOs and using 1,620 different types of kits.

It was the first time that such a complex, factory-level modification was made at PAF Base Sargodha. The complexity of these major tasks can be guaged from the fact that fewer than ten countries, out of thirty-two operating F-16s worldwide, opted for in-country accomplishment, whereas the rest sent their aircraft to Lockheed, USA for retrofit installation.

By the end of 1998, Falcon-Up modification was accomplished on two

146

aircraft, whereas seven aircraft were OCU modified. Further modifications had to be stopped because of the latest US sanctions, but studies were immediately begun in order to face this new challenge.

Maintenance of the Engines

The F-100 Shop was established at PAF Base Sargodha for the scheduled maintenance on the PW-F100-200 engine. In 1989, it was upgraded to extend the maintenance and engineering support to WP-7B and ATAR engines of F-7 and Mirage aircraft respectively.

The upgrading of the F-100 engine core module from 1800 to 4000 cycles was started in 1985. This was a major project involving a major disassembly/assembly of the engine. During the upgrade in 1991, problems arose in storing the fan module augmentor duct while the engine was disassembled. Since storage stands were not available in sufficient numbers, they were manufactured locally and the upgrade was completed on all the F-100 engines by 1996. In 1986, a package of Time Compliance Technical Order (TCTOs) was received, that dealt with the improvement in lubrication and fuel system of the engine. These TCTOs were accomplished on all the engines by 1989. Additionally, by 1998, the F-100 Jet Engine Intermediate Maintenance (JEIM) team had built four complete engines from knockdown kits it had on its inventory.

The F-100 test cell had been made dependent on the crash trolley that was always required during any test run. In May 1993, the development of the Halon cylinder facility made it possible for the engine run to be carried out without the presence of the crash trolley.

The month of April 1997 is remembered as a milestone in the history of the F-100 test cell. In this month, a major project of upgrading the test cell for the PW-F-100/200E engine was completed. With the induction of F-100-PW-200E engines, it became mandatory to modify the test cell so as to accommodate the 200E engine series also. As the kits had already been received for this upgrade, the F-100 test cell team took up this job as a challenge and went out of their way to accomplish it with the assistance of the technical representative from Pratt & Whitney, USA.

Adventures All Around

PAF Base Masroor has the unique privilege of servicing and operating almost every weapon system of the PAF. In 1989, the Chinese built F-7P aircraft was inducted, and second-line maintenance facilities were established for it at the Base. In the period 1990-91, it was selected to undertake the task of preparing ex-Australian Mirages for operational use, though later the project was assigned to PAC Kamra. In 1997, 7 Squadron was refurbished with Retrofit of Strike Element (ROSE) modified Mirage aircraft. The Base ensured a smooth transition by providing adequate support in the training of the technicians. Similar facilities were extended by the Base in September 1998 to the first batch of ex-French Air Force Mirages.

The Engineering Wing, Chaklala, in addition to its designated task, has also performed special tasks to enhance existing capabilities. Some of the notable achievements are the induction of the fuel nozzle tester, the dynamic balancing of the propeller, the induction of the video analyzer boroscope, and the development of a voltage regulator/generator test stand. In addition, the establishment of the propeller life extension facility and recovery of three T-56 engines out of 10 BCR held at 101 ALC were also achieved.

In 1996, WP-7 type 'E' engines were inducted at 102 AED for overhaul, and the task was successfully accomplished in 1997. Between 1996 and 1998, the twin cell test bed was upgraded, and a modification of exhaust deflectors was carried out to facilitate testing of engines after overhaul/EFM. This would ensure the timely availability of serviceable WP-7 engines for supporting the F-7 fleet of the PAF. In 1998, CATIC approved the skill level of the manpower at the depot as well as the quality of its production for WP-7 engines.

C-130 PDM Inspection

In the late eighties, the C-130 aircraft of the PAF were due for overhaul, commonly known as Programme Depot Maintenance (PDM). This inspection was to be performed as per USAF document FD 2060-86-52153. The inspection required extensive non-destructive inspections (NDI) of critical areas including removal, cleaning, inspection, repairs and rigging of all major assemblies of C-130 aircraft. This was a highly specialized job demanding high calibre skills.

The PAF did not have the required infrastructure or skills to undertake such an extensive project and, therefore, some of the C-130 aircraft were sent for PDM to Singapore and Peru. In the meantime, the PAF set out to establish PDM facilities and started training its technicians. Finally, the project was launched and the construction of a hangar was undertaken. The first PDM was begun in February 1993 and successfully completed in February 1994. It not only saved valuable foreign exchange but also helped the PAF to establish a unit not found in many other countries of the world. This was yet another great achievement, leading to the PAF's avowed goal of self-reliance.

Besides the PDM, the facility is capable of undertaking all types of major structural repairs and modifications on C-130 aircraft. Thus, the PAF is no longer dependent on foreign countries for the upkeep of its C-130 fleet. In the 1995-96 timeframe, the unit undertook an avionics upgrade modification, enabling the C-130 aircraft to have INAS on board the aircraft. A highly motivated and dedicated team of engineers and technicians made the modification. By this time the PDM unit had earned an international reputation as a base for C-130 overhaul and modifications. As a result, various foreign companies showed their interest in having joint ventures with this unit in order to further expand the facilities for undertaking such tasks. So far the PAF has undertaken ten PDM inspections and carried them out with a high degree of skill and professionalism. At present, the unit is looking forward to establishing an Outer Wing Improvement Programme (OWIP) and Quick Engine Change (QEC) housing overhaul facilities, so that other areas are also well covered and the PAF can become fully self-reliant.

The Allouette-III Overhaul

The PAF uses Allouette-III helicopters for rescue operations. These helicopters were overhauled at the Pakistan Army workshop No. 503 at Dhamial. The average time for the overhaul varied between eighteen to twenty-four months, thereby resulting in the problem of Allouette availability in the PAF. Furthermore, all of the overhaul requirements as specified by the manufacturer were not satisfied. Since the schedules and overhaul schemes were not meeting its requirements, the PAF decided to establish an Allouette-III overhaul facility at 102 AED.

The project for setting up an Allouette-III overhaul facility started in July 1996, and a team of officers and airmen was trained at Dhamial and subsequently in Romania. The fixtures required for the overhaul were manufactured locally at 102 AED. The first helicopter for trial overhaul and on-the-job training (OJT) was inducted in June 1997. It was completed in April 1998 and all aspects of subsequent overhauls including logistics and training were addressed during this period. The second helicopter was completely overhauled in a record time of just twenty weeks. This undertaking has helped the PAF to substantially reduce the cost of overhaul as well.

This facility not only meets the PAF's recurring overhaul requirements of the Allouette-III fleet but has also enabled the recovery of some parts/spares including glass reinforced plastic parts etc., which were earlier discarded or sent to the manufacturer for repair.

Setting Up the Precision Measurements Equipment Laboratory (PMEL)

The Standard and Calibration (S&C) Squadron was established at 107 AED in the early 1960s, to meet the limited requirements of repair and calibration of test equipment. In the early 1980s, the need for enhancing the role of S&C Squadron was felt by virtue of a major influx of new weapon systems in the PAF. A study was carried out by a team of foreign experts from AGMC, USA, who proposed the establishment of the PMEL. In 1989, all the prerequisites for the present PMEL were met and it became operational in providing calibration and repair support to all PAF Bases/units and other services. The PMEL is capable of calibrating 500 items per month.

In addition to the calibration/repair of PME, the unit has other functions. It has been equipped with a satellite receiver bench that monitors worldwide information in the southern zone of the country. It also encompasses a laboratory to address issues related to temperature, pressure, linear measurement, angular measurement and electro-mechanical equipment.

Calibration and maintenance documentation was carried out manually in the early stages of PMEL (S&C). In 1986, it was changed over to IBM System-36 module Calibration Management System (CMS) and in mid-1997, it was further improved to System 3090 of ALMS module CMS.

The Mirage Aircraft Upgrade

The Mirage aircraft avionics upgrade project named as Retrofit of Strike Element (ROSE) was conceived in 1992. The upgradation of the aircraft commenced in April 1995 and was successfully completed by 1998. The avionics package included inertial navigation system (INS), head up display (HUD), multi-mode radar, airborne video recording system and self-protection systems like RWR, chaff and flares. No. 25 squadron was re-equipped as a transient squadron for ROSE modified aircraft in April 1996. Later, 7 squadron and the CCS (Mirage) squadron were allotted ROSE modified aircraft by August 1997. At present, Griffo fire control radars from Italy are being installed by the PAF on these Mirage-III aircraft.

In 1996, a project was launched to upgrade the avionics of the Mirage-V (ROSE-II) aircraft. SAGEM of France are presently doing this and the aircraft are being delivered to the PAF after the avionics upgrade. These aircraft are equipped with forward-looking infra radar (FLIR) instead of fire control radar. All ROSE-I and ROSE-II aircraft thus carry sophisticated and the latest avionics equipment like the navigation and attack unit (NAU), head up display (HUD), radio altimeter, coloured airborne video tape recorder (AVTR), etc.

Air Chief Marshal Parvaiz Mehdi Qureshi, the CAS, inspecting the first batch of recently inducted Mirages overhauled and upgraded in France, 2 October 1998

The T-37s Receive New Life

The T-37 aircraft have been operating in the PAF since 1962. Their initial structural life was 8,000 hours of flight. The fleet was reaching the limit of its service life during the early-1990s. To further enhance their life, the T-37 Structural Life Enhancement Programme (SLEP) was started in 1993. This was a major depot level project, which was to be accomplished by Sabreliner Corporation, USA. However, the PAF decided to undertake this difficult project within Pakistan, using its own resources. Sabreliner representatives came to Pakistan and trained one officer, twenty airmen, and thirty civilian technicians for this purpose.

This project included five major structural modifications in the wing, fuselage, and the horizontal and vertical stabilizer area. The project work started in November 1993 at the Engineering Wing, PAF Academy, Risalpur. A total of twenty-seven aircraft were successfully modified in a professional manner. To complete this modification, the SLEP team worked very hard and not only produced an excellent quality of work but also proved that the PAF technical know-how and skills were second to none. Through this project, the life of each aircraft was enhanced by an additional 7,000 flying hours. It also helped to save millions of dollars in foreign exchange. All this has been accomplished with the help of locally trained manpower, attached to the PAF Academy from different units, mostly from 102 AED.

The successful and safe completion of SLEP is a noteworthy achievement of the

Wing Spar Modification being carried out on a T-37 aircraft under the SLEP programme at the PAF Academy, Risalpur

PAF Academy Risalpur; as many as eleven aircraft were SLEP modified in a single year. Among the aircraft that underwent SLEP modification, three were extensively damaged and had been on the ground for a period ranging from seven to eighteen years. The PAF team, however, successfully recovered all three aircraft, performed SLEP, and made the aircraft airworthy.

The Crotale 4000 Maintenance

Until 1989, 108 AED provided maintenance facilities to the Crotale 2000 weapon system but not to the Crotale 4000 system. Efforts were made to acquire the requisite equipment and additional facilities and the repair capabilities were enhanced to support the Crotale 4000 system as well. Subsequently, facilities

were established to overhaul the older pieces of this weapon system. The necessary infrastructure has also been put in place to overhaul the 150 HP power pack that is fitted in the Crotale vehicle. Thomson-CSF, France, is providing necessary technical assistance and guidance in the overhauling of the first batch of power packs.

Other Notable Achievements

A number of modifications were accomplished on the PAF aircraft by 102 AED during the period 1988 to 1998. These include twenty-seven Structural Life Enhancement Programmes (SLEP), in that the major share of work was with the depot's team at the PAF Academy. Besides this, twelve re-wiring modifications on T-37 aircraft, seventeen modifications on MM-3 of A-5, ten Tow-banner modifications on F-6 and FT-6 aircraft and forty landing light, HUD and, bombs delay system modifications for F-7 aircraft were also accomplished by 102 AED.

Field Training Detachments (FTDs)

The PAF has always paid special attention to the training of its personnel. For the technical staff, a number of Field Training Detachments (FTDs) are established throughout the air force. The purpose is to ensure that a continuous and well organized training programme is run under a single training agency at a Base. The maintenance crew training programme consists of formal training at an FTD, followed by informal training imparted by supervisors at work centres. For other technicians, training is conducted under the supervision and monitoring of the OJT flights. With this objective in mind, FTD for the F-16 aircraft was established at PAF Base Sargodha and the Mirage FTD was shifted from PAF Korangi to Masroor in 1991. PAF Base Masroor was also equipped with two Mirage simulators for the operational training and conversion of pilots. The Mirage-V simulator was installed in 1984 and the Mirage-III simulator was shifted to Masroor with its FTD. The FTD for FT-5 aircraft is established at PAF Base Mianwali, with the aircraft mock-up, whereas PAF Base Peshawar houses FTD for A-5 aircraft and Allouette-III helicopter. The F-7 FTD is located at PAF Base Rafiqui with excellent training facilities and mock-up. In all the FTDs, modern training aids and related facilities are provided to ensure a high standard of skills and proficiency amongst the pilots, engineers, and technicians of the air force.

The Pakistan Aeronautical Complex

The history of the Pakistan Aeronautical Complex (PAC) dates back to the period immediately following the war between India and Pakistan in 1965. At that time, under the pretext of equity and fairness, the Johnson administration clamped a total embargo on the supply of arms to Pakistan, including aircraft spares. It was in the aftermath of this bitter experience that the PAF seriously felt the need to diversify its sources of supply. Soon after the war, the Mirage and F-6 weapon systems were inducted in the PAF from France and China, respectively. It was also considered to be in the long-term interest of the country to establish an indigenous maintenance support base. This is how the idea of setting up an aeronautical maintenance facility was conceived. The PAC owes its existence to the PAF, for not only was the idea first conceived at the Air Staff level, but the PAF also contributed its own expertise and resources to establish this much needed facility.

Today, the PAC can boast of the most modern and technically advanced facilities. It has provided tremendous support in maintaining the PAF fleet. Besides major overhauls of aircraft, the PAC undertook a number of upgrading programmes that have enhanced the PAF potential despite the crippling sanctions.

Strengthening the Fighting Force

The Royal Australian Air Force (RAAF) purchased its Mirage-III O and Mirage-II D aircraft in 1964 from Dassault Aviation, France. These aircraft were withdrawn from service by the RAAF in 1988, after they had flown between 2,000 and 5,059 flying hours. In the same year, the Australian government put out a tender for the sale of fifty used

Mirage aircraft. The PAF showed interest in the package deal and a joint team from the PAF and PAC Kamra visited Australia in July 1988 to evaluate the Mirages offered by Australia. The team conducted a very comprehensive evaluation survey and submitted its recommendations to the CAS. After government approval, a contract for purchase was finalized between Pakistan and Australia in 1990.

When these aircraft arrived in Pakistan, the MRF carried out R-4+ inspections on each to make them airworthy and to give them a new lease of life. But these were extensively used aircraft and therefore, required special care. Keeping in view the inspection requirements in the period after 1997, Air Headquarters tasked MRF to carry out an ageing study on one of the ex-Australian Mirage aircraft that had flown maximum hours after the R-4+ inspection. Experts from MRF inspected one

such aircraft using NDI techniques, and after a thorough study, a special 2P+ inspection package was prepared. Following this study, Air Headquarters decided to let these aircraft complete a life cycle of 960 flying hours. The 2P+ inspection was also the responsibility of MRF. This was an additional responsibility entrusted to the factory, and was accepted as a challenge by the officers and technicians involved in this task.

Tackling the F-7P Overhaul

In August 1988, the PAF inducted a new weapon system—the F-7P fighter interceptor aircraft. This aircraft is the Chinese version of Soviet Russia's Mig-21, a tried and tested weapon system. The aircraft came in various batches and was quickly inducted into the air force. Although no match for the F-16 weapon system inducted in 1983, the

Engine installation symmetry being carried out during the F-7P overhaul at the F-6 Rebuild Factory, Kamra

The former Prime Minister of Pakistan, Mohtarma Benazir Bhutto, being briefed about the first locally rebuilt F-7P aircraft at the PAC Kamra by Air Marshal Dilawar Hussain on 8 February 1994

performance of this sleekly designed aircraft highly impressed the operators. At that stage, the need to set up its rebuild facility was visualized by the management of the F-6 Rebuild Factory (RF). The project preliminaries were initiated in October 1989 and the contract with the Chinese for technical assistance was signed on 1 September 1990. It was the first time in the history of the country that the F-7P rebuild programme was completely and successfully handled in Pakistan. Before this in-country facility was established, all aircraft of Chinese origin had to be sent to China for overhaul. A team was sent to Chengdu Aircraft Factory, China for the initial training. After the training of officers and technicians in China, the team returned to prepare for the commencement of the project. The preparations included training

additional manpower, selected from the experienced group of technicians already deployed on the overhaul of other Chinese version aircraft. By the time that the rebuild requirement of these existing aircraft had more or less stabilized; it was considered more beneficial to employ experienced hands in establishing the F-7P overhaul line.

A 62-member Chinese technical specialist team arrived at F-6 RF on 12 March 1993. By then, all preparations had been made to start work. It was a big day in the history of F-6 RF—the first F-7P aircraft, with the serial number 88-509 was inducted on 31 March 1993 for trial overhaul. Initially, three aircraft were inducted for the trial production that was successfully completed between March 1993 and May 1994.

The roll-out ceremony of F-7P aircraft was another milestone in the history of the

154

F-6 Rebuild Factory. The factory wore a festive look on 8 February 1994 when the first F-7P aircraft was handed over to the PAF. An interesting situation arose when the aircraft, after a final paint, bore the tail number 88-515 instead of 88-509. There was no time then to make corrections. The roll-out ceremony was held with the aircraft bearing the wrong tail number!

The Prime Minister of Pakistan was the chief guest for the occasion, which was also attended by a number of foreign dignitaries and senior officials of the PAF. The ceremony turned out to be very impressive and colourful. Replying to the welcome address delivered by the Director General PAC, Air Marshal Dilawar Hussain, the PM said:

> I would like to congratulate the Director General, officers, and men of the Pakistan Aeronautical Complex and our Chinese friends for a job well done. My special felicitations go to the engineers and technicians of the F-6 Rebuild Factory for the successful overhaul of the first F-7P aircraft. As you return this aircraft today to the Pakistan Air Force, you can take pride in the fact that you have added to the war potential and operational capability of the air force. You should also stand tall for having accomplished this task within the scheduled time period...

The Mirage Aircraft – Milestones Achieved

The Fuselage Repair Facility
The need to set up a Fuselage Structural Repair Facility at MRF had been felt for a long time. The requirement to establish this facility was based on the premise that the cost of repair and transportation of damaged aircraft structures abroad was exorbitant. In addition to this, the time period involved in repairs abroad was very long. This perception led to the decision to establish a local

structural repair facility for this purpose. The purchase order for the fuselage repair jig was placed on 13 March 1988, training was imparted to the MRF personnel in France from November 1988 to April 1989, and the repair jig arrived in December 1989.

The construction of a hall for the fuselage structural repair facility within the old hangar was completed in time for two French technicians to install the jig. The installation was completed within a month. It enhanced the induction capacity of aircraft, and the old hangar was converted into a structural repair facility.

Doctoring the Aircraft Wings
The wing refurbishing facility for the Mirage aircraft was planned to be established in the old hangar, side by side with the fuselage repair facility. This facility was meant to repair cracks in rib 4 by replacing the rib, repairing the decanting hole, refurbishing the main spar, replacing the rear lower panel of the wing, and replacing ribs 1 and 2 with that of thicker material. Most of the jigs and fixtures, and ground equipment were recommissioned from the ex-Australian equipment received in 1991. The jig was modified and converted from a production jig to a repair jig with the technical assistance of Dassault Aviation in 1992. The re-adaptation of the ex-Australian jig saved foreign exchange amounting to 1.3 million French francs. Another jig called the 'lifting and turning jig' was also purchased from France at a cost of 1.4 million francs. This jig also was required to be used in the same facility.

Meanwhile, cracks in rib 4 of the main spar and lower panel of wings forced the PAF to put ten wings from the fleet out of action. The MRF was asked by the PAF to establish a wing repair facility expeditiously. This venture was also taken up by the PAF and MRF jointly and turned into a real success, when the wing repair jig was installed in early 1995. The training of PAC personnel was imparted by Dassault Aviation at MRF while working platforms were manufactured locally, which yielded substantial savings in foreign exchange. Ever since the commissioning of this facility, thirteen wings have been refurbished.

Upgrading the Avionics

To upgrade the avionics of the current Mirage fleet, a contract was signed in January 1992 between the PAF and a French company, SAGEM, for the avionics upgrade of Mirage-III aircraft. The decision was strategic, and was taken after long deliberations. Pakistan could not just sit idly while the enemy continued to invest heavily in acquiring the latest weaponry. At the same time, the PAF had to be cautious in spending the meagre resources at its disposal in view of the precarious economic conditions prevailing in the country. The initiative to upgrade the Mirage aircraft was, therefore, a timely step. To achieve this, the PAC Kamra infrastructure was to be used for integrating the system and manufacturing of hundreds of mechanical parts in the form of kit 'A' items and wire-looms. The top management was committed to saving foreign exchange by making use of the PAC potential.

Initially, Kamra Avionics and Radar Factory (KARF) was assigned the management of the first programme, called Project ROSE. Consequently, the first Mirage aircraft (a two-seat version, DP) was inducted by KARF on 13 April 1992. This date came to be known as 'T0' (Time Zero) for the DP aircraft modification. One more Mirage III EA was undertaken for upgrade by KARF on 5 August 1993. KARF did not have the technical platform to accomplish maintenance, structural modifications and wiring changes on the aircraft. Therefore,

while KARF managed the project, a large amount of work on the aircraft was performed through the assistance rendered by MRF. To remove certain functional and administrative anomalies, Project ROSE was shifted to MRF on 13 January 1994. According to this decision, KARF was only to retain the programme for setting up Intermediate Level facilities for the maintenance and inspection of upgrade equipment.

Assisting Allied Countries

The Mirage Rebuild Factory at Kamra was set up while keeping in mind the overhaul requirements of the PAF and of similar jobs from other countries, particularly the Gulf states. The production line of MRF was experiencing a lean period between 1987 and 1990. Under these circumstances, the United Arab Emirates (UAE) was offered the services at MRF, for overhauling their Mirage aircraft. As a result, the PAC was able to conclude a contract with the UAE. In December 1987, a contract was signed between the government of Pakistan and the UAE for the overhaul of twenty-six Mirage aircraft at the MRF. Under the contract, the responsibility for the provisioning of spares lay with the UAE, while MRF was to provide the maintenance services by overhauling the aircraft. Later on, due to difficulties encountered by the UAE Air Force for the procurement and provisioning of spares, this project had to be terminated after the overhaul and delivery of only six aircraft.

A New Life for the Engines

The Engine Overhaul Wing at the MRF was formally established in March 1982. It was initially tasked to carry out a General Overhaul (GOH) of the ATAR 09C engine

The roll-out ceremony of the first UAE aircraft overhauled at the MRF, Kamra

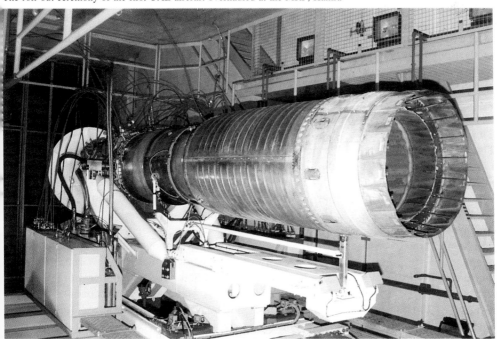

The multi-engine test bed installed at the MRF, Kamra

and its accessories installed on the Mirage aircraft. Until 1990, an average of twenty engines, twenty jet pipes with junction sections, and 1,750 accessories were produced each year. Apart from the general and light overhaul of complete engines and jet pipes, support was also extended to the PAF for the repair and overhaul of accessories. Due to the general nature of the facilities available, assistance was also provided in repairing parts of other engines in operation with the PAF, such as the J-69 engine.

In 1991, the MRF was tasked to service and commission the ATAR engines of the ex-Australian Mirages. The overall production task of engines was increased from twenty-four to thirty-six engines per year. The available resources at MRF were geared up to ensure the achievement of the enhanced task by 1993. The requirements of the PAF gradually increased further, from between twenty-four and thirty-six engines per year to sixty engines per year. Despite a shortage of manpower, (which had not been increased correspondingly with the enhanced production), the existing resources were used to their fullest, enabling the assigned tasks to be completed.

An F-100 engine being overhauled at the MRF, Kamra

The F-100 Engine

The PAF inducted the F-16 weapon system in 1983. To achieve self-reliance in maintenance of this weapon system, it was considered essential to establish overhaul and depot repair facilities for the F-100 engine, which powers the F-16 aircraft. The MRF was considered the most logical choice because of the extensive engineering facilities and expertise already available under the ATAR engine project. A four-member combined team of the United States Air Force (USAF) and Pratt & Whitney (P&W) surveyed the site and the engine

rebuild facilities in mid 1985. In early 1986, a project team, headed by Wing Commander Athar Qureshi, was formed and charged with the responsibility of its execution. After considerable discussions with the USAF and the manufacturer, a Letter of Offer and Acceptance (LOA) worth about $47.5 million was signed and approved by the DP Division in January 1987, and subsequently by the Defence Committee of the Cabinet (DCC) in May 1987.

To get the basic know-how for rebuilding the F-100 engine, thirteen officers and sixty-one technicians were trained in the USA in twenty-one different specialties. The organization of the Engine Group was also restructured and a number of new work centres were added. For economy of effort and effective utilization of facilities, the engine rebuild complex was reorganized according to its functions. Subsequently, both

ATAR as well as F-100 engine assembly and disassembly operation were moved into the newly constructed building. The existing rework and inspection areas were also expanded and another building was completed in 1996, to meet F-100 engine inspection requirements.

The F-100 programme received a setback after the enforcement of the Pressler Amendment in 1990, banning the supply of any kind of military equipment or assistance to Pakistan. In order to continue the programme at MRF, it was decided to meet the deficiencies of support equipment and spares for completing overhaul facilities of F-100 modules, and to carry out increased life cycle (ILC) modifications of core modules. The commercial contract with P&W that had already been initiated to meet urgent requirements, was finalized on an immediate basis. Thereafter, all the deficient equipment and spares were procured on BOA (commercial contract) with an initial Letter of Credit (LC) valued at $2.0 million.

After the passage of the Brown Amendment, the PAF was to receive the upgrade kits for the PW-F-100-220E engine. Now, the complete upgrade programme is carried out at MRF. It involves major modifications and the reworking of F-100 parts, assembly of engine, and test bed check. The first PW-F-100-200 engine was received for upgrading in November 1996 and the upgrade was completed on 19 August 1997. Under this programme, thirteen engines had been upgraded by the end of 1998.

In June 1988, it was decided to establish the Jet Fuel Starter (JFS) overhaul facilities at MRF, at a cost of $1.33 million, that included formal training of personnel in Holland. Through this facility, ninety-eight JFSs were overhauled at MRF by the end of 1998.

Manufacturing the Engine Parts

The experience and expertise acquired in carrying out the overhaul and repair of high performance aero-engines has brought MRF officers and technicians to a stage where they can step into the field of the progressive manufacture of aero-engine parts. Since October 1983, this matter has been pursued with SNECMA. Following the visit of an MRF team to confirm the parts to be manufactured and subsequent training of technicians in France, the manufacture of eleven hardware line items (pins and nuts) of the ATAR 09C engine commenced in November 1995 and was completed in December 1995. By the end of 1998, fourteen line items had been manufactured, whereas another thirty-five line items are under development.

The combined team of the USAF and P&W, which surveyed the MRF facilities in the middle of 1985, also recommended adding a number of machines and testers. This followed a contract with the US goverment and, as a result, thirty-three machines and testers were received initially in 1989-90. The delivery of six machines was stopped under the Pressler amendment, but released later after the Brown amendment was passed. In addition to this, seventy-five more machines were received by the middle of 1996 under a commercial contract with P&W. Later, another fourteen testers/ machines were added to this facility and by the end of 1998, sixteen F-100 engines were successfully tested.

To meet the automation requirements for the F-100 engine rebuild, the combined USAF and P&W team had, during their site survey of MRF in mid 1985, suggested the installation of a computer system in the Engine Group. Consequently an IBM mainframe 9375-060 system was installed in the Engine Group in October 1989, under the FMS contract. Its configuration comprised

159

16 MB of memory with two disk drives of 850 MB each and a number of terminals and printers. Two software modules were developed, one for shop floor management and the other for inventory management, known as Depot Management Information System (DMIS) and Depot Automated Inventory Management System (DAIMS), respectively. In January 1990, it was decided to also load ATAR engine data on the mainframe computer. In 1994, a study was carried out at MRF for automating the inventory of aircraft and their components. The existing capability of the system was not sufficient to meet the additional inventory management and shop floor requirement. Accordingly, an upgradation in the system was effected to suit the requirements.

The Karakorum-8 (K-8) Trainer

Aircraft manufacturing is a very specialized activity. Before embarking upon such a project, there are many variables that must be taken into account. There is the question of economic feasibility, engineering expertise, technical facilities, production processes and equipment, and last but not least, the market prospects. For a developing country like Pakistan, it is not an easy decision to undertake such a venture because aircraft manufacturing requires huge investments and commitment of resources. Even in the developed world, aircraft manufacturing projects are usually joint ventures involving many countries and a host of firms.

However, notwithstanding the difficulties involved, the AMF found an early opportunity to participate in the manufacture of a jet aircraft. The PAF had begun to think about replacing its T-37 trainer jets in the early 1980s. In 1983, Air Headquarters suggested to PAC that it should collaborate with CATIC

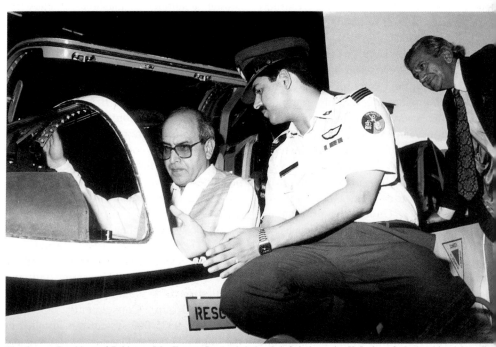

The former President of Pakistan, Mr. Farooq Leghari, being briefed about the K-8 aircraft during his visit to the PAC, Kamra on 1 December 1994

n upgrading the L-7 aircraft that was later to be purchased as a replacement for the T-37 aircraft. The Chinese were then working on its design. Responding to the interest shown by Pakistan, they agreed to design a new jet trainer, L-8, taking user-defined basic parameters into account. This was the beginning of the joint venture or co-project of a jet trainer aircraft, renamed Karakorum-8 which came to be known as the K-8.

The K-8 is a low wing, tandem seat, all-metal jet-trainer with side intakes. It is capable of providing basic and advanced training. It is fully aerobatic, has excellent flight characteristics, manoeuvrability, and spin recovery. The prototype aircraft had achieved a top speed of 807 KPH at 700 meters, and has a climb rate of 5,900 ft/min. The maximum service ceiling of aircraft is 42,000 ft. This aircraft is fitted with a Garrett TFE-731-2A turbofan engine producing 3,600 lbs static thrust at sea level. The engine has demonstrated its low fuel consumption and low noise. The main features of the engine are its convenient operation, easy maintenance, and high reliability. These are also characteristic of the aircraft.

The first general agreement to jointly design and develop a basic jet trainer with advance features was signed between China and Pakistan, on 21 August 1986. AMF participated in this programme on the basis of sharing 25 per cent of the development cost. The development cost estimated in 1986 was $24 million out of which Pakistan's contribution was $6 million.

The design phase of the K-8 started in May 1987. For participation in this phase, a team of nine engineers flew to Beijing on 27 August 1987. Each member was assigned a specific design area or speciality depending upon his academic background and experience. This team was to stay at Nenchang for a period of fifteen to twenty-one months, depending upon the members

respective specialities. Under this agreement, twenty-one engineers, two pilots and twenty-eight technicians participated in aircraft design, tooling design and manufacture, piece part production, sub-assembly, final assembly, as well as flight and ground test phases. They made meaningful contributions towards the overall programme.

The first prototype aircraft flew in January 1991, after which the AMF participated in the flight test phase of the programme. One prototype aircraft was flown to Pakistan in March 1993 as per the provisions of the first general agreement.

In May 1992, after the verification of the basic design parameters during the flight test phase, the Chinese launched a Small Batch Production (SBP) phase in which fifteen K-8 aircraft were manufactured. This phase ended in December 1995. Under the co-production plan, the AMF had five major sub-assemblies in its share. These included horizontal stabilizer and elevator, vertical stabilizer and rudder, engine cowling, front section of the fuselage and engine access doors.

The PAF decided to carry out a detailed evaluation of the K-8 aircraft, before making a final decision about its induction. On 9 April 1994, a contract for the purchase of six K-8 aircraft was signed between DGMP and CATIC. These aircraft were to be used by the PAF for evaluation. Six K-8 aircraft were purchased with comprehensive transfer of technology clauses, and the aircraft arrived in Pakistan in November 1994. Since then, the PAF Academy, Risalpur has been operating the aircraft.

In May 1992, when basic tactical and technical specifications had been verified through flight tests and twelve basic parameters had been achieved, the Chinese decided to launch the SBP Phase. In this phase, it was proposed to manufacture fifteen K-8 aircraft and enhance the tooling to facilitate the smooth transition into the serialized production phase. These aircraft could be given to potential customers for evaluation, and during production, some modifications for improvement of aircraft systems and performance were to be incorporated. Negotiations were started in 1991 and the AMF decided in principle to participate in this phase. The second general agreement was thus signed on 27 May 1992 for participation in the SBP phase on the subject of investment sharing. The AMF's share of investment was $6 million. In this phase, AMF was also to acquire the manufacturing capability for the five sub-assemblies.

Later, PAC and CATIC reached an agreement for regular production of K-8 sub-assemblies at PAC Kamra. The work share of PAC was to depend on its established capability/capacity. The assemblies manufactured at PAC were to be installed on the aircraft manufactured in China.

Since then, the transfer of technology has been achieved for some major sub-assemblies. The first phase of sub-assembly work was completed with the manufacture of eight sets of horizontal stabilizers locally. Following this, the technology transfer for vertical tail and engine front cowling started in June 1996. By now PAC has completed Transfer of Technology (ToT) for three sub-assemblies, i.e. horizontal tail, vertical tail and engine cowling. During the ToT phase, a total of nine horizontal tails, four vertical tails and five engine cowls were manufactured and dispatched to China. In continuation of the ToT process, a contract has been signed under which the capability to manufacture the front fuselage shall be acquired by the end of the year 2002.

A joint sales and marketing agreement with the Chinese for K-8 aircraft promotion in the international market was also signed on 22 April 1993. Conceptually, it calls for the formation of a joint team of three members from both sides. All expense incurred on sales promotion activities and participation in air shows would be met from a joint fund in which each side would contribute 50 per cent of the costs. This agreement with CATIC was to come into force in April 1999. Both sides had formulated the broad outlines of a joint marketing strategy for projection of the aircraft in the world market. The first major event was joint participation at the Paris Air Show where the K-8 was taken for static/aerial display. Both sides were jointly pursuing negotiations with the Sri Lankan Air Force for the sale of the aircraft. The PAF also planned to participate in the Dubai Air Show in November 1999.

The Super Mushshaq

The Mushshaq aircraft has been in service with the PAF and the Pakistan Army since the 1970s. The AMF had acquired manufacturing rights from the SAAB Scania of Sweden. The AMF had successfully managed to maintain very high standards. In this context, the reliability of its prime product, the Mushshaq aircraft, has always remained very high. Despite this, certain users (especially the Pakistan Army) wanted a more powerful engine to enhance the Mushshaq's capability of operating from short, unprepared fields. Another desired feature was a higher rate of climb in hot ambient temperature conditions. The aircraft's deficiency was due to the design limitations of the Lycoming 10-360-A1B6 four cylinders engine which was installed on it. The Mushshaq was fulfilling training needs and other designated roles, but user feedback showed that more power, a better rate of climb, and a higher cruise speed were additional, desirable features that needed to be incorporated.

As a first step, in 1979, AMF engineers and the original designers undertook a study

Major General Prince Turki Bin Abdul Aziz, Deputy Commander, Royal Saudi Air Force prepares to fly a Pakistani built Super Mushshaq trainer aircraft during his visit to PAF Academy, Risalpur, 20 October 1998

to install a Teledyne Continental Motors (TCM) six cylinders engine with 210 horsepower rating, instead of the Lycoming four cylinder engine which had a rating of 180 horsepower. The additional feature of the TCM engine was the presence of a turbo charger. This programme continued for over six years, by the end of which, the new version of the aircraft, called the Shahbaz, was manufactured and Federal Aviation Agency (FAA) certification was sought. However, the project, which was jointly undertaken by AMF, SAAB Scania, and Teledyne Continental Motor Corporation, failed to produce the desired improvements to the satisfaction of the users, even though it cost over $2 million.

Due to the persistent demand of the operators to enhance the performance of the Mushshaq and to brighten its export potential, this issue remained under active consideration. Finally, an indigenous project was initiated in December 1995 to select a suitable alternative engine for the Mushshaq upgrade programme. Two guiding principles had been set out for the programme: the installation of a more powerful engine, and minimum structural changes in the basic airframe. The goal envisaged appreciable enhancement in basic performance parameters like speed, rate of climb, manoeuvrability, and aerobatic characteristics, without entering a region where design changes in the basic structure would become necessary. With this in mind, an engine of the Lycoming family was chosen for retrofit. The rationale behind this choice was that the maintenance facilities available with the users could be readily utilized and additional infrastructural costs would be avoided. The spare parts would be compatible and separate inventories would not be required. There was, however, to be no major impact on life cycle costs. The Lycoming 10-540-V4A5 six cylinders normal aspirated engine was thus selected. This engine is rated at 260 HP at 2,700 RPM. Installation of this engine would have ensured that additional power would be available to improve the basic flying parameters.

There were several other technical considerations while selecting this engine. Some of the major issues pertained to the design of the engine mounts, the installation of accurate and reliable electrically operated instruments, an electrical trimmer system, and an effective air-conditioning system.

The fact that all the above objectives were realized in a period of less than one year reflects well on the engineering effort that had gone into this programme. In a period of less than three months, the design was finalized for the engine mount, its manufacturing completed, and a test rig locally designed and manufactured to verify the design load limits calculated for the engine mount. Such was the speed at which this project was pursued.

The design of the new engine cowling was undertaken concurrently with studies for the design of an electric trim system, and the installation of electrically operated instrument and environmental control systems. The selected engine, instruments, and other materials were imported and installed. The aircraft then started a series of test flights, flown by a highly qualified and experienced test pilot of the AMF. The first test flight was successfully completed on 15 August 1996, only eight months after the start of the project.

A new name for the upgraded version of the Mushshaq aircraft was under consideration. There were several proposals and many names were suggested. In the meantime, a team of journalists visited PAC in the middle of March 1997 to receive a briefing on ISO-9000 certification. During the visit the aircraft happened to come under discussion, and next morning newspapers carried banner headlines calling it 'Super Mushshaq'. This is how the new version of the Mushshaq aircraft found its name.

The selection of a propeller compatible with the new engine installed on the Super Mushshaq is yet another issue being handled. Three different types of compatible propellers have been installed and tested on the Super Mushshaq. They include the MT 3, the Hartzell 3 and the McCauley 3 blade propellers. The installation of these propellers on the aircraft has caused no problems and the flight tests have proved successful with no adverse effects on the performance of the aircraft. The aircraft shows varying performance due to the different propulsive efficiencies of the three propellers. The changes are, however, marginal and the aircraft is safe to fly in the operating envelope without any problems with all three propellers. This exercise has afforded potential users the opportunity to select any of the three propellers for their Super Mushshaq. The indigenous development of the Super Mushshaq has been achieved at a very nominal cost and has lent new confidence to PAC engineers and personnel.

The Super Mushshaq will find a definite place in our defence services because of its enhanced performance. The installation of the advanced avionics package from Bendix King with a built-in Global Positioning System (GPS), effective environment control system, electrically-operated instruments, and the installation of an electrically-operated trimmer system will make Super Mushshaq a potent contender in the aviation market amongst other aircraft of its category. At present, the PAC has two fly-worthy Super Mushshaqs; both with the AMF.

Different countries have shown an interest in buying the Super Mushshaq for their Air Forces. The Royal Saudi Air Force (RSAF), the Royal Jordanian Air Force (RJAF), the Sri Lankan Air Force (SLAF), the Lebanese Air Force (LAF), and the Royal Thai Army (RTA) have shown varying degrees of interest in the aircraft.

Making Tools Selectively

The AMF has enough potential to become an aircraft manufacturing enterprise of international standards. The technical facilities, competence of personnel, technological expertise, and production capability which exist today are limited only by certain extraneous factors. But slowly, it is moving forward. It is inducting new technologies and skills, new manufacturing facilities, both generic and specific, and finally it is creating a nucleus of highly trained personnel in aircraft manufacturing skills. This is its guarantee against stagnation.

One such facility that came up in the recent years is a comprehensive tooling facility with the ability to design and manufacture tooling for the production and assembly of aviation standard structures. It is an inescapable requirement for any manufacturing concern engaged in the production of aircraft parts and sub-assemblies, or even in the assembling of aircraft structures. Conceptually, the backbone of any manufacturing facility is its tooling shop.

The establishment of a comprehensive tooling facility at PAC Kamra was contemplated in 1989. The envisaged facility has the capability to design and manufacture all types of dies, moulds, fixtures, and jigs/gauges. The contract for the transfer of technology from the Chinese was concluded in 1992 and in July 1997, an establishment of eighty-five personnel, including thirteen officers, was authorized by the government. Meanwhile, the facility has been made operational since January 1995 by using the available manpower from the factory. The major projects undertaken by the Tooling Facility include design and manufacture of ROSE Project tooling, fabrication of tooling for K-8 horizontal tail, rudder and engine cowling, repair of worn out Mushshaq tooling and design and fabrication of Super Mushshaq tooling.

Modernization in Manufacturing Capability

The AMF is currently working on a programme to modernize its general engineering and machining facilities. For future manufacturing requirement capabilities, a five-year modernization programme was taken up by the management, to convert machining processes from conventional to CNC/NC machines. A CNC machining centre backed by state-of-the-art inspection and measurement facilities has been established. An EP 50 milling and boring machine was procured from Germany in December 1988. Another machine, a CNC MAHO 1600S, which is a four-axis simultaneous positioning milling machining centre, was commissioned in August 1995. Its control unit has the ability to operate with computers of a high level such as main frame computers or a CAD/CAM system. It is equipped with a sixty pocket automatic tool change system and has the ability to store all the relevant data of tools such as length, radius, and location. The CNC Lathe CTX-600 is a two-axis turning machine in which twelve tools can be posted in a turret head. Among the modern facilities there also exists a 6-axis CNC folding press. Additionally, in 1995, a new welding shop was constructed along modern lines in which separate booths for different types of welding machines have been established.

The Kamra Avionics and Radar Factory (KARF)

Following the Soviet invasion of Afghanistan in 1979, there was an increase in the air defence activities that led to the enhanced deployment of radars. This period saw extensive use of the newly acquired MPDR-45E radars in rough and rugged terrain and hostile environments. They were fast becoming due for major servicing or rebuild; so were their power generators and associated equipment. It was estimated that the cost of overhaul for one radar would be equivalent to Rs 21 million in foreign exchange. Taking the annual rebuild requirement into account, the cost was enormous. In due course of time, Control and Reporting Centres (CRCs) and high-looking TPS-43 radars would have also become due for rebuilding. In view of this urgency and compulsion, the PAF decided to establish an appropriate facility locally, and to acquire self-sufficiency in radar maintenance and overhauling as well. It is certain that the F-6 and Mirage overhauling projects, and their obvious benefits, guided the Air Staff's decision to establish a similar radar facility. Consequently, a study group was formed and based on its response, it was decided to set up a project within the PAF to plan the establishment of overhauling facilities for radar and generators. This project suffered some delays and ultimately materialized on 7 August 1983 when Air Chief Marshal Anwar Shamim, Chief of the Air Staff, laid

Generators being overhauled at the KARF, Kamra

166

the foundation stone of the Radar Maintenance Centre (RMC) at Kamra.

The first MPDR-45E radar was inducted for overhaul in November 1987. A team of German experts provided assistance during the experimental rebuild. This process was completed in May 1988. In July 1988, Air Chief Marshal Hakimullah, the then Chief of Air Staff, handed over the first overhauled MPDR-45E radar to the Air Defence Command in a ceremony held to mark that occasion. Subsequently, the rebuild of MPDR radars commenced on a regular basis and, almost simultaneously, it was followed by generator overhauling activities.

As the operations expanded, more skilled personnel were employed to increase the production. The success of the project led the Air Headquarters to consider expanding its scope so that it could undertake the repair and manufacture of certain avionics systems as well. This revised role required extensive funding which could not be provided from the PAF budget. It was at this stage that the PAF decided to propose to the government to convert the existing set-up into a defence production project and place it directly under the Defence Production Division as Kamra Avionics and Radar Factory (KARF). Thus, Kamra Avionics and Radar Factory, the fourth factory of the PAC and the first of its kind, started operating with Air Commodore Rafi-ul-Qadar as its first Managing Director in April 1989.

The Rebuilding of Radars and Generators
The participation of the factory team in rebuilding the MPDR-45E radar proved so effective that a regular stream of radars started to be fed to KARF for rebuilding. As a consequence, foreign technical assistance was reduced to two resident representatives who also left after another six months. Thus,

by the end of 1988, the project was run entirely by the local staff. The production was sustained at two radars per year and efforts were made to induct more production processes and machinery to enhance the output. The Microwave Shop was equipped with advanced RF test and diagnostic equipment, including network analyzers, spectrum analyzers, and microwave test sets etc.

In early 1994, the PAF felt the need for more radar overhauls. The factory accepted the challenge and a dedicated team of engineers and technicians brought about a record increase in production which amounted to five radars in the fiscal year 1994-95, and implied a 150 per cent increase. Since then, this performance has become the benchmark for others. Simultaneously, an aggressive deletion programme was pursued, which resulted in curtailing the import of expensive assemblies from abroad and provided a boost to local repairs. All this resulted in considerable savings in foreign exchange.

The successful rebuilding of the MPDR-45E radar showed potential for overhauling the equipment employed in radar operations, and so attention was focused on the rebuilding facilities of Siemens 20 KVA power generators used with MPDR-45E radars in the field. Following some extensive studies, it was decided to establish generic facilities that could cater for all types of power generators in the future. As such, the rebuilding of multiple types of generators, such as 100/62.5/125 KVA and 50/400 Hz, was also introduced and successfully carried out. Meanwhile, a large number of 5 KVA generators, manufactured by Hanomag and Siemens, needed overhauling. These had been inducted during the early 1980s, to support the development of radio relay units for passing radar track data to the Control and Reporting Centres (CRC). The KARF

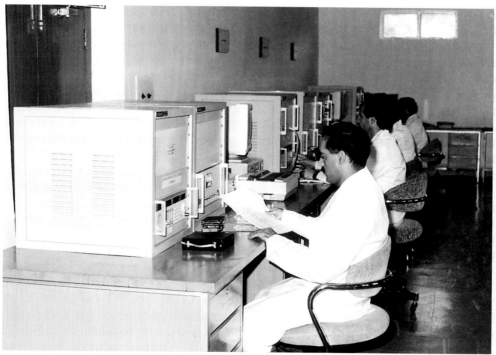

The RWR production facility at the KARF, Kamra

undertook the rebuilding of these generators and also cleared the backlog.

Soaring Towards Excellence

The PAF has a fleet of modern aircraft to fulfill its operational commitments, backed by a suitable ground environment. However, the sophisticated advances in air defence and the weapon systems of the enemy necessitated that the PAF adopt measures that ensured the survivability of its aircraft over enemy territory. One way to achieve this objective was by incorporating system upgrades in order to increase the operational effectiveness of the PAF aircraft.

Accordingly, the PAF decided to equip its fleet with modern Radar Warning Receiver (RWR) systems. It was also decided that instead of buying the RWR system off-the-shelf, it should be produced in Pakistan.

This would not only be cheaper but would also give the local industry exposure and experience with respect to the latest technology. The PAF conducted extensive tests and trials on each model of the RWR equipment offered by different countries like the United States, Italy, France, and China. In June 1988, free evaluation of Chinese RWR on A-5 and F-7P aircraft of the PAF was offered, and a co-production agreement was signed between CEIEC, China, and DGMP on 19 November 1992. This contract provided for the establishment of co-production facilities, the building of related infrastructure, and the procurement of equipment. KARF was selected to undertake this project at Kamra.

Meanwhile, a case for the establishment of the RWR co-production facility at KARF was taken up with the Defence Production Division. It was approved on 7 May 1995 and got the final approval from the Defence Committee of Cabinet (DCC) on 20 May 1995. The production line was successfully set up to facilitate the processes of commissioning and operation. KARF personnel were required to be trained on these techniques in China. For this purpose, a batch of three officers and fourteen technicians was sent to Chendgu, China, for four different courses in specialized fields for the duration of one to two months.

An eighteen-member Chinese technical assistance team arrived at KARF in November 1994 for providing assistance in the production of the pilot batch. The production was planned in two phases. In the first phase, RWRs were to be produced from Completely Knocked Down/Semi Knocked Down (CKD/SKD) kits received from China, while in the second phase, RWR sets were to be produced through a deletion programme. The production started in March 1995 and the first RWR was produced in the same month. With the completion of the first phase, the Chinese team left.

Meanwhile, an expunging programme was initiated to reduce dependence on foreign vendors for a supply of kits for production. DGMP contacted a number of vendors and provided the specifications for indigenous manufacture. Some vendors indicated their interest in developing the Line Replacement Units (LRUs); the contract was awarded to Shaheen Aero Traders on 29 June 1995. After successful production of the prototype, the second phase of production was launched in May 1996.

In the aftermath of the Afghan war, the PAF decided to upgrade its fleet of combat aircraft with a new generation airborne radar capable of providing improved operational performance. The upgrade envisaged the improvement of the fire control capabilities by extending the range of the airborne intercept radar and improving acquisition and processing capabilities. Reputed international avionics manufacturers were approached to present their proposals for the supply and co-production of suitable airborne fire control radars. After having selected Kamra as the venue to establish the co-production facility, a contract was signed in June 1993 with Messrs FIAR, an Italian firm, for co-production of their Grifo-7 airborne radar. This facility, however, could also be used for the manufacture/repair of a wide variety of avionics equipment such as radars, communication equipment, and IFF etc.

Meanwhile, an F-7P aircraft was assigned for the conduct of survey and test flights from 15 November to 20 December 1993 in order to gather technical data on mechanical, thermal and electrical characteristics of the aircraft. A specialist team from KARF comprising electronic, electrical and mechanical engineers participated in the trial phase. In December 1993, the FIAR survey team submitted a report certifying the feasibility of the Grifo-7 installation on F-7P aircraft. To facilitate the accomplishment of this task, KARF personnel were detailed for training in Italy.

The PAF opted for the avionics upgrade of its Mirage-III aircraft in the early 1990s. After extensive negotiations, a contract was signed in 1992 with Messrs SAGEM, France, for carrying out the upgrade of the Mirage fleet under the aegis of Project ROSE. This project was directed at achieving a complete refurbishment of the Mirage navigation and attack system with a state-of-the-art avionics package. With this upgrade, the ageing Mirages not only got a new lease of life but also acquired the latest navigation and attack capabilities comparable to the front-line fighters of today.

This project envisaged the local manufacture of hardware parts and wire-looms, followed by system integration and the installation of radar. Initially, this project

The keys of the first locally rebuilt CRC being presented to the AOC, ADC by the Director General, PAC, Kamra

was started at KARF but later it was shifted to the Mirage Rebuild Factory due to reasons related to aircraft handling facilities. This contract also envisaged the setting up of Integrated Logistics Support (ILS) for the upgraded avionics at Intermediate and Depot levels. KARF was found to be a suitable place for setting up these facilities. A team of officers and airmen underwent an extensive training programme with the leading avionics manufacturers of Europe. The ILS Workshop, commissioned in August 1996, contains Automated Test Stations for testing and repairing of ROSE Line Replaceable Units (LRUs) within the environmentally controlled and anti-static premises. The facilities of this workshop are also being extensively used to test the new equipment before installing it on the aircraft.

The Control and Reporting Centres (CRCs) are the nerve centres of the PAF's Low-Level Air Defence System and have been conducting round-the-clock operations since their induction. Due to extensive use, these CRCs approached their recommended operational hours and/or field deployment life rapidly, and became due for rebuilding.

By the mid-1980s, Project-786 was engaged in establishing the rebuild facilities for ground radars and it was felt that this project could also sponsor the rebuilding of the CRCs. In April 1990, it was decided that studies for establishing different projects might be carried out by PAC and P-786. One of these studies pertained to the planning and implementation of the rebuild facilities for the CRC system. The report of this study was forwarded to the DP Division on 28 July 1990, with strong recommendations for establishing the CRCs rebuild facilities. After prolonged deliberations, the project was approved in the DP Board meeting held in May 1995, which envisaged a saving of Rs 422 million in the first rebuild cycle alone.

The quantum of work in rebuilding the CRC can be judged from the fact that approximately thirteen workshops and forty types of workstations needed to be made operational. The Siemens Low Level Air Control System (SILLACS) of air defence consists of MPDR and CRC systems. Therefore, the existing facilities for the overhaul of the MPDR system and its ancillary equipment could also be used for the CRC Rebuild Project. For this purpose, some additional facilities such as Display Processing Shop, Data Processing Shop, Data Communication Shop, Auxiliary Equipment Shop and Computer and Peripherals Shop were established. The first CRC was inducted for rebuilding in July 1997 and was completed in March 1998. When this book went to press, four CRCs had been rebuilt at KARF.

Achieving Quality Standards

At the PAC, the campaign to upgrade the quality system to ISO standards began, following a directive issued by the DP Division in 1994, that made it mandatory for its entire establishment to acquire certification by December 1997. The preparatory work at PAC started soon afterwards, and in the first phase of this programme, the MRF was selected for implementation of the ISO-9000 system. This effort received momentum after Air Vice Marshal A. Rahim Yousefzai took over as the Director General, PAC. He took a keen interest in the programme and provided active support. While the Director General pushed for the implementation of this programme, the Managing Director MRF, Air Commodore Niaz Hussain (later Air Vice Marshal), came forward to implement this system at a time when very little was known about it in Pakistan. Only a few organizations, and none from the defence industry, had initiated this programme. There were mental barriers, and its usefulness was being questioned. However, the MD, MRF took up the challenge and proved the efficacy of the system by actually implementing it in

ACM Parvaiz M. Qureshi, the CAS, inspecting the 100th Mirage overhauled at the PAC, Kamra

his organization. The MRF became the first defence industrial unit in Pakistan to get ISO-9000 certification, in September 1995. It was a significant achievement in pursuit of quality and excellence.

The other three factories of the PAC Kamra soon followed suit. In February 1997, the F-6 Rebuild Factory was certified to ISO-9002 standards by a French certification agency, AFAQ International. It was the same company that had certified MRF, earlier in 1995. Later in March 1997, the AMF and the KARF were certified to the same standards by a German certification body, DQS. With this, all four factories of the PAC were now certified to the internationally recognized ISO-9000 quality management standards. The Pakistan Aeronautical Complex thus earned a unique distinction of class. The PAC now leads all other sectors of industry, both public and private, by example, working towards a quality culture and an awareness of standards.

The achievement of ISO-9000 certification is the beginning of a new journey for PAC. Since the time when the MRF started the ISO campaign, quality has swept across the rank and file of PAC as a movement. It has been a matter of intense discussion, debate, agreement, and disagreement amongst the officers and technicians. In the course of preparing for ISO certification, an overall improvement in procedures and attitude towards work has taken place.

Over the years, the PAC has moved from strength to strength. The cost of establishing aircraft and radar overhauling facilities within the country has already been paid back and the investment amortized for some time now. In the last few years, there has been great emphasis on enhancement in production, improvement in the quality of production, and reduction in wastage. Without adding new infrastructure or employing extra manpower, the factories of PAC have gone far beyond their originally assigned role and task. There is a visible urge to do more and do it better, in order to cross the threshold and launch the PAC as a real competitive aircraft industry at par with other big names in this field. With the establishment of the PAC, our dependency on foreign sources of supply for maintaining weapon systems has been vastly reduced. The PAC has also saved the nation from recurring and crippling bills in foreign exchange. With opportunities for export now beckoning, the future looks more promising. Hopefully, the PAC will one day provide both economic and military muscle to the nation.

6 HUMAN RESOURCES—GROOMING AND CAREER DEVELOPMENT

War is not an affair of chance. A great deal of knowledge, study and meditation is necessary to conduct it well.

Frederick Wilhelm, II

'One machine can do the work of hundred men. No machine can do the work of one outstanding man'. By saying this, Elbert Hubbard was actually pointing to the kind of person that an organization, keen to progress in the modern world of science and technology, would like to induct into its ranks. The PAF is consistently endeavouring to inculcate this state of excellence amongst its personnel. Young minds, in their formative years, are inducted, educated and honed to the specific requirements of the

PAF. The public schools run by the PAF, its training institutions and other in-Service training facilities thus put in a considerable effort to groom and train young minds. Besides academic and technical training, these institutions also boost the trainee's physical, mental, and moral standards. These measures eventually help to develop the qualities of command and leadership, loyalty and honesty, determination, and the will to compete and succeed even in times of great stress and strain.

The search for talent starts at an early stage. PAF's public schools at Sargodha and the one recently revived at Lower Topa, act as nurseries for the officer cadre. Youngsters from the eighth grade onwards go through a

Air Chief Marshal Muhammad Abbas Khattak, Chief of Air Staff, awarding the Quaid-e-Azam trophy to Fury House for overall best performance at PAF College, Sargodha on 31 December 1995

cycle of stringent selection criteria prior to their induction into these public schools. They become eligible for training at the PAF Academy, Risalpur after clearing their Intermediate examination, and after passing the tests of the Inter-Services Selection Board (ISSB) and Central Medical Board (CMB). The successful completion of training at the Academy culminates in the award of the B.Sc. degree. The graduating cadets, besides getting their commissions in the rank of Flying Officer, either earn a flying wing (for pilots), or the badges of other branches.

Both professional grooming, as well as in-Service training with a broad-based education continues, and is spread over the entire career of an officer. There exists a network of very fine institutions where the professional excellence of an officer is enhanced progressively. Likewise, airmen, who are simple matriculates when they enter the PAF, receive professional training as well as a general education in a wide array of institutions. The Service environment as a whole is quite conducive to learning. In almost all the training institutions, special emphasis is laid on the art of communication, both verbal as well as written.

The PAF College, Sargodha

The standard of general education in the civil sector leaves much to be desired, therefore the candidates at the time of selection are sometimes deficient in academics, extra-curricular activities, and leadership qualities. As such, the quality of human resource for induction in General Duties (Pilot) GD(P) and College of Aeronautical Engineering (CAE) courses has deteriorated considerably. Recognizing that public schools contribute a sizeable number of officers to the armed forces, the

Reunion group photograph of the old Sargodhians at PAF Officers Mess, Islamabad on 19 August 1998

174

AF College, Sargodha was converted back into a public school in 1989. The conversion of the PAF College, Sargodha into a pre-cadet training institution proved beneficial. As a public school, the PAF College Sargodha has proved to be a nursery for the PAF Academy, Risalpur. All the students of this college have put on an excellent performance at the Academy in both GD(P) and CAE courses. Statistically speaking, a total of 634 cadets graduated from this College and reported to the PAF Academy Risalpur for further training during the years 1986-1990. Aviation Cadet Syed Azkaar Hussain, a Sargodhian from the 23rd Entry won all the trophies, including the Sword of Honour, in the Passing Out Parade held on 16 May 1998. Similarly, Aviation Cadet Shuaib Salamat of the CAE, who won the Sword of Honour, and the CAS Trophy in November 1998, was also a Sargodhian.

The PAF College, Lower Topa

The Air Board meeting held on 16 June 1996, decided that the PAF Intermediate College, Lower Topa be converted into a public school by the year 1998. It was to induct cadets on open merit into the GD(P) and Engineering Branches of the PAF. Wing Commander (retired as Group Captain) Haroon-ur-Rashid Abbasi was deployed as the Project Director, PAF College, Lower Topa.

The PAF College, Lower Topa is situated in the proximity of Murree. In the midst of lofty mountains covered with tall pine trees, the buildings present a magnificent view. The primary aim of the institution is to educate and train suitable Pakistani boys for the Intermediate Examination of the Federal Board of Intermediate & Secondary Education (FBISE), Islamabad, in a healthy environment. The objective is to mould them

Air Commodore Khayyam Durrani ACAS (Education), awarding a trophy at the first prize distribution ceremony of PAF College, Lower Topa

175

Cadets on parade at the first Parents Day of the PAF College, Lower Topa

Topians Reunion—1998

into confident and disciplined young men with a strong character, and qualities of command and leadership.

Group Captain M. Tariq Qureshi (now Air Commodore) arrived on 11 May 1998 to take charge as the Principal of the revived PAF College, Lower Topa. Teachers from PAF College Sargodha and other PAF institutions joined on 8 June 1998. On 27 June 1998, PAF College, Lower Topa was revived after a gap of more than thirty years, with a pledge to set new standards of excellence. Air Marshal Aliuddin, the then Vice-Chief of Air Staff, formally inaugurated the College. The Annual Reunion of the old students of PAF College, Lower Topa was held on 5 July 1998. This was the first occasion that young students of the recently revived College were also present. The former Sindh Governor, Lieutenant-General (Retd.) Moinuddin Haider, an ex-Topian, was the Chief Guest on the occasion.

The Chief of the Air Staff, Air Chief Marshal Parvaiz Mehdi Qureshi, visited the institution on 28 October 1998. While recording his impressions in the visitors' book, he observed that 'the Base was bestirred to become a seat of learning'.

The first term was both eventful and challenging. The teaching staff and students bore hardships and work diligently to achieve their objectives. The pioneering role of the founding members was in keeping with the best traditions of Lower Topa. In doing so, they have lived up to their motto, 'I will Dare'.

In the first phase, two houses were revived, i.e. Babur and Iqbal. The third house (Aurangzeb) was to be established by March 1999. It is pertinent to place on record that in spite of several limitations, the revival had been accomplished successfully.

Air Vice Marshal Pervez A. Nawaz, DCAS (Trg.), with the newly inducted staff of PAF College, Lower Topa

The Search for Quality Human Resources

New Challenges

Over the years, due to a host of factors, including materialistic trends in society, the element of risk and uncertainty in the flying career, and the sharply declining educational standards in the country, the PAF's recruitment teams have been finding their job increasingly difficult. Rather than being genuinely attracted to the thrills of this profession, most candidates turn out to be mere job seekers. They represent the lot who cannot make the grade for professional institutions, and find it convenient to try their luck in the armed forces. They apply simultaneously to all the three Services and at times, even after selection, opt to proceed on the first call from any of the three Services. The percentage of the youth that are fit to qualify the stringent criteria of ISSB and CMB, is very small and has to be shared by the three Services. That is why, during the last decade, it had become increasingly difficult to make up the required numbers while ensuring that quality is not compromised. The Selection Statistics Table reflects interesting trends.

These statistics show that the number of civilian candidates who turn up at the Selection Centres, despite some fluctuations, is not consistent. Their success rate at the ISSB is merely 6.6 per cent and at CMB, 70 per cent. This is despite the fact that from 1995 onwards, the PAF College, Sargodha contributed an average of thirty-five students per year. If the number of candidates from Sargodha is subtracted from the above figures, the success rate at the ISSB drops to just over 5 per cent. In comparison, the success rate for candidates from the PAF College Sargodha, in ISSB and CMB is 74.6 per cent and 81 per cent, respectively. The problem assumed such proportions that it was deliberated upon at the Air Board level

SELECTION STATISTICS: GD(P) COURSES

Year	Reported at I&SCs	Selected for ISSB	Recommended by ISSB	Med Fit by CMB
1988	9,621	2,272	219	160
1989	(No Selection was carried out during the year)			
1990	4,076	1,210	104	72
1991	4,645	1,798	150	104
1992	2,304	947	86	68
1993	10,559	2,471	187	142
1994	6,908	2,524	136	88
1995	3,590	2,384	162	97
1996	8,687	3,605	137	89
1997	5,042	2,407	148	101
1998	7,956	2,359	136	110
Total	63,388	21,977	1,465	1,031
Success Rate	–	34 per cent	6.6 per cent	70 per cent

June 1996. The then CAS, Air Chief Marshal M. Abbas Khattak, gave a directive that the PAF Public School at Lower Topa was to be revived where a parallel stream of potential GD(P) candidates would be inducted and groomed. This step did not come a day too soon, and after the necessary spade work, PAF Public School, Lower Topa started functioning from 27 June 1998. On a long-term basis, the problem will be resolved only when two separate streams of GD(P)/CAE candidates from both the PAF Public Schools will not only make up the required numbers but will also ensure an adequate inflow of healthy, educated and motivated youth into active PAF Service.

Publicizing for Recruitment

The PAF has entrusted the task of publicity to the Directorate of Recruitment. All PAF Information and Selection Centres (I & SC Centres) carry out publicity the whole year around. The PAF calendar remains the main item for publicity, and is published and released on 7 September every year. The pages of the calendar highlight PAF activities in peacetime. There are other items of public interest like posters, stickers, souvenirs and aircraft models that are put up for sale at affordable prices. Besides this, the officers commanding PAF I & SC Centres personally visit various schools and colleges to motivate the students to join the PAF. The air force image is also projected through attractive advertisements in print and electronic media on national days. An All Pakistan Bilingual Declamation Contest is held once a year at the PAF Academy. In this contest, both male and female speakers from colleges across the country are invited to the Academy, and they spend about four days here. During their stay, besides a busy schedule of high quality speeches on a large variety of subjects, the civilian students and their accompanying staff/chaperones get a first hand impression of life in the PAF.

For the Golden Jubilee celebrations of the PAF in 1997, the Air Staff chalked out a comprehensive command-level programme. DCAS (Training), as the chief coordinator, was tasked to monitor the progress of all the events and to ensure their completion by the due date. The Directorate of Recruitment had printed a special PAF calendar, posters, stickers, banners and souvenirs to mark the celebration.

The Selection of Airmen

The recent modernization and sophistication in aviation technology has ushered in the inevitable demand for the induction of quality manpower in the airmen cadre. Keeping pace with the latest technology, selection of recruits for the aero-technicians and aero-supports group is conducted along scientific lines. The marking of papers is carried out by computer and Scantron, under the supervision of the Preliminary Airmen Selection Board at the PAF I & SC Centres. The results of provisionally selected candidates are transmitted via computer to the Directorate of Recruitment. The final merit list, duly compiled and prepared on computers, is despatched to I & SC Centres. Call-up letters are then sent to the selected candidates. In order to search and identify quality manpower, selection by mobile teams is also carried out. Academic and intelligence test papers are prepared and replaced frequently. The process of computerization, which was initiated at all the PAF I&S Centres in 1993, has almost been completed. The PAF has come a long way in establishing a transparent and efficient system of selection and recruitment.

The Establishment of a Human Resource Laboratory (HRL)

A research-oriented Human Resource Laboratory (HRL) was established at the Directorate of Recruitment in March 1994, with an aim to develop flying aptitude tests, i.e. the defence mechanism test, and attention diagnostic method and computer-based psychomotor ability tests. These tests have been constructed by using local resources. They will be included in the selection cycle of GD(P) courses after their predictive validity is established.

The HRL has also developed two intelligence test batteries, one in 1997 and another in 1998. The computerized trade specialty allocation tests, i.e. mechanical, practical, and clerical aptitude tests were developed and validated in 1998. In addition, personality tests and performance evaluations were also constructed to facilitate the selection of candidates for Special Purpose Short Service Commission (SPSSC), Education Instructors and Religious Teachers.

Fair Selection

Keeping in view the requirements of advanced technology and ever-increasing complexity of equipment, the PAF follows a very strict and careful approach in selecting its airmen. The candidates are extended all possible help and facilities by the Centres to assist them in preparing for the tests. The Centres strictly adhere to the rules and regulations to ensure absolute fairness in the selection process.

The introduction of a computerized system of testing and marking, frequent changes and construction of new intelligence and academic test batteries, and close supervision has eliminated the chances of any malpractice or compromise. At present, the PAF can proudly claim that it has a fair and transparent selection system.

The Induction of Women in the PAF

Female officers were first inducted into the PAF in 1977. Initially, six female psychologists were inducted into the officers' cadre out of which one rose to the rank of Wing Commander. The others left the PAF after completing ten years of service. In 1993, the PAF took a bold step and recruited women for all branches, except GD(P) and ADWC. The first batch of four lady cadets inducted for Education and Data Automation branches joined the first Service Orientation Course on 6 February 1993. Boarding and lodging during their training created some problems, but this was resolved by accommodating them initially in the PAF Officers' Mess. The subsequent lady cadets were lodged in the Under Officers Block of the Cadets Mess. So far, over seventy lady cadets have been trained at the Academy and have been commissioned in various branches, namely Education, A&SD (Administration and Special Duties), Accounts, Data Automation, Engineering, Meteorology, and Legal.

Initially, the PAF had set the quota of female officers to 5 per cent of the total strength of officers, to be achieved by the year 1999. However, in view of the enthusiastic response and an excellent performance by women, the policy was revised in 1997 and they are now allowed to compete with men on open merit. With the regular induction of female officers in the specified branches, they have now settled down in comparatively more secure PAF environments. They have proved to be highly motivated and dedicated and are thoroughly committed to the duties assigned to them. In the next phase, the PAF plans to open up operational branches for women, albeit in a limited way. For example, women will pilot slow flying aircraft like light communication, transport and helicopters, and also be inducted in some selected jobs in ADWC Branch. Thus, the PAF, in its own way, is contributing to gender equality, which is the declared policy of the Government.

Training the Air Warriors

Cadet Training

Candidates with the educational qualification of F.Sc. or an equivalent are inducted into the Academy for flying training at the College of Flying Training (CFT). Under the three-year training scheme started in November 1995, Aviation Cadets undergo one year of Academic and General Service Training. Successful completion of this process qualifies them to continue their academic training, leading to the Primary Flying Training (PFT) Phase.

During the PFT Phase, they fly Mushshaq aircraft, on which they learn composite flying. Upon successful completion of this phase, the Cadets move onto the Basic Flying Training (BFT) Phase, which is spread over two terms. During this phase, the cadets fly T-37 or K-8 trainers. (The training on K-8 started in October 1996.) They are trained in some advanced phases of flying, thus forming a basis for their future operational training. The successful completion of this phase culminates in graduation, and the award of their flying wings. In the decade under review, continuing importance was attached to the high quality of flying training in the Academy, staffed by competent and dynamic QFIs in the BFT Wing. Such instructors help in imparting realistic and exacting flying training. The BFT Wing has kept pace with modern requirements and has set up a computer room to facilitate the sharpening of operators' skills. Phase briefs and ground-training activities are now conducted using computers and multimedia programmes while the practice of using computer simulation for the training of cadets is gathering momentum.

The under-training officers of the Civil Services Academy pay a visit to the BFT Wing every year. A number of foreign dignitaries from China, Turkey, Jordan and England visited the Wing during the last ten years and expressed their satisfaction at the well organized programme being run by the BFT Wing. The cadets of the PAF Academy had an opportunity to visit the Jordanian and Turkish Air Force Academies in June 1997 and October 1997, respectively. These cadets also represented the PAF in the Golden Jubilee Celebration Parade of Turkey in 1998.

Para-motor Glider Training

To facilitate the Aviation Cadets in their quest for adventure and aviation sports, the Para-motor Gliding Club was established at the PAF Academy, during August 1998. The club owns seven gliding machines and is functioning under the auspices of the Cadets' Wing. An exclusive team of Cadets' Wing officers has been made responsible for the maintenance and operational conduct of the gliding activity. The instructional team also includes two qualified and competent para-jump-training instructors. Cadets can learn para-motor gliding as a hobby in their third term. Simple to operate and easy to handle, the gliders are very successfully providing real flying experience and balancing in the air to aviation cadets of all branches.

The Paratroop Training Set-up

The Paratroop Training set-up at the PAF Academy has been established as per the requirements and safety standards of the Army's Paratrooper Training School, Peshawar. GHQ was requested to advise HQ,

SSG for the certification of paratrooper training facilities at the Academy. These efforts by the PAF Academy are intended to provide an adventurous outlet for Aviation Cadets without disturbing their training routine. Additionally, those cadets already trained to para-jump at the Academy's facility would subsequently be required to spend a much shorter duration at the Army Para School, thereby saving valuable training time.

Academic Training

Introduction of the Semester System
The academic training of GD(P) courses, supervised by the Directorate of Studies, CFT, changed from the composite academic to the semester system from 12 January 1991. The 95 GD(P) was the first course to graduate under the new system. Austerity and pragmatism were the two factors that spurred this change. The Academy had a two-pronged objective behind this conversion. The new scheme of studies afforded an overlap between academic and flying training, and thus reduced the overall training period of Aviation Cadets by six months. Besides, it introduced a greater similarity between the academic systems of the College of Aeronautical Engineering and the College of Flying Training.

Construction of the New Convocation Hall
In the proximity of the new Academy Complex, a superbly designed convocation hall saw its completion in the first quarter of 1995. The Convocation Ceremony of 97 GD(P) course on 27 May 1995 marked the inauguration of this facility. The building is immaculately furnished and has a seating capacity of 440.

Engineers' Training—The College of Aeronautical Engineering (CAE)
After passing through the pre-entry selection process, an engineering candidate joins the PAF Academy, Risalpur for a period of three years, where the initial General Service Training and BE courses commence simultaneously. The training at the CAE is conducted in six departments of study, namely Humanities and Science, Avionics Engineering, Aerospace Engineering, Military Science, Industrial Engineering and Professional Continuation Education.

The training programme also includes Islamic and Pakistan Studies, Military History, and Airmanship. The serving officers of the PAF and the sister Services, members of other organizations and officers from friendly countries are entitled to avail the course offered by the CAE. The college remained affiliated with the NED University, Karachi until 1995, after which it became affiliated with the National University of Sciences and Technology (NUST). Upon successful completion of the three-year training programme, students are awarded BE degrees from the affiliated University and the PAF Cadets among them are commissioned in the rank of Flying Officer.

Split MS Programme
A split MS programme in collaboration with the NUST was started in September 1997, with an intake of five student officers. All of them were sent abroad to complete their theses at foreign universities. Subsequently it was decided that from the second MS course onward, only two top students, one each from the disciplines of Avionics and Aerospace, would be sent abroad to complete their research work.

The Self-Financing Scheme

A self-financing scheme was introduced at the CAE in July 1994. The scheme was introduced to provide an opportunity to civilians to acquire this education. Besides professional knowledge, the scheme provided civilian students with an opportunity to receive leadership and educational training at their own expense without any pre-condition to join the PAF. In the future, according to the revised induction policy, civilians would only be inducted through the NUST. The wards of Army, Navy and PAF personnel are also inducted as per the existing policy.

Advanced and Specialized Training

Fresh graduates of the GD(P) Branch from the PAF Academy are sent to the Fighter Conversion Unit (1 FCU) located at PAF Base Mianwali. The duration of a fighter conversion course is about six months. During the course, students fly a total of ninety sorties on FT-5 aircraft, which includes instrument flying, close and battle formation, navigation and some advanced manoeuvring.

During the FCU course, students are evaluated in the following areas: flying skill, ground studies, and discipline. At the end of the course, two trophies are awarded: one for the best performance in flying and the other for the best overall performance. To keep students up-to-date with the latest technological advancements, and to trigger their mind towards subjects of common interest, the student officers are required to give lectures. In those lectures, the students are graded for their knowledge and public-speaking ability. Educational visits to different military and civil organizations are also undertaken. During the last ten years, the average induction per course was twenty-six; the attrition rate was 12.37 per cent and the average number of students who graduated per course was twenty-four.

After graduating from the FCU, students are posted to the Operational Conversion Unit (OCU). During the period under review, 25 Squadron remained an OCU for F-6 aircraft until 26 October 1995. The squadron was then disbanded. Meanwhile, 19 Squadron was re-equipped with the F-7P aircraft in 1990, and in its new role, it started to function as an OCU. Therefore, from 1990 to 1995, there were two OCUs working to produce operational pilots on F-6 and F-7P aircraft. After 1995, the Operational Conversion Course was restricted to the F-7P aircraft only. After graduation, the pilots are posted to operational squadrons operating F-7 or A-5 aircraft.

As a pilot grows in service and experience, he may be selected for conversion onto the Mirage or the F-16 aircraft, purely on merit under a well-defined criteria. In operational squadrons, pilots continue to train in accordance with the war role of their units. They become pair leaders, and then section leaders. With a minimum grand total of 500 hours and a specified on-type experience, pilots are selected for the Combat Commanders Course (CCC), which is an important milestone in a fighter pilot's career.

In the past, pilots required for transport, light communication aircraft (LCA), and helicopters were selected from amongst officers with varying degrees of flying experience and service seniority. Because these officers came from different backgrounds, this policy often limited the effective utilization of some of these aircrew and, also caused career and management difficulties. In order to redress these problems, a new policy was evolved in 1997, laying down the selection criteria for Transport, LCA and Helicopter career groups.

A small number of pilots are selected for the C-130 Co-pilot Course directly from the successful graduates of the Academy. Selection is based on merit and carried out by the Air HQ. The Transport Conversion School (TCS) conducts all training on the C-130 aircraft. Cadets suspended from the Academy are not eligible for any kind of pilot training in the PAF and are then considered for ground branches only. Those selected for the ADWC Branch are sent to the Air Defence Training School for the Basic course followed by Advanced training. Those cadets who are suspended from flying, but have a sound academic record, are considered for the Navigation Branch. Similarly, officers from ground branches, having previous flight experience, can also be detailed for a Navigation course in the TCS provided that their commissioned service does not exceed two years.

Officers who are suspended from the FCU, OCU, or from a fighter squadron are eligible for flying duties on Transport, LCA and Helicopters. Initially, all such pilots are inducted for the Helicopter Conversion Course which is conducted by No. 81 Search & Rescue Squadron based at Peshawar. It also conducts Qualified Helicopter Instructor Courses. Besides its search and rescue role, the squadron started to function as the PAF's Helicopter Flying School in May 1995. After attaining the status of captain and completing 250 hours on helicopters, pilots are posted to 41 Squadron where they gain experience on the LCA. Pilots are selected from the common pool of available pilots whenever a C-130 co-pilot course is planned.

Flying Instructors' Training (FIT)

At the PAF Academy, another very prestigious flying training institution, namely the Flying Instructors School (FIS), is also maintained. The role of the FIS is not only restricted to the training of the PAF pilots as instructors but it also includes training officers of the sister Services, i.e., the Army and the Navy. Due to its high standards, the FIS has also earned a high reputation outside the country. It trains instructors from friendly countries of the Middle East, Far East and Africa. The FIS is also responsible for maintaining the high standard of teaching at the College of Flying Training (CFT) and the FCU. Moreover, the re-categorization of the instructors in all three Services is an additional responsibility of the FIS. The school conducts two courses each year with an induction rate of approximately twenty-four to twenty-six students in each course. This 22-week course is aimed at teaching instructional techniques in the air along with a more detailed and comprehensive study of Aero-Science subjects.

The Training of Logistics/BLPC/Admin. and MDA Officers

As a result of the amalgamation in 1990, the College of Logistics at the CAE only conducted short refresher courses for Engineering Officers in the Supply speciality until April 1993, when it was closed down and direct induction of Supply Branch Officers was stopped. The professional training of Administration and Staff Duties (A&SD), Air Traffic Control (ATC), Legal, Meteorological, Accounts, and Branch List Permanent Commission (BLPC) officers is now conducted at the PAF Academy. Other than the Special Purpose Short Service Commission (SPSSC) scheme, where people with appropriate qualifications are directly inducted from the civil sector, suspended cadets from CFT and CAE are also selected for training in the Maintenance Data Automation (MDA) Branch. Their professional training is conducted at the

PAF's School of Computer Sciences, Badaber.

In order to provide unified training in the Administration and Air Traffic Control disciplines, a Department of Administration and Air Space Management (DA&AM) was established at the Academy, in June 1994. The Air Traffic Control (ATC) School, established in October 1989 at the PAF Base Masroor, was shifted to the Academy in August 1992, which later was designated as DA & AM. The department has conducted eight A & SD (ATC) courses since its inception at the PAF Academy, from which 103 students have graduated. Out of these, seventy-seven were those suspended from the CFT or the CAE and twenty-six were directly inducted from the civil sector. Prior to this, two A & SD (ATC) courses were held at the ATC School, Masroor. Before the amalgamation of A & SD and the ATC Branches, pure A & SD courses were run at the Academy.

The Induction of Simulation Systems in the PAF

The development of the computer-aided simulation system has revolutionized training methodology. Simulated Computer Based Training (CBT) provides an excellent way to impart low-cost but realistic training. The PAF embarked upon the development of CBT for all its training institutions in 1998. A consolidated package was prepared by the Training Branch, which could be split over a three-year period, to ensure that by the turn of the century, the PAF would be abreast with other more advanced countries of the world. All the training institutions of the PAF have greatly benefitted from this programme.

The Computer Literacy Programme

The Training Branch introduced a computer literacy programme for all PAF officers. The aim of this programme is to train the officers without requiring them to move out from their parent bases. For this purpose, a mobile team of computer experts was given the task of visiting all the operational bases and conducting computer courses after regular working hours. According to an estimate, all PAF officers were to be computer literate by the end of 1999. They are able to operate Microsoft Windows, access the Internet, use e-mail programmes and are adept at using the MS Word and Power Point softwares.

New In-Service Education Scheme for PAF Officers

Career progression is a step by step process. Officers' Promotion Examinations (OPEs) were introduced in the then RPAF in 1951. The progressively senior courses were designated as 'B', 'C' and 'Q'. OPEs 'B' and 'C' were administered by the Directorate of Education, at Rear Air HQ, Peshawar and the 'Q' examination by the PAF Staff College, Faisal. OPE 'B' was compulsory for promotion to the substantive rank of Flight Lieutenant, 'C' for the substantive rank of Squadron Leader, and 'Q' for selection to attend the then PAF Staff College.

The Individual Staff Studies (ISS-III) Correspondence Course was first introduced in the PAF in 1970 to replace the Staff College Qualifying Examination 'Q' with a planned, guided, and supervised correspondence course under the aegis of the PAF Staff College. The purpose of this system was to eliminate the drawbacks of a subjective system of qualifying examination. Later, the College of Staff Studies was established at PAF Base Faisal as a part of the then PAF Staff College, to conduct In-Service Correspondence Courses for PAF Officers.

In 1978, it was decided to further expand the scheme and replace the OPEs 'B' and 'C' with appropriate correspondence courses. Hence, OPEs 'B' and 'C' were re-designated as ISS-I and ISS-II, respectively and were administered by the College of Staff Studies, Peshawar.

A review of the system in August 1991 resulted in approval by the Air Staff of a revised Education Scheme. There were some doubts about the availability of officers for the resident courses. A further study revealed that the scheme was workable. The CAS, Air Chief Marshal Farooq F. Khan, authorized its implementation from November 1993 onwards.

According to the new scheme, the PAF follows a building-block approach to educate its officers. The professional education of officers is spread over their entire career. They have to undergo various courses at different stages of their career, culminating in the Air War Course. A fresh graduate from the PAF Academy is given some time to stabilize in his profession and service. After this brief period, besides professional courses, he is exposed to various Service courses at regular intervals. These are the Basic Staff Course, Junior Command and Staff Course, Senior Command and Staff Course, and finally, the Air War Course.

Basic Staff School (BSS)—The First Step in the Ladder

The Basic Staff Course (BSC) lasts for nine weeks, and facilitates the smooth assimilation of young officers, in their third year of service, into the PAF's working environment and prepares them for their future staff and command appointments. The course is conducted at the Basic Staff School, Badaber.

Under the new scheme of training, it is mandatory for all PAF officers to pass the BSC course to qualify for the substantive rank of Flight Lieutenant. During the course, student officers are exposed to various concepts in the disciplines of Staff Communication, Administration, Air Force Law, Management and Air Operations.

The BSS is an independent unit and has been placed under the Training Branch for functional and administrative control. An experienced faculty looks after the instructional and academic assignments. Instructions are imparted through lectures, discussions with the help of suitable multimedia training aids, and exercises that could be oral, written, or practical.

Director-level guest speakers are invited from almost all the important directorates of Air Headquarters and from both the sister Services in order to acquaint the budding officers with the role and task of these establishments. Students are also taken on educational visits and field trips. A one-week Pakistan Studies tour is organized exclusively for allied officers.

To infuse fresh spirit into the training environment, the principle of interactive education has been introduced. Student officers are now encouraged to learn through each other's experiences. Evenings are used for games and learning, as well as practical work on computers. The internet is available to officers who can explore this unlimited treasure-house of knowledge. Oral communication exercises have been merged into current affairs to achieve the twin benefits of communication skills as well as information. The use of multimedia is compulsory during all presentations by student officers. The informal subject of morality and military code of conduct has been introduced to give student officers an opportunity to understand ethical values and their advantage to individuals and society. To dovetail these essential elements of training which help to keep pace with the spirit of the age, the duration of the original eight-week course was enhanced to nine weeks.

Junior Command and Staff Course—The Second Step

The Junior Command and Staff Course (JC & SC) further builds up on the objectives of the BSC in order to provide working knowledge to the officers to handle command and staff appointments compatible with their service experience. It is also a prerequisite for promotion to the substantive rank of Squadron Leader. The JC & SC is conducted by the College of Staff Studies (CSS) located at Rear Air Headquarters, Peshawar.

After passing the BSC, officers are detailed for the year-long JC & SC. In their sixth year of service, officers from the General Duties branch are detailed for this course while officers from the ground branches are detailed in the seventh year of service. Courses commence each year on 1 March and 1 September. Those officers who qualify tutor-assessed exercises appear in an examination, which is held twice a year in the month of March and September. The subjects covered during this course include English, Organization and Administration, PAF Law, Air Operations, International Relations and a specialist branch subject.

The JC & SC is a one-year corres-pondence course comprising three phases, with each phase spread over twelve weeks. The course is conducted through tutor assessed exercises. In each phase, the officer is required to solve one exercise on each subject with the exception of the

engineering branch subject, which has two papers. The College of Staff Studies (CSS) prepares and despatches study material and exercises for each phase to student officers. They are then required to submit the solved exercises to the CSS for evaluation, as per schedule. After completion of a phase, the CSS despatches study material and exercises of the next phase along with the evaluated exercises of the previous phase.

The qualifying grade in each exercise is 50 per cent. An officer who fails to achieve this grade is asked to repeat the exercise. A repeated exercise is not graded more than 50 per cent, if otherwise found satisfactory. Should an officer fail to pass even the repeat exercise, his case is referred to the Review Board for relegation to a junior course. Submitting at least five exercises is essential for promotion to the next phase. On passing all the exercises, the officer undergoing the JC & SC becomes eligible to take a written examination. (Each course consists of two parts, 'exercises' and a 'written' examination). Exercises carry 25 per cent of the marks, while the written examination carries 75 per cent of the total marks. Final assessment is made on the basis of total marks obtained in the exercises and written examination. The passing grade is a minimum of 50 per cent in each subject. Officers securing first and second positions with 70 per cent or more marks in aggregate are awarded the Chief of Air Staff's Commendation Certificate.

The Senior Command and Staff Course

Upgrading the Staff College to Air War College created a vacuum in the PAF officers' training system. Not everyone who had qualified the JC & SC could go to the Air War College, yet there was a need for grooming additional mid-level commanders and staff officers. In order to bridge this gap, a Staff Wing was established at the Air War College to conduct the Senior Command and Staff Course (SC & SC) for those officers whose seniority level fell within twelve to fourteen years of commissioned service.

The course is conducted in two components: the Correspondence Component (CC) and the Resident Component (RC). The CC is spread over a period of one year and by implementing the distance learning concept, the officers are tasked to submit written assignments. This part of the course is conducted in two phases. During each phase, officers are tasked to submit five assignments on subjects like Staff Studies, English, Management, International Relations, War Studies and Employment of Air Power. The assignments are regularly assessed and students are debriefed about their performances in each. The Correspondence Component Cell of the SC & SC was initially formed at College of Staff Studies, Peshawar in 1992, which was later moved to the Air War College on 30 December 1995.

At the end of the academic year, officers who pass the correspondence component are sent to the Air War College for the Resident Component of the course. This component consists of an intense eleven-week course. The main focus of this component is on general comprehension, verbal and written communication, staff-work, and leadership and management skills. The course is conducted through lectures, syndicate discussions, individual presentations and written assignments. Guest speakers are also regularly invited to speak on various topics of interest. The curriculum of the resident component is divided into six academic clusters, i.e. Communication, Staff Studies, Air Power, Armed Forces of Pakistan, International Affairs, Pakistan Studies, and Management and Leadership. The final item in the course is a war game planning exercise.

During the resident component, close supervision and guidance are provided to the members by way of personal involvement of the faculty in general, and the sponsor Directing Staff (DS) in particular. The course is a pre-requisite for all PAF officers to be promoted to the rank of Group Captain. At the end of the course, a 'psa' certificate is awarded to the graduating officers. A B.Sc. (Hons.) degree is also conferred on those officers who already hold the B.Sc. degree.

Until December 1998, the Staff Wing had conducted twenty-two courses in which a total of 597 officers had qualified. The course has not only provided the PAF with competent staff officers and mid-level commanders, but has also promoted inter-branch harmony among the PAF officers.

The School has four Directing Staff members viz. DS (Tutorials), DS (Plans), and DS (Research), headed by a Chief Instructor. The DS (Army) and DS (Navy) are shared between the Staff Wing and the War Wing. The course is considered equivalent to the one conducted by the (Army) Command and Staff College, Quetta. The School regularly participates in Exercise Tri-Brachial with other staff colleges once a year. The induction of a limited number of allied officers is also under active consideration. The top two students of the course are awarded the CAS Commendation Certificate. All those who receive final grade of B+ (65 per cent or above) are considered for a Staff College Course abroad. Visits to industrial areas, Southern Air Command, and operational squadrons are part of the syllabus. The curriculum is continually updated. Computers are being added to facilitate day-to-day work.

The Air War Course—Grooming for Higher Echelons

The highest course in the PAF is the Air War Course, which is a one-year resident course at Air War College (AWC). Unlike other courses, only selected officers undergo this course, which is designed for up to thirty-two officers of the rank of Group Captain and its equivalent from the PAF, Pakistan Army, Pakistan Navy, and Air Forces of the friendly countries. The college is affiliated with the University of Karachi.

The approach towards imparting instruction at the Air War College is based on the university tutorial system, with some modifications to meet the peculiar military requirements. The course is divided into four syndicates of six to eight officers each. Each syndicate has a Sponsor Directing Staff (DS). The DS is not a typical tutor but, as the name suggests, one who directs and guides the participants throughout the course. The course participants are called members. They are encouraged to study on their own but the respective DS is constantly at hand to provide guidance. Typical study activities comprise lectures, discussions, presentations, spoken and written exercises, seminars, study tours and war games. These exercises and activities are in most cases evaluated collectively by all the faculty members. The final reports

The former President of Pakistan, Mr Ghulam Ishaq Khan and Air Chief Marshal Farooq Feroze Khan at the inauguration of the PAF Air War College at PAF Faisal on 8 December 1991

are written after a thorough analysis of each student's performance by the Tutorial Committee, which comprises the Commandant and the entire faculty. The aim of this course is to prepare selected officers for the assumption of key command and staff appointments where they would be required to develop, manage, and employ air power as a component of national security. The course is designed to enable participants to:

a. Think clearly, speak logically, write effectively and apply these principles to command and staff duties.
b. Comprehend essential dimensions of military history, philosophy, and strategy with special emphasis on the study and application of air power.
c. Assimilate and perceive the rapid diffusion of technology, and development of military doctrine leading towards the most effective employment of air power.
d. Develop an understanding of the geo-strategic environments, inter-state relationships, and their influence on national security.
e. Study Pakistan's economic and industrial growth and power potential.
f. Study contemporary theories of management and leadership and their relevance to military situations.
g. Understand the genesis of Pakistan and the determinants of its survival.

The duration of this course is forty-five weeks. The available training period consists of 246 days, equivalent to 1,722 hours. During the course, students carry out both individual as well as group research. There are a number of in-country tours to military and civil establishments, and a foreign study tour at the end of each course. There are also other activities that are typical to any other war course. At the end of the course, the students qualify for an MSc. degree (Strategic Studies) or a degree in BSc Hons. (War Studies) from the University of Karachi.

With ISO-9001 certification achieved recently, the College is sure to enhance the quality of its graduates by following a well-documented, well-implemented and audited international quality management system. The commitment of the top management of the AWC to continuously improve and update its training process is indeed the real engine of change for the better. The College, throughout its existence, has been a torch-bearer of quality and consistency. With ISO-9001 certification, this glorious tradition of the AWC will be carried into the new millennium.

The Courses Abroad
The PAF has continued to interact with the advanced Air Forces of the world in order to upgrade its professional competence. To achieve this objective, a variety of foreign courses are arranged either on payment or on a reciprocal basis. The Directorate of Training (Officers) is responsible for the formulation of policy and for arranging the training of PAF personnel overseas. This is implemented through an Annual Training Programme that is formulated each year. So far, under this programme, officers have been sent for staff and war courses to sixteen countries, including USA, UK, France, Germany, and Australia.

Civil Courses for PAF Officers
In-country training at the country's civilian institutions is also pursued by the PAF with equal enthusiasm. Courses are arranged at top management schools and institutions. MBA courses, of one to two years duration, are arranged at the College of Business

Management, the American Management Association, Preston University, and the Islamic University. The Training Branch also makes arrangements for MSc. in Strategic Studies at the Quaid-e-Azam University, Islamabad. Short courses are also available at the Pakistan Institute of Management Sciences, NIPA, NUST and the Pakistan Institute of Quality Control.

Training the Backbone of the PAF—Its Airmen

Basic Trade Training at Kohat

The basic and trade training of airmen upon their initial entry is carried out at PAF Base Kohat. Kohat's air base has a long and colourful history dating back to the early-1920s.

Pre-Trade Training School (PTTS)

At the start of the training at the PTTS, Kohat, all newly inducted recruits undergo trade allocation tests, which basically aim to screen out those who lack the aptitude for adjustment in the PAF environment. These also aim at awarding a trade that best suits each recruit's aptitude, capacity, and ability.

The Personnel Selection and Research Cell (PS & RC), which works directly under the Directorate of Recruitment at Rear Air Headquarters, Peshawar, conducts the trade tests of recruits. The trade test comprises Intelligence Tests, Mechanical Aptitude, Practical Aptitude, Clerical Aptitude and Interview.

Recruits with a science background are placed in the Aero-tech group, whereas those with an Arts background are placed in the Aero-support stream. The whole system is computerized and works under the close supervision of the Director of Recruitment. Trades are allocated on the basis of merit

and on the available vacancies in different trades.

Since July 1992, the PTTS has been regularly training three entries per year with an overall strength of 2500 to 2700. With a vigilant eye on high standards and dedication to quality, the unit has consistently maintained the passing out results as high as 92 per cent on an average.

The airmen's training also underwent changes from 1988 to 1998. Being the lifeline of the PAF, it received the close scrutiny and attention of policy-makers. Thus, the PAF witnessed structural as well as qualitative changes in the training of airmen. The changes, though not very frequent, have been effected, taking into account the pressing requirements of the PAF, and of the fast changing trends in technologies in the contemporary world.

In 1985-1986, the Apprentice scheme was renamed the 'Aero-tech Stream'. This course is meant for aircraft related trades viz. for Radio, Radar, Airframe, Engine, Electrical, Instrument, Photo and Armament. Later, *ab initio* training was completely stopped and the Aero-tech Stream was introduced for all the other trades. Initially, the training duration for Aero-tech Stream was three years while the Aero-support Stream had a training duration of one to two years, depending upon the trade. In 1990, the training duration of Aero-tech Stream was reduced from three years to two years and three months. Similarly, the duration of the Aero-support Stream was reduced from two years to one year. Presently, both Aero-technicians/Aero-support undergo thirty-one weeks of GST-cum-Academic training at the PTTS, Kohat followed by a maximum of eighty-seven weeks of technical trade training at the Trade Training Institutions for Aero-technicians. The non-technical trades, i.e., Aero-support have different training periods. These vary from sixteen to forty-seven weeks for different trades. Training for Aero-support trainees is imparted at the Administrative Trade Training School, (ATTS) and at other non-technical trade training schools such as, the Aero-Medical Institute (AMI), Computer Training School (CTS) and School of Logistics (SOL), Kohat.

Responding to the rapid development in technology, the PTTS has set up a state-of-the-art computer cell functioning on modern lines. The cell had been established with five PCs and allied peripherals. Three computer orientation courses for instructors have already been conducted. The base auditorium has recently been completely renovated with new fittings, soft furnishings and stage sophistication. The facility is basically utilized for extra curricular activities viz. Naat-o-Qirat competitions (the recitation of religious hymns and the Holy Quran), Declamation Contests and Dramatics. Besides these, Base functions and ceremonies of the PAF Inter College are also staged in the hall.

The worn-out, unlevelled, and small sized Parade Square of the PTTS had been enlarged and reconstructed to accommodate maximum number of flights of all the five squadrons viz. Rafiqui, Alauddin, Iqbal, Rashid Minhas, and Munir. The unit has thus become self-sufficient in conducting all kinds of general service training, and assemblies of all the trainees of PTTS within its premises.

The quality of the unit's magazine, earlier named 'Nigah Buland', has been considerably improved and its frequency of publication increased under the new title 'CONCEPTS', standing for 'Contributions by Cerebrals of Pre-Trade School'.

A new course in the English Language under the name 'Shaheen English Language Series' (Books One, Two and Three) has been completed by a team comprising the instructors of the English Department. The new series helps to widen the trainee' vocabulary, aids in English-language comprehension and communication, and also provides a broader spectrum of General Service Knowledge, Technical Vocabulary and Writing Skill. In addition to this, steps have been taken to update the précis of Mathematics and Physics with expanded topics to fulfil the technical requirements of the trainees. This new syllabus was to be introduced in the year 2000. Classes to teach the recitation of the Holy Quran (Nazra Quran) have been launched for trainees unlettered in the Holy Quran. The strength of participants ranges from four to six hundred per entry. Special classes for those wishing to commit the Holy Quran to memory (Hifz) are conducted under the supervision of Education Instructors. This effort, too, will indeed yield positive results.

The Administrative Trade Training School (ATTS), Kohat

The ATTS imparts advanced trade training to the personnel allocated to the Accounts, MT Mechanic, MT Driver, Fire Fighter, Secretarial Assistant, Provost, Administrative Assistant and Meteorology trades in the PAF. In addition, in-Service courses for MTD and Stenography are also conducted. All courses pertaining to the officers training have been discontinued at the ATTS during the last decade. To improve the spoken English of the trainees, a language laboratory LLS-700 was established in 1989.

The School of Logistics (SOL), Kohat

The School of Logistics provides effective and meaningful training to the Aero-Support Supply and Catering Assistants. It also imparts Mid-Level Logistics Management and Equipment Phase training to the

Engineering Officers. Additionally, the SOL runs courses in Automated Logistics Management System (ALMS) for in-Service men, civilians and officers of the Supply Branch. The School has thirty computer terminals for the training of officers and airmen. Since 1992, the average results have been 97 per cent.

At present, foreign trainees from the UAE and the Sri Lankan Air Force are attending various courses conducted by the SOL. In the years to come, trainees from Saudi Arabia are also likely to attend the School.

Advanced Training

After completing their initial training at Kohat, the airmen are ready for more specialized training in the different trades allotted to them, and this takes place at the PAF Base Korangi Creek.

The School of Electronics (SOE)

The School of Electronics train airmen in the radio and radar (Air and Ground) trades along with the Ground Signaller Operator (GSO), Radar Operator and ATC (non-technical) trainees arriving from PTTS, Kohat. From 1986 onwards, the Apprentice streams have been renamed as the Aero-Techs and Aero-Supports (Technical). Trainees from the Aero-Tech stream undergo eighty-three weeks of training at the SOE, while those from Aero-Support have a training schedule of forty-seven weeks. A simulator for Radar Operators was inducted in the early nineties and a refresher cell was also established with a mini press to revise and print the training notes, and trade manuals for the trainees. The Soldering Lab, Morse Code Lab and the Aircraft Model Room have also been upgraded and modernized. The SOE to date has trained a large number of personnel not only from the three Services, but also from

the departments of Plant Protection, Civil Aviation and personnel from several friendly countries. The output of this unit stands at 1000 technicians per year. A total of 267 courses have been conducted with a total strength of 8861 trainees during the last decade. Basic computer training has also been initiated in the various training courses of the SOE since 1998.

The School of Aeronautics (SOA)

The SOA imparts the necessary training to trainees of the Airframe, Engine, Instrument and Electrical trades. To train these airmen in contemporary specializations, the school has a dedicated team of highly educated officers and trained instructors. To improve the academic qualification of airmen, qualified education officers and instructors, with specialized degrees in their subjects, have been posted to the Education Training Squadron of the SOA. Special emphasis has been placed on spoken and written English. The 'BBC (Follow Me)' programmes are now taught with the help of audio-visual aids, and the trainees are frequently taken to the language lab to improve their comprehension and vocabulary. To inculcate discipline amongst airmen, the SOA lays strong emphasis on their drill and general service training activities.

To add interesting diversions to the SOA's demanding environment, the school has introduced a number of co-curricular activities. Regular After Dinner Literary Activity (ADLA) sessions have been institutionalized in the School. The ADLA sessions are conducted regularly in the trainees' mess. To provide the trainees with on-the-spot learning and practical knowledge, educational visits are also arranged. They are taken to the PAF flying bases, the Navy's harbour installations, industrial units, museums, libraries, and places of historical interest to widen their mental and educational horizons.

At the end of the training, incentives are given to the trainees in appreciation of their hard work. Distinction holders in the end-term examination are awarded badges and a merit certificate. On completion of their training, those scoring 80 per cent and above in the overall performance, are awarded six months seniority.

The JCOs Academy

The PAF's JCOs represent the most important intermediate supervisory leadership link in the PAF's chain of command. Accordingly, before a Senior Non-Commissioned Officer (SNCO) rises to that highest non-commissioned rank, he is required to attend the JCOs Academy located at Korangi Creek. The syllabus includes English Language, Leadership, Management, Pakistan Studies, PAF Law, Organization and Administration and Drill commands to prepare the selected SNCOs for higher appointments.

The Academy has so far conducted forty-six regular courses and has turned out over 5,800 SNCOs from 1986 to 1998. Out of these graduates, over 401 SNCOs have earned distinction certificates by scoring 80 per cent and above.

The System of Promotion Examinations (QE Series for Airmen)

It is important for the PAF to ensure that the advancement of its recruits is based purely on their performance, which is assessed through a fair but strict evaluation process.

This is carried out through well-designed qualifying examinations and tests. The Central Trade Test Board of the PAF performs this function under the control of the Air Headquarters' Directorate of Training (Airmen). The CTTB conducts examinations at training institutions along with the other qualifying examination, viz. QE-I, II and III of airmen twice a year. The categorization of MTDs also comes within the purview of CTTB.

After passing the appropriate examination, an airman becomes eligible for promotion to the next rank. The qualifying marks for each subject were 60 per cent prior to September 1993 and were brought down to 50 per cent in the subsequent boards. In 1996, the frequency of QE boards was reduced from three boards per year to two boards a year. The decision was taken in view of providing enough time, both to the candidates to prepare for the examinations, and also to enable the bases and CTTB to complete the prerequisites for examination and result compilation.

The CTTB's new trade manuals were prepared and distributed in September 1997. These trade manuals were prepared keeping in mind the changes in different policies, and the introduction of new concepts based on new technical data. The CTTB is, at present, shouldering the responsibility of dealing with the examination affairs of about 10,000 airmen per year, at various levels.

7 BACKING UP THE FORCE—THE ORGANIZATION AND ADMINISTRATION

Organizational and administrative changes are normal features of any dynamic organization and so it is with the PAF. Being a forward-looking and vibrant force, the PAF readily adapts to positive changes. When a problem in the field or at Headquarters level affects the operational effectiveness of the PAF, it is referred to the Air Board, where the senior leadership of the PAF examines and deliberates on the possible solutions. While input from the field is invariably given due weightage, the problem is resolved through the collective wisdom of the leadership.

During the last decade, several decisions were made, which may have appeared controversial at the time, but in the long run proved useful—a tribute to the PAF commanders who are known for their professional and vigorous style of leadership. One such decision related to the amalgamation of the engineering branches. Before debating this issue at the Air Headquarters, a thorough study was carried out by a team of officers especially assigned for the purpose. The team studied the system in vogue in other air forces before putting up their recommendations. Similarly, the Air Secretary's Office was reorganized into the Personnel Branch, and the management of all personnel is now being looked after centrally by this branch. The Air Combat Evaluation System replaced the old and redundant practice of routine inspections. The PAF's own Operational Readiness Inspection organization gave a new meaning to this concept.

The system of checks and balances, a responsive leadership, inherent flexibility, and a vibrant and caring administration are what make this a special service—and an elite one in the professional sense.

Management of Human Resources

Two different departments traditionally handled the human resource management in the PAF. The Assistant Chief of Air Staff (ACAS) (Personnel-Organization) was looking after the airmen and civilians, while the Air Secretary, in the rank of Air Commodore, was responsible for the entire career management of the officers' corps. Since the Branch Principal Staff Officers (PSOs) were senior in rank and status, they impinged on the authority of the Air Secretary and were prone to making independent decisions. Virtually all decisions were being taken by the Branch PSOs. This had reduced the Air Secretary's Branch to the status of a post office. The then CAS, Air Chief Marshal Farooq F. Khan, took note of the decline in the Air Secretary's authority, and in 1992, directed that the Air Secretary should assume greater responsibility. In June 1994, the CAS expanded the areas of responsibility of the Air Secretary and ordered a reorganization, culminating in a Personnel Branch headed by an Air Vice Marshal.

Keeping in view the disadvantages of the scattered management system, the concept of a centralized Human Resource Management system was introduced, combining all the personnel management departments under the DCAS (Personnel). As a result, the functions of the Director Civilian Personnel (DCP) and the Director of Personnel (D of P) along with the Pension Cell are now supervised by ACAS

(Personnel-Airmen/Civilians), while the PAF Record office, headed by its Officer Commanding, is also placed under the DCAS (Personnel). ACAS (Personnel-Officers) looks after matters related to officers of all branches. All Deputy Air Secretaries and Assistant Air Secretaries are now re-designated as Directors and Deputy Directors respectively. The Deputy Chief of Air Staff (Personnel), who heads the Personnel Branch, has four Air Commodores under him, i.e. ACAS (Personnel-Officers), ACAS (Personnel-Airmen/Civilians), ACAS (Work Study), and OC Records.

With this new reorganization, the Personnel Branch initiated a number of studies pertaining to its field, to identify on scientific lines the areas that needed immediate attention. The first was the officers' promotion policy and its spectrum, which had certain lacunae. Until 1993, the cases for temporary promotion up to the rank of Wing Commander were moved on files. The composition of the Promotion Board, the promotion criteria, and thresholds for various ranks were not clearly defined. After deliberations at various levels, a policy letter was issued to consolidate all information on the subject. New instructions are now available in a single document that spells out the service requirements and the composition of Branch/General Promotion Boards. A higher collective body now makes promotion decisions.

Temporary promotions are now subject to the availability of establishment vacancies, clearance by the promotion boards, and final approval by the Chief of the Air Staff. A mini-board, chaired by the DCAS (Personnel) and attended by the PSO of the respective branch, decides cases concerning promotion from Squadron Leader to Wing Commander. For Group Captains and above, approval by the Government of Pakistan is an additional requirement. To facilitate decision-making during the Promotion Board

meetings, computerized data is displayed. It includes personal information, OER scores, professional and other courses, posting history along with graphical comparison of an officer with his contemporaries. A computer generated Initiating Officers' trend is also displayed.

The Branch simplified the procedure for the award of the Professional Excellence Badge to the entitled officers. It also succeeded in getting the PAF quota enhanced for the non-operational military awards. A large number of vacancies in the selection ranks were also upgraded.

In addition, the reorganized Personnel Branch made significant contributions in areas such as the induction of officers into the Civil Service, easing the problem of promotion blockage, and streamlining the procedure for retirement, extensions of service, etc. The posting policy of officers, criteria for detailing them on different courses, and their post-retirement rehabilitation policy were also revised. Decisions regarding the overseas deputation of officers are now made in a meeting organized by the Personnel Branch and chaired by the VCAS.

The emergence of the Personnel Branch has been an important development. There now exists a dedicated work force consisting of mostly mainstream officers who continually review policies and oversee their implementation. They are concerned with the career advancement of officers and their post-retirement rehabilitation. Centralized management under a separate PSO has enabled the Air Force to optimize its human resource potential to the maximum.

The Reorganization of the Directorate of Work Study

The Work Study team assists the Air Staff and field commanders as a decision support ool, for efficient employment and management of resources. The team applies analytical methods to organizational problems for the optimum use of available resources, and helps achieve desired organizational goals. Recognizing its importance, the PAF had, right from its inception, established an influential Directorate of Work Study and placed it at par with the then PSOs and other Air Staff in the Air Headquarters' organization.

With the passage of time, the organization of the PAF underwent a gradual change. While the rank/office structure of PSOs, Air Staff and Directors were upgraded, the Directorate of Work Study did not receive the attention it deserved. The resources allocated to this establishment were not adequate, thereby rendering it rather ineffective.

The Air Staff had long felt that the specified role and task of the Directorate was not well defined and the organizational structure needed revamping. Therefore, in November 1998, the 'Role and Task' of Work Study was replaced with a well defined 'Mission and Objectives'. In addition, a new and effective organization representing all the major branches of the PAF was also approved for the Directorate. In order to provide the Directorate with qualified analysts, suitable officers were trained in the relevant disciplines in recognized institutions before deploying them on the job. The post of Director of Work Study was also upgraded to that of ACAS (Work Study); Air Commodore Maqbool Shah was the first ACAS (Work Study) of the PAF.

The Role of the Personnel Branch in the Career Planning of Officers

An issue often talked about in the Personnel Branch is whether an officer himself is the main architect of his future career. This is true to an extent, but not altogether. Officers are encouraged to adopt a professional approach towards career progression and are motivated to attain distinction through the true application of their abilities in whatever assignments they undertake. Professional excellence, dedication, and hard work make an indelible impression on one's superiors and influence career advancement positively.

Confidential Record (CR) dossiers contain a complete record of every officer. In addition to Officers Evaluation Reports (OERs), they also contain various training reports. A CR dossier contains the Inter-Services Selection Board (ISSB) Report, End-of-Courses Report, awards and appreciation/discipline letters. All other information of a sensitive nature, important in career progression, is also placed in the dossier. These dossiers are invariably consulted at the time of all postings, courses, promotions, etc. DCAS(P) and respective PSOs use these dossiers as background information to decide on applications and petitions etc. Dossiers of Air Vice Marshals and above are kept with the CAS (Chief of Air Staff) and those of Air Commodores and below are kept in the Career Planning Section of the Personnel Branch.

All incoming OERs (Officer's Evaluation Reports) are monitored and scrutinized for omissions and errors before being processed through the PSOs etc. Letters of guidance and advice are also issued, based on those reports. All recommendations for awards, and discipline cases are also processed through the Career Planning Section.

The promotion policy is basically dictated by the pyramidal structure of the service. Promotions can only be made within the limits of this structure and are characterized by a decreasing number of vacancies as one goes higher. Each branch has its own established vacancies therefore, both the number of promotions, and thresholds of one branch cannot be compared with another.

Promotions of GD(P) (General Duty Pilot) Branch serve as a reference point for those in other branches.

Based on this concept, the Personnel Branch endeavours to promote the maximum number of officers to higher ranks within the available thresholds. This ensures a reasonable longevity of career with a minimum possible disturbance in the Inter-Branch Seniority (commonly referred to as 'Inter se Seniority'), and within the available deployment options. The scope for promotions is calculated on the basis of a number of constants and variables. The constant factors are existing established vacancies, anticipated new vacancies and the retirements taking effect. Variable factors include the availability of inter-service vacancies, pool vacancies, vacancies loaned from other branches, and finally, deputation and secondment. The promotion threshold is based on the number of vacancies available. The data is prepared and presented to the Air Board. After the Promotion Board, the cases for selection ranks are forwarded to the MoD for approval. Ranks are issued only after approval by the government, and as and when actual vacancies become available. Presently, officers below the rank of Air Commodore can be considered for promotion in two consecutive Promotion Boards. If an officer is not cleared for promotion, it does not necessarily mean that he is not competent; it is because others are better than he is. In the ultimate analysis, it all depends on comparative performance, and the number of places available. Uniformity in the performance criteria of different boards cannot be guaranteed. Luck definitely plays its part in terms of competition and available vacancies.

The 'Inter se Seniority' is only meant for protocol arrangements; it has nothing to do with promotion. No promotion policy document talks of 'Inter se Seniority', but over the years, this has become a complex issue and is open to all kinds of interpretations. According to the Air Board directive, it is to be fixed with the date of the promotion of an officer to the substantive rank of Squadron Leader. However, this limit serves as a guideline and remains flexible, thus accommodating the peculiarities of a branch structure and the number of vacancies available. The Personnel Branch endeavours to minimize this disturbance.

All officers are considered for promotion to the next rank prior to retirement. Some officers, who are not cleared for promotion but are still considered useful to the Service, are granted an extension beyond service limits. Only the federal government can, however, grant extensions beyond the age limit.

The procedure for career planning existed even during the tenure of the Air Secretary Branch. However, after the reorganization of the Personnel Branch, the availability of a professional and dedicated work force, and a PSO heading the Branch, procedures are much more streamlined. The introduction of computers as tools for decision-making has revolutionized the working of the Personnel Branch. Decisions regarding promotion cases are now systematic and transparent.

Airmen Career Management

The PAF Record Office

Since its establishment, the PAF Record Office had been functioning as part of the Admin. Branch. In February 1994, the Record Office was placed under the Air Secretary Branch and later, during reorganization of the Air Headquarters in March 1995, the Record Office was placed directly under the DCAS (P).

Airmen Information System

The Computer Section of the Record Office was established in 1972. The data collected at that time was restricted to the coding of entries from PORs on diskettes at the Computer Centre, Habib Bank Plaza, Karachi. After some years, this computerization process was shifted to the Directorate of Data Automation, Badaber. A dedicated team of computer experts was detailed by the Directorate to examine the efficacy of the existing system. The system was analysed, designed and various useful inquiry figures and printing formats were prepared for the users. At that time, IBM System-36 was used for the purpose. Recognizing the importance of this database, the entire system was transferred to an advanced version of the IBM, and a printer was installed at the Computer Centre, Peshawar. Service information relating to all airmen is now updated and maintained on the computer, which includes basic personnel data, posting history, promotion history, career examinations, annual evaluation reports, qualification courses, data for promotion boards, retirement data, and war deployment of airmen etc. These facilities have been extended to all main offices by providing a terminal to each office. The system has also proved useful for the higher authorities, different directorates, and civil departments like the Directorate of Housing, Central Accounts Office (CAO), Directorate of Accounts, Shaheen Foundation, Civil Aviation, and other government departments.

Introduction of the Rank of the Assistant Warrant Officer (AWO) in the PAF

The nomenclature of ranks of non-commissioned personnel in the PAF and its equivalent in the other two services has always been a contentious issue. The rank of Chief Technician had no equivalent in the Pakistan Army and Navy and was thus creating some confusion at the Inter-Services level. Due to time-scale promotions in vogue, there was a gradual accumulation of personnel at the rank of Chief Technician. As a result, the existing strength in this rank stood at 160 per cent of its authorized establishment. To resolve both these problems, the rank of Assistant Warrant Officer (AWO) was recently introduced in the PAF. Like all JCO (Junior Commissioned Officer) ranks, promotion to this rank would be subject to availability of establishment vacancy. About one thousand Chief Technicians have now been converted to AWOs. The Air Force plans to convert all Chief Technicians to the AWO rank during the next four years.

Reorganization of the Directorate of Public Relations (Air)

For over two decades, the office of the PRO (Public Relations Officer), Air Force constituted a small detachment of the ISPR (Inter-Service Public Relations), headed by one officer. In 1989, the first PAF officer (Wing Commander Sultan Mahmood Hali) was posted as PRO, Air Force. It was during this period that the reorganization of this office was taken up. Video documentaries and training films were prepared as tools to project the PAF more effectively. The ISPR detachment was given additional manpower and the office was designated as the 'Directorate of Public Relations (Air)', with the Director of Public Relations as its head. Since then this Directorate has been working to fulfil its mission, which has become more demanding with the ever increasing freedom of the press and the growing media awareness in the country.

The Directorate of Public Relations (Air) has done a commendable job in highlighting the achievements of the PAF during the decade under review. Some of its notable achievements include the popular TV serial 'Shahpar', the production of video and audio cassettes eulogizing the PAF through music and song, and contributing special supplements in newspapers on the PAF's achievements etc.

Revamping the System of Inspection

Most modern air forces depend on sharpening their operational skills, and keeping the force ready for its assigned role, on a system of inspection that reports directly to the air force commander. Air Marshal Asghar Khan had set up the 'Inspectorate', with a Chief Inspector as its head, in February 1959. Its mandate was to inspect bases and units, and to gauge the progress in the implementation of Air HQ policies. The system worked quite efficiently for the first ten to fifteen years. The senior Air Staff at Air Headquarters and all the field commanders took its reports very seriously and many deficiencies of the air force were thus removed. However, changing circumstances over a period of time necessitated a review of this organization. It was, therefore, decided in 1991, to upgrade the department to 'Inspector General's Branch', and to give it a larger mandate to assess the PAF's status of operational readiness.

The Inspector General's Branch has made a significant contribution towards the operational readiness of the PAF. It has brought to the fore shortcomings of units and bases in carrying out their wartime roles. It has guided and assisted the commanders in continuously evaluating the performance of their assets. Additionally, the confidence and the ability of PAF personnel has improved over the years, and procedures have been refined to ensure instant response in an emergency.

This change in role has given the inspectorate function renewed importance. In the field, personnel have started responding to it positively. Besides the dynamic methods adopted in the new concept of inspections, the attention that its reports receive at the top level ensures that every one understands its importance. The emphasis of the Inspector General (IG) is now on the net outcome of the mission given to the squadrons. The IG's team focuses on the deficiencies that have a negative impact on the mission.

Air Vice Marshal Abbas Mirza was the first Inspector General under this revised scheme. He undertook visits to some of the modern air forces for this purpose. He visited the United States Air Force (USAF) and looked at their system in totality and also at what the air force expected from the inspectorate. Clearly, there were two objectives to be achieved. One was the routine work—the audit that needed to be done to determine how the bases were performing. The second, and more important issue was the operational preparedness of the air force. In the Pakistan Air Force, this was monitored by the Operations Branch, who issued orders and also monitored their implementation. This was organizationally wrong. The IG was given a free hand to check operations and to give suggestions. The first task was to look into the system of inspecting a base. In the old system, the Inspectorate normally used to take three to four weeks to inspect a base. Under the new scheme of things, the inspection period was cut down to just seven days and the warning time given to the bases was limited to a maximum of forty-eight hours.

The IG divided his inspection report into three parts—one for the base, one for the PSOs, and the third for the CAS. The Chief's report was to be a maximum of three pages that concerned the wider implications for the entire air force. PSOs read what they had to do for the base and took action accordingly. The report for the base highlighted the areas they could tackle at their own level without looking for help from higher formations. That is how the system was streamlined. The operational exercises were also made more realistic. For example, the 'Flat Out' exercises now involve operational flight plans, other aspects of war plans, such as runway repair capability, ammunition and loading etc. The squadrons have launchers that have to be checked in the event of a war. During initial inspections, when the IG team visited bases, they asked squadrons to load up actual bombs on the aircraft for a particular target, as per war plans. Then the exercise 'Flat Out' was closely monitored. As a result of this effort, there emerged a whole range of issues that needed to be addressed.

Air Vice Marshal Abbas Mirza believes that the IG branch made an impression on the bases. The reports that came out from the inspections were ready to be put into action, and the branch itself began to be taken seriously. The bases started working to ensure that they were ready at all times, and that their procedures and systems were fully functional.

According to the revised mandate, the role and task of the IG's Branch are to:

a. Keep the Chief of Air Staff informed on the overall efficiency of bases and units.

b. Establish a system of accountability by making field commanders responsible for their actions.

c. Bring to the notice of the Principal Staff Officers deficiencies and problems pertaining to their area of responsibility, which require executive action at Air Headquarters.

d. Provide field commanders with factual, unbiased and detailed reports on the state of the concerned unit along with constructive advice.

e. Recommend measures to remedy faults and overcome difficulties.

The revised mandate envisaged formal inspections of PAF bases and units by the Inspector General's team on behalf of the Chief of the Air Staff. They were required to check for operational preparedness, efficiency of management, adequacy of facilities, effective utilization of available resources, and to see that rules, regulations and directives were complied with. The IG's Branch was required to carry out, on a single team concept, Audit Inspection, Operational Readiness Inspection (ORI), Assessment of Combat Efficiency of Squadrons (ACES), Air Defence Excellence Competition (ADEX), and evaluation of different command level exercises.

Audit Inspection

Audit inspections of bases and units are conducted once every three years. Adequate time is provided to bases for preparation. These inspections focus on peacetime functions and programmes, and evaluate the performance of units against established standards and criteria. These are accomplished with thoroughness. The accountability of commanders at various tiers at the base is also undertaken during these inspections.

Operational Readiness Inspection (ORI)

The ORI is an undeclared biannual event undertaken with a warning of seventy-two hours only. Various contingencies simulating wartime operational scenarios are included in the ORI. The basic emphasis during ORIs is on assessing the combat readiness of bases and air defence units.

The ORI is divided into three phases for the purpose of evaluation. Initial response constitutes the first phase, during which the base or unit is assessed for actions taken for transition from peace to war. Combat employment is the next phase in which the ability of the base or a unit to manage its assets in support of operational missions and contingencies is assessed, as is the level of proficiency of various operators. The third phase of an ORI evaluates the ability to survive and operate. In this phase, the overall effectiveness of command, and the control and decision-making abilities of key staff are analysed. This phase evaluates how well a base survives during an enemy onslaught and then recovers from the degradation of operational facilities and infrastructure during war.

ACES—Assessment of Combat Efficiency of Squadrons

To assess the combat efficiency of combat squadrons, an improved system of ACES categorization has been in force since 1989. All operational squadrons are evaluated once a year. For these evaluations too, a warning of only seventy-two hours is provided. This evaluation is done by the Inspector General's branch.

ADEX—Air Defence Excellence Competition

Like ACES, an Air Defence Excellence competition for eligible and designated air defence units has been held on a yearly basis since 1993. The aim of this competition is to improve the operational efficiency, and combat preparedness of air defence units. The evaluation is also designed to standardize mission-oriented training and operational procedures amongst air defence units. The IG's Branch is now in charge of conducting the ADEX competition.

Evaluation of Exercises

Exercises at the armed forces level in general, and at the air force level in particular, have been conducted in the PAF since its inception. However, the decision to assign the task of assessing the performance of participating formations to the IG's Branch was made in 1993. Since then this branch has undertaken the assessment of High Mark-93 and High Mark-95.

Revision of the PAF's Evaluation Systems

ACES

The Air Combat Evaluation System has helped to promote the operational readiness of the fighter squadrons, and has contributed directly towards the overall efficiency of the PAF. The evaluation criteria and the scoring system evolved in 1986 was revised by the Directorate of Operations in 1989 to meet changing requirements. However, the ACES competition has been the subject of constant criticism by squadron commanders because of its inability to bridge the gap between the F-16 and other squadrons as regards human and technical resources. In order to give all the participating squadrons an equal chance to compete for the ACES trophies, the IG's Branch undertook a series of discussions with the Operations Branch and squadron commanders of fighter squadrons to amend the rules and provide a level playing field for all competing squadrons. It included the evaluation of weapon-loading exercises in terms of training violations, and skill level and management. It also divided the ompetition into three sub-groups, i.e. multi-role (F-16), Tactical Attack (Mirage and A-5) and Air Superiority (F-6 and F-7) Squadrons. Winners of each of these groups now compete for the ACES top squadron trophy.

ADEX

On the pattern of ACES, a scheme of systematic evaluation was instituted for the air defence units in 1993, called the Air Defence Excellence Trophy (ADEX). The sole objective was to improve operational efficiency and enhance combat readiness. With the passage of time, and with experience gained during previous evaluations, certain anomalies and dichotomies were observed in the assessment criteria and methodology. The IG's branch addressed these problems by revising and updating the criteria governing ADEX. The revision focused on renaming the trophy and on the grouping of compatible air defence units according to their specialty so that each group could compete for a trophy, while Sectors could compete for the Overall ADEX trophy.

Ombudsman

The IG's Branch also looks after the office of the Ombudsman in the PAF. This office was instituted in 1969, much before it came into being on the national scene. Presently, the Inspector General Air Force acts as the Ombudsman, and is directly responsible to the CAS for this purpose. Uniformed and civilian personnel can send applications to him about the following subjects:

a. Defects or weaknesses in the organization, structure, or administrative system of the PAF.

b. Breaches of law, regulations, instructions, orders, or policies. Also the misuse of official position, corruption, or any other action by an individual, which is against the interests of the Service or the applicant.

The Ombudsman has no executive authority to implement his findings or recommendations. However, in the revised charter of duties he has been given the option of reopening a case and asking for a review or investigation by an independent agency. The Ombudsman does not entertain anonymous letters. He also does not disclose the identity of an applicant if there is danger of victimization, or if the applicant requests anonymity. In case the allegations are found to be false or deliberately malicious, the Inspector General can order disciplinary action against an applicant under the PAF Act. On receipt of an application, it is first ascertained whether the applicant had exhausted all normal channels for redress of his problem. It is then decided whether the matter merits further attention. If so, the case is sent to the concerned agency for comments. Viewpoints from both sides are studied in light of Air Force policies and guidelines. An advisory letter is dispatched both to the applicant, providing him with the Ombudsman's opinion, and to the concerned agency so that it may review its decision or action as appropriate.

The Amalgamation of the Engineering Branches

The Pakistan Air Force continued with the Royal Air Force system of maintenance until the United States Air Force maintenance concept was adopted, and the US assistance programmes began in the mid-1950s. The AFI 69 of 1959 identifies the Maintenance branches of the Pakistan Air Force. According to Paragraph 3 of the AFI, the Maintenance Branch would consist of the following sub-branches:

a. Maintenance Technical (Engineering)
   - (MT Engg.)
b. Maintenance Technical (Electronics)
   - (MT Elect.)
c. Maintenance Technical (Armament)
   - (MT Armt.)
d. Maintenance Equipment
   - (Maint. Equip.)
e. Maintenance Data Automation
   - (MDA)

Although these sub-branches were headed by one PSO, viz. DCAS (Maintenance), each one had its own independent maintenance command, maintenance policies and the officers had independent career progression within their own sub-branch. At the bases, all the components were placed under the Officer Commanding Maintenance Wing, who used to be an MT Engineering officer. Similar arrangements prevailed at Air Headquarters and only an MT Engineering officer was selected as DCAS (Maintenance). This arrangement continued until 1985, when, keeping in view the important role of electronics in modern warfare, MT Electronics was separated from the Engineering branch and placed under a separate PSO, i.e. DCAS (Electronics) at Air Headquarters. At PAF bases, activities pertaining to electronics were placed under a separate Officer Commanding, who was designated OC Electronics Wing.

This arrangement continued for a little less than five years when the higher command felt that after the creation of Electronics as a separate branch, the delineation of responsibilities between the Aerospace and Electronics sub-branches had become diffused, in so far as it related to the responsibility for maintenance and availability of airborne weapon systems. To rectify this growing aberration, the then Chief of Air Staff, Air Chief Marshal Hakimullah, directed the two branches to

present a concept of maintenance with a view to determining the areas of responsibility for each branch. During the presentations, which were made on 3 October 1989, the Electronics Branch recommended the amalgamation of the maintenance branches at the Air Headquarters level. Based on this recommendation, the CAS inquired whether this concept could be extended to include the field level as well. The CAS was of the opinion that the inter-branch rivalry in the engineering cadre had reached such proportions that it was becoming counter-productive to the cause of the Air Force, and amalgamation would put an end to the growing problem of branch parochialism. The CAS believed that although pride in one's own branch was understandable, when it turned into unbridled hostility towards another branch, the problem demanded immediate resolution. He believed that a qualified engineer should be able to perform the role of an engineering officer in the flying squadrons, as well as in the second and the third line maintenance functions. Moreover, at the time the air force did not require specialization in Aerospace and Electronics to that extent. He was convinced that graduates from the CAE could easily perform all the tasks that the technical sub-branches were required to accomplish.

To study and work out the modalities of the amalgamation, the CAS appointed a Committee for the Amalgamation of Maintenance Branches (CAMB), comprising the following:

a. Air Vice Marshal Abbas H. Mirza
   AOC NAC
b. Group Captain Niaz Hussain
   D of Elect. Engg.
c. Group Captain M. Anwar Khokhar
   ACAS (Armt.)
d. Group Captain M.T. Saleem
   DWSM (A)

The CAS directed the CAMB that the amalgamation was to be put into effect as early as possible, with minimum dislocation and disturbance. At that time, the strength of the five sub-branches together was 1,365. This included 496 officers of MT Engg., 487 of MT Elect., 119 of MT Armt., and 204 from Maint. Equip. sub-branches. Besides this, the MDA branch consisted of 59 officers.

Preliminary Confabulation

The team began its deliberations in HQ Northern Air Command, Peshawar. Air Commodore Muzammil Saeed, Commandant CAE, was co-opted as a member of the team to study the impact on the training aspects at the CAE. In addition, the team decided to interact with senior officers of the maintenance sub-branches so that it did not work in isolation, and received the benefit of the experience and input of the officers who were likely to be affected by the amalgamation.

Soon it became obvious to the team that amalgamation aroused spirited responses. The reactions of maintenance officers varied widely. Some were enthusiastic about the change while others were doubtful and openly voiced their concern. It was also apparent to the team that amalgamation could pose problems in the initial stages of its implementation due to the fact that the PAF had not followed a uniform system for the induction of maintenance officers. The PAF had, within its fold, short course officers without a broad-based engineering background, graduate officers from the CAE, as well as those inducted directly from the civil colleges, and Branch List Permanent Commission (BLPC) officers. As a result, the views and apprehensions of each category of officers towards amalgamation were different.

The Sub-branches of Data Automation and Logistics

Initially, the CAMB favoured amalgamating the Data Automation sub-branch with the Maintenance branch. However, after detailed discussions, it was decided to let the Data Automation sub-branch remain as it was, primarily because the sub-branch was very small and did not interfere with the amalgamation problem to any great extent.

According to the definition of the Maintenance Branch, the Equipment Branch (later called Logistics/Supply) also formed a part of the branch and was to be studied for amalgamation. This branch, primarily responsible for the procurement, receipt, warehousing and issue of PAF technical and non-technical stores, had no engineers but Equipment officers who had varying educational qualifications obtained from civil colleges. These officers were given only a short phase course at the Academy before being commissioned as Supply/Logistics officers. After deliberation by the CAMB, it was proposed that, with the amalgamation of maintenance branches, technical officers should also perform the role of supply officers.

The amalgamation of the Maintenance Branch, therefore, meant the integration of the MT Engg., MT Elect., MT Armt., and the Maint. Equip. sub-branches to form one Engineering Branch.

The Rationale for Amalgamation

A study conducted at that time revealed that about 88 per cent of the technical officers (excluding the BLPC cadre) were graduate engineers. These officers had engineering degrees in either Mechanical (Aerospace) or Electrical (Avionics) fields. In each major field, the engineers had broad-based (about 15 per cent) knowledge of the other specialty. In terms of actual hours of study, this 15 per cent amounted to nearly 200 hours of theory and 165 hours of practical work. Furthermore, the graduate engineers' major field study consisted of about 45 per cent of the total training curricula. The remaining 40 per cent was devoted to Humanities, Industrial Engineering and Military Science subjects.

It was, therefore, fairly certain that a graduate engineer was suitably qualified to assume maintenance posts in either the avionics or aerospace fields. The Armament Officer had background knowledge of both avionics and aerospace engineering. The cross-utilization of the graduate engineer in any of the three technical areas (aerospace, electronics, armament) would not pose any major problem provided some weapon system-specific training was imparted to an officer before his assignment. In a similar manner, at the senior or middle management level, the cross-utilization of technical officers would be made through familiarization training.

The CAMB also examined the issue of the possible loss of efficiency in the branch in the initial stages of the amalgamation. It was thought that as an increasing number of officers would be utilized in inter-disciplinary assignments, the efficiency of the Engineering Branch would ultimately improve substantially. It was expected that any loss of efficiency experienced in the formative stage of the process of amalgamation would be overcome, and efficiency would eventually exceed existing levels to a large extent. There was also an expectation that a reduction of officers made by removing the duplication of jobs, would make the PAF a more efficient organization.

30 October 1989. The committee stated, during its discourse, that an attempt to amalgamate the Maintenance Branches had been made in 1969-70. It was shelved because at that time only 10 per cent of PAF's engineers were from the CAE, while the rest of the maintenance officers had only done short courses and did not possess a broad-based engineering background. However, by 1989 the situation had changed and 88 per cent of all technical officers were CAE graduates, and their rank structure varied from Flying Officer to Group Captain.

During the presentation, it was evident that the opinions and perceptions of the participants varied drastically. Finally, however, a consensus was reached amongst all the participants and the CAMB was asked to study the proposed organizational set-up, and to examine the advantageous aspects of the organization and function of the Falcon (F-16) system. The Falcon Project is primarily a concept that provides both financial and supply control to the weapon system and takes these functions away from logistics.

The committee was also asked to reconsider the function of Supply Officers and address the factor of cost if the PAF was to have technical officers functioning as Supply Officers as well. The committee had suggested a new name for the branch as General Duty Engineering. However, this was not accepted and the team was asked to propose a new name. The other issue to be addressed was having 'generalist' officers as opposed to 'specialist' officers. Finally, the CAS directed the CAMB to make an exclusive presentation to him and the PSOs by the end of November 1989.

Preliminary Findings of the CAMB

The CAMB submitted its preliminary findings to the Commanders' Conference on

Final Presentation

The presentation to the CAS and his PSOs was made on 27 November 1989 and all the pertinent points were discussed in detail. The CAS agreed with the Committee's suggestion of 'Engineering' as the new name for the branch. He also approved that in future technical officers would perform supply functions as well. A new organization was put up to the CAS based on the F-16 system, which also received provisional approval. The CAS directed the Committee to visit a few European Air Forces in addition to the USAF and study their systems of induction, and the functioning of technical officers, as well as the level of specialization required. Finally, the CAS asked for a proposed timetable for the implementation of the amalgamation, and for a final presentation on the subject. The CAMB gave its final presentation to the Commander's Conference on 30 January 1990. After detailed discussions, the CAS directed that the implementation of the programme should start forthwith. A presentation was also given to all the officers of the technical branches from the rank of Group Captain upwards.

Implications of the Amalgamation
The amalgamation of Maintenance Branches necessitated a review of the implications, such as the ground rules for the preparation of an integrated list of the amalgamated branch, adjustments required in the syllabi at the CAE, additional in-service courses, career progression of the affected officers, and reorganization at the PAF bases and Air Headquarters.

Foreseeable Problems
During the course of its study, the CAMB pointed out a number of problems that could emerge in a 'Common List' after amalgamation of the officers of the existing maintenance sub-branches. Some of these were:

a. Inter-branch seniority—resulting from varying durations of the initial training course.
b. Graduate engineering course officers, who held different temporary/local ranks although their commissioning dates and seniority were the same.
c. Restricted sub-branch initial training for short course officers precluded their cross-utilization in the Engineering branch.
d. The effect on promotion prospects of individual sub-branches because of the existing allotment of vacancies. It was revealed that MT Engg. would be adversely affected at the senior ranks (Wing Commander and above), MT Elect. would be adversely affected at the Squadron Leader level and MT Armt. would gain at all ranks.

The foremost problem, however, that arose in the immediate amalgamation of all branches into a single Engineering branch was the formulation of a fair seniority list that could obviate existing anomalies in promotions, whilst ensuring equal opportunities for the future.

Implementing the Amalgamation Plan
In pursuance of the directive of the CAS issued on 1 March 1990, all the technical branches, excluding the Data Automation Branch, were merged into a unified Engineering Branch. This was a critical task which could lead to serious repercussions, and which could adversely affect the careers of certain officers. The Engineering Branch would, after the amalgamation, have only one DCAS and he would be called DCAS (Engg). Also, the Ministry of Defence (MoD) would have to be approached to make the relevant changes in the appropriate AFIs etc. Since there would be only one air force list for these officers, adjusting seniority was

considered extremely problematic. The Supply and Armament cadre of officers would be totally eliminated and replaced by one set of engineering officers. The training courses at the PAF Academy would have to be changed to accommodate the teaching of both the aerospace and electronic disciplines. The Supply branch would cease further induction, and the present lot of Supply Officers would continue to serve their tenures in the service. Similarly, officers who had joined the air force before the bifurcation of the engineering branches would suffer by having their careers curtailed. It was recommended by the CAMB that no extensions were to be given to these officers regardless of their competence. The careers of these officers had to suffer in the larger interest of a unified engineering branch. Also, cross-training courses were to begin at the Academy for Flight Lieutenants and Squadron Leaders of both the disciplines who were to be responsible for all engineering functions.

A two volume report was prepared after many hours of heated debate, both within the team and the air force in general. The Amalgamation Scheme was very controversial and led to difficulties and insecurity among the Engineering and Supply Officers. The full report was delivered to the CAS, with a recommendation to adhere to the programme spelled out in the report. Unfortunately, the report was not implemented fully, and extensions were given to some officers. This deviation was lamented by the CAMB leader, AVM Abbas Mirza who commented that it was sad to see the institution succumbing to inter-branch rivalry. He believed that the amalgamation would have worked if the commanders had withstood the pressures of vested interests.

Although the Amalgamation Scheme was implemented in 1990—all the selected engineering branches merged and joined in a single seniority list—in the practical sense amalgamation was never implemented as recommended by the CAMB. The respective sub-branches maintained their separate entity up to the rank of Wing Commander and continued working as before. The amalgamation took practical shape only at a few bases from the rank of Group Captain and above where Electronics and Armament officers were deployed as OC Engineering Wing. With the exception of the then Air Commodore (now Air Vice Marshal) Niaz Hussain, an electronics officer who remained Managing Director MRF, Kamra, the situation at depots and factories remained almost unchanged, and officers in all ranks were posted in the areas of their own specialty. So amalgamation, as visualized in the CAMB report, has not been implemented except in the sense that now there is only one engineering branch.

Speaking on this issue, Air Vice Marshal Niaz Hussain, the DCAS (Engg.), commented:

> With amalgamation there was a feeling that personnel would become general duty officers and specialization would go overboard. But this was not so. We have been working in the system for about nine years and specialization is still there, till at least to the rank of Wing Commander. When the officer graduates from the CAE, he goes along a specialized track either in avionics or aerospace field and, until he becomes a senior Wing Commander or a Group Captain, there is no crossing. Amalgamation really comes at the senior level like in the Army, when they wear the Colonel's rank, they do away with their arms and become staff officers. So that is where the amalgamation comes in. OC Engineering Wing can be an aerospace officer, an electronic officer or an armament officer.

Theoretically, the Logistics Branch was also amalgamated in the Engineering branch. However, in practice it was kept separate because the existing group of logistics officers lacked any engineering training, and hence could not go into any engineering function that related to pure engineering and direct operations. What the amalgamation committee foresaw was to do away with the induction of special supply officers and to allow the engineering officers to look after all the aspects of logistics. Some engineering officers were trained and assigned logistics duties but later, the question was raised whether an engineer was wasted when employed as a stock-specialist at a depot. Now the air force is reconsidering the issue and may opt to continue with the specialty of logistics/supply within the Engineering Branch, and induct officers for supply instead of letting graduate engineers go into the supply function.

Reasons for Deviation

Discussing the deviations from the CAMB recommendations, Air Vice Marshal Abbas Mirza, the CAMB leader, was of the opinion that amalgamation of the technical branches in the PAF was strongly favoured by the then CAS, Air Chief Marshal Hakimullah. The CAS was of the opinion that a qualified PAF engineer should be able to perform the role of an engineering officer in the flying squadrons as well as in the second and third line of maintenance. On the other side of the argument was the fact that aerospace and electronics had become so specialized that the two were totally different disciplines. Moreover, the Supply and Armament officers felt threatened in connection with their careers, and feared that they would be phased out over a ten-year period. As such, the idea of amalgamation was seen to be self-destructive by a large majority of the engineering officers.

There was mixed reaction to the decision of amalgamation. The DCAS (Electronics) and the DCAS (Engineering) held divergent views on the subject, and there were disagreements amongst the non-engineering branches as well to the proposed change. Many senior officers felt that the proposal to amalgamate was precipitated by heightened inter-branch rivalry in the higher echelons and could have been dealt with differently. The problem lay with the personalities and not with the system. Any system can be made to work or fail but it has to be ensured that service interests take priority over personalities.

On this issue, Air Vice Marshal Afzal, a former DCAS (Engg.), stated:

> In developed countries, technical re-presentatives of the manufacturers are available to advise and supervise any major activity. As we are sitting thousands of miles away from the manufacturers, and do not have the required technical expertise in the PAF for maintenance of the aircraft, we had the apprehension that if the amalgamation took effect from the grass roots level then we would cease to have access to specialist officers for the maintenance. So, when I became DCAS (Engg.), I decided that I would keep specialization up to the Wing Commander level, and beyond that we would go for selection and amalgamation. I implemented this policy after convincing the CAS that unless we ensured this specialization up to a certain level we would not be able to maintain the highest standards of flight safety. The Air Board and the CAS agreed and we continued with specialization upto the Wing Commander level. Beyond that there was amalgamation. This is what they are following even today.

Advantages

The advantages to be gained from the decision to amalgamate included the expectations of enhanced promotion prospects through the opening up of all assignments for engineering officers, recognition of merit, and the end of branch parochialism. The implementation of this policy opened all the available slots for engineering officers irrespective of specialty. In addition to this, it also removed the anomaly of job duplication and clearly defined the responsibility for maintenance. Amalgamation of technical branches was thus aimed at shaping the branch into a more efficient organizational set-up.

Commenting on the advantages of amalgamation, Air Marshal Aliuddin, the former VCAS, said:

> I remember that in the pre-amalgamation days, we used to talk of 10 per cent NORS being acceptable and 20 per cent to 30 per cent huge 'Red Bars' in the Air Staff Presentations were a matter of routine. These are now down to 2, 3, 4 or 5 per cent, and the availability of these aircraft has never dropped. It was inherent in the concept of amalgamation that there would be optimum utilization of our manpower, and equal opportunity and career progression for all our officers; nobody would drop out in the widely held conviction that engineers of all types were equally capable of doing the job. In my judgement that has happened, although you will keep coming across commanders who will say, 'No, do not give me an electronics officer, give me a technical engineering chap'.

Air Vice Marshal Niaz Hussain, the DCAS (Engg.) was of the opinion that:

> The advantage of amalgamation is that inter-branch rivalry is finished. There used to be a lot of inter-branch rivalry, particularly between the former MT Engg. and MT Elect. officers. As far as career tracks and promotions were concerned, amongst people of the same course, some were Air Commodores and some Group Captains, depending upon the vacancies. By amalgamation, equal opportunity has been given to everybody and so there is cohesion in the branch and it is working exceedingly well. As the number of graduate engineering officers in the Air Force is increasing, serviceability and reliability are improving. Another very important benefit that is visible in our maintenance management are our vastly improved NORS rates. The datum line for NORS is 5 per cent and it is steadily decreasing. The first time it came down lower than 5 per cent was in 1997 and it remained there in 1998 and 1999. So amalgamation has not been bad for the Air Force in so far as two things are concerned: one, it has finished inter-branch rivalry and it is now a cohesive branch; two, there has been a definite improvement in management so far as our weapon systems and our assets are concerned. Serviceability, reliability and NORS rates are really healthy and stable. So amalgamation has been good. Specialization still continues, and R&D still continues in specialized activities in aerospace and avionics, so that advantage is not lost.

The general consensus on the amalgamation of the engineering branches is therefore, that it has proved beneficial for the PAF.

8 NEVER TO BE FORGOTTEN—CARING FOR THE DEDICATED WARRIORS

The PAF allocates a good proportion of available resources to the general well-being of its personnel in order to make their lives comfortable in normal times, as well as in times of distress and emergency. Almost all amenities generally required by an individual or a family, are available within the PAF premises. PAF provides for basic facilities such as health, education, sports, and the general welfare of its personnel, both serving and retired, in order to relieve its rank and file of occupational and domestic pressures, and to enable them to concentrate on their primary task. The PAF also extends the maximum possible attention to the welfare of its retired personnel, by looking into their rehabilitation, and into any other problems they may encounter. It makes certain that their entitlements are disbursed promptly. This strengthens the bonds that retired personnel have with the PAF. Overall, the PAF has tried to fulfil its responsibilities towards both serving and retired personnel.

Medicare

Stringent medical standards are laid down for the selection of officers and enlisted personnel, varying with the requirements of the branch or the trade into which entry is sought. Once a candidate joins the service, he or she needs to maintain the same degree of fitness to progress in the chosen career.

At the same time, the PAF takes very good medical care of its personnel. This is one of the most important obligations of a service that expects the best out of its men and women. Medical services are provided at different levels to achieve this objective.

PAF Hospitals and Health Care Units

PAF Hospitals were constructed and upgraded gradually in terms of manpower, equipment, and capability since independence. However, during the last decade (1988-1998), in addition to the renovation of the PAF Hospital, Masroor, new hospitals were constructed at Sargodha, Rafiqui, Mianwali, PAC Kamra, and Islamabad. The PAF presently has sixteen medical squadrons, which render a wide spectrum of preventive and primary health-care services to the base population, including polio and viral immunization programmes. Six of these squadrons, viz. Malir, Faisal, Korangi Creek, Samungli, Peshawar, and Risalpur, do not have staging hospitals as their locations are attached to the nearby Military or Naval hospitals. All these units have the Base Sick Quarters where less serious medical problems are dealt with. The remaining units have attached staging hospitals, where pathology, radiology, and physiotherapy services are available.

At PAF Hospital, Rafiqui, the Labour Room, Isolation Ward and Radiology Departments were completed in the year 1986 and then, in another effort, the hospital's capacity was increased to ninety-nine beds. PAF Hospital, Mianwali has been functioning efficiently. An ENT specialist was posted there in the year 1990 and three years later, the capacity of this hospital was also raised to ninety-nine beds. The PAF Hospital, Kamra was formally inaugurated in October 1986. Its capacity was increased from 125 to 157 beds in November 1990. This hospital has an excellent operation theatre and an Intensive

Care Unit equipped with modern equipment. The capacity of the PAF Hospital, Masroor was enhanced by ninety-nine extra beds to 299 in 1989. A Children's Ward/Labour Room and a new Operation Theatre (OT) were also constructed in 1991.

PAF Hospital, Islamabad

A fifty-bed PAF hospital was planned in the capital city once the Air HQ shifted to Islamabad. This hospital was constructed in six phases, and was completed on 24 April 1995. It was expanded in March 1998 to house a hundred beds, and its operation theatre became functional in June 1996. Since then, the hospital has started providing surgical treatment in almost all the major specialties. It caters to the needs of both serving and retired PAF personnel stationed at Islamabad, Chaklala, Kahuta and the surrounding areas. The hospital is housed in a new building and has well-equipped departments of medicine, surgery, and gynaecology. The radiology and pathology laboratories also have state-of-the-art equipment. The two fully equipped operation theatres have facilities such as cardiac monitors, pulse oximeter, defibrillators and Cardiopulmonary Resuscitation (CPR) equipment. Thus all types of surgical procedures are undertaken here. PAF Hospital, Islamabad also has a four-bed intensive care unit equipped with the latest technology, which has greatly enhanced its capability.

PAF Hospital, Sargodha

Initially established as a small institution, the PAF Hospital, Sargodha has developed progressively. In 1988, it was upgraded from 240 to 299 beds along with the planned construction of a burns unit, new wards and an officer's block. The project was completed by the end of 1989 when the hospital assumed its present shape with separate female and male wings, an officer's ward, a medical Intensive Treatment & Care (ITC) Unit and a surgical ITC. The burn centre was still under construction at that time. By the end of January 1995, the hospital building was fully established with a separate intensive care unit, both for medical and surgical cases. The burn centre, however, was converted into an Operation Theatre.

New electro-medical equipment was introduced at the time of the upgrade. In 1992, facilities pertaining to Ultrasound, Dialysis, ECG + Cardiac Monitoring System and Radiography were installed. Later, a Physiotherapy department was established with modern equipment. In 1995, a new water supply system for the hospital was also set up.

Between 1996-1998, a complete renovation of the hospital took place, including the replacement of old equipment and the provision of new apparatus. Attention was given to the environment to make it more congenial.

Over the years, the hospital has also made major progress in the academic field. It is now recognized by the College of Physicians and Surgeons of Pakistan as a post-graduate training institute. A conference room and a library have been set up for seminars and academic sessions, and to provide reading material for students. This will help prepare doctors for new challenges in their profession.

PAF Dental Hospitals/Units

The PAF has fourteen dental units located at the PAF Hospital, Islamabad, PAF Academy, Risalpur and PAF Bases Masroor, Peshawar, Sargodha, Chaklala, Korangi Creek, Rafiqui, Mianwali, Kohat,

Lahore, Faisal, Samungli, and Kamra. The No. 11 Dental Unit located at Lahore was established in 1988. The units at Sargodha, Chaklala, Kamra, Masroor, Faisal, and Peshawar have two dental chairs each, and the rest are single-chair units.

Medical Care of PAF's Civilian Employees and their Families

According to the regulations for Medical Service of the Armed Forces 1978, civilian employees of the PAF are also entitled to free medical treatment. The families of employees above grade five are entitled to out-patient facilities only. Although the families of civilian employees in grades one to four are not entitled to out-patient facilities at service hospitals, the PAF continues to provide them with free consultation and treatment. This also includes dispensation of free medicine to the extent that availability of non-public funds will allow.

Research and Analysis

The Directorate of Medical Services undertook an anthropometric survey in 1998. The various positions assumed by air crew during flight provide an important guideline for aircraft design. The measurements of eighteen such positions were taken to study the ejection seat integration, and cockpit layout design. The aim of this was to ensure that the design of the aircrew station was efficient, safe and comfortable for people of varying statures. Ten PAF bases were visited during the course of this study. Pilots up to the rank of Group Captain were included in the study. The percentile data in respect of each measurement was then calculated. This data will contribute greatly to future research and equipment design.

Education

Educational Facilities at PAF Formations

The PAF has several very fine academic institutions established at various PAF bases. These institutes provide quality education to the children of serving and retired PAF personnel. In view of the gradual increase in the strength of the students, there has been a steady expansion in the facilities of the existing institutions. At the beginning of 1988, there were 24,800 students and 1,047 teachers. Now, the total strength of teachers is 2,014 (with 1,007 non-teaching staff) and 42,761 students.

The PAF, at present, maintains twenty-five educational institutions, which have a steady record of progress in both academic as well as extracurricular activities. Owing to the ever-increasing strength of the students, quite a few of these institutions were upgraded to a higher level during the past ten years. However, with the shifting of Air HQ to Islamabad, the PAF Degree College, Peshawar was downgraded to the intermediate level because most of its students shifted to Islamabad with their parents.

These institutions functioned efficiently mainly due to the PAF effort to induct highly qualified teachers and not to compromise on standards.

The introduction of computer education at PAF institutions has been one of the most significant developments of the past decade. Well-equipped computer laboratories have been developed, and properly qualified instructors employed to acquaint the students with computer usage, and its applications in different fields. Students have evinced a keen interest in computer education.

New construction, as well as repair and renovation of the existing buildings was undertaken with a view to providing more

A group of students from PAF Schools and Colleges photographed with the Chinese Cultural Attache, prior to its departure for China on 3 July 1989

space to meet the ever-expanding needs of the PAF's educational institutions. As a result, the student-teacher ratio in the classrooms is now at an acceptable standard. Accommodation has been provided to the teaching staff as well, and a number of PAF bases now have sufficient accommodation, located within the PAF premises, reserved for teachers.

General Education Schemes

First conceived in 1984, this programme was aimed at providing facilities for the professional betterment and self-improvement of the PAF personnel. Several education schemes have been implemented.

Books, dealing with general as well as professional subjects, are provided to PAF staff. Book reviews are one of the most powerful means to inculcate reading habits amongst the PAF officers. According to the book review programme launched in January 1984, every officer is required to review a book of his own choice every year. The copy of the book review is forwarded to the Directorate of Education, Rear Air Headquarters at the end of each applicable quarter on a regular basis.

The Adult Education Programme, another constructive activity, was initiated in February 1994. The programme is open to PAF airmen and civilian employees, and it also provides education to employees from

214

deprived sections of the society. A good number of personnel participate in this programme.

Branches of the PAF Writers' Forum, initiated in recent years at all PAF Bases, serve as a platform for improving the writing skills of officers and help to generate articles for the PAF journal, 'Shaheen'. Since 1984, the PAF Book Club has been providing quality books to PAF officers at a nominal cost to help them maintain a personal library. The club was asked to provide three books to its members every year. So far, it has provided forty-one books to its members. There were more than 3,350 members recorded in December 1998. Complimentary copies of each book are also sent to the President of Pakistan, the Prime Minister and chiefs of the sister Services. Retired officers are also allowed to be members of this club.

Motivation and Religious Affairs

Apostle rouse the believers to the fight. If there are twenty amongst you, patient and persevering, they will vanquish two hundred, if a hundred, they will vanquish a thousand of the unbelievers: for these are a people without understanding.

(Al-Quran, Surah Anfal : 65)

Jehad is one of the pillars of Islam. The Directorate of Motivation and Religious Affairs, Rear Air Headquarters is tasked to assist in maintaining military discipline, and in keeping alive the fighting spirit of the PAF personnel. The Directorate of Motivation backs up the endeavours of the commanders of PAF bases and units, to enhance the overall efficiency of the PAF by improving discipline, morale, motivation, sense of duty, character, and good social conduct. All possible measures are employed to properly educate and train PAF personnel to act as custodians of the trust reposed in them by the nation for the defence of the ideological and geographical boundaries of the country. The PAF operates sophisticated weapons of war but depends more on its men and women to win its battles. It is the spirit of the PAF human resources, and the competence and commitment of its leaders that brings victory even against heavy odds.

The Directorate of Motivation and Religious Affairs is required to:

a. Frame policies of motivation and religious education.

b. Select Religious Teachers (Officers and JCOs), and arrange for their training and administration.

c. Supervise the duties of Religious Teachers, and to advise them as and when required.

d. Provide counselling and guidance for religious, managerial and psychological problems.

e. Deliver lectures on motivational themes, and religious teachings at PAF bases and units on a regular basis.

f. Make arrangements for the religious education of PAF personnel, and their children.

g. Arrange special short courses in Arabic for personnel earmarked for deputation to Arab countries.

At the base level, the Directorate of Motivation and Religious Affairs arranges motivational lectures and, provides Quranic education and knowledge of the *Hadith,* (Islamic Jurisprudence), and religious schooling *(Maktab)* in the PAF mosques. It also conducts regular and special Arabic classes, and arranges for sermons to be delivered to congregations on Friday, Eid-ul-Fitr and Eid-ul-Azha.

215

The PAF in the Sports Arena

Physical fitness among PAF officers and other personnel has always played a vital role in achieving and maintaining a high standard of operational preparedness. It is a fact that organized sports help to inculcate an *espirit de corps*, and improve the physical fitness and mental alertness of a fighting force. The School of Physical Fitness, initially established at Peshawar, was shifted to PAF Base Kohat in 1998. A large physical fitness detachment was set up at PAF Base Korangi Creek and smaller Physical Fitness Teams (PFTs) were established at all the bases. The basic purpose behind this was to provide the bases with their own PFTs in order to promote more interest and achievements in the field of sports.

Realizing the significance of sports, the PAF pursues a policy of promoting sports, both within the Service and at the inter-Services and national level. For this purpose, a Directorate of Sports was established at Rear Air HQ, working under ACAS (Admin.), which provides approximately Rs. 6.2 million annually to PAF bases and units for the improvement of sports facilities. These funds are generated through public funds and the non-public Central Sports Fund to which contributions are made each month by the uniformed personnel of the PAF.

The PAF Sea Survival School was established at PAF Base Korangi Creek in 1986. Its aim is to conduct Sea Survival Courses for the PAF personnel. The unit has conducted twenty-six such courses upto December 1998, with an average intake of 100 officers per course. The Sea Survival School also provides rescue services at the

Student officers practicing fire and shelter making during the Desert Survival Course

216

Student officers on a route march during the Mountain Survival Course

base in emergencies like cyclones, hurricanes and tidal waves.

The PAF Yacht Club, Korangi was commissioned in 1989 to impart sailing and windsurfing training both to service personnel and enthusiasts from the civil sector. The club has conducted forty-eight sailing and windsurfing courses till December 1998, with an average of twelve students per course. A new club hangar was established in 1990 for the storage of rescue crafts and sailboats. It also has classrooms, a workshop, survival bay, etc. In 1993, a water sports stadium was constructed and in 1996 the old Halton Block was renovated and converted into the Club House with new fixtures.

The PAF Yacht Club won the national windsurfing title in 1993, and has since maintained the honour. The club represented Pakistan in the thirteenth Asian Games held in Bangkok in December 1998. The club has also won gold medals in the Inter-Services Sailing Championship. The sailors of the club represented Pakistan at Bahrain in 1989, the UK in 1990, Hong Kong in 1994, Singapore in 1995, China in 1997 and 1998, and Bangkok in 1998.

The Ski Federation of Pakistan

The Ski Federation of Pakistan was established in December 1990. Base Commander, PAF Base Kalabagh is the Secretary of the Federation. The Federation is a member of the Pakistan Sports Board (PSB) and the Pakistan Olympic Association (POA). The Ski Federation of Pakistan is also provisionally affiliated with the International Ski Federation (ISF). The Ski Federation of Pakistan has organized seven National Ski Championships.

The PAF team which won the National Skiing Championship with Air Chief Marshal Farooq Feroze Khan, Chief of the Air Staff at AHQ, Chaklala on 3 April 1991

The Ski Federation represented Pakistan in the third Asian Winter Games held in Harbin, China, in Iran's first 'Ten Days of Dawn' competition in 1996, and in the second 'Ten days of Dawn' in 1998, and in Germany in the German Armed Forces Ski competition. In 1999, it was scheduled to participate in the fourth Asian Winter Games at Kangwon, South Korea, the ninth Asian Children's Ski Championship, Iran, and the Asian Coaches Seminar, Kazakhstan. In addition, every year the Ski Federation of Pakistan organizes basic ski courses for the youth of the country at PAF Base Kalabagh and the PAF Base Naltar. It was scheduled to participate in the Basic Ski Training at Iran in the year 2000.

Other Sports Activities

Annual Inter-Base Competitions in Football, Volleyball, Basketball, Hockey, Cricket, Swimming, Water-polo, Boxing, Squash, Tennis, Golf, Kabaddi, Athletics, Shooting, Skiing and Sailing are organized by the PAF. The Base scoring the maximum points is awarded the 'Strongman Trophy', and a cash prize of Rs. 50,000.

The PAF has made significant contributions in sports at the national level too. The PAF Sports Control Committee has been regularly organizing such National/ International Tournaments as the National Ski Championship, the CAS International Squash Championship, the CAS Open Golf Championship, the CAS Khyber Cup Open

ACM Hakimullah, Chief of the Air Staff, awarding the Strongman Trophy for best performance to the Base Commander, PAF Base Sargodha on 1 March 1989

Tennis Championship, and the CAS Challenge Cup Polo Tournament. In 1988, the CAS Open Windsurfing Championship was also introduced.

PAF athletes have performed admirably in both national and international tournaments. A five-member PAF athletics team comprising of Corporal Technician Samin, Corporal Technician Hamid, Corporal Technician Basharat, Junior Technician Abid, and Senior Aircraftman Afzal represented PAF in the Royal Malaysian Air Force International Half Marathon Race held at Kuala Lumpur. Out of ten countries, the PAF attained the fourth position in the race.

The PAF always encourages promising sportsmen. They are inducted in the PAF, and are provided with facilities to excel in their field.

PAF Golf Club, Islamabad

Air Chief Marshal Jamal A. Khan conceived the idea of the PAF Golf Club, Islamabad in 1987. Squadron Leader Nasim Zafar Baig, Education (now Wing Commander) was tasked with the completion of this project. The L-shaped nine-hole golf course spread over twenty-eight acres of land in front of the PAF Officer's Mess, Islamabad (another project begun by the same air chief) was built under Squadron Leader Nasim's supervision. Tree plantation and landscaping started in February 1988 after the proposed map of the course was formally approved by the CAS.

219

Wing Commander Nasim Z. Baig after winning the Inter-Base Golf Championship Trophy

Air Vice Marshal Sardar M. Asif, the then DCAS (A) was appointed the first President, and Squadron Leader Nasim Zafar Baig, the Pioneer/Honorary Secretary of the PAF Golf Club, Islamabad. The PAF Golf Club is a popular rendezvous for serving and retired PAF officers, as well as for other club members, and guests from the diplomatic corps.

Outstanding Athletes

Squadron Leader (Retd.) Sardar Khan was awarded the Commendation Certificate by the former President of Pakistan (Late General Muhammad Ziaul Haq) for the effective supervision of the National Camp and for improving the standards of the Pakistan football team. The standard of football has been steadily improving in the PAF. In the National Championship, 1998, the PAF football team was the runner-up. From time to time, a number of basketball players from the PAF have been selected for the combined Services Basketball Team. The Pakistan Squash Federation is run by the PAF and the Chief of the Air Staff is its President. Every year, the PAF organizes Squash Tournaments called the 'Chief of the Air Staff Championship'. Since 1990, the PAF Cricket team has been regularly participating in the Patron's Trophy Grade-II. During 1997 and 1998, it had the honour of playing in the finals. Wing Commander Mahmood Ahmed of the PAF was appointed as a member of the Disciplinary Committee in the Board of Control for Cricket in Pakistan (BCCP). The honorary services of Flight Lieutenant (Retd.) M. Riaz Malik and Chief Warrant Officer (Retd.) Mushtaq Ahmad Qazi, Warrant Officer Shafique, Wing Commander Saeed R. Butt and Air Vice Marshal Syed Ata-ur-Rehman are being utilized by the Pakistan Volleyball Federation in different capacities. Recently, in 1998-1999, Senior Technician Zulfiqar represented the national side in the thirteenth Asian Volleyball Championship held at Bangkok, and in the Al-Rashid International Volleyball Tournament held at Dubai (UAE).

Wing Commander Nasim Zafar Baig is a renowned golfer. He was selected as a member of the PAF Golf team in 1984, and represented the PAF in the Inter-Services Golf Championship until 1998. He has bagged seven gold medals, and seven medals for the PAF in the Inter-Services Golf Championships from 1984 to 1997. He has won over a hundred National and Provincial Trophies. Wing Commander Nasim Zafar Baig also won the PAF Golf Championship in 1998. This officer has to his credit the design of the PAF Golf Course, Korangi Creek (1984), and that of the PAF Golf Course, Islamabad (1988), as mentioned earlier.

Providing Shelter—The PAF Housing Schemes

In 1982, the government approved an Army Housing Scheme for out-going officers of the armed forces. The PAF was somewhat late in establishing a set-up to undertake housing projects for its officers. Subsequently, a separate scheme for the PAF officers known as Air Force Officers' Housing Scheme (AFOHS) was approved in October 1992. The AFOHS was formally launched in July 1993 with the establishment of a Directorate of Housing at Air Headquarters. The main task of the Directorate was to ensure housing for retiring PAF officers within the policy framework outlined by the government, and the rules formulated by Air Headquarters.

Development of Construction Sites

On the eve of launching the first batch of construction, only two sites, i.e., Rawalpindi and Faisal (Karachi) were earmarked. The next site to be developed was Tufail Road Lahore, which was established on 31 December 1995. Construction on the Peshawar site was initiated on 1 January 1997. Additionally two new sites, i.e. Walton (Lahore) and Malir (Karachi) have also been introduced. 427 houses were to be completed by the end of December 1999.

Insurance Coverage

The AFOHS members are provided insurance cover against death. An insurance scheme was introduced in 1994 with a nominal monthly contribution of Rs 150 per member. Under this scheme, on the demise of an AFOHS member, a free house is allotted to the widow, and the next of kin of the deceased officer. Coverage is given up to the officer's Struck Off Strength (SOS) date and any amount deposited by the member towards construction cost, is refunded to the next of kin with the exception of the registration fee. Till 31 December 1998, thirty-three houses had been allotted to the widows, and next of kin of deceased AFOHS members.

Establishment of the Directorate of Housing

The Directorate of Housing has been expanding gradually to meet the tasks entrusted to it by the Air Staff. Initially, the Directorate was looking after three projects: the Tarnol Housing Scheme, Fizaia and AFOHS. In August 1996, it was decided to bifurcate the existing set-up into two separate directorates known as the Directorate of Housing and Directorate of Estate Projects. The Directorate of Housing was entrusted with the responsibility of managing the affairs of the AFOHS.

AFOHS Detachments

Detachments of the Directorate of Housing have been established at each AFOHS site to supervise construction activities, and to ensure that the policies of the Air Headquarters are implemented promptly. The detachment is generally headed by a Squadron Leader/Wing Commander who is assisted by a carefully selected staff-member to ensure that the directives emanating from the Air HQ are executed in letter and spirit.

Tarnol Housing Scheme

The Tarnol Housing Scheme, has about 800 residential plots, and is spread over an area

ACM Muhammad Abbas Khattak, Chief of the Air Staff, at the inauguration of the Tarnol Housing Scheme on 25 October 1996

of about 4000 kanals (one kanal is equivalent to 500 square yards). It is one of the larger housing schemes, situated on Fateh Jang Road—about seven kilometres from the Tarnol railway crossing. The scheme was launched to accommodate both officers and airmen. The development work started in 1996. After facing some problems in the initial years, the project is now on track. The Directorate is presently handing over plots, in different phases, so that the allottees may begin construction of their houses.

Fizaia Housing Scheme

Situated on the Lahore-Islamabad Highway, the Fizaia Housing Scheme was launched in 1989. It has 250 residential plots, and is spread over an area of 450 kanals. After the completion of the development work, the construction work began at a reasonably fast pace. The project was successfully completed in all respects and was eventually handed over to the Residents' Committee.

The Pakistan Air Force Women's Association (PAFWA)

The Pakistan Air Force Women's Association (PAFWA) was set up in December 1965 with a view to providing social, educational, and economic support to the lower paid employees of the PAF, and their families. Since its establishment, the Association has contributed significantly towards this end in spite of its limited resources. In April 1985, the Air Board revised the working of the PAFWA, and a new organization plan was formulated to accomplish the objectives and purposes of the Association:

. The social, educational and economic amelioration of low paid employees of the PAF.
. The undertaking of relief work independently, and in collaboration with national agencies, to provide assistance to those in distress, and to provide relief to calamity victims.
. Vocational and educational training programmes.
. Religious and national motivation programmes.

Organization

The new organization of the PAFWA is split into two levels, the Air Headquarters and the Base structures:

Air Headquarters. The Chief of the Air Staff is the Patron-in-Chief of the Association and his wife acts as the President of PAFWA. The wife of the VCAS is designated as the Vice President. ACAS (Admin.) is the Chief Liaison Officer, PAFWA (CLO, PAFWA). A Central Council consisting of PSOs, AOCs and their wives formulate policies and also guide the PAFWA in various activities.

Base. The Base Commander acts as the Patron and his wife as Chairperson Markaz-e-PAFWA. If the Base Commander's wife is not in a position to devote herself to this task, the Base Commander nominates a suitable chairperson in consultation with the CLO, PAFWA. A Local Council, consisting of volunteers or wives of nominated officers, JCOs and airmen is constituted with the approval of the Base Commander. A lady doctor from the base is also inducted as a member. The Local Liaison Officer (LLO,

PAFWA) appointed by the Base Commander co-ordinates the PAFWA activities at the base level.

Institutions of the PAFWA

College of Education for Women, Chaklala

The College of Education (COE) for Women, Chaklala is affiliated with the University of Punjab. The Principal of the COE (W), Chaklala is appointed by the Central Council.

The College offers both graduate and post-graduate degrees in Education, as well as a Certificate in Training (CT). The B.Ed. classes are held in two shifts: morning and evening, with the former accommodating 300 students and the latter over 170 students. The M. Ed. programme, being more recent, had a strength of fifty-two students (1998), all of whom secured first divisions. The overall results of the college have been exceptional and outstanding.

Rehana Jamal Mujahida Academy, Peshawar

Established in 1989, the Rehana Jamal Mujahida Academy (RJMA) is located at Peshawar. The person in charge of the Academy is appointed by the Central Council. The administrative and functional orders relating to the Academy are issued by the CLO, PAFWA who also acts as the Patron of the Academy.

The Academy conducts three-month courses in the areas of cooking and baking, cutting and flower/feather work, art and painting, car driving, typing, English language, beauty care, computers and swimming. A good number of students enrol for these courses, and the results have been outstanding.

Begum Farzana Farooq Feroze Khan, unveiling the plaque of the newly constructed block at the College of Education for Women, Chaklala on 19 February 1994

Begum Riazuddin Sheikh with the Principal and other faculty members at the inaugural ceremony of the first M.Ed. course held on 1 September 1998 at the PAF College of Education for Women, Chaklala

Begum Pervez Musharraf giving away the award to Miss Sadia Sher Khan at the convocation of a B. Ed. course held at the PAF College of Education for Women, Chaklala on 25 April 1999

Mrs. Oliver M. Rana Singhe wife of the Commander, Sri Lanka Air Force visiting the PAF College of Education for Women, Chaklala on 9 October 1997

PAF Finishing School Chaklala

The PAF Finishing School for Women was established at the PAF Base Chaklala in March 1996 to impart high quality, modern, and sophisticated education to selected young ladies. The education aims at developing in the students the art of presenting themselves confidently, improving communication skills, and enhancing their knowledge of contemporary subjects. The PAF Finishing School for Women renders a valuable service to empower women, in recognition of their right to acquire varied skills, to shoulder their responsibilities with expertise and ease.

Seven courses have been conducted since March 1996, and a total of 163 students have successfully graduated from the institute.

Mashal-e-Ilm School/PAFWA Primary School, Badaber

Mashal-e-Ilm School at PAF Base Chaklala and the PAFWA Primary School, PAF Camp Badaber are under the functional control of Central PAFWA. However, the administrative control of both the institutions lies with the Base Commander, PAF Base Chaklala and OC, Rear Air HQ (Unit), Peshawar, respectively. These schools offer primary education to the children of lower paid PAF employees.

PAF Schools for Special Education

Schools of Special Education have been established at PAF Bases Faisal, Masroor, Sargodha, Lahore, Chaklala and Peshawar to cater to the needs of disabled children.

Marakaz-e-PAFWA

There are eighteen Marakaz-e-PAFWA offices, one at each Base. The local Markaz-e-PAFWA endeavours to organize various educational and vocational training courses depending upon the particular needs. The

Begum Samina Abbas Khattak inaugurating the PAF Finishing School at Chaklala on 31 July 1996

226

Special children with Mrs Rukhsana Nazir, Principal, PAF College of Education, and the principals of other academies and schools, during a visit to the PAF Junior Montessori, Chaklala on 11 August 1998

Marakaz-e-PAFWA regularly conducts classes in knitting, cutting, stitching, embroidery, typing, adult education and Quranic education.

PAFWA Montessories

The methodologies pertaining to Montessori teaching are considered very apt for pre-school children. Consequently, eighteen PAFWA montessories have been set up at various bases. These are placed under the functional control of the Central PAFWA, but their administrative control is exercised by the respective bases. The montessories at Islamabad, Chaklala, and Lower Topa were opened after 1988, however, the one at PAF Camp Badaber was reopened in 1998. The montessories at the other bases were opened before the decade under study.

Exhibitions and Achievements

The PAFWA holds a variety of activities, throughout the year, to enrich the quality of life at the bases and to keep its basic objectives alive. All the activities mentioned below reflect a strong and positive image of the PAF and attract a large number of people:

Annual Exhibition and Fair. The Annual Handicraft Exhibition and Fair helps to raise funds to sustain the operations of the PAFWA. The function is held strictly in accordance with policies which lay down the parameters for these events.

Talent Exhibition. Since 1990, the PAFWA has held a talent exhibition every year in Islamabad. The basic purpose of this

Begum Hakimullah distributing prizes at the Children's Day celebrations at PAF Base, Chaklala on 21 October 1990

exhibition is to revitalize the role of women in the PAF. The PAFWA strives hard, through these exhibitions, to highlight the creative talents of the PAF ladies.

PAFWA Literacy Programme. This scheme was initially launched at Chaklala, and later adopted throughout the PAFWA. The main objective of the programme was to provide basic education to those families and dependants of PAF employees who did not receive regular schooling. PAFWA fulfils this aim in collaboration with the Prime Ministers' Literacy programme for women.

PAFWA Stalls at Youm-e-Fizaia. PAFWA Stalls were earlier arranged at all PAF Bases on the occasion of 'Youm-e-Fizaia', (Air Force Day, celebrated on 7 September each year), but since 1997, these are set up only at the major bases of the PAF, i.e. Chaklala, Peshawar, Masroor, Rafiqui and Sargodha. These are very well-attended.

PAF Community Centre, Islamabad. The PAF Community Centre was established at Air Headquarters, Islamabad on 11 October 1997. The Centre offers courses to the PAF families in aerobics, cooking, cutting and stitching, knitting, machine embroidery, hand embroidery, and beauty care.

The Celebration and Observance of National and Religious Occasions. National and religious occasions are normally organized and observed at all the PAFWA Branches in accordance with the Central

228

Begum Samina Abbas Khattak giving away prizes to the young artists of PAF schools and colleges at an exhibition of their paintings held at the National Art Gallery, Islamabad on 15 October 1995

The former Prime Minister of Pakistan, Mohtarma Benazir Bhutto, inaugurating the Pakistan Air Force ladies' talent exhibition held at the PAF Officers Mess, Islamabad on 2 December 1995

Council's guidelines imparted by CLO, PAFWA.

Other PAFWA Welfare Measures (1988-1998)

During the past decade, Rs. 2,160,000 were paid as a one-time grant to lower level employees of the PAF from the Central PAFWA fund. Rs. 321,000 were spent on the purchase of hearing aids for PAF personnel. Rs. 75,814 were given in scholarships to the children of PAF personnel, and an amount of Rs. 3,646,000 was distributed amongst the lower level employees, both Muslim and Christian, of Air HQ Chaklala/Islamabad and Rear Air Headquarters, Peshawar, on the occasions of Eid-ul-Fitr and Christmas. In addition, quilts worth Rs. 475,000 were purchased for distribution amongst the lower level employees of PAF Bases, Samungli, Lower Topa, Sakesar, Kalabagh, and Cherat. Rs. 4,585,154 were donated out of the Central PAFWA fund to several PAF Schools and other organizations to assist in their day-to-day operations.

Shaheen Foundation

Established in 1977, the Shaheen Foundation has consistently striven to enhance and provide welfare benefits both to the serving and the retired personnel of the PAF, including civilians and their dependants, through the funds generated by its industrial and commercial enterprises. A number of profitable ventures have thus been launched, maintained and upgraded with time. Some of the main features of the Foundation's welfare programme are the provision of job opportunities to the retired PAF personnel, the grant of scholarships to the dependants of beneficiaries, lump sum grants in case of death or injury to a beneficiary, and the construction of houses for the families of beneficiaries.

Shaheen Airport Services

The Shaheen Airport Services (SAPS) was established in 1982 with the aim of extending ground handling services to scheduled and non-scheduled airlines at Karachi Airport. It has since expanded its operations to include Lahore, Islamabad and Peshawar. SAPS is a member of the IATA Ground Handling Council. It provides wide-ranging services to several international carriers. In addition, it also provides complete ground support to almost all the domestic airlines with the exception of PIA, which has its own facilities. It also extends its services to visiting aircraft from friendly countries. The SAPS has its own workshop for maintaining a high state of equipment serviceability and reliability. Besides the provision of ground handling equipment, SAPS has also established an airfreight unit, a car rental service, a meet and assist service, and a ground engineering service. SAPS has set up modern terminals for imported cargo at Karachi and Lahore to enhance its warehousing and handling capabilities. An Export Hangar had also been constructed at Lahore in 1997. This provides an effective outlet to air bonded export from the dry ports at Sialkot, Faisalabad and Lahore. SAPS has emerged as a very successful venture. Nearly 60 per cent of Shaheen Foundation's total revenues come from SAPS.

Shaheen Air International

When the government deregulated the airline industry, the Foundation launched Shaheen Air International (SAI) in 1993 as a joint venture with a concern in the private sector. Like any new commercial venture, Shaheen

Secretary Defence, Lt. General Iftikhar Ali Khan (Retd.) and AVM Nafees Ahmed Najmi (Retd.), Managing Director of the Shaheen Foundation, with officials of the Shaheen Air International (SAI) at Islamabad airport on 21 December 1997 to mark the resumption of SAI flights

Air met with many difficulties in the beginning. To exist under the shadow of a well-established, government owned airline like the PIA and to compete with it, when it was dictating aviation policy, was an uphill task. The main factor which adversely affected the commercial performance of private airlines in Pakistan, at the time of their inception, was that PIA enjoyed many privileges like tax exemption, monopoly on foreign routes, and full government support, all of which were not available to private airlines.

However, within a short span of time, and in spite of many odds, SAI gained popularity among business executives and discerning travellers due to its efficient service, both on ground and aboard the aircraft. On 23 October 1994, SAI was granted the status of Second National Carrier, which enabled it to commence international operations. In January 1996, the Shaheen Foundation acquired the shares of its joint venture partner, Akber Group, which held 49 per cent of the shares and thus the airline became a fully owned enterprise of the Foundation. With complete control of the SAI, the management embarked on restructuring the organization with an emphasis on redefining the human resource requirements, fleet structure, route planning, financial outlays, etc. The basic objective of undertaking such an exercise was to increase the airline's productivity and revenue generation while maintaining its original standard and dynamism. The airline has operated aircraft like Boeing 737-400, B-707, Airbus 300, and TU-154. This would not have been possible without possessing a pool of trained manpower from a proper aviation-related

231

discipline. Till December 1998, Shaheen Air International had transported over 500,000 passengers with a load factor of over 80 per cent. The SAI has had its ups and downs but its performance is constantly improving, and it has been breaking even for some time now.

Shaheen Air Cargo

Shaheen Air Cargo (SAC) was established in 1993, primarily to increase the cargo uplift capacity out of Pakistan in order to serve the national export needs. Shaheen Air Cargo is one of the two national freighter operators with international destinations. It provides time-effective services at competitive rates. It has also flown chartered flights to transport United Nations peace-keeping troops to Bosnia, Cambodia, Haiti and Somalia. To cater to the growing needs of the cargo sector, the cargo Head Office was moved to Lahore, with branch offices at Rawalpindi and Karachi. Shaheen Air Cargo has also operated chartered flights to the Commonwealth of Independent States (CIS), Sri Lanka, Russia, South Africa and the Middle East. In the near future, the SAC will operate a domestic express air cargo service to link major towns in Pakistan.

Shaheen Aerotraders

Shaheen Aerotraders was established in 1988. The subsidiary which represents foreign principals, is involved in import and export, and arranges bonded warehouse facilities for aircraft parts imported from China. The firm is actively involved in manufacturing upgrading, refurbishing, overhauling and repairing electrical and electro mechanical high-tech equipment. Shaheen Aerotraders represent well known foreign principals including GEC Marconi, UK; Information Handling Services, USA; Ilford, UK; and Grinel, South Africa. Its dedicated efforts have now resulted in the growth of services in Avionics, Engineering and Shaheen Pharma.

Shaheen Insurance

In 1996, the Shaheen Foundation launched an insurance company with a paid-up capital of Rs. 60 million. Its Head Office is at Karachi, and its regional offices are located at Islamabad, Lahore, Faisalabad and Peshawar. The company has established a good reputation in the market and has become one of the better known insurance companies in Pakistan. It has entered into joint partnership with Hollard Insurance Company of South Africa, which has worldwide interests in insurance, shipping, and banking. Shaheen Insurance also provides cover to Shaheen Air International, and Shaheen Air Cargo. Furthermore, it may introduce new products like health insurance, legal insurance, etc., in collaboration with its partners from South Africa.

Shaheen Complex

The Foundation decided to go into real estate development as a source of continuing financial returns to support its welfare activities. The first Shaheen Complex was constructed in Karachi during the 1980s at the busy intersection of M. R. Kayani Road and Dr Ziauddin Ahmed Road. After SAPS it is the second main contributor to the Shaheen Foundation's total revenue. The second complex is presently under construction at Lahore. This will be a nine-storey commercial building. Similar complexes will also be constructed in other cities in due course of time.

Shaheen Knitwear

Since 1981, Shaheen Knitwear had been progressing gradually. Anticipating the expansion of exports to Europe, and the increased workload of local 'cut-to-pack' contracts, Shaheen Knitwear took steps to cater to this requirement, and a lot of maintenance, upgrading and purchase of new stitching and knitting tools was initiated. The present export earning of Shaheen Knitwear is estimated at $ 1.2 million per year.

Hawk Advertising and Communication Consultants

Since 1977, Hawk has grown into a sound advertising agency. It is equipped to undertake all kinds of assignments pertaining to the field of advertising. Skilled and qualified executives with adequate experience and innovative ideas run all its departments. It is an All Pakistan Newspapers Society (APNS) accredited agency, which maintains an impressive list of satisfied clients; most of them have been with it for a reasonably long time. In keeping with modern market compulsions, Hawk has grown countrywide. With its Head Office at Karachi, and branches at Lahore and Islamabad, Hawk is acknowledged as one of the leading advertising agencies in the country in terms of the quality of its work.

Shaheen Systems

Shaheen Systems was established in 1989 to provide professional computer expertise to Pakistan's computer users. Shaheen Systems employs a team of well-trained, and experienced professionals, and offers a host of services to its clients. Besides developing software, it has its own workshops for the maintenance and repair of computer hardware and allied equipment and photo-copiers. During the last decade, Shaheen Systems has been engaged in conducting computer literacy courses at PAF Bases besides working on a large contract to develop Computer Based Training Systems for the PAF.

Shaheen Pay TV

Shaheen Pay TV was initiated in 1995 as a joint venture between Shaheen Foundation and a private consortium. It emerged as the first cable TV network in Pakistan, and has a state-of-the-art multi-point, multi-channel distribution technology. The project provides an attractive opportunity to the private sector to develop programmes of international quality, which will also be available on satellite. The project has, however, been shadowed by certain doubts about the transparency in the award of licences to its partners. The project still has immense prospects financially. Efforts are in hand to resolve the issues related to share-holding.

FM-100

FM-100 is Pakistan's first 24-hour music channel established as a joint venture with the private sector in 1995. Broadcasting from Karachi, Lahore and Islamabad with its unique signature tune, 'Assalam-o-Alaikum Pakistan', the channel became an instant success with listeners. It presents a delightful array of scintillating music catering to the taste of a variety of listeners.

Employment in the Country and Abroad

One of the major welfare activities of the Shaheen Foundation was to facilitate employment of retired PAF officers, airmen, and its civilian employees within the country and abroad. The Foundation maintains a pool of highly disciplined, trained and experienced retired PAF personnel on its waiting list, and makes their services available to meet manpower requirements for its clients. The Foundation has already provided manpower to a number of air forces in the Middle East and many local organizations. The UAE Air Force Selection Team visited Pakistan in August 1998 to induct retired PAF personnel. It selected 693 airmen of which the first batch of seventy-eight technicians was sent to the UAE on 28 October 1998. A total of 1,250 retired personnel have been sent to various destinations by the Foundation so far. The registration of ex-airmen has been computerized to promptly meet the specific requirements of the clients. The Foundation continues to strive for the rehabilitation of a large pool of retired PAF officers and airmen with varying job specialties.

Scholarships
The Shaheen Foundation awards substantial amounts in scholarships every year to children of PAF personnel—both serving and retired. It provides scholarships and merit certificates to outstanding students of classes IV to IX studying at both the PAF and the government schools located within the PAF Bases. About 2,300 students receive these scholarships every year.

Shaheen Fellowship Scheme
Through this scheme, financial support is being provided to the deserving children of serving and retired personnel below the rank of Squadron Leader, in the officer cadre, JCOs/Airmen, and equivalent PAF civilian employees. The fellowship is also awarded to those who obtain admission in a professional institution affiliated with a recognized Pakistani university in the disciplines of BE, BCS and BBA. During 1998, seventy-eight applications were received out of which thirty top students were selected for annual scholarships of Rs. 20,000 each. The daughter of a Shaheed (martyr) was also selected as a special case.

Shaheen Excellence Award
A lump sum amount of Rs. 50,000 is given to the children of serving or retired PAF personnel who secure first position in the SSC or HSC examinations from any Board of Intermediate and Secondary Education in Pakistan.

Hajj Expenses
Every year the Shaheen Foundation provides funds for four low-paid PAF civilian employees selected by the CAS to perform Hajj. Additionally, Shaheen Foundation provides articles like Ahram, Aba, baggage stickers, name tags, and tag clips to the PAF Hajj contingent.

Medical Welfare Scheme (MWS)
The MWS was launched in 1986 to provide coverage to serving officers and airmen against death and medical down-categorization. The scheme provides a cover of Rs. 100,000 to officers against a monthly premium of Rs. 55, and Rs. 33,000 to airmen against a premium of Rs. 18. During 1998, a sum of Rs. 1,266,000 was paid to fourteen persons as compensation.

Strategy for Future Growth
In its formative years, the Foundation went into diversified fields, and did not develop a long-term strategy. It has now decided to expand into areas of its strength, and avoid certain fields where it does not have the requisite expertise. Its core business and future growth is likely to be in aviation-

related projects, and in services rather than industry. The Shaheen Foundation has also started arranging foreign investment for large infrastructure projects.

As a first step in the education sector, Shaheen Foundation established the Shaheen Public School in Islamabad at the end of 1998. The school management is committed towards achieving the high standards, and new concepts involved in a modern education system.

The Shaheen Foundation has always been consistent in its effort to explore new avenues of growth. It has been the endeavour of the Foundation to identify and make long-term investments in profitable ventures of national importance including airline, air cargo, airport handling, knitwear, real estate, computer and insurance. Today, Shaheen Foundation stands as one of the major contributors to the national economy.

The Foundation continues to increase its welfare activities. Education, health care and post-retirement rehabilitation are its major areas of focus.

PAF Retired Officers Association (PAFROA)

The PAFROA began as a volunteer organization on the personal initiative of retired officers. The following regional PAFROAs have been functioning since the dates mentioned against each:

	City	Date of inception	
a.	Lahore	02 January	1990
b.	Peshawar	12 April	1992
c.	Karachi	13 February	1993
d.	Rawalpindi/ Islamabad	07 September	1994

In 1994, the Secretary, PAFROA Rawalpindi/Islamabad suggested to the then DCAS (Admin.) that the Association should be organized on the pattern of the Royal Air Force Association. He received a positive response, and the matter was further pursued. Consequently, the Association was given the official patronage of Air Headquarters. A Central Coordination Committee was set up at Air Headquarters under the chairmanship of Air Marshal Aliuddin, the then DCAS (P) and later DCAS (Admin.) in 1995. At present, the chairmanship is with DCAS (Admin.). Since 1995, the Committee has been holding its meetings regularly. The main objectives of PAFROA are:

a. To provide a forum to PAF retired officers and their families for social get-togethers and interaction.

b. To discuss matters of common interest and, where possible, to assist one another in an individual capacity.

c. To identify the problems faced by officers after retirement, and where necessary, to seek assistance from Air Headquarters.

Each set-up has an elected President and a Secretary to run its routine affairs. Other office bearers are also elected. The regional PAFROAs hold their meetings regularly. Matters of common interest, requiring the assistance of Air Headquarters, are referred to the Central Coordination Committee for consideration and further action. So far, a number of problems faced by retired officers have been successfully sorted out.

PAFROA's regular meetings, and consistent efforts to pave the way for the welfare of the retired officers have yielded some useful results. Matters related to the provision of accommodation for retired officers in the PAF messes all over Pakistan have been approved. Provision of dental facilities by PAF Dental Units and a 50 per cent concession on travel by Shaheen Air International (SAI) for families of retired personnel has been approved quite recently. The burial arrangements for PAF retired officers and their spouses in the PAF graveyards have also been authorized by Air Headquarters. Shaheen Foundation has arranged a limited number of plots for retired PAF officers in different Housing Societies.

Cases regarding pension and grant of concession to them as senior citizens are currently being processed by the government. Additionally, all PAF units and agencies have been advised to extend maximum respect and courtesy to the retired officers while corresponding with them. These are but a few areas of achievement. Much more is expected in the coming years.

Lady Officers' Winter Working Uniform   Lady Officers' Summer Working Uniform

Air Officers' Working
Dress

Officers' Ceremonial
Uniform

Officers' Winter Working
Uniform

Officers' Mess Kit

Airmen's Summer
Working Uniform

Airmen's Winter Working
Uniform

PAF Musician Uniform

9 THE TEAMS

Commands and Bases

Commands, Bases, Wings, Units and Squadrons are the sinews of the PAF and their role in the accomplishment of the Air Force Mission is central. Any significant change in their tasks, any development in their operational capabilities, or achievement in the air or on the ground, directly affects the Service as a whole. These entities are, in fact, the strength and the glory of the PAF. They function round the clock, to their maximum potential, to help maintain a high quality of work in the Service. Owing to the unexpected events of the decade between 1988-1998, these constituent elements of the PAF had to work under considerable stress, and they did so with constant readiness and dedication. It is, however, a pleasure to record that most, if not all of them, rose to a level that exceeded expectations, and helped make the PAF what it is today.

Air Defence Command

In October 1991, after the reorganization of Air Commands, Air Defence Command was rejuvenated and took control of the air defence system to make it more responsive to the future requirements of national air defence. The operational and functional control of all air defence units, that was earlier vested in the Regional Air Commands after their creation in 1982, reverted to Air Defence Command. This change-over was introduced during the tenure of the then AOC Air Defence Command, Air Vice Marshal Anwar-ul-Haq Malik.

After the reactivation of Air Defence Command, a total of seventy-nine routine and two major air defence exercises viz. High Mark-93 and High Mark-95 were conducted between June 1991 and December 1998. In the wake of the nuclear tests conducted by India in May 1998, exercise Bedaar-98 was also carried out, deploying all the air defence assets at their operational sites, within the shortest possible time.

Apart from exercising operational and functional control over air defence units through Sector Headquarters, another important function of the Command is to categorize air defence weapon controllers for the award of 'A' and 'B' categories. The Central Categorisation Board and Evaluation Team (CCB & E) was initially established at Air Headquarters (Directorate of Air Defence) in 1975. In July 1977, it was placed under the Headquarters Air Defence Command. In April 1990, the CCB&E was once again moved back to the Directorate of Air Defence. Finally in August 1994, the organization of CCB&E was reinstituted under the Headquarters Air Defence

Command. The CCB&E team is headed by a President, who is assisted by two members viz. Member Categorisation, and Member Evaluation. The team regularly visits all Air Defence units for the award of 'A' and 'B' categories. This classification is based on theory and practical tests. The team also monitors the local categorization i.e. Category 'C' tests in GCI units and operational status in SOCs and SAM units.

The Air Defence Command carries out studies and arranges seminars to evolve new procedures, tactics, techniques, and to inculcate professionalism in the ADWC officers. In October 1992, a tri-Services study was carried out to analyze the air threat to Pakistan in the backdrop of the Gulf War. In October 1993, a comprehensive study was conducted, the object of which was to visualize future Air Defence requirements of Pakistan in the year 2000 and beyond (PADS-2000). The team was headed by Air Vice Marshal Parvaiz Mehdi Qureshi, and included senior officers from ADWC and the Engineering Branches as members. In February 1997, a seminar on national defence against air attacks and C^3I/C^3 CM systems was held. Finally, a presentation on the Evaluation of Air Defence Units and career planning of ADWC officers was conducted. High level defence delegations from China, Saudi Arabia, Iran, Jordan, and the Philippines visited Headquarters Air Defence Command during the period.

Regional Air Commands

The functions of policy formulation, and the monitoring of its execution had remained vested in the Air Headquarters till the early 1980s. In the absence of any operational field formations, such as the Corps in the Army, contacts between the PAF and the Pakistan Army and Navy existed mainly at the headquarters level. Consequently, the required coordination and close understanding between the fighting elements of the three Services did not develop. This led to serious problems and some unfortunate set-backs in the operations during the two wars with India.

The PAF had grown into a sizeable tactical Air Force by the early 1980s, and by the mid-1980s, it had a strategic role as well. This necessitated a separation of functions of policy formulation and its execution. This organizational change was successfully experimented through the establishment of the Southern Air Command on 25 January 1981. This step proved beneficial in promoting the required level of coordination among the fighting elements of the three Services. The formation of Regional Air Commands in northern Pakistan had also become essential since areas in this region constituted the most sensitive territory, and the venue for major land battles during the two wars with India. Since these territories faced threats from two sides, a close understanding between the fighting elements of the PAF and the Army became an even more critical imperative of Pakistan's national strategy.

It was proposed, therefore, that the Northern and Central Air Commands be created from within the existing establishment and resources of the PAF. Formal government approval for their creation was received on 17 May 1982. Thus, the Northern Air Command and the Central Air Command came into being on 1 July 1982.

The area of responsibility of each Regional Air Command generally conformed to the existing boundaries of the groups belonging to the Pakistan Army Corps. Initially, the Air Commands were provided with manpower and resources from within the existing establishment, but as anticipated, this directive was subsequently reviewed.

The Regional Air Commands were to exercise operational and functional control over the specified Bases/Satellites, Sector Headquarters, early warning and GCI units, Sub-Control Centres, MOUs, SAM squadrons, and balloon defences. Besides, AAA of the Pakistan Army, Navy and Janbaz Forces were to be integrated into the air defence system.

Policy formulation, and the direction and control of the entire PAF continued to rest with Air Headquarters, in keeping with the principle of the 'Indivisibility of Air Power'. The conduct of operational training, liaison with counterparts of the other Services and the conduct of any other role assigned by Air Headquarters was to form the basic role of Regional Air Commands. The role and task thus stipulated for the Regional Air Commands were:

a. During peacetime, they will conduct all air operations in accordance with the policies of Air Headquarters, and coordinate tactical operations with Army/ Navy formations in their respective areas of responsibility. The Commands will review, and when needed, evolve new tactics and concepts of operations, and suggest organizational changes.

b. During war, each Command will operate as Regional Battle Headquarters of one central command i.e. the Chief of Air Staff's Command Operations Centre (COC), and the CAS will assume direct command and control of all PAF resources in order to fully exploit the flexibility of the available air power. Each RAC will operate as a regional battle headquarters and be in effect an extension of the Chief of the Air Staff's COC.

The Northern Air Command

The headquarters of the Northern Air Command were established at Peshawar. For the purpose of monitoring air defence operations in its area of responsibility, SOC Sakesar was first linked with NAC in the manual mode, but was later replaced with the automated SOC North at Chaklala.

Soon after its inception, the Northern Air Command was involved in a hot situation involving active air operations. On the eastern side, it faced the challenging task of defending the Kahuta Complex against possible surprise air strikes by the enemy. This involved round the clock vigil, high ADA status, random CAPs and the highest alert state of surface to air weapons. A colossal effort was invested in terms of air surveillance and weapon deployment, to create deterrent defences. F-16s from Sargodha and other interceptor squadrons from Minhas and Peshawar provided fighter CAPs while Crotale SAMs and AAA constituted terminal defences. Air surveillance was provided by a CRC deployed near Chaklala, linked up with its chain of low-looking MPDRs deployed along the eastern border from Muzzafarabad to Mangla. To ensure detection in the valleys, extensive reconnaissance was carried out throughout Azad Kashmir for the deployment of radars at the selected sites. This was an extremely challenging and dangerous task to accomplish in the difficult terrain. It was only the motivation and dedication of the personnel involved that made it possible to execute the whole task without any mishaps. The ADGE so established, the aggressive use of interceptors on CAP, and the state of high readiness successfully deterred the enemy from embarking on any misadventure.

The western front had been active for almost three years— since the 1979 Russian intervention in Afghanistan. The hot pursuit operations by the Afghan Air Force accross Pak border forced Pakistan to conduct wartime air operations during peacetime. For more than ten years, the PAF had to fight an undeclared war. In all, there were 2,476 air violations by Russo-Afghan jet fighters, helicopters, and transport aircraft, involving 7,589 aircraft—(the summary of these violations is given in Appendix 'A'). It was a gigantic task to support the forward radars and MOUs located in the toughest and the unfriendliest terrain. There were also fifteen defections involving thirteen Afghan and two Russian pilots—(the details of the aircraft that landed in Pakistan are given in Appendix 'B').

The magnitude of violations warranted a continuous vigil for the timely detection and interception of intruders. Despite the large network of radars, the entire air space could not be lit up because of the hilly terrain. The Afghan helicopters exploited the hilly contours and valleys to avoid detection, and mostly got away without being challenged. Mounting of round the clock CAPs was an expensive option, one that the PAF could ill afford. However, despite all constraints, the PAF did manage to contain air violations of jet fighters to a large extent. The list of PAF Claims/Awards during the Afghan war is given in Appendix 'C'.

The situation had eased considerably after the withdrawal of Russian forces from Afghanistan. A significant reduction in air space violations was observed in 1989. A total of forty-seven air violations occurred in 1989 as compared to the 201 in 1988. Almost all of these were close border violations with a penetration of 2-3 NM, and they took place during a turn, while operating over or close to the border. Despite the large reduction in enemy air activity, vigilance was continued in order to counter violations. Interceptors were scrambled whenever the enemy aircraft reached the Line of Defence (5 NM short of the border). Due to shallow enemy penetrations of only 2-3 NM, however, no engagement took place throughout 1989. The pattern remained the same during 1990. A planned withdrawal of air defence radars and MOUs was also affected as part of a de-escalation plan implemented in 1990.

The Central Air Command

The Central Air Command was assigned different peacetime and wartime roles. Its most significant peacetime role is to establish and maintain close contact with the Army at a senior command level, so as to facilitate a mutual understanding of each other's operational environments, plans, and tasks. The Command was also to concentrate on achieving the highest possible operational efficiency of the combat elements and related resources placed under its jurisdiction.

The wartime role of the Central Air Command required it to operate as a regional battle headquarters, and in effect an extension of the Chief of Air Staff's Command Operations Centre (COC).

The Central Air Command started functioning with effect from 1 July 1982. In the ensuing organizational restructuring, the air defence elements in the field were placed under the Regional Air Commands, and Headquarters Air Defence Command was left with monitoring functions only. The post-1982 reorganization did not take into account the fact that the Air Defence network had to work alike during peace and war. After exhaustive review and deliberations, the operational and functional control of the air defence organization was transferred to Headquarters Air Defence Command with effect from 1 September 1991.

Headquarters CAC functioned as an interim measure from PAF Base, Sargodha in the CCS building from July 1982 to 5 September 1987. However, on 6 September 1987, the CAC Headquarters shifted to its permanent location near Sargodha. Ever since the formation of the Central Air Command, it has very effectively implemented and executed the Air Headquarters policies, and ensured the necessary coordination and understanding between the fighting elements of the two Services. The Command has also planned and conducted several exercises to enhance the war preparedness of its bases and satellites.

The Southern Air Command

The Southern Air Command has been a model of inter-Service cooperation. It has been closely interacting with the Pakistan Army and the Pakistan Navy. Successive AOCs have progressively enhanced this co-operation. During the last decade, numerous naval exercises were held with active PAF support.

The operational exercises in which the SAC has been actively involved are High Mark-93, High Mark-95, the Inspired Alert series of exercises in collaboration with the US Navy, Live Missile Firing, Fire Power Demo-89, ISAC-96, and others.

The inauguration of the PAF Museum at PAF Faisal was held on 14 August 1997, as part of PAF's Golden Jubilee Celebrations. The then Chief of Air Staff, Air Chief Marshal Muhammad Abbas Khattak was the Chief Guest. Ever since this project was conceived, the SAC had been spearheading the effort to complete it in time.

An Air-to-Air and Surface-to-Air Missile Firing Camp was conducted at Army Air

Defence Range, Sonmiani, from 16 April to 26 April 1998, under the supervision of Headquarters SAC. In May 1998, PAF Bases Shahbaz, Sukkur and Mirpurkhas were activated prior to the nuclear tests conducted by Pakistan.

In September 1998, Exercise Pathfinder was conducted at Air Headquarters. Both NAC and SAC had been tasked to make presentations on an issue of vital national importance in light of the changed strategic environments in the region. As a result of the study, valuable suggestions were made to Air Headquarters for the formulation of an air strategy for the coming years.

During 1998, the SAC arranged a seminar for the officers of 5 Corps and 4 Air Defence Division. The purpose of the seminar was to highlight the aerial threat and the envisaged air operations in the South. DGAI presented a briefing on the IAF and its capabilities, in the year 2000 and beyond. This was followed by a detailed presentation on the nature of air operations likely to take place in the South, in any future conflict. Detailed discussion and a question and answer session, chaired by the AOC, SAC followed the presentation. About 250 officers of 5 Corps and No. 4 Air Defence Division attended the seminar. They included the Corps Commander and most of the senior field commanders. In his closing remarks, the Corps Commander acknowledged the initiative of the SAC, which had benefited a large number of officers.

The SAC continues to receive a large number of high-ranking foreign delegations the whole year around.

PAF Base Sargodha

PAF Base Sargodha has traditionally housed the PAF's most sophisticated weapon systems. During the 1965 war, it had both F-86 and F-104 squadrons. Similarly, the

French Mirage weapon system found a place at this base soon after its induction. Even now, two F-16 squadrons, the Combat Commanders School, and a Rescue Squadron are located on this Base. During the Afghan war, this base was in a state of round the clock alert that lasted a decade, to deal with air violations by the Russo-Afghan aircraft. The pilots of 9 and 11 Squadrons had to keep their vigil day and night, flying CAP sorties to safeguard the western borders as well as the strategic installations of Pakistan. Prior to the nuclear tests by Pakistan, the F-16 aircraft were moved to their new location within a few hours.

The airfield infrastructure at Sargodha was kept in an immaculate condition all along. This included periodic surface treatment as well as the filling of joints and cracks in the main and secondary runways and taxi tracks. Some new fighter pens were also constructed in 1988-89. In March 1993, the old NDB transmitter G-9 was replaced with the new transmitter ND-4000. In October 1994, the old TACAN AN/TRN-26 was replaced with the

The former prime minister of Pakistan, Mr. Nawaz Sharif, inspecting the cockpit of an F-16 aircraft at PAF Base Sargodha on 7 December 1992

new AN/FRN-45. A TWCC display was installed in ATC and an MPDR Radar was connected with PC in August 1996.

During the last decade, the fighter squadrons of this Base participated in all the operational exercises, with excellent results. The exercises included Zarb-e-Momin, High Mark and Fire Power Demo in 1989, High Mark in 1993 and 1995, Saffron Bandit in 1994 and 1997, Armament Competitions in 1989 and 1996. No. 9 Squadron won the Maintenance Efficiency Trophy in 1990, 1993, 1996 and 1997. Besides, the same squadron was declared Top Gun in 1991, 1997, and 1998. Another fighter squadron of this base, No. 11 Squadron, won the Inter-Squadron Armament Competition and the Sher Afhan Trophy in 1989 and was the Top Gun in 1993, 1994 and 1995. PAF Base Sargodha had the honour of winning the

Inter-Base Maintenance Efficiency Trophy in 1994 and 1995. The Base also won the Rahim Khan Inter-Base Flight Safety Trophy in 1988, 1990, 1991 and 1998.

No. 114 AED was established in 1989 near Sargodha. It was also upgraded and enlarged to meet the required specifications for a storage and maintenance depot. In 1991, F-100 JEIM successfully conducted a One Time Inspection (OTI) on all the F-100 engines, in response to two turbine failure incidents experienced by the PAF. This was the first time that such extensive work was undertaken on these engines at the intermediate level. During the period from April 1994 to December 1996, a safety modification of Leading Edge Flap Actuators (LEFRA) was successfully carried out on thirty-two F-16 aircraft. This was a depot level task that was undertaken locally, as

American assistance was not available due to the Pressler restrictions. All the aircraft cleared the first FCF Code 1. In January 1997, the F-16 Upgrade Cell was established to carry out OCU and Falcon Up programmes, which again were depot level jobs.

During the period 1988-98, additional married and single accommodation for officers and men was completed at the Base. A Jamia Mosque with a capacity for more than two thousand worshippers was inaugurated on 26 January 1998. The mosque has a spacious courtyard and an elegant minaret. The structure has changed the complexion of the entire residential area. A beautiful park surrounds the mosque.

PAF Base Sargodha has been providing excellent educational facilities to the children of PAF employees. PAF Cadet College, Air Base Intermediate College and PAF Model Intermediate College are located close to the Base and are rated as the finest educational institutions in the area. PAF Modern School was merged with PAF Model Intermediate College on 23 November 1998. Computer education facilities are available at all the PAF educational institutions.

The PAFWA at PAF Base Sargodha has been conducting adult literacy classes for PAF women, and provides free education for the wards of the lower income employees at an Iqra School, which was established in 1995. A modern Play-Land Montessori also exists at the Base. Many vocational courses are regularly conducted for the women at the Base.

PAF Base Sargodha has an excellent record in the field of sports. It has retained the 'Strongman Trophy' for six consecutive years (1993 to 1998).

The administration has endeavoured to provide PSI markets in the residential camp to meet the day to day requirements of the residents. The CSD store, Utility Store, and Sunday Bazaar facilities have also been established at the doorstep of personnel living in family quarters. To provide better recreational facilities, parks have been developed since 1988 in the residential areas for the airmen, officers, and their families. Another park for the children of the lower income employees was developed in the colony where they live.

PAF Base Masroor

In its fifty-eight years of existence, PAF Base Masroor has witnessed many great events. It has grown from a single transport squadron base to the largest operational base of the PAF. By virtue of its size and location, it poses unique administrative challenges for smooth and effective functioning.

Five Commanders of the Masroor Base, viz. Group Captains M. Nur Khan, A. Rahim Khan, Air Commodores M. Anwar Shamim,

246

Farooq Feroze Khan, and M. Abbas Khattak rose in rank to command the PAF. Two other chiefs, Air Marshal Zafar Chaudhry and Air Chief Marshal Zulfiqar Ali Khan, were Commanding Officers of 32 FGA Wing located at the Base.

In the last decade, Masroor's flying squadrons and air defence units participated in a number of operational exercises, for example, High Mark-89, Zarb-e-Momin, High Mark-93 and 95, Saffron Bandit-92, 94 and 97, and the Inspired Alert series, in collaboration with the US Navy from 1995 to 1997. The Base hosted the Inter-Squadron Armament Competition in 1996 and participated in live missile firing at Sonmiani range in 1998.

The Engineering Wing also played a vital role in supporting and enhancing the operational effectiveness of Masroor. It had the privilege of servicing and operating nearly every weapon system of the PAF. After the induction of the Chinese F-7P aircraft in the PAF, second-line maintenance facilities of the system were established at the Engineering Wing. In 1990-91, the Wing was entrusted with the onerous task of making the ex-Australian Mirages ready for operational use. In 1997, 7 Squadron was re-furbished with ROSE modified Mirages, and the Wing ensured its smooth transition by providing adequate support in the training of technicians, by conducting a number of courses at its Field Training Detachment (FTD). In 1998, the first batch of the ex-French Mirage aircraft commenced operations from at Masroor and the Wing, once again provided complete technical support by training the technicians and establishing second-line maintenance facilities.

In 1991, the Mirage FTD and the Mirage III simulator, were shifted from PAF Base Korangi Creek and established at the Engineering Wing, Masroor. DEFCOM exchange was commissioned at the Base in 1998.

The PAF Hospital, Masroor, which was originally established as a seventy-five bed hospital in 1957, has been gradually renovated over the years. In 1989, its bed capacity was increased from 200 to 299. In the same year, a new Children's Ward and Labour Room were constructed. In late 1998, a new building for the Operation Theatre was constructed and equipped with a second table. The hospital was provided with ultrasound equipment during the same year.

In 1985, the Tactical Air Support School (TASS) was established at Masroor, to train army officers as Forward Air Controllers (FACs), Airborne Forward Air Controllers and Ground Liaison Officers (GLOs). The school, besides conducting various courses of FACs and GLOs, also undertakes studies and analysis of new techniques and procedures of land-air warfare. The TASS has so far successfully trained 2,072 Army officers as FACs and GLOs. Through its own initiative and efforts, the school was successful in preparing comprehensive SOPs for the use of GPS-100 in close support missions, and in compiling the Manual of Air Recognition pamphlet.

PAF Base Rafiqui

The role of PAF Base Rafiqui in peace and war is to maintain a high state of readiness, to provide realistic training to operational elements, and to generate an air defence effort as required. It supports and looks after three Forward Operating Bases (FOBs) and several lodger units.

With the induction of the F-7P aircraft in the PAF, the Field Training Detachment (FTD) for the aircraft was established at PAF Base, Rafiqui in March 1988. The in-country training to PAF personnel is conducted at

In February 1996, it was decided to consolidate the functions performed by the Training Control, Field Training Detachment (FTD), and On-Job Training (OJT) Flight. The Ground Training Squadron (GTS) was established for the purpose. This set-up has facilitated a continuous and well organized training programme for the entire Base, under one training complex.

The Base took on the task of constructing a 4,000 feet Katcha landing strip at Thal Range for exercise High Mark-97. The construction of the initial 500 feet was started on 4 March 1997, using Rapid Runway Repair equipment. The first landing of the MFI-7 aircraft on the initial 500 feet was made on 6 March 1997. The strip was then extended to 4,000 feet and it was formally inaugurated on 26 March 1997 by the Air Officer Commanding, Central Air Command.

the FTD to prepare an efficient maintenance crew for the F-7P weapon system. Familiarization and first-line maintenance courses on F-7P are also conducted regularly.

PAF Base Rafiqui provides education to the wards of its personnel as well as civilians, through a PAF College that was upgraded to

The former president of Pakistan, Mr. Ghulam Ishaq Khan, inspecting the cockpit of an F-7P aircraft at PAF Base Rafiqui on 7 February 1990

the degree level in 1991. The college has established itself as an institution of considerable repute among the local colleges. It lays great emphasis on both the physical and intellectual development of its students.

The Base also has a reasonably sophisticated hospital, which provides medical and health care to its personnel. There are also a number of parks and playgrounds for children. The Airmen's Children's Park and Lake, Sabre Montessori and Zoological Gardens were established in December 1997 by the Base's administration on a self-help basis. The PAFWA is well established and quite active, not only within the Base premises but also in the civil sector.

During the last decade, the PAF Officers' Club was constructed and the PAF Hospital was extended. A swimming pool facility for the airmen, a railway underpass to facilitate personnel plying between the Base and colony, and finally the Fizaia Welfare Filling Station and Fizaia Superstore were established to benefit the Base personnel and the local population alike.

PAF Base Samungli

No. 31 Wing located at this Base comprises 17 and 23 Squadrons of the PAF. Both squadrons played an active part in the Afghan War, with F-6s on their inventory. During 1988, these squadrons performed ADA duties at Chaklala, in rotation. In March 1989, they participated in the PAF Fire Power Demonstration held at Sonmiani Range, Masroor. The squadrons also participated in almost all the major PAF exercises and competitions during the last decade. PAF Base Samungli also exercises administrative control over three different air defence squadrons, which provided excellent air surveillance and medium level ground controlled interceptions during the Afghan war.

When 25 Squadron was re-equipped, the F-6 aircraft belonging to the squadron were despatched to PAF Base, Samungli, in December 1995. These aircraft were surplus to the requirement of the Base. Instead of putting them in storage, the Base authorities decided to set up a new unit named Field Maintenance Unit (FMU), to maintain those aircraft in reduced flying status. Thus, with very little manpower and resources at its disposal, the Base has been able to keep those aircraft in serviceable condition for the last three years. This concept proved extremely fruitful when almost all FMU aircraft had to be made available for operation at a day's notice during the May 1998 nuclear tests.

PAF Base, Samungli had the rare distinction of defending some vital assets during the critical period in May 1998, by carrying out extensive operations from the parent Base as well as from both of its FOBs—Shahbaz and Sukkur. The CAP missions were provided by the F-6s of 17 Air Superiority Squadron during the day, while night operations were conducted by F-16s of 9 Multi Role Squadron. No. 314 Ground Combateers Wing, located at the Base, actively participated in providing enhanced security cover to the F-16 aircraft.

PAF Base Samungli extends good educational facilities to its personnel through a PAF Intermediate College. Medical needs are met through a twenty-five bedded PAF Hospital situated in the main premises of the Base. The PAFWA activities at the Base are also lively and constructive.

PAF Base Minhas

The construction of Minhas airfield dates back to the Second World War. It was constructed over the site of a disused airstrip that was built by the British, ostensibly as one of the measures to stop the Soviet hordes from marching into the subcontinent. After the 1971 war, it was decided to establish the Pakistan Aeronautical Complex (PAC) near Kamra Village, in district Campbellpur. The airfield,

named after Kamra village, was originally constructed to serve the PAC. However, with the arrival of the F-16s in 1982, the PAF needed another main operating base for this weapon system. In order to counteract the growing threat to our strategic VP, Kamra was considered a suitable base from where the air defence effort could be generated with relative ease. This consideration was later validated by the important role that the Base played in subsequent years.

After the Soviet intervention in Afghanistan in 1979, hostile aircraft gradually increased their air activity over the Pak-Afghan border. By the 1980s, it had become essential for the PAF to have a back-up base for Peshawar, for its air defence effort against the Afghan air violations. In 1984, therefore, the Air Staff decided to establish a fighter base at Kamra which would facilitate minimum reaction time against the Soviet-Afghan threats, besides any other threat to our strategic installations at Kahuta. After building an infrastructure of the bare essentials, the Base was given care and maintenance (C&M) status in February 1984. As tension heightened on the western border, Kamra (Minhas) was upgraded to a 'one squadron Base' in July 1984, under the command of Air Commodore M. Ehtisham Akram.

While the Afghan war was at its peak (1987-1989), the construction of major facilities at PAF Base Kamra continued. When plans for the new Base headquarters building at Kamra were being made, Air Headquarters wished it to face the runway, so that it would provide a view of the landing and departing aircraft from the Base Commander's office. The administration at the Base, however, missed the point, and the building came to face the mountains, Afghanistan, and the lands beyond! During the withdrawal phase of the Soviet Forces from Afghanistan the fighting touched new levels of desperation. As the end drew nearer, Kamra flew more and more and the Base Headquarters continued to be built, brick by brick, very slowly. It was finally completed, the war trophies were mounted, and the Soviet-Afghan war ended. In March 1989, the SU-25 wing, with its Red Star marking from a downed Soviet fighter, and the AIM-9L missile pointing towards the western sky, went up on the pedestals, and the Base Headquarters was inaugurated.

The first squadron to be deployed at PAF Base Minhas was 5 Squadron, equipped with Mirage-III aircraft, in July 1984. It was replaced by 18 Squadron, equipped with Mirage-V aircraft in April 1989. During this period, Kamra became one of the two premier bases of the PAF to house F-16 aircraft. No. 14 Multi-Role (MR) Squadron, equipped with F-16, shot down five Afghan aircraft on the western border between April 1987 to November 1988. Later, in 1989, 18 Squadron moved out and 15 Squadron, equipped with the old workhorse, the F-6 aircraft, was deployed on the Base. In July 1993, 15 Squadron was re-equipped with the F-7P aircraft. In September 1993, 14 Squadron was re-equipped with F-7Ps while its F-16s were re-grouped at Sargodha. At present, the Base is established with one F-7P squadron and one ROSE-II modified Mirage squadron.

The first F-7 four-ship formation aerobatics team was formed at Minhas. It made its first demonstration to AOC Northern Air Command on 21 December 1993. In September 1998, the first batch of Forward Looking Infra Red (FLIR)-equipped Mirage Vs of 25 MR Squadron arrived from France.

In 1988, the Maintenance Wing was providing second-Line maintenance to support one F-16 and one Mirage squadron. In July 1990, the Maintenance Wing was re-designated as the Engineering Wing. A

RRR Squadron was established in June 1991. To provide an all weather landing facility for the aircraft, Instrument Landing System was installed at the Base in December 1992. At present, the Engineering Wing is providing second-line maintenance facilities to F-7 aircraft, and those for ROSE-II modified Mirages are being established.

PAF Base Peshawar

The fighter wing at Peshawar consists of two fighter squadrons and a rescue squadron. Peshawar is a joint user airfield, where the civil air traffic density has almost doubled since 1988. Earlier, there were eighteen flights per day but now there are thirty-five to forty flights per day. Peshawar airport is now connected with eight different international airports. Accordingly, the runway, navigation and approach aids have been augmented with the help of the Civil Aviation Authority (CAA). Precision Approach Path Indicators (PAPIs) were installed in 1990, new runway lights in 1991, and Runway End Identification Lights in 1996. Runway carpeting was completed in December 1998.

PAF Base Peshawar was the first Base to be affected by the Soviet invasion of Afghanistan in 1979. The fighter squadrons at the Base remained in varying states of readiness throughout the Afghan war. The Base was also asked to establish an ADA flight at Chaklala in 1985, to augment the defence of strategic installations. After 1986, the Base provided air escort for PIA and C-130 traffic, to and from Chitral. During those years, there were several hot scrambles, but no kills were scored as the sensor cover and ROEs in force at that time did not permit PAF fighters to effectively engage the enemy intruders.

The past decade witnessed the relocation of several squadrons to and from PAF Base Peshawar. No. 41 Squadron was the first one to move out in August 1988, and become part of 35 CAT Wing, Chaklala. No. 16 Squadron moved in from Rafiqui in June 1989 and 15 Squadron was shifted to Minhas in August 1989. No. 316 GC Wing was formed at the Base in July 1991 and was later shifted to Kohat in April 1994. Another important development on the Base was the establishment of a Helicopter Flying School, which started basic helicopter conversion and helicopter instructor courses with effect from 1995. The Quaid-e-Azam's aircraft, which had been lying at Peshawar for a long time, was shifted to Faisal in November 1996, to become part of the PAF Museum. Another important event was the closure of the Jamrud Range in September 1997, which was handed over to Peshawar Development Authority (PDA). The Range that had over the years helped many young pilots learn their basic gunnery, and master dropping of live ordinance; that had witnessed the fury of live ammunition dropped by PAF

stalwarts during fire power demonstrations, finally passed into history.

The fighter squadrons of this Base participated in all the Command and Region level exercises during the last decade. No. 16 Squadron won the Inter-Squadron Maintenance Trophy in 1990 and the ACES Trophy in 1997. No. 26 Squadron won the ACES Trophy in 1996 and the Sarfraz Rafiqui Trophy in 1992, 1994, 1995, and 1998.

The Base hosted many inter-base, inter-Services and national level championships in sports like tennis, golf, hockey and squash. The tennis lawns of Peshawar Officers' Mess continued to attract top tennis players of the country for the CAS Khyber Cup Open Championship. The three schools and colleges being administered by the Base meet the educational needs of approximately 5,000 students of the PAF as well as other residents of Peshawar. The surroundings of the Officers' Mess were maintained and improved. The Mess not only serves as a venue for functions, but is also available for ex-Sargodhian and Pakistan Air Force Retired Officers Association (PAFROA) reunions. A gymnasium was established in the Officers' Mess in 1991 and in the Airmen's Mess in 1999. Peshawar had the honour of winning the Inter-Base Tennis Championship in 1990 and 1999. The Base was the runner-up of the Inter-Base Cricket Championships, held in 1989 and 1993.

PAF Base Mianwali

PAF Base Mianwali was upgraded to a full-fledged operational base in August 1974. It was established primarily to conduct flying training. The nature of its peacetime role and task were shaped by this consideration. To accomplish this task, the Base has been organized into three conventional wings with their integral units and sections. Amongst the

A ground control approach radar and Magasync tape recorder at ATC were installed in the late-1980s. In order to keep pace with technological advancements, the induction of the Bird Repellent System, the setting up of SATCOM and DEFCOM, the installation and maintenance of Global Positioning System and radio altimeter on the aircraft, were undertaken by the Engineering Wing. The Wing had to expand its maintenance capabilities when 19 Squadron, equipped with newly inducted F-7P aircraft, was raised at the Base in 1991. The establishment of the F-7P hangar further increased the maintenance capabilities of the Aircraft Engineering Squadron. The setting up of ALMS in 1994 automated the record keeping. The installation of the barrier assemblies added a new dimension to the role of AGES. Subsequently, the tail hook barrier for the F-16s was installed, to enable the Base to serve as a diversionary site for these aircraft.

A lot of construction took place at the Base between 1988 and 1998. This included the construction of a tarmac, a hangar, and a perimeter wall around the airfield, and additional, 'married accommodation' for the officers, JCOs and airmen.

The PAF Inter College, Mianwali, has earned a reputation for producing excellent academic results. The college won the Chief of the Air Staff Trophy in 1990, 1993, 1994, and 1995, for outstanding performance in the SSC and HSSC examinations.

lodger units, the Base exercises administrative and functional control over the PAF Hospital, the Dental Unit, a DSG Company, and a Data Automation Detachment.

No. 1 Fighter Conversion Unit was shifted from Masroor to Mianwali in November 1975 on a permanent basis, and was equipped with the Chinese FT-5 aircraft. In November 1976, 14 Squadron arrived at Mianwali, which was to function as an Operational Conversion Unit for the F-6 aircraft. In 1986, after having graduated over a hundred fighter pilots, the squadron moved to Minhas to be re-equipped with F-16s. The role of the OCU was then taken over by 25 Squadron, which moved from Sargodha to Mianwali for this purpose. No. 25 OCU remained a part of 37 Combat Training Wing until January 1996 when it was shifted to Minhas to play a different role. In 1991, 19 Squadron was moved to Mianwali to act as an Operational Conversion Unit on F-7P aircraft. In December 1998, 18 Squadron moved from Rafiqui to this Base in order share the load of 19 OCU.

PAF Academy Risalpur

The PAF Academy Risalpur, in line with its avowed objective, continues to impart high quality training to aviation cadets, and to graduate them as pilots, engineers and professional officers of ground branches. Of late, it has expanded and progressed, keeping pace with the latest developments in flying training and aviation technology.

The College of Flying Training (CFT) now consists of a Flying Training Wing, the Directorate of Studies, the Engineering Wing and the Flying Instructors' School (FIS). The Primary Flying Training (PFT) Wing and the Basic Flying Training (BFT) Wing have been placed under the command of the Officer Commanding Flying Training Wing. The last decade also witnessed the induction of K-8 aircraft into the PAF. Six aircraft were officially handed over to K-8 Evaluation Flight by the then Prime Minister of Pakistan at a ceremony held at the Academy in January 1995. The Flight now imparts basic flying training to student pilots.

The air displays by the PAF aerobatics team, the Sherdils, which had remained suspended for some time, were revived in June 1996. Their feats have since become a continuing

Air Vice Marshal Imtiaz Haider, the then Air Officer Commanding PAF Academy, Risalpur presenting the historical picture of Quaid-i-Azam to Air Marshal M. Asghar Khan

254

legend. A new Academy aerobatics team, comprising four pilots of the K-8 aircraft, has been developed, and is known as 'Academy Hawks'. The Academy Hawks performed their first air display at the graduation ceremony held in May 1999. The Hawks thrilled the spectators with their performance. Wing Commander Nayyar Iqbal Wasti led the first display. Flight Lieutenant Nadeem Akhtar, Flight lieutenant Asif and Squadron Leader Nauman Altaf also took part.

The PFT Wing was awarded the Masroor Hussain Flight Safety Trophy for achieving the highest accident free flying in 1989, 1996, and 1998. The Engineering Wing of the Academy was awarded the Turowicz Inter-Base Maintenance Efficiency Trophy for the period 1998-99.

The Directorate of Studies was initially established with two departments, viz. Humanities and Aerosciences. Somewhat later, the departments of Aviation Sciences, and Administration and Airspace Management (A&AM) were added, to provide integrated training. The Directorate of Studies is currently imparting academic training to all GD (P) and Non-GD courses. The academic training of GD (P) courses at the Directorate of Studies saw a major shift from the composite academic system, to the semester system, in January 1991. The new scheme of studies afforded an overlap between academic and flying training, and thus reduced the overall training period of aviation cadets by six months. In addition, it promised more harmony between the academic systems of the College of Aeronautical Engineering and the College of Flying Training. The regular induction of lady cadets in the PAF was started in February 1993. They are now trained at the Academy for commission in various ground branches.

Air Marshal M. Asghar Khan inspecting the Guard of Honour at PAF Academy, Risalpur on 13 April 1997 to commemorate Quaid-i-Azam's historical visit to the then RPAF College, Risalpur

A new, superbly designed convocation hall, with a seating capacity of 440, was constructed in the proximity of the new Academy Complex, in 1995. A Para Motor Gliding Club was established in 1998. In addition to the Para Troop Training, a Riding and Polo Club has also been established at the Academy.

On 13 April 1997, the Golden Jubilee of the Quaid-e-Azam's visit to the then Flying School at Risalpur was celebrated. The first Pakistani C-in-C PAF, Air Marshal M. Asghar Khan (Retd.), was the Chief Guest on the occasion, while five other former Chiefs of the Air Staff attended the ceremony.

A sports complex near the Officers' Mess was inaugurated recently, to provide extensive sports facilities, both indoor and outdoor, to the officers and their families. Earlier, a gymnasium had been inaugurated to provide facilities to airmen for physical fitness exercises. The PAF Degree College, Risalpur was upgraded to Degree level in the disciplines of BA, B.Sc., and BCS (Bachelor of Computer Science).

The College of Aeronautical Engineering (CAE) was established in July 1965 at Korangi Creek, with Colonel John H. Blakelock, USAF, as its first principal. After having functioned for twenty-one years at Korangi Creek, the CAE was shifted in May 1986 to Risalpur. Its relocation led to centralized officers' training, and the promotion of comradeship and early bonding between the fliers and engineers of the PAF.

Being part of the PAF Academy, the CAE has undergone tremendous advancement after 1988. In order to cope with modern technologies, its curriculum was upgraded, labs and workshops were improved and the latest computational facilities were added. The role and task of the institution has also been progressively revised. In addition to training prospective and serving engineering officers of the PAF and the trainees of other organizations for their BE degree in Aerospace and Avionics, the CAE has now been assigned the additional role of imparting postgraduate education and undertaking research and development in the relevant

A view of the newly constructed Blakelock Auditorium at the CAE

disciplines. Its affiliation with the National University of Science and Technology (NUST) in 1995 has paved the way for its students to pursue postgraduate programmes in some international universities of repute.

PAF Base Chaklala

PAF Base Chaklala houses and supports the air transport element of the PAF. But during the Afghan war, when the threat to our nuclear installations seemed imminent, the infrastructure at the Base was upgraded to maintain regular Air Defence Alert (ADA) and Combat Air Patrol (CAP) operations.

The old Base Headquarters and Accounts Squadron buildings were demolished to provide the requisite space for the construction of a new VIP lounge complex, and new alternative buildings were constructed. The project was completed in three phases. In phase I, the BHQ was shifted to its new building (July 1991). Phase II involved the shifting of the Administration Wing to the new building (July 1992). Finally, the Accounts squadron was housed in the new building in May 1995, as phase III of the project.

The VIP lounge and suites at Chaklala were constructed in collaboration with the Government of Saudi Arabia, who provided funding for the project. After its completion, the project was taken over by the Base on 17 October 1996.

Previously, there were no Programme Depot Maintenance (PDM) facilities at the Base for C-130 aircraft. Consequently, a huge amount of foreign exchange was required to have PDMs carried out abroad. This situation warranted the establishment of a PDM facility that met international standards in-country. The project was given to the Base, and it was successfully completed within a very short period of time. In February 1992, 130 Air Engineering Depot (AED) emerged as the first C-130 PDM establishment in Pakistan. Although it experienced problems typical to a newly established unit, the first PDM on the first C-130 aircraft was completed within six months. The depot has thus far accomplished PDM of nine aircraft, with an average time of four months per aircraft.

In 1989, the PAF decided to establish the Automated Logistic Management System (ALMS) at Chaklala and Karachi. In January 1991, the project was started at Chaklala, and it progressed so swiftly that by July 1993, the first aircraft (Mirage) had been switched over to ALMS. By May 1996, all the PAF aircraft were converted to this system.

To centralize the transport element of the PAF, 41 VIP Communication Squadron was shifted from Peshawar to Chaklala in 1988. Due to a shortage of space, the squadron was initially housed in containers and cabins. The squadron started its operations on 30 August 1988. In November 1996, the squadron was shifted to the building which had been newly constructed, to house the offices of No. 35 Wing.

Due to its peculiar location, Chaklala had always been at the center of various administrative and operational activities. It is the Base which provides administrative support to contingents participating in the Pakistan Day parade every year. The Base also provided administrative facilities to the RAF's Red Arrows, during the air show held at Islamabad in 1998. At present, the Base is providing administrative support to approximately fifty lodger units.

The Base provides excellent educational facilities to both serving and retired PAF personnel, wards of sister Services, as well as civilians. The schools at Chaklala and Jinnah Camp are presently maintaining an intermediate level of educational institutions, in the fields of Science, Computer Science, and Humanities. Both the institutions have produced outstanding results in academic and extracurricular activities.

The Pakistan Air Force Women's Association (PAFWA) at this Base has completed a number of projects pertaining to the welfare of the personnel, with a particular focus on lower income employees working at the Base. At Markaz-e-PAFWA, free training in sewing, cooking, flower arrangement, etc., is provided to the families of lower income employees. The Mashal-e-Ilm primary school, established at the Base in 1988, extends a high quality education to the wards of low income personnel, and also provides work opportunities to educated young women.

The Base Central Library, located in the Education Squadron, was renovated in 1998. It is accessible to all PAF personnel, both uniformed and civilian, and their wards. A Hobbies Club for uniformed personnel is also located within this squadron. The club provides training and practice in electronics, photography, aero modeling, and calligraphy, under the close supervision of experts.

PAF Base Faisal

PAF Base Faisal, which is well known for its traditional roles of supply and maintenance, developed quickly both in scope and size. By 1985, the Base had assumed full flying and operational services, and presently it caters to all PAF flights heading from south to north and the other way around. A number of well developed maintenance and logistics depots of the PAF such as 101 ALC, 102 AED, 103 ALC (Dett), 104 AED (Dett), and 107 AED, are situated at Faisal. The Base provides administrative facilities not only to these depots but also to the PAF Air War College, Southern Air Command, Central Technical Development Unit (CTDU), Defect Investigation and Analysis Cell (DIAC), Supply Provisioning Section Dett (SPS), and the PAF Information and Selection Center, Karachi.

The importance of the Base was duly recognized when the Air Headquarters decided to set up the PAF Museum at Faisal, not only because of the availability of space, but also because of its well established in-house engineering facilities. The personnel of the Base put in untiring efforts to complete this task and eventually, on 14 August 1997, the museum was inaugurated by the then CAS, Air Chief Marshal M. Abbas Khattak. Since then, the museum has attracted both Service personnel and the general public. In another venture during 1988, the Base made a considerable contribution towards the completion of the new PAF Air War College premises.

In 1992, a Hobbies Computer Club was established at the Base to enhance computer literacy among airmen, civilian employees, and their dependants. The Club had conducted thirty such courses by 1998.

The PAF Intermediate College Faisal was taken over by the Shaheen Foundation in 1980. However, in 1988, it was returned to the jurisdiction of the Base. The college was upgraded to the degree level in 1994 and shifted to the new college campus, which contains a well-equipped science laboratory. Since then, a new subject, (Computer Sciences) has been introduced into the curriculum. The present strength of the college is well above 3,500 students. The college has so far done well in providing quality education to the Base personnel.

Until 1988, PAF Base Faisal had faced an acute shortage of water. New overhead tanks were constructed to meet the situation. A community water filter plant was installed in the Airmen's Camp in 1996 and another in 1998. Both plants are accessible to the residents twenty-four hours a day, and the airmen and civilians living in all the camps are its beneficiaries. After the installation of the filter plants, a substantial decrease in water-borne diseases was noted.

During 1996-97, the Base expanded its housing facilities for civilian employees by constructing forty-eight 'living out' quarters. The PAFWA is very active on the Base in welfare activities throughout the year, and it undertakes special programmes on Eid, Christmas, and other occasions of national importance.

PAF Base Malir

After its establishment in 1948, the Base functioned as a training institution for signal and radar technicians, until the late 1960s. From the early 1970s, the Base assumed additional responsibilities for training and maintaining the PAF's mobile and fixed air defence elements, in a high state of readiness. After the induction of PADS-77, the Base expanded. It did so particularly after the establishment of two Control and Reporting Centres in the early-1980s. The same period also witnessed the deployment of a high powered TPS-43 radar in addition to the old vintage FPS-20 radar.

No. 105 AED was redesignated as No. 105 Air Ordnance Depot (AOD) in 1988, and renamed as No. 105 Air Engineering Depot in

1990. The unit's revised assignment included overhaul, modifications, and major inspection and evaluation of combat stores. The depot was responsible for providing technical advice, and for the on-site recovery of stores.

A Munitions Training School (MTS) was established at the depot in June 1987, to promote a better understanding of the latest weapon systems among the senior armament supervisors, and to disseminate the knowledge gained as a result of R & D being carried out at the depot. Provost training was shifted to Kohat in 1989, and the training School of GCs was also moved to Kohat in 1994.

The No. 312 Ground Combateer Wing at Malir has been imparting training in the field of ground defence to the personnel of friendly countries. It also conducted the SSG course for airmen, and administered basic Judo and martial arts training to ASF personnel and the PIA Cabin Crew. This Wing continues to train personnel in activities such as unarmed combat, the martial arts and the use of explosives, etc. The Wing also took on the responsibility of escorting VIPs and providing trained personnel as air guards. The 312 Wing renders assistance in the planning and implementation of ground defence for the units of SAC. The personnel of the Wing also perform ceremonial guard duties at the Mazar-e-Quaid starting from 1 September till 31 December each year. In addition to all this, the Wing is responsible for holding security and ground defence related courses for PAF personnel.

In 1987, the PAF Model School at Malir was upgraded to the Intermediate College level. By the end of 1998, the college had a strength of over 1,500 students, along with approximately a hundred teaching staff. In 1997, two jogging tracks were established, one at the main sports complex and the other near the officers' residential area. A gymnasium was added to the indoor sports facilities during the same year.

PAF Base Lahore

PAF Base Lahore, comprising the base technical area, residential areas, and other operational units, is spread over seven different locations, including PAF Walton. Although a lot of capital work and abnormal repairs were carried out during 1988-1998, most of the buildings, which are fifty to eighty years old, have deteriorated over the years. Because of its historical importance, Lahore attracts many visitors, both local and foreign. As such, PAF Base Lahore is frequently visited by VIPs from within the country and abroad, throughout the year. PAF Base Lahore also has a PAF Intermediate College, which has risen within a short time to a level that is appreciated by parents, students, and the general public alike. It has maintained outstanding results in the Matriculation as well as in the F.Sc. examinations.

The Base extends administrative support to a number of operational units, including a Control and Reporting Center (CRC), two radar squadrons, the Air Defence System

School (ADSS) deployed at PAF Walton, and two Mobile Observers Units. There is also another very busy unit called the Information and Selection Center, which conducts a number of recruitment cycles throughout the year. During the mid 1980s, 245 and 246 MOU Squadrons were permanently shifted from Lahore to other locations. Later, 242 MOU Squadron, which was numberplated in June 1989, was re-equipped and reactivated in September 1991 and shifted to PAF Base Rafiqui.

The Base hosts regular Inter-Base and national championships in cricket, hockey and football. The Officers' Mess, which has a rich history of over seventy years, provides an excellent venue for sports and recreation.

PAF Base Korangi Creek

PAF Base Korangi Creek was established by the Royal Air Force in 1923 to provide embarkation and disembarkation facilities to the RAF and other British personnel arriving by civil or military amphibious aircraft. Its other function was to receive and dispatch cargo carried by these aircraft. The Base today has the primary role of providing advance trade training and general Service knowledge through the School of Education (SOE) and the School of Aeronautics (SOA), to the airmen from technical trades. The Base has been maintaining the JCO's Academy and the College of Education (COE) since 1986. The JCOs Academy provides senior supervisory level training to the NCOs of the PAF, who are likely to assume the responsibility of Junior Commissioned Officers in future. The COE imparts training in Instructional Technique (IT) to airmen as well as officers. The College of Education also helps the retiring NCOs and JCOs to enhance their educational status by providing them with the opportunity to acquire a Bachelor of Education (BEd) from the Karachi University.

PAF Base Korangi Creek, by virtue of its unique location, plays a vital role in the air defence of the southern and coastal regions of Pakistan. The Base has the necessary infrastructure for the deployment and operation of related modern weapon systems. It also holds great potential for the growth and development of this infrastructure, and promises to meet any requirement that might arise. Two MOU Squadrons are deployed at the Base to give advance warning of enemy raids on the southern borders of Pakistan.

During the past decade, a jeepable track was developed along the seaside within the Base area. A stadium for water sports, a cricket ground with a jogging track around it, hockey and football grounds were also developed. Further developments include the establishment of the unique family park 'Creek View Park,' and two childrens parks within the Base.

In recent years, the Sea Survival School and the PAF Yacht Club have received special attention. Arrangements have been made to provide water sports training to airmen in the early stages of their career. The Yacht Club has been renovated and an all-weather yachting facility is now available at the Base. A big picnic platform and a seaside stadium have been constructed to encourage picnics, and sea sports. Besides, the Base Golf Club has been revived and is now fully operational, providing golf facilities to its members and visitors.

PAF Base Kohat

Established in 1922, Kohat is one of the oldest bases in the subcontinent. Until 1947, Kohat operated with two fighter-bomber squadrons. Soon after independence, Kohat was entrusted with the additional responsibility of imparting training to newly inducted recruits in the PAF for which the Recruits Training Centre (RTC) was shifted from PAF Lahore to PAF Kohat in 1948. Soon thereafter, the centre was renamed the Recruits Training School (RTS). In 1987, this institution was again renamed,

the Pre-Trade Training School (PTTS) with a redesignated role of training Aero-Tech and Aero-Support technicians. No. 9 Squadron, the last flying unit to operate regularly from Kohat, ceased operations from this airfield in 1961. Thereafter, Kohat has remained primarily a training base of the PAF.

The PTTS campus is situated in the picturesque valley of Kohat, and is the largest unit of the Base. The school comprises five squadrons named after Shuhadas (martyrs), and heroes of the PAF, namely, Minhas, Iqbal, Munir, Alauddin, and Rafiqui.

The huge PTTS campus presents an attractive view against the background of the Kohat hills. The unit is self-sufficient in most respects, and it comprises administration and education blocks in the centre of the campus, flanked by a parade ground and twenty-four residential barracks. Seven sports grounds, two messes and an exquisite mosque are close by. The older part of the campus was constructed in 1948 and extensions were made in 1955 and 1977 to accommodate the growing number of trainees. The campus is spread over an area of around seventy acres, and has the capacity to accommodate 2,400 trainees. The well-equipped library has a stock of about 27,000 books. The school also has the latest audio and visual aids, a graphics section, science laboratories, a computer cell, hobbies and dramatic clubs.

The school is entrusted with the task of moulding young recruits from diverse civilian backgrounds into disciplined airmen. This is a radical change in the life of the new entrants who often find the new regimen very rigorous and demanding. It is the school's mission to bring about change with a persuasive and motivational approach.

From 1968 onwards, a large number of airmen from friendly countries have been undergoing training at the RTS. To cater to these airmen, a separate training unit, called the Allied Training Squadron (ATS) was established for foreign trainees.

The unit maintains an antique tower clock housed in the centre of the main building. The chimes of the clock at quarterly, half-hourly and hourly intervals are a familiar sound to the entire valley.

The Base also exercises administrative control over 316 GC Wing and the School of Logistics (SOL). Both units were shifted to Kohat from Peshawar and Risalpur, respectively, in the 1990s.

PAF Base Sakesar

Until 1992, the administrative and functional control of PAF Base Sakesar rested with the Headquarters Northern Air Command. The Base was later placed under the Headquarters Central Air Command.

The Base has two main units, the 401 Squadron and the Air Defence Training School (ADTS). The former performs an operational watch, to provide coverage for the aerial borders of Pakistan, while the latter imparts basic training to Air Defence Weapon Controllers.

Initially, 401 Squadron was a part of the Operations Wing of the Base. It became an independent high-level radar squadron in June 1992. The radar performed well for two decades, but after its performance deteriorated, the analogue receiver was replaced with a digital one in 1988. The radar was hooked to automation in 1992.

During exercise High Mark-93, the squadron was tasked to provide recovery services to strike aircraft, operating in the Fox Land area of exercise. In addition to recovery, the squadron was asked to remain on standby to carry out spoofing on a radio channel in order to confuse the enemy jammer. The equipment remained serviceable throughout the exercise period. A total of fifty strike aircraft were provided with recovery service. During the Afghan war, the squadron provided surveillance.

The maintenance of radar used to be the responsibility of the Engineering Wing. However, in 1992, the responsibility of all maintenance activities pertaining to radar, automation, and communication systems, was transferred to 401 Squadron.

The ADTS is an institution where basic air defence training is imparted to the cadets. The school also conducts advanced air defence courses, and training courses for foreign students when directed by the Air Headquarters. Before the establishment of the ADTS at PAF Base Sakesar, the training of ADWC officers was conducted at 229 Squadron, PAF Korangi Creek. In order to provide realistic practical training, one MPDR-90 Radar was permanently deployed at the base recently, to facilitate practice in live interceptions by the students.

The Sakesar jungle was preserved while the boundaries of the Base were defined in 1986. The Base had only one entry and exit

AVM Parvaiz Mehdi Qureshi, AOC Air Defence Command shaking hands with officers at PAF Base Sakesar, 1993

Air Chief Marshal Farooq Feroze Khan, CAS, PAF shaking hands with officers during his visit to Sakesar, 1992

towards the eastern side via Nowshera. The need for a road which linked the Base with Quaidabad City and PAF Base Mianwali, had been felt for a long time. Following two years of relentless effort by the Base authorities, the road linking Sakesar with Mianwali and Quaidabad was commissioned. In terms of educational & recreational facilities, the PAF Modern School, Sakesar (Prep to Class V) was established in 1996-97, and two parks were developed at the Base.

PAF Base Lower Topa

The history of Lower Topa starts from 1930 when the British Air Force established a small summer training establishment for its officers and men, in the scenic Murree Hills. Some traces of the presence of the Royal Air Force personnel at Lower Topa date back to 1897 and 1913. A grave in the cemetery at the Lower Topa bazaar and a building at the base, bear indelible imprints of those years. Lower Topa became a regular RPAF station in May 1950, and it provided administrative services to the school that trained airmen in non-technical trades.

In 1985, the Base assumed its new operational and administrative role. It was tasked to establish and facilitate the deployment of the School of Intelligence (SOI), a radar squadron and a Mobile Observers Unit (MOU) at the Base. The recent revival of the PAF public school at Lower Topa necessitated some changes at the Base. These included the shifting of the SOI and the radar squadron to alternative locations. PAF College, Lower Topa started functioning with effect from 12 June 1998, as an independent pre-cadet institution parallel to PAF College, Sargodha.

The primary aim of the PAF College, Lower Topa is to educate and train suitable Pakistani boys for the Intermediate Examination of the Federal Board of Intermediate and Secondary Education (FBISE), Islamabad, in a healthy environment. In their formative years, they are moulded into confident and disciplined young men with a strong character and exceptional leadership qualities. Besides this, Lower Topa also facilitates special Adventure and Survival Courses for PAF personnel from time to time.

PAF Base Kalabagh
PAF Base Kalabagh, located at an altitude of 8,600 feet above sea level is at a driving distance of about four hours from Rawalpindi. The Base provides an excellent training and recreational resort for PAF personnel and their families during all seasons of the year. Since its establishment

as a full-fledged Base in 1975, it has conducted several survival courses such as Ski and Snow Survival, General Survival, Desert Survival, Sea Survival and Adventure courses. These courses are conducted at multiple locations. The Ski and Snow Survival courses are held in Naltar Valley, Sea Survival in the coastal areas, Desert Survival in Thar and Cholistan, and Mountain Survival at Kalabagh and the northern areas. However, Adventure courses are conducted at various changing locations. The areas normally chosen are the Khunjrab Pass, Shandoor Pass, Nanga Parbat, Rakaposhi, Deosai Plains, Kaghan and Naran Valleys and Azad Kashmir, etc.

In addition to its own role and task, PAF Base Kalabagh is also responsible for coordinating and overseeing the functioning of the Ski Federation of Pakistan, which was established at Kalabagh in December 1990. The Base Commander Kalabagh is appointed

the Secretary of the Federation. The Federation is a constituent member of the Pakistan Sports Board and the Pakistan Olympic Association, which is provisionally affiliated with the International Ski Federation (ISF).

By February 1999, the Ski Federation of Pakistan had organized eight National Ski Championships. It also represented the country in international ski competitions twice in 1996, in the '3rd Asian Winter Games' held in China, and the 'Ten days of Dawn' in Iran. Later, in 1998, it represented the country in 'Armed Forces Ski Competition' in Germany and 'Ten Days of Dawn ISF Ski Competition' in Iran.

To meet the educational requirements of children at Kalabagh and its surrounding areas, the PAF Model School, Kalabagh was established as a primary school in 1980, and upgraded to the middle standard in 1983. In 1989, it was further upgraded to the secondary level and was finally raised to Intermediate College level in 1996. By the end of 1998, the College had a strength of 200 students and seventeen teaching staff.

In November 1996, an unfortunate incident occurred at Naltar, in which the PAF Officers' Mess caught fire. As a result, the wooden building was completely destroyed along with the fittings and furniture. In August 1997, the first phase of reconstruction of Officers' Mess was completed in which the Officers Mess building, ten BOQs, the overhead water tank, and several external services were provided. Phase II and III expansion programmes have been included in capital works of the fiscal years 1998-99 and 1999-2000, respectively. Phase II covers four BOQs and one classroom, whereas a VOQ Block and Sunroom have been included in Phase III.

Operational Squadrons

No. 1 Fighter Conversion Unit

This unit was established in 1975 to train newly graduated pilots from the Academy, on the aircraft acquired from China. Though initially it acted as a fighter conversion platform for F-6 aircraft, it continued to perform this role even after the induction of F-7Ps and A-5s.

The unit has the primary peacetime role of training newly commissioned officers, (with limited experience on the slower T-37s), to fly supersonic jets. No. 1 Fighter Conversion Unit (FCU) administers intensive and challenging courses each year. Maintaining its tradition of flight safety, the unit won the Masroor Hussain Flight Safety Trophy during 1992, 1995 and 1998.

In 1987, the unit was assigned the wartime role of air defence. This change of role not only necessitated a change in the war plans but also inspired flying instructors to refresh their skills as intercept pilots. During

ISAC-96, the FT-5 aircraft fired an AIM-9P, which connected with its target successfully, demonstrating the capabilities of this old hero of the Korean war. In addition, the unit regularly took part in major command level operational exercises. On 23 April 1998, during an air-to-air missile firing, the FT-5 successfully launched an AIM-9P, (an IR guided air-to-air missile), on target, demonstrating that the system is fully capable of living up to the standards of a fighter aircraft in any future conflict.

1 FCU has conducted forty-five Fighter Conversion Courses since it was established. During the last ten years, 450 students have graduated from this prestigious institution. The average induction per course was twenty-six, the attrition rate approximately 12 per cent and the average number of graduates was twenty-four.

No. 2 Squadron

During the last decade, this squadron was assigned to perform a variety of tasks, viz.

the training of pilots, the arranging of ground controlled interceptions to train air defence controllers, and aerial target towing for all three services. After the induction of F-7P aircraft in August 1990, the squadron's role was expanded to include air defence. At that time the squadron was also split into two separate flights, designated as 'A Flight' and 'B Flight' for F-7P and T-33/RT-33 aircraft, respectively. On 7 July 1993, the T-33/RT-33 aircraft were phased out, and the squadron's role was confined to air defence only. In October 1993, the squadron was renamed the No. 2 Air Superiority Squadron.

Apart from the essential quarterly exercises, the squadron participated in many operational and air defence exercises. They included all the Saffron Bandit exercises, the Armament Competition-96, Inspired Alert exercises with the US Navy, Excercise High Mark-95 and Air-to-Air Missile Firing-98. The squadron participated in several inter-Service exercises such as 'Sea Spark', and an Army exercise at Kotri in 1991. The squadron won the Non-AI Air Superiority ACES trophy during 1997.

No. 5 Squadron

The No. 5 Tactical Attack and Reconnaissance Squadron is the second oldest fighter squadron of the PAF. It is one of the few squadrons that conducts operational missions even during peacetime. It is responsible for trans-frontier photo reconnaissance the year round. The pilots of this illustrious squadron use special reconnaissance pods to photograph the entire eastern border from the Himalayas to the Arabian Sea. The entire operation is divided into several parts, and is conducted in close coordination with friendly radars and escorts. The results of reconnaissance flights are disseminated among the Armed Services of Pakistan.

The squadron uses four different types of Mirage aircraft. This alone makes it a unique squadron, as it has to face multiple maintenance and operational problems. Despite this, the squadron won the Inter-Squadron Maintenance Efficiency Trophy in 1991, 1992 and 1995. During ISAC-96, the squadron was placed first among all the conventional weapon systems and was judged to be fourth over all.

The squadron completed fifty years of existence in 1997. An impressive ceremony was arranged on 25 October 1997, to celebrate this event, and a large number of serving and retired PAF officers were invited to PAF Base Rafiqui. The then CAS, Air Chief Marshal Abbas Khattak, Air Chief Marshal Hakimullah and other war veterans of the squadron, including Air Commodore (Retd.) Imtiaz Bhatti and Group Captain (Retd.) Cecil Chaudhry, graced the occasion. The squadron arranged a historical presentation for the guests during the event, which lasted for two days.

The squadron participated actively in all the PAF operational exercises. The

Air Chief Marshal Khattak, CAS, Air Marshal Qureshi, VCAS, with senior retired officers at the fiftieth anniversary of No. 5 Squadron

specialist role of photo reconnaissance keeps the squadron's operations dispersed to multiple locations round the year. Monthly ADA duties and different training cycles further increase the operational responsibilities of this squadron. During peacetime, the squadron fulfilled another kind of assignment by actively participating in the last election and census duties. The No. 5 squadron Falcons take their name from the squadron crest painted on their mirages.

A historical gallery has been set up in the squadron headquarters to preserve the past and its glories. The main features of the gallery include photographs of the pioneers, different trophies won by the squadron, crests, and other photographs of historical significance. This squadron occupies an important place in the PAF as is evident from the number of visits paid to the unit by important national and foreign personalities. Delegations from the Pakistan Army and National Defence College are also regular visitors to the squadron.

No. 6 Squadron

Whenever fighter squadrons are to be deployed to FOBs, this transport squadron delivers men and material at a very short notice. Besides undertaking domestic assignments, the squadron is often tasked to uplift service freight from other countries. An annual Hajj flight takes PAF personnel to Jeddah to enable them to perform their religious obligation. The squadron has also been flying the PAF Air War College on its educational tours abroad. The countries visited in this connection include the USA,

China, England, Australia, North Korea, Germany, Egypt, Syria, Cyprus, Singapore, Malaysia, and Sri Lanka.

The squadron has always supported the Pakistan Army in several types of operations. These missions include paratrooping and para-drop to all drop zones of the country. When the difficult mountainous terrain of the northern area hinders the transportation of men and material of the Pakistan Army, this squadron comes to their rescue by evacuating casualties and injured personnel from the field. The squadron conducts aerial drop missions at Paiju Drop Zone by flying through the most difficult valleys in the world. During the last decade, it has flown thirty-four such sorties, on average, each year. The Pakistan Navy also seeks help from the squadron whenever it needs it. One such exercise named Sea Spark was conducted in October 1989, during which C-130 aircraft provided tactical and logistic support. The squadron also helps PIA with domestic flights to the northern areas. Search and rescue missions were flown in July 1989,

after a PIA Fokker was lost while flying from Gilgit to Chaklala. Special flights were also conducted in November 1994 to convey stranded PIA passengers bound for Gilgit.

The squadron has always been quick to react to emergencies, both inside and outside Pakistan. This squadron is ever ready to extend its services in times of emergency, such as after earthquakes and floods. After the Gulf War, a C-130 carrying relief goods was sent to Kuwait in March 1991. Similarly, the squadron flew a large number of flood and earthquake relief missions to friendly foreign countries.

A large mob of Afghan nationals attacked the Pakistan Embassy in Kabul in September 1995. The embassy was destroyed and one of the staff members died while the rest were seriously injured. On 7 September 1995, a C-130 aircraft with Group Captain Nayyar as Mission Commander was sent to Kabul for the recovery and evacuation of the embassy staff. The aircraft landed under extremely hostile conditions and the crew still managed to evacuate the personnel within half an hour. During this operation, another C-130 aircraft kept flying over Kabul in order to relay the prevailing situation to the Air Headquarters. Many such delicate missions have been flown to different parts of Afghanistan under very trying conditions to rescue, negotiate, and seek peace.

During May 1998, prior to the nuclear tests conducted by Pakistan, the squadron carried 12,66,615 lb load in seventy-one sorties, which is an achievement that its personnel remember with pride.

No. 7 Squadron

After bidding farewell to the 'Heavies' (B-57s) on 27 December 1983, the agile and sleek A-5s became the flying machines of 7 Squadron. During 1988, the maintenance of the A-5 fleet was going

through a turbulent phase, so the men and material of this squadron were distributed among other units. The squadron was temporarily disbanded during the second half of 1988. On 13 November 1989, when the squadron was re-established with A-5s that had been overhauled in China, it took hardly any time to retain its operational status. The squadron participated in all the operational exercises conducted by the PAF. In May 1990, the Air Headquarters declared this squadron as an OCU for A-5 aircraft. A batch of newly graduated fighter pilots from the FCU reported to the squadron and completed their operational conversion successfully. Unfortunately, owing to the limitations of the aircraft ejection seat, many aircrew fatalities took place on A-5s. Therefore, the fleet was grounded again. During this transitional period, all the aircrew except the officer commanding, were attached or posted to other squadrons. On 1 July 1991, PAF Base Masroor received the first batch of Martin Baker zero-zero seats and all the

A-5s started flying again within a span of two months.

Air Headquarters decided to re-equip No. 7 Squadron with ex-Australian Mirage-III aircraft, and thus the A-5s were transferred to Peshawar. Pilots experienced on Mirage aircraft were initially posted to the squadron to make it operationally stable. Those pilots were dubbed the 'Magnificent Seven' in the squadron history book. They were tasked with the responsibility of restoring the operational status of the squadron, as soon as possible. After the first three Mirages had been received from PAC Kamra, the dawn of 24 November 1991 witnessed the first training sorties being generated by the squadron.

During 1992, the squadron continued to gain proficiency on the newly inducted weapon system. On 15 February 1993, the squadron's entire flight line assets were swapped with those of 22 OCU. While this change kept the squadron waiting for the allotment of role and task by the Air Headquarters, it remained busy while integrating this new weapon system in the squadron. In November 1992, the squadron participated in the exercise Saffron Bandit, for the first time. The squadron also participated in all the operational exercises including High Mark-93 and 95, and air-to-air camp in 1995. The squadron stood fourth overall in the armament competition held in 1996.

The squadron received the ROSE modified ex-Australian Mirage aircraft during 1997. It proved its mettle in the annual air-to-ground weapon delivery exercises. The squadron participated in the Live Missile Firing Camp, held at PAF Masroor in 1998. It had the honour of guarding the aerial frontiers over Balochistan, prior to Pakistan's nuclear tests. At present, the squadron operates the maximum number of ROSE modified aircraft. After the induction of the new airborne radar, the squadron's role will be changed from a tactical to a multi-role unit.

No. 8 Squadron

The No. 8 Tactical Attack Squadron is the only squadron in the PAF that provides maritime support missions to the Pakistan Navy, in addition to carrying out its normal operational commitments as a strike platform. The squadron aircraft are capable of carrying the Exocet Antiship Missile (the destroyer of Sheffield—the Royal Navy ship in the Falklands War). Although the squadron was at full operational status, the inventory of the squadron was completed after the induction of six Mirages in December 1993.

During the last decade, the squadron had the opportunity to participate in a number of operational exercises during which its performance remained exceptional. The squadron was deployed at Sargodha in 1990,

1992, 1995, and 1997 in connection with SCUP and Saffron Bandit exercises. As a strike platform, the squadron was pitched against F-6, F-7 and F-16 aircraft and it engaged all its assigned targets successfully. The CCS duly acknowledged the immaculate planning, professional execution, and high standards of flight safety particularly during the mass raids conducted by the squadron.

For DACT camps, the squadron was deployed to bases and satellites like Samungli, Minhas, Shahbaz and Multan. Besides, various squadrons were also invited to the home base for the same purpose. The squadron pilots were continually exposed to the entire inventory of the PAF during the period. The innovation and initiative remained the hallmark of the squadron's weapon employment, exhibiting extremely high standards of training. During exercise High Mark-93 and 95, the squadron lived up to its reputation of sustaining back bending operations from Chander and Shahbaz, and performed exceptionally well without compromising on flight safety.

The squadron maintains a close liaison with the Pakistan Navy. Exercises such as Sea Spark and Nasim-ul-Bahr are regularly conducted, covering the entire coastal region of Pakistan. A squadron contingent is required to activate the Pasni airfield and conduct operations from both the coastal airfields simultaneously. During one of the Nasim-ul-Bahr exercises, Wing Commander Shahid Latif, the Officer Commanding of the squadron, fired an Exocet missile against a decommissioned Pakistan Navy ship, PNS Shahjehan, scoring a direct hit.

The squadron also participated in the ISAC-96. Among the sixteen operational squadrons participating in the event, this squadron earned the second position. During exercise Inspired Alert, the squadron had the unique opportunity of facing USN combat aircraft such as F-14 and F-18, and it put up an impressive performance in a series of these exercises during the period 1994 to 1997. The squadron also conducted successful mass raids against Naval ships, with precision, and achieved exceptional results. It took part in the Missile Firing Camp-1998, and it emerged in first place amongst the tactical attack squadrons for the ACES trophy, in 1996. All along, the squadron continued to strive for the safety standards. These efforts earned for the Base the Flight Safety Trophy in 1997. On 24 September 1992, Flight Lieutenant Ali and Flight Lieutenant Mazhar intercepted a stray Indian Naval Battleship, INS Talwar, in Pakistan's territorial waters. These young men ushered it out of our territorial limits and such an occurrence has not been repeated.

The Griffins, 1996

No. 9 Squadron

No. 9 Multi Role Squadron is the seniormost squadron of the PAF and has always been considered its most elite unit. The F-86, F-104, Mirage, and the F-16 aircraft have been on the inventory of this squadron. Since Air Marshal Asghar Khan, seven Chiefs of the Air Staff have been members of this squadron. Undoubtedly no other PAF Squadron pilot can be as proud of his history as a Griffin. This squadron celebrated its fifty year (1943-1993) anniversary on 14 October 1993. The Griffins, in their unique style, made the occasion a memorable one by arranging a whole day of festivities. All the retired Chiefs of Air Staff, PAF were invited, together with all serving and retired Griffins of the rank of Air Commodore and above. The day's activities included visits to the squadron headquarters, ADA hut, and flight lines, besides a spectacular static display of various aircraft. The squadron commander made a comprehensive presentation on the history of the squadron.

The squadron was awarded 'Best Combat Ready Squadron', 'Combat Flying Training' and 'Maintenance Efficiency' trophies for the year 1991, and earned the title of 'Top Gun-1991'. The squadron again won the 'Inter-Squadron Maintenance Efficiency Trophy' for the year 1993. The Griffins led the Pakistan Day fly-past contingent and won the 'Best Formation Trophy' for the year 1996. It also earned the coveted title of 'Sher Afgan' by securing the first position in the ISAC-96. Squadron Leader Aasim Zaheer was declared 'Sher Afgan' of the

273

The Griffins of No. 9 Squadron

A group photograph of the No. 9 Squadron at its Golden Jubilee celebration competition. The Griffins had the distinction of being the 'Best Multi-Role Squadron' of the PAF in 1996. It also won the 'Maintenance Efficiency' trophy for the year 1996-97. In 1997, it earned the 'War Preparedness' and 'Best Combat Ready Squadron' trophies for the year 1997, and was yet again declared 'Top Gun' for the year 1997. The Griffins achieved the unique distinction of holding the dual titles of 'Sher Afgan' as well as 'Top Gun' in 1997. The Squadron was deployed at PAF Base Samungli on 27 May 1998 to provide air defence cover in connection with the nuclear tests. It successfully accomplished the deployment at very short notice.

Wing Commander Azher Hasan, officer commanding, 9 Squadron, PAF, appeared in a live television interview on PTV World in connection with the 'Defence Day Celebrations—1998'. It was an acknowledgment of the squadron's performance and the meritorious services rendered to the PAF and to the nation. Wing Commander Azher Hasan, in his interview, talked about the history and contributions made by the squadron in times of peace and war.

The squadron took part in all the operational exercises that the PAF normally conducts. These included DACT camps, Saffron Bandit, High Mark exercises, multinational exercises and numerous air defence exercises. Five pilots of this squadron moved to Masroor with their aircraft on 7 October 1996 to participate in the ISAC-96. The team won the 'Sher Afgan Trophy'. The squadron came out as the best amongst the finest in the Air Force. It participated in the Pakistan Independence Day Golden Jubilee fly-past on 7 September 1997, along with the Turkish Air Force team of four F-16 aircraft, that had flown to Pakistan especially for the purpose. The squadron also participated in the air show at the Capital Park Islamabad, arranged by the PAF on 24 November 1997 to mark the

Golden Jubilee Independence celebrations. Wing Commander Azher Hasan performed solo aerobatics.

The No. 9 squadron was regularly visited by VIPs, and foreign dignitaries including the President and Prime Minister of Pakistan, Chairman JCSC, C-in-C US Central Command, and several other foreign Chiefs of the Air Staff.

No. 11 Squadron

After playing a significant role in the Afghan war, this squadron maintained its legendary traditions during numerous operational exercises in the last decade. It made a landmark contribution to the history of the PAF by winning the 'Top Gun' trophy of ACES, three years in a row, in 1993, 1994 and 1995.

While deployed at Masroor in February 1990, the squadron carried out LGB trials at Sonmiani air-to-ground range and also participated in exercise Hit Hard XII.

In July 1991, the squadron participated in a DACT camp against 5, 18 and 20 Squadrons. There was an imminent threat to our nuclear installations in early 1992, and the squadron had to fly the national contingency 'Thunderbolt' for a period from 19 February 1992 onwards. During the last decade, the squadron remained very busy during all the operational, air defence and multi-national exercises that were conducted from time to time, including the High Mark series of exercises, as well as Saffron Bandit, DACT camps, Inspired Alert etc. Besides, the squadron is also an operational conversion unit for the F-16 aircraft; therefore, the Squadron is also responsible for conducting these courses. The squadron achieved a unique distinction when all of its instructors gathered on-type flying experience in excess of 1,000 hours.

During High Mark-93, the squadron achieved 100 per cent of the allotted task; the squadron earned 225 kills out of all the shots claimed. ATLIS attack had a 100 per cent success rate. The squadron secured third position in the ISAC-96, held at Masroor.

After the nuclear tests by India in May 1998, the tension on the borders heightened. The PAF was put on higher alert and the squadron moved to its wartime location on 24 May 1998. In spite of the very hot weather and the degraded facilities at the satellite, the squadron measured up to the task, and successfully and satisfactorily performed the day and night ADA duties till Pakistan's own tests were completed on 28 May 1998.

The Inspectorate team visited the squadron on 28 October 1991 and termed the inspection as exceptional. The ACES team visited the squadron on 8 February 1993 and the squadron won three out of the four trophies, including 'Top Gun' for the year 1993. During the ORI of 1995, the squadron won the ACES trophy for the second consecutive time, winning three out of four trophies again. In 1996, the squadron achieved a landmark in the history of the PAF by retaining the coveted ACES trophy for the third consecutive time. During ACES inspection in 1997, the squadron secured the second position, staying very close to the 'Top Gun' squadron for the year 1998.

The squadron had the honour of receiving a number of important visitors, including the Prime Ministers, Chairman Joint Chiefs of Staff, the Defence Minister and the Chief of the Air Staff.

No. 12 Squadron

The role of the No. 12 squadron is to transport VIPs, both home and abroad. It is also responsible for the calibration of navigational aids throughout the country. The squadron flies the President, the Prime Minister, the CAS, foreign heads of state, and other important dignitaries. A C-130 carrying the President of Pakistan, Chairman

Joint Chief of Staff, the American Ambassador to Pakistan, and several others from Bahawalpur to Chaklala, crashed on 17 August 1988, killing everybody on board. The Officer Commanding 12 Squadron, Wing Commander Mashood, was the captain of this ill-fated aircraft.

On 31 January 1989, Group Captain Maqsood, Wing Commander Sabahat and Wing Commander Inam operated the first VIP flight on a Boeing 707. From 24 June to 8 July 1990, the squadron flew eleven relief flights to Tehran on the Boeing 707 aircraft. The Prime Minister of Pakistan was flown to Kuwait on 25 March 1991. This was just after the Gulf War, when the Kuwait airport had no navigational aids and the city was engulfed in thick clouds of smoke rising from the burning oil wells. From 14 to 22 May 1991, the squadron flew six relief sorties to Dhaka.

In 1994, a PIA Boeing 737 was officially handed over to the PAF for VIP commitments. Initially, eight officers were sent abroad for training. They continued their line training with the Boeing Company instructors in Pakistan. The Boeing 737 flew its first VIP sortie with the President of Pakistan, Mr Farooq Ahmad Leghari, on 13 December 1994. The operating crew included Wing Commander Jamal, Wing Commander Anjum and the Squadron Leader Aasim.

On 7 November 1995, after take-off from Darwin (Australia) with President Farooq Ahmed Leghari on board, the No. 1 engine of the Boeing 707 caught fire, and suffered severe damage and the rupture of a fuel tank. Wing Commander Kamal, who was occupying the captain's seat at that time, landed the aircraft safely at Darwin.

From 15 to 20 October 1995, a number of missions were flown to Kandhar and Mazar-e-Sharif on DA-20 and F-27 aircraft, as part of the shuttle diplomacy between Pakistan and Afghanistan. During 1997, a number of peace missions were flown to various cities of Afghanistan including Kabul, Mazar-e-Sharif, Kandhar, and Shabbarghan, carrying Mr Iftikhar Murshad, Additional Secretary of Afghanistan Affairs and others, for negotiations between the Talibans and Iran. During one such mission on 12 July 1997, while flying at night from Mazar-e-Sharif to Peshawar, the aircraft, an F-27, was diverted to Mazar-e-Sharif due to an in-flight emergency. Because of lack of communication facilities and poor lighting conditions on the runway, it was about to be shot down by the Afghans who mistook it for an enemy aircraft. However, it landed safely. Wing Commander Khalid Kamal was the captain of the aircraft.

As in the previous year, extensive peace missions were flown to Afghanistan carrying the Additional Secretary of Afghanistan Affairs, Foreign Office Officials, a Saudi Prince, and an Iranian delegation. These dignitaries were meeting for negotiations, and to ease tension between Iran and Afghanistan. As a result of these peace missions, the Government of Afghanistan released five captured drivers initially, and all the remaining prisoners later, who were then flown to Islamabad on a Fokker aircraft.

During the month of July 1997, the Chief of the Air Staff, Air Chief Marshal Parvaiz Mehdi Qureshi was converted on DA-20, and flew his first mission to Lahore on 28 July 1997.

From January 1993 to April 1994, the squadron flew 181 hours on the Boeing 707 aircraft, in support of the United Nations' peacekeeping mission in Mogadishu (Somalia). Between May 1993 and June 1998, the squadron flew 590 hours for missions to Ankara, Colombo, and Almaty as chartered flights for Shaheen Air Cargo.

No. 14 Squadron

This squadron had been an OCU for the F-6 aircraft until September 1986, when it was re-equipped with the F-16 multi-role aircraft and shifted to Kamra. The squadron's stay at Kamra (later renamed Minhas) proved to be extremely fruitful. During the long Afghan war, the squadron flew extensive combat air patrol missions over the western borders. The ever vigilant presence of the Tail Choppers on the border earned them five kills.

On 16 April 1987, Squadron Leader Badar Islam, with Squadron Leader Khalid Pervez Marwat as his No. 2, shot down an Afghan SU-22 with an AIM-9L missile. Squadron Leader Saif-ur-Rehman was controlling the formation. On the night of 4 August 1988, an SU-25 was shot down and its Russian pilot, who ejected, was taken prisoner. The pilot of this aircraft was Colonel Alexander Rutskoi, who later rose to the position of Vice President of the Russian Federation. Squadron Leader Athar Bukhari was the pilot of the F-16 while

Squadron Leader Taufiq Raja controlled this night interception.

On 12 September 1988, Flight Lieutenant Khalid shot down two Mig-23 aircraft; Squadron Leader Irfan-ul-Haq was the controller. Again on 3 November 1988, Flight Lieutenant Khalid Mehmood shot down an Afghan SU-22. The young Afghan pilot who ejected was later handed over to the Afghan Government. Squadron Leader Saif-ur-Rehman controlled this formation.

On 9 September 1993, a nine-ship F-16 formation made a farewell fly-past over Minhas to say goodbye before departing for Sargodha. During the month that followed, the squadron was re-equipped with the latest Chinese F-7P aircraft, under the command of Wing Commander Abbas Petiwala.

On 1 November 1998, the Tail Choppers celebrated their fiftieth year. Air Vice Marshal (Rtd.) M. Khyber Khan, the first Squadron Commander of 14 Squadron, reviewed the Golden Jubilee Celebration parade. The Squadron Commander, Wing Commander Khaleel Ahmed, commanded the parade while Flying Officer Faisal Gul was the colour bearer. The parade was dovetailed with the fly-past of the 'Missing Man Formation'. This fly-past, led by Wing Commander Arshad Mahmood, was meant to pay tribute to the martyrs of the squadron.

No. 15 Squadron

The Cobras continued to defend the western borders and faced Afghan intruders boldly until the end of the war. They flew innumerable scrambles as well as CAP missions throughout the conflict. The squadron got relocated to Minhas in June 1989. In July 1993, the squadron bade farewell to its aging F-6 aircraft and was re-equipped with the Chinese F-7P fighter interceptor aircraft. In the same year, in August, Skardu was activated and safe

Air Chief Marshal Parvaiz Mehdi Qureshi with former Chiefs of Air Staff, AVM Khyber Khan and members of the No. 14 Squadron at its Golden Jubilee, 1 November 1998

operations were conducted despite inclement weather and problems associated with high altitude operations.

The squadron continued to participate actively in all the operational exercises conducted in the PAF, like DACT, High Mark series of exercises and Saffron Bandit. The squadron flew the maximum number of sorties in High Mark-95. It created a new record in the PAF's history by scoring an 'A' in the air-to-air firing camp held at Masroor in January 1996. The aircrew displayed their professional skill during the Pakistan Day Fly-Past on 23 March 1997 and won the Best Formation Trophy.

As a consequence of the PAF Force Re-structuring Programme, the squadron was numberplated on 31 October 1997 and the F-7P aircraft on its inventory were distributed among other F-7 operating units. The unit will be re-equipped with ex-French Mirage aircraft and is scheduled to be reformed at its new location, Rafiqui. The squadron will then take up the role of a tactical attack squadron.

No. 16 Squadron

In 1988, this squadron was stationed at PAF Base Rafiqui, and was equipped with A-5 aircraft. The year was full of operational commitments. In addition to one Flat Out and two Wide Awake exercises, the squadron carried out the Long Shadow Exercise in February, and Hit Hard-VI, VII and VIII in April, June, and August 1988, respectively. In addition, the Fake-XIV and Shako Exercises were also carried out. The squadron also participated in a Durandal bomb drop exercise at Sonmiani range in December. In the later half of the year, 1 vs. 1 DACT missions were carried out, evaluating the performance of the A-5 against the F-7P in close combat.

In 1989, apart from taking part in Hit Hard exercises, the squadron participated in

the Armament Competition. During the Fire Power Demonstration that followed the competition, the squadron carried out level delivery of MK-82 bombs. During the month of May, five more aircraft were added to the squadron's inventory. In November 1989, the squadron was deployed at PAF Farid for Exercise High Mark. At the end of the year, the Inter-Squadron Dive Bombing Competition was held between 16 and 26 Squadrons, which the 16 Squadron won.

During 1990, the squadron carried out one Flat Out and three Wide Awake exercises. Exercise Tondo-II, III, and IV were also carried out. In the middle of year, the Officer Commanding, Wing Commander Zafar, went to China to carry out evaluation trials on A-5M and F aircraft. The squadron pilots also went to Sargodha to undergo SCUP.

During 1991, three FT-6 aircraft, fitted with MB seats, were added to the inventory of the squadron. In addition to the exercises Flat Out and Wide Awake, the squadron also participated in Exercise Combat-VI, Sore Eyes-III, and Condor-II. During November, the squadron moved to Multan and during its stay there, it flew 115 sorties with 100 per cent serviceability and reliability.

During 1992, the squadron carried out four Wide Awake and three Flat Out exercises. The Squadron also participated in DACT Camp in April and May. In June, Exercise King Cobra was held in which the squadron achieved 100 per cent results. During 1993, in addition to the routine exercises, the squadron carried out DACT in the month of May and participated in High Mark Exercise in October. During 1995, the squadron participated in the exercise Saffron Bandit followed by exercise High Mark.

In January 1996, the squadron proceeded to Masroor for air-to-air firing. During this year, three Wide Awake and three Flat Out exercises were also carried out. During 1997, the squadron participated in exercise Fire Fox in March. This was an Air Defence exercise aimed at generating low level tracks for interceptors.

The year 1997 was full of squadron movements. The squadron was deployed twice to Minhas for a DACT Camp, and to Murid and Minhas as the runway of its parent base was being re-carpeted. The squadron was also deployed at Chaklala for ADA duties. The last deployment was at Sargodha for participation in the exercise Saffron Bandit. The squadron also participated in the fly-past on 7 September in connection with Pakistan's Golden Jubilee celebrations. Besides, the squadron carried out routine Wide Awake and Flat Out exercises. In one of the Wide Awake exercises, the canopy of an A-5 aircraft flew-off in the air, while it was proceeding to range. The aircraft landed safely at the home base. It was during this year that operations on the Jamrud Range were discontinued as it was handed over to civil authorities.

In April 1998, the squadron participated in Exercise Zarb-e-Aahen and exhibited a high standard of professionalism that was appreciated by the Corps Commander who had witnessed the entire exercise. In appreciation of the performance of the squadron pilots, he visited the squadron along with AOC, NAC, Air Vice Marshal Pervaiz Mirza, and presented a memento to the squadron. The squadron was awarded the ACES Trophy for the best performance, from among all tactical attack squadrons, in the year 1997.

No. 17 Squadron

During the Afghan conflict, this squadron carried out ADA duties from PAF Base Samungli. From July to October 1988, it carried out ADA duties at Chaklala under the command of Wing Commander Shaukat Haider Changezi. The squadron participated

in the PAF Fire Power Demonstration at Sonmiani Range on 25 March 1989, a performance which was witnessed by the then Prime Minister. The squadron also participated in ISAC-89 and won the trophy in the non-INAS aircraft category, while Flight Lieutenant Arif Khan was declared No. 1 pilot in the 'Sher Afgan-89 Armament Competition' among the non-INAS aircraft. In November/December 1989, the squadron participated in the Exercise 'Zarb-e-Momin' while operating from PAF Base Farid and PAF Vehari. In March 1990, it participated in the Pakistan Day fly-past while operating from PAF Base Peshawar. The squadron also won the 1990 ACES Trophy. In October 1996, the squadron participated in ISAC-96, held at PAF Base Masroor. The squadron pilots also carried out banner tow duties for ISAC-96. Wing Commander Khalid Chishti (then Squadron Leader) was declared the Best Shot on the F-6 weapon system.

In 1998, prior to the nuclear tests at Chaghai, the pilots of 17 Squadron carried out standing CAPs under the command of

Wing Commander Muhammad Jamil Memon.

No. 18 Squadron

In 1989, after a brief stay at Kamra, No. 18 Squadron moved back to Rafiqui. The squadron was re-equipped with F-7P aircraft, and fifteen pilots were posted to the squadron. Later, during the same year, the squadron took part in exercise High Mark. Many dignitaries, including the Bangladesh Air Chief and COAS visited the squadron during the period 1990 to 1991. In 1993, the squadron pilots visited Jordan to establish stronger ties with the RJAF, a gesture which was reciprocated by a visit from pilots of 9 Squadron of the RJAF in 1994.

In 1994-95, the squadron participated in different exercises like Saffron Bandit, Twilight, Sky Guard-III, and High Mark-95 and performed extremely well.

The year 1997 brought new laurels to the squadron when it won the 'Air Superiority' and the 'Top Gun' trophies. It was the first

F-7P squadron to have won the highest honour of the PAF.

Buster-I was the last exercise in which the squadron participated from Rafiqui. The end of the year 1998 witnessed relocation of the squadron to PAF Base Mianwali. The squadron was supposed to become an Operational Conversion Unit by the start of the year 1999.

No. 19 Squadron

No. 19 Squadron participated in the exercise High Mark-89 from Risalewala. That was the last exercise in which F-6 aircraft were used by the unit. The squadron was re-equipped with F-7P aircraft at Rafiqui in July 1990, under the command of Wing Commander Gulrez. After the re-equipment, the squadron carried out Exercise Flat Out on 17 and 19 March 1991. It also participated in Exercise Tornado-VII on 9 and 10 June 1991. The first four FT-7 aircraft were ferried from Hotian, China and were inducted in the

squadron on 7 August 1991. The squadron was tasked to conduct the first Operational Conversion Course on F-7P aircraft. Ten student pilots reported to the squadron for No. 1 OCC, which commenced on 3 September 1991. The squadron was tasked to participate in Exercise Condor-II on 9 December 1991.

DACT was conducted with A-5s in April 1992, and Exercise King Cobra-II on 6 June 1992. Air Vice Marshal Shafique Haider and Air Vice Marshal Aliuddin visited the squadron and flew two sorties each on FT-7. An Army exercise named Flash Point was carried out between 8-13 December 1992. The squadron was deployed at Chaklala from 25 January 1993 to 4 February 1993.

The squadron had its first major accident on 31 August 1994, when a student pilot, Flying Officer Imran Yousaf, crashed while trying to land an F-7P aircraft after it lost its canopy. He was fatally injured.

On the night of 13 October 1997, all the aircraft in the squadron were badly damaged by a hailstorm which had struck Mianwali.

The year 1998 remained uneventful, and the squadron continued to perform the role of an Operational Conversion Unit. The squadron had successfully graduated a total of 176 pilots till the graduation of 13 OCC.

No. 20 Squadron

In mid-1987, the PAF decided to induct the Chinese F-7P aircraft into its fighter fleet, to replace the veteran F-6s. Seven pilots proceeded to China for initial conversion on F-7P aircraft, on 8 May 1988. On 20 June 1988, Wing Commander Ghazanfar took-off in the first F-7P aircraft and was followed by Squadron Leader Asif in the second aircraft. Following the ferry of F-7P aircraft from China to Pakistan, 20 Squadron became the first squadron to operate these aircraft. On 12 August 1988, seven pilots along with ground crew and the Project Zodiac team,

proceeded to Hotian in order to ferry an additional ten F-7P aircraft. The ferry was completed on 16 August 1988. On 31 August 1988, the DCAS (M) visited the squadron and inspected the maintenance facilities for F-7P aircraft. During the rest of 1988, the squadron flew many mutual air combat missions and later, it flew such missions against other aircraft like the A-5, the Mirage, and the F-16s, in order to develop tactics in dissimilar air combat.

On 7 February 1989, the squadron participated in the first operational exercise viz. Hit Hard-X. The CAS visited the squadron during the annual inspection of the Base on 14 February 1989. During the same month, the squadron took over the role of converting pilots on the F-7P aircraft. On 23 March 1989, four F-7P aircraft flew in the fly-past for the first time in the history of the PAF. In August 1989, four FT-7s were ferried from Hotian to Peshawar. On

18 August 1989, twelve fresh graduates of 1 FCU reported to the squadron for the first Operational Conversion Course on F-7P. The squadron participated in the Air Force Day celebrations for the first time on 7 September 1989. No. 1 OCC graduated on 11 October 1989. The CAS visited the squadron on 3 November 1989, stayed with the squadron for a couple of days, and also flew the aircraft. During Exercise High Mark-89, the pilots of 18 Squadron as well as ten of its aircraft took part in the exercise as part of 20 Squadron.

On 7 February 1990, the re-equipment ceremony of the squadron took place. President Ghulam Ishaq Khan was the chief guest on this occasion. Twenty-four aircraft led by Group Captain Toor took part in the Pakistan Day fly-past on 23 March 1990. Twenty F-7Ps were ferried from Hotian to Peshawar and then to Rafiqui on 19 April 1990. In August 1991, three officers from the Sri Lankan Air Force were attached to the squadron for conversion on F-7P. On 15 October 1991, the Chief of the Air Staff of the Royal Air Force, Air Chief Marshal Sir Peter Harding, flew an FT-7 aircraft with the Officer Commanding 20 Squadron, Wing Commander Adeeb.

During the rest of the period, the squadron participated in a number of routine and command level exercises, including DACT camps held from time to time, High Mark exercises, Saffron Bandit, air-to-air firing, air defence exercises, and armament competition, etc. When PAF decided to induct F-7Ps of Hand Shake-IV in June 1993, most of the pilots detailed to ferry them were from this squadron. On 14 July 1996, AVTR modification was started on all the aircraft of the squadron. A number of VIPs also visited the squadron during this period.

No. 22 Squadron

Ever since the induction of the Mirage aircraft into the PAF in 1967, 9 Squadron had been conducting operational conversion courses on them. After the induction of F-16 aircraft into the PAF, 9 Squadron was re-equipped with F-16s and its role was changed from an OCU to a Multi Role Squadron. In order to fill the gap thus created, 22 Squadron was raised in 1985 to take over the role of operational conversion of pilots on Mirage aircraft.

The Mirage Operational Conversion Course consists of forty-six sorties that are equivalent to about forty hours of flying, per student. The duration of the course has varied from four to eleven months, depending upon the availability of dual-seat aircraft and other commitments of the squadron. However, with the increase in the number of dual-seat aircraft in the squadron, the course duration was reduced to four to five months only. The Operational Conversion Course begins with a comprehensive ATT spread over a period

of one month, followed by the flying phase. Apart from the typical syllabus of an Operational Conversion Course, the squadron lays special emphasis on air-to-ground attack, including bombing, followed by level as well as pop up strikes. From 1988 to 1998, the squadron was able to conduct sixteen operational conversion courses, graduating 158 fighter pilots.

During the last eleven years, the squadron participated in numerous operational exercises. Some of them were conducted in coordination with the Pakistan Navy. The squadron participated in the Armament Competition and Fire Power Demonstration in 1989, as well as High Mark-89 and-93. Besides, the squadron flew in exercise Inspired Alert in 1994, 1995, and 1997. During this series of exercises, the squadron's pilots flew DACT missions against the F-18 aircraft of the US Navy. In 1998, the squadron's pilots were detailed to ferry ex-French Mirage aircraft from France to Pakistan.

In January 1993, the squadron was equipped with ex-Australian Mirages, and its own aircraft were handed over to 7 TA Squadron. In the same year, the ACES team awarded an 'A+' grade to the squadron in armament loading exercises. Despite being a training unit, the squadron has an impressive flight safety record.

No. 23 Squadron

In January 1988, 23 Squadron participated in air-to-air banner firing. It provided air defence of the western borders from PAF Base Samungli, during the Afghan conflict. A detachment of the squadron consisting of twelve pilots and ten aircraft, commenced air defence duties for Kahuta, at PAF Base Chaklala, with effect from 4 April 1988. In March 1989, the squadron participated in the Fire Power Demonstration held at the

Sonmiani Range. The squadron was awarded Inter-Squadron Flight Safety Trophy for the year 1988. The squadron moved to Chander for participation in Exercise High Mark-89/ Zarb-e-Momin. The activation for this exercise lasted for a month, from 22 November to 23 December 1989. A detachment of the squadron was attached to PAF Base Sargodha for flying duties between 19 February to March 1990. On 14 March 1990, the squadron moved to PAF Base Masroor for air-to-air firing and DACT Camp.

Four officers and five aircraft went to PAF Base Peshawar to take part in the fly-past ceremony on 23 March 1991. The squadron shifted from its old underground building to its new premises in the Flying Wing Headquarters in the second quarter of 1991. In September 1991, the squadron moved to Mirpur Khas to participate in an air defence exercise. In November 1991, the squadron moved to PAF Base Farid, where it carried out another air defence exercise. The squadron had the honour of winning

Sarfraz Rafiqui Flight Safety Trophy twice in a row, for the years 1990 and 1991.

During Exercise High Mark-93, the squadron was deployed at PAF Risalewala. During 1995, it took part in Exercise Saffron Bandit as well as Exercise High Mark. In February 1997, the squadron moved to PAF Shahbaz for DACT with F-16s. The Governor of Balochistan visited the squadron on 12 August 1997.

In May 1998, the squadron was deployed at PAF Base Sukkur. The activation of Sukkur continued for about a week, ending soon after Pakistan successfully conducted its nuclear tests. The squadron, under the command of Wing Commander G. M. Abbasi, and supported by Wing Commander Irfan Idrees, Squadron Leader Khan Maqbool, Flight Lieutenants Anwer Karim, S. Atta, Waqas Mohsin, Zeeshan Saeed, Aamir Shaukat, Ali Asher, Nadeem Afzal, and Nasir Jamal, had the honour of taking part in this operational commitment.

No. 24 Squadron

No. 24 EW Squadron was formed in 1962 at PAF Base Peshawar. At that time, it had RB-57F aircraft on its inventory. The squadron was numberplated in 1967 after the withdrawal of RB-57 by the USAF. The squadron was revived in 1987, following the induction of two DA-20 aircraft fitted with a modern EW suite. The primary role of the squadron is to provide dedicated ESM and ECM (EW) support to the PAF during both war and peace. The squadron also conducts training of electronics and air defence officers, on the EW concepts, equipment and operational tactics. Most of the maintenance is done at the squadron level, which includes first and second-line maintenance, and servicing of EW suite along with major and minor repairs. The data collected through the EW missions is analyzed by electronic

warfare officers to evaluate enemy tactics and establish the enemy's electronic order of battle.

The squadron participated in various PAF exercises in both ECM and early warning roles. The first major exercise in which the squadron took part was Zarb-e-Momin in 1989, during which twenty-one ECM missions were flown. During Exercise High Mark 89, 93, and 95, the squadron flew seventeen, fourteen, and sixty-five missions, respectively. Communication and radar jamming was carried out successfully and spoofing was very effective. Also, friendly forces were provided with valuable and timely warning of intruding aircraft. In 1997, during exercise Saffron Bandit, thirty-five missions were flown. In this exercise, the squadron provided ECM training to the pilots and controllers, and almost the entire air force was exposed to operations under degraded environments. Moreover, lectures covering the capabilities of the DA-20 were also delivered to the participating squadrons.

The squadron participated in almost all the air defence exercises conducted within the PAF during the last ten years, besides taking part in various joint exercises with the Army and the Navy. In the joint exercises, practice to operate in EW environment was given to the Army and the Navy, and the susceptibility of their equipment to jamming was analyzed. Some of the important exercises included Naval ECM Exercise in 1991, Exercise Sky Guard in 1994, Jiddat in 1995, Sea Lion in 1996, and Sea Hawk and jamming of Army Fire Control Radar in 1997. In 1998, jamming was carried out against Sky Guard Radar and LAADS of the Army Air Defence System.

The squadron also carried out ESM during Exercise Inspired Alert-94 and 95, and Sea Spark-95, to find out the capabilities of the radar and the tactics used by participating aircraft. The squadron flies extensively to ensure complete coverage on all the enemy exercises. The data collected during these exercises is analyzed to determine the enemy's operating tactics and deployment of assets. Besides, the assets of this squadron form an integral part of trans-frontier photo-recce missions that are carried out from time to time.

No. 25 Squadron
On 27 August 1986, 25 Squadron was permanently shifted to PAF Base Mianwali to be merged into 14 OCU as the latter was nominated to become the third F-16 squadron of the PAF. It was tasked to conduct operational conversion of the graduates of 1 FCU on F-6/FT-6 aircraft. On 17 October 1989, the squadron moved to Sargodha as the re-carpeting of the runway at Mianwali airfield was in progress. The squadron moved back to Mianwali on 30 March 1990.

The 31st OCC was the last F-6 conversion course to be graduated by 25 OCU, after

which the squadron's assets were withdrawn and allotted to 17 and 23 Squadrons. The last F-6 of 25 Squadron took-off for Samungli on 9 December 1995.

The squadron was relocated at PAF Base Minhas on 25 January 1996. It formed a staging flight for ROSE modified Mirage aircraft. The squadron completed trials on all such aircraft in 1998. These Rose-I modified aircraft now form part of 7 Squadron and CCS Mirage squadron.

The squadron was re-designated as 25 TA Squadron and assigned the specialist night attack role with effect from March 1997. On 29 September 1998, the first two Mirage-V EF (Rose-II) aircraft were ferried to Minhas from France. The squadron is presently waiting for the next Rose-II Mirage ferry before it can become a full-fledged operational squadron.

No. 26 Squadron

In the year 1989, apart from Flat Out and Wide Awake exercises, the squadron took part in air-to-air firing camp at PAF Base Masroor. The squadron also took part in the Inter-Squadron Armament Competition and the officer commanding, Wing Commander Wali Mughni, was declared the 'Sher Afgan'. During the month of April 1989, the squadron's pilots ferried the aircraft to China for overhaul. The squadron was Runner-Up in ACES for the year 1989. It also took part in Exercise High Mark-89.

During 1991, MB seats were installed on four A-5 aircraft. During 1992, the squadron participated in a DACT Camp, which was held at PAF Base Minhas. Apart from some air defence exercises, the squadron also conducted routine exercises like Flat Out and Wide Awake. The squadron won the 'Sarfraz Rafiqui Flight Safety Trophy' for the year 1992.

In 1993, the squadron participated in exercise High Mark-93 while operating from Murid. The squadron won the 'Chief of the Air Staff Professionals Trophy' along with the 'Sarfraz Rafiqui Trophy' for the year 1994. During Exercise High Mark-95, the

squadron was deployed at Jacobabad. In 1996, the squadron won the 'Sarfraz Rafiqui Trophy' as well as the ACES Trophy.

A Turkish delegation comprising two officers and three cadets visited the squadron during the year 1997. The squadron also participated in Exercise Saffron Bandit during the same year. In 1998, a contingent of three A-5 and as many pilots from the squadron took part in the Live Missile Firing Camp held at Masroor. From 14 to 30 September 1998, the squadron participated in the DACT camp held at Minhas. In that camp, ten A-5 aircraft and all the pilots of 26 Squadron took part. The other participating units were 8 and 16 Squadrons.

In October 1998, the squadron was deployed at PAF Base Sargodha with 8xA-5 aircraft and ten pilots to complete armament cyclic training for 1998. During the nineteen-day stay from 5 to 24 October 1998, the squadron flew 246 armament sorties.

Combat Commanders' School (CCS)

The Combat Commanders' School continues to fulfill its mission of training fighter pilots and air defence controllers. During the past twenty three years, CCS has graduated 350 fighter pilots and 186 combat controllers including a controller from the UAE Air Force.

Besides fulfilling its peacetime role of conducting Combat Commanders' Courses, the unit also evaluates all PAF fighter squadrons and carries out research and development on aerial and ground attack tactics. The CCS Mirage and F-7 Squadrons also continue to train for their wartime roles.

In addition to the usual Combat Commanders' Courses (CCCs), two Fighter Weapon Instructors' Courses (FWICs) were also conducted for junior leaders, bringing the total to three such courses. Later, FWICs were discontinued to accomodate the more urgent need for imparting training to senior supervisors, who could in turn train junior pilots in the squadrons. The school has so far conducted three FWICs and twenty-seven CCCs.

In order to keep pace with the ever-changing aerial threat and environment, CCS reviews its course contents continually. New study and flying phases involving EW and BVR threat have been added and others augmented with changing fighter tactics. The CCS continues to emphasize the develop-ment of courage, aggression and *esprit de corps* in an air battle, and a deep awareness of the threat posed to the country.

The CCS participated in all the operational exercises conducted by the PAF, that included Exercises Hit Hard-XIII and High Mark-89/ Zarb-e-Momin. The CCS staff acted as umpires in High Mark-95. The School also supervised and conducted the Inter-Squadron Armament competition, Sher Afgan-1989 and 1996, at PAF Base Masroor.

To keep the PAF's fighting elements at the peak of their efficiency, CCS was given the responsibility of conducting annual visits to all the fighter squadrons to enhance their combat awareness and assess their combat efficiency. Later, in June 1990, Air Headquarters instituted the Squadron Combat Upgradation Programme (SCUP). Two fighter squadrons, along with a few pilots from F-16 and air defence weapon controllers, participated in each cycle which lasted for a month. Four such cycles were conducted till October 1990.

To further consolidate the professional architecture of the PAF, SCUP was replaced by Exercise Saffron Bandit in September 1992. This exercise provided a more complicated, near realistic, and demanding environment to the participants. The CCS has supervised all Saffron Bandit exercises while continually improving the flying and air defence syllabi.

Research and development in the realm of tactics and conducting weapon trials also forms an important part of the school's responsibilities. Its working influences almost every operational dimension of PAF activity. The school has also remained actively involved in future projects aiming at new induction and upgradation. In the same context, Squadron Leader Athar Bukhari visited China in May 1992 and became the first Pakistani pilot to fly an F-8 II aircraft. Squadron Leader Khalid P. Marwat was attached to the ROSE Project for upgrading Mirage-III avionics. Wing Commander Raza recently concluded successful trials of LGB deliveries from Mirage III aircraft.

On 10 July 1988, Air Chief Marshal Hakimullah, the then Chief of the Air Staff, made the historic announcement of inducting F-16 aircraft into the school's curriculum. On 16 July 1988, an F-16 instructional unit was established at CCS. With the induction of the F-16 weapon system in the CCS, PAF's tactical doctrine experienced a

qualitative improvement. The introduction of F-16s in the course not only helped refine tactical employment of the weapon system, but also brought greater awareness amongst the aircrew flying the more conventional aircraft.

The next advance in hardware came in 1993, when F-7P aircraft replaced the aging F-6s. F-7P has a more pilot friendly reputation as compared to its predecessor— the sturdy F-6 Farmer. The new aircraft also had better avionics, and in particular, the radar warning receiver and chaff and flare dispenser gave it an advantage over the Mirage-V in the sister squadron.

To keep CCS in the forefront of weapon system induction and development of system specific tactics, Air Headquarters once again re-equipped the CCS Mirage squadron with the latest ROSE-1 modified Mirage-III EA, in 1998. The ROSE modified Mirages afford the latest avionics suite in the PAF so far. The induction of F-7s and the ROSE modified Mirage-III EA gave more impetus to the progressive evaluation of the PAF tactical doctrine.

In 1986, Air Chief Marshal Jamal A. Khan thought of raising a fighter gallery at Sargodha to impart a greater sense of history to the PAF officers and men. On his directive, work on a specifically designed building in the CCS complex started the same year. At the same time, carefully selected aircraft models were procured from England and America. However, it was only in 1994 that the officer commanding CCS Mirage was entrusted with the task of furnishing and decorating the gallery. A team comprising eight officers, airmen, and civilians, with the full availability of base resources, completed the project in a manner that was highly appreciated by all visitors. Fighter Gallery was inaugurated on 28 July 1994.

The gallery, which was the first of its kind in the PAF, was developed around many well-blended themes, the chief among them being a chronological depiction of the evolution of combat aviation. The PAF's evolution was presented in a tastefully decorated section with the help of large scale models of almost all the PAF aircraft. The Fighter Gallery became popular with visitors and remained an essential part of visit programmes of all the dignitaries visiting PAF Base Sargodha. All assets of the gallery were shifted to the PAF Base Faisal on 24 December 1996, which then became part of the newly developed PAF Museum.

On 19 October 1987, Air Chief Marshal Jamal A. Khan presented the Combat Commander's Creed to the CCS. The laser-etched text on the teak board that now hangs prominently in the CCS building reads:

A Combat Commander of the Pakistan Air Force:

- ¤ Shall uphold the credo "Commitment, Courage, Competence."
- ¤ Shall always expose himself to danger ahead of his subordinates or at least share risks equally with them.
- ¤ Shall hold the conviction that there is no difference between call of duty and call of honour.
- ¤ Shall never seek self advancement or glory in the air at the cost of a comrade.
- ¤ Shall always choose, when faced with two equally adverse options in combat, the more honourable course.
- ¤ Shall boldly express his pride and sincere belief in the righteousness of his profession.

The school has benefited a good deal from the evolution of tactical thought in the air forces of advanced countries. To study the progress of other air forces and the changes in their operational training concepts, the school staff made visits to renowned training institutions of the US, British, German, French and Turkish Air Forces. On 11 October 1988, Group Captain Zahid Anis (now Air Marshal), Officer Commanding CCS, delivered a lecture on 'Air intercept Operations over Mountainous Terrain' at the Dutch Weapon Instructors' School in the Netherlands.

Many local and foreign teams and dignitaries visited the CCS during the last decade. General Larry D. Welch, Chief of Staff, USAF, came in November 1988, the Chief of the Bangladesh Air Force and Admiral Iftikhar A. Sirohi, Chairman JCSC, visited in 1991. In 1993, the then Prime Minister of Pakistan, Nawaz Sharif, Lieutenant-General Ahmed Bin Ibrahim Behery, Chief of Staff, Royal Saudi Air Force, and General Vincent Lanata, Chief of Staff, French Air Force, visited CCS. General Merril A. McPeak, Chief of Staff, USAF, General Zhang Wannian, Chief of General Staff, PLA China, and General Halis Burhan, Commander, Turkish Air Force, were other notable dignitaries that visited the school.

Important visitors in 1994 included the then President of Pakistan, Farooq Ahmad Khan Leghari, Lieutenant-General Guido Vanhecke, Chief of Staff, Belgian Air Force, and Air Vice Marshal Muhamad bin Mahfoodh, Comander, Royal Air Force of Oman. Major General Muhammad Ali Qadah, Chief of Staff, Royal Jordanian Air Force and General Artuo T. Enrile, Chief of Staff, Philippines Armed Forces visited CCS in 1995. Air Chief Marshal Pambudi, Chief of Staff, Indonesian Air Force, visited in 1996.

In 1997, for the first time, PAF opened the doors of the CCS to officers from friendly countries. Captain Abdullah, an air defence controller from the UAE Air Force, was given a seat in No. 26 CCC. Captain M. Mattar, a pilot from the UAE Air Force also joined the same course as an observer. He was later inducted in No. 27 CCC on Mirage aircraft.

No. 41 Light Communication Squadron

On 23 June 1966, 41 Light Communication Flight was formed at PAF Base Peshawar. At that time, the flight was equipped with one Beechcraft, one Aero Commander and one T-6G aircraft. The task assigned to this flight was communication of service personnel, freight and mail. Four new Cessna-172 aircraft were inducted in the year 1974-75, and three out of these were later allotted to other bases. Two more aircraft, i.e. one Beech Baron (B-55) and one Cessna-172 were added to the flight in 1979 and 1982, respectively. The Aero Commander was phased out in 1991 and is now placed in the PAF museum.

On 13 August 1985, 41 Flight was upgraded to a squadron. On 29 August 1988, the squadron shifted to PAF Base

Chaklala, where it was initially housed in pens and mobile huts. On 2 April 1991, four more Cessna aircraft were purchased from PIA and added to the squadron's inventory. In October 1987, one Piper Seneca-II aircraft belonging to the Pakistan Atomic Energy Commission was allotted to this squadron. In 1993, a Chinese built twin engine Y-12 aircraft was attached with the squadron for trials and was finally inducted in the PAF in July 1996. Training of the air and ground crew for this aircraft was conducted in China. The second Y-12 aircraft was added to the squadron on 1 December 1996. The squadron thus achieved all-weather, day and night capability. On 4 January 1995, one MFI-17 aircraft was also allotted to the squadron to carry out single pilot operations. In November 1997, the squadron offices were accommodated within the building of 35 CAT Wing Headquarters. Pilots of this squadron ferried Y-12 aircraft from Pakistan to Iran on different occasions.

At present, the squadron is operating two Y-12s, one Beech Baron (B-55), one Piper Seneca-II, five Cessna-172, and one MFI-17 aircraft. The squadron has, a total of twenty-five pilots, including six QFIs. In 1997-98, nine pilots of this squadron were converted on F-27 aircraft. These pilots share VIP flying on this aircraft with the aircrew of 12 Squadron.

The squadron also operates from disused airfields and *kutcha* strips whenever necessary. This includes operations from Thal Range, Jauharabad, Dera Ghazi Khan, Arawali, Parachinar, Muzaffarabad, Sialkot, and Chashma.

No. 81 Search and Rescue Squadron

No. 81 Search and Rescue (S&R) Squadron started to function as a Helicopter Flying School from 7 May 1995. A number of books

required for the conversion course and Qualified Helicopter Instructor (QHI) course were procured through different sources. Patter books were procured from the Royal Air Force, UK. A local patter book was prepared at the school. Most of the lectures and phase briefs are conducted using the latest instructional aids like computers and multimedia. One additional helicopter was allotted to the squadron for training purposes. The first QHI course was conducted to train instructors for the Helicopter Flying School. Subsequently, the conduct of QHI courses on a regular basis was authorized from 14 November 1997.

The squadron has a total of three helicopters. Apart from the instructional role, S&R also form an essential part of squadron duties. The area of operation of the squadron in the S&R role is 70 NM around Peshawar airfield. During the last ten years, the squadron has flown twelve actual search and rescue missions.

No. 82 Search and Rescue Squadron

Ever since its establishment in 1967, 82 S&R Squadron has been providing rescue coverage to all flying within a seventy nautical mile radius of Sargodha, daily, from dawn to dusk. During the last decade, the squadron continued to fly the French built Allouette-III helicopter. In June 1997, the PAF purchased four Allouette-III helicopters from Romania, and one of those was allotted to this squadron.

Realizing the utility and versatility of the rotary wing aircraft, commanders have now started employing helicopters for tasks other than typical S&R missions. Some of them are aerial photography for the ISPR and helping the cause of flight safety by hunting wild boar within the airfield parameters. The squadron took part in major exercises like High Mark in 1993 and 1995, and Saffron Bandit in 1992 and 1997. During the last decade, the squadron carried out on an average two successful actual rescue missions per year, including a very daring and risky night rescue mission in September 1989. By undertaking leaflet drop missions, the squadron played its role in educating, and seeking the cooperation of civilians around Sargodha in tackling the bird menace. It also carried VIPs whenever required to do so. The squadron proved equal to the task whenever called upon to carry out flood recce and relief missions or to convey critically injured persons to hospitals in major cities. During an ORI in 1997, the squadron was tasked to provide video camera footage of all the contingencies in order to provide situation updates to the field commanders sitting in the Base Operations Room.

In 1998, the squadron was tasked to locate all vulture nesting sites around Sargodha airfield. The flight safety squadron later eradicated those sites, thereby reducing the number of bird-related accidents. During the last decade, the squadron remained heavily committed and extra vigilant in providing rescue coverage and other associated services to the air force as well as to the civil sector whenever called upon to do so. During the last ten years, the squadron has progressively matured into a team of highly trained and professional S&R pilots.

No. 83 Search and Rescue Squadron

Ever since No. 83 S&R Squadron was established in 1972, it has been operating the French built Allouette-III helicopters. In 1997, after four Allouette-III helicopters were purchased from Romania, one of them was handed over to this squadron. The squadron has been providing S&R coverage from dawn to dusk to all military and civil aircraft within a radius of 80 NM around PAF Base Rafiqui.

During the last ten years, the squadron has successfully carried out, on an average, one actual rescue mission per year. In April 1998, the squadron flew an actual rescue mission at night. Apart from providing S&R coverage during all operational exercises, the squadron has been playing its role in educating the local population about the bird hazard to flight safety by dropping leaflets from the air. During an Operational Readiness Inspection (ORI) of the Base, whenever the squadron was tasked to fly missions for identification of bomb droplets after a raid, it proved equal to the task. In 1992, the squadron successfully accomplished the task of flood recce, when the area around the Base came under water due to heavy flooding in the river Chenab. The squadron also participated in certain air defence exercises during 1998-99. The aim of these exercises was to assess the operational readiness of the air defence system and to give practice to the air defence

missile units against raids by combat helicopters.

No. 84 Search and Rescue Squadron

No. 84 Search and Rescue Squadron, named 'Dolphins', was established at PAF Base Masroor in 1986. The squadron's motto is 'Alert and Vigilant'. In 1988, the squadron was tasked to assemble six helicopters that had been inducted into the PAF S&R fleet, from the UAE Air Force. The squadron took up this challenging task and with the help of local expertise, managed to assemble all of them prior to their allocation to different S&R squadrons. Two of those helicopters were allotted to this squadron. During the last decade, the squadron has flown 4,000 accident free and AOR free hours on these helicopters.

In October 1996, during ISAC-96, besides performing extended S&R duties from dawn to dusk, the squadron was also tasked to fly communication sorties to and from the Sonmiani Range. During the last decade, the

squadron accomplished seventeen actual S&R missions in which twelve survivors and five fatally injured pilots were evacuated from the crash site to the Base.

No. 85 Search and Rescue Squadron
This squadron was established on 13 March 1986 at PAF Base Samungli. It started its duties under the command of Squadron Leader M. Farooq Azam. Since then the squadron has been commanded by nine different officers commanding.

The squadron is responsible for providing S&R facilities to PAF Base Samungli as well as the Civil Aviation Authority, from dawn to dusk. The squadron also provides S&R coverage to Shahbaz and Sukkar whenever these bases are activated. The routine duties of the squadron include continuation training of squadron pilots, casualty evacuation and limited communication duties, including VIP flights. The squadron is self-sufficient in all types of periodic maintenance i.e. 200, 400 and 800 Hours Inspections (both engine and airframe). The squadron was initially established with one Alouette-III helicopter but received one more in October 1987. The squadron carried out six rescue missions and several search missions during the last five years.

No. 86 Search and Rescue Squadron
In September 1983, the Rescue Flight that was the predecessor of this unit was equipped with one Aloutte-III helicopter, and started its operations at PAF Base Mianwali. At that time, the flight had only three pilots with Squadron Leader Muhammad Arif as Officer Incharge. The role of this flight was to provide S&R coverage within the flying area of PAF Base Mianwali. The rescue helicopter was also used for transportation of VIPs. In October 1987, another Aloutte-III helicopter

was added to the flight. In February 1993, the Chief of the Air Staff upgraded this Flight into a full-fledged Rescue Squadron, which was named No. 86 Search and Rescue Squadron. The first squadron commander was Squadron Leader Raja Zafar Abbas.

Air Defence Units

Headquarters Norsec, PAF
Soon after the Soviet invasion of Afghanistan in 1979 and with the increase in hostile air activity on Pakistan's western borders, an additional sector was established at Sakesar on 15 April 1980. Base Commander, Sakesar, Group Captain Nasim Ullah Khan, in addition to his own duties was designated as Sector Commander. Operations from this sector continued till November 1985, when it was shifted to PAF Chaklala.

The sector had the unique experience of actively participating in the Afghan war. In 1988, five Afghan/Soviet aircraft were shot down within the area of responsibility of this

sector. In addition, one helicopter, one MIG-17, one AN-12, one SU-22 and three MIG-21s of Afghan/Soviet air forces also defected or landed for other reasons at Parachinar, Miran Shah, Qila Abdullah and Peshawar, between 1988 and 1990.

Apart from participation in routine air defence exercises, Headquarters Norsec participated in Exercise High Mark-89 alongside Exercise Zarb-e-Momin as part of Blueland Air Force. An important feature of the exercise was the first ever employment of the function of Air Space Management during Air-Land operations.

In the wake of nuclear tests carried out by India in May 1998, all the air defence units of this sector were deployed on their designated sites to participate in exercise Bedaar-98.

Headquarters Censec, PAF

After the shifting of Headquarters No. 1 Group to Sargodha in 1958, a sector operations centre was established in a rented house in Sargodha in 1959. Two C & R officers, Flight Lieutenant A. Moiz Shahzada and Pilot Officer Rab Nawaz were among the pioneers who started operations from this sector. At that time, Type 21 radars comprising 225 and 226 squadrons (deployed at Lahore) and 223 and 224 squadrons (deployed at Wegowal near Sargodha) were the only radar units which passed surveillance data on speech circuits to the sector. The first live interception by this sector was conducted on 10 April 1959 by Pilot Officer Rab Nawaz when an Indian Air Force Canberra was shot down flying on a reconnaissance mission near Rawalpindi.

After the commissioning of the FPS-20 high-level radar at Sakesar in 1960, the sector operation centre was also shifted from Sargodha to Sakesar, and its role was changed to that of a Master GCI station. This arrangement continued till May 1972 when it was shifted back to Sargodha under the command of Group Captain N. Rehmat Khan and named Headquarters No. 1 Sector. Operations during the India-Pakistan wars of 1965 and 1971 were conducted while the sector was operating from Sakesar.

General Ziaul Haq, President of Pakistan, visited this sector on 1 November 1984 and inaugurated the new automation system.

Between 1988 and 1998, a number of routine and major air defence exercises were conducted by this sector. Exercise High Mark-89 was held from 14 November 1989 to 20 December 1989, and the entire operations of Foxland Air Force were conducted from this sector. Exercise Saffron Bandit was conducted by this Sector from September 1994 to March 1995. Headquarters No. 1 Sector was redesignated as Headquarters Censec, PAF on 30 April 1991.

The sector was awarded the air defence excellence trophy, ADEX, twice in the years 1996 and 1998.

Headquarters Sousec, PAF

The history of this sector dates back to 1952 when it was established at PAF Base Korangi Creek within the premises of No. 229 squadron's building. In November 1955, it was renamed Headquarters No. 2 Sector, PAF instead of the Karachi sector. Two FPS-20 high-level surveillance radars were acquired from the USA in 1959, and one of these radars was commissioned in Badin in 1960. On 27 January 1962, Headquarters No. 2 Sector was also shifted to the operations room of the Badin radar, and its role was changed to that of a Master GCI station accordingly. The sector continued its operations from Badin till 1972 when it was shifted back and re-established at PAF Base Korangi Creek under the command of Group Captain M. Anwar Shamim. All low/ high-level operations during the India-Pakistan war of 1971 were conducted from this sector. Finally, in May 1984, the sector was shifted from PAF Base Korangi Creek to PAF Base Faisal. In July 1991, the sector

was renamed as Headquarters Sousec, PAF. After the induction of automation equipment under PADS-77, operations of the sector were changed from manual to an automated mode on 1 November 1985. The introduction of automation resulted in a quantum leap in the overall efficiency of the sector as a near real time surveillance picture enabled the battle staff to make a better threat assessment and initiate timely tactical action.

Between 1988 and 1998, the sector participated in forty-two routine day/night air defence exercises, including High Mark-95 and Bedaar-98. Located in the Karachi area, a number of inter-Services exercises with the Pakistan Navy were also conducted during this period. Between 1995 and 1997, joint PAF/US Navy exercises of the 'Inspired Alert' series were conducted by the sector.

The sector was awarded the air defence excellence trophy, ADEX, in the year 1997.

Headquarters Wessec, PAF

The Soviet invasion of Afghanistan in December 1979, and the subsequent intensely hostile activity on Pakistan's western borders compelled the PAF to establish a full-fledged sector operations centre. Headquarters No. 4 Sector was thus established on 8 April 1981 to function as a mini sector operations centre in a manual mode at PAF Base Samungli, under the command of Wing Commander Safdar M. Khan.

The operational and functional control of Headquarters No. 4 Sector was vested with Headquarters Southern Air Command, whereas administrative control rested with Air Headquarters. In the beginning of 1986, an underground building was constructed and the sector's operations room was shifted to it. It was formally inaugurated by AOC, Southern Air Command and No. 4 Sector was redesignated as Headquarters Wessec, PAF on 2 May 1986.

Between September 1988 and July 1991, a total of eight medium/high-level air defence exercises were conducted by this sector. However, with the de-escalation of air activity on the western front, it was finally decided to close Headquarters Wessec with effect from 7 March 1992, and its area of responsibility was merged with Headquarters Sousec. The air defence assets of Wessec were directly placed under Headquarters Sousec and the status of the sector was changed to care and maintenance (C&M).

In view of the large area of responsibility of Headquarters Sousec, which covered almost half of the country's airspace, it was decided by the Air Headquarters in July 1997 to reactivate Headquarters Wessec with a redefined area and redistribution of air defence assets. Consequently, Headquarters Wessec was made operational in a manual mode on 13 January 1998 under the command of Group Captain Mahmood Jaffar.

Since its re-activation, two routine air defence exercises named Hill Top-I and Hill Top-II have been conducted in 1998. During

exercise Bedaar-98, all the assets under the control of this sector were made ready to be deployed at short notice.

No. 481 Control and Reporting Centre

No. 481 Air Defence Wing was established in December 1979 at PAF Base Lahore under the command of Group Captain Ihsanullah Khan. It was equipped with German origin Siemens display trucks, equipment truck, communication truck, maintenance truck, generators, and associated equipment. Additionally, a combination of MPDRs was also allotted to the wing. Later, in May 1986, the unit was renamed as 481 CRC Wing and finally the present name 481 CRC was announced in October 1987.

Since its induction, the CRC is carrying out its peacetime role from its present location at PAF Base Lahore. Apart from taking part in routine air defence exercises, the CRC also participated in High Mark-93 with its complete compliment of MPDRs. Deployment of the unit commenced in mid-October 1993,

and continued till the end of December 1993. A ground defence exercise, in which CRC, along with all its sensors, was deployed, was also conducted in October 1996.

In the wake of nuclear tests conducted by India on 11 May 1998, the CRC, along with seven MPDRs, was deployed at designated sites to participate in exercise Bedaar-98. Round the clock operations were provided till the exercise was called off on 1 June 1998.

The CRC was awarded the air defence excellence trophy, ADEX, for the year 1993.

No. 482 Control and Reporting Centre

Raised in December 1979, the unit started its operations from PAF Base Masroor under the command of Wing Commander Aftab A. Khan. Later, it moved from Masroor to its peacetime location at PAF Base Malir in April 1983. Apart from participation in routine air defence exercises, the unit also participated in a number of joint PAF/Pak Navy exercises, namely Sea Spark and

Shamsher-e-Behr series. The controllers of this CRC have performed GCI duties on board naval ships, to defend them from air strikes, on a number of occasions. From 1995 to 1997, the unit also participated in joint PAF/US Navy exercises named 'Inspired Alert' series. An additional task assigned to the unit was to evaluate the naval radar AGROS-73 acquired by the Pakistan Navy in 1997. This unit has been specially entrusted to conduct operations for this naval radar during exercises and emergencies.

In March 1997, the unit airlifted its MPDR-90S radar from PAF Base Faisal to PAF Shahbaz to participate in Exercise Hilltop. A highly complicated task was skilfully and successfully accomplished by the unit personnel.

Soon after the nuclear tests conducted by India, the unit deployed its MPDR-45 radar in the Sukkur area at a very short notice on 21 May 1998. This far-off and difficult deployment for exercise Bedaar-98 was completed smoothly. The radar handled a number of CAP missions that were launched to counter any aerial threat to our nuclear installations.

No. 483 Control and Reporting Centre

No. 483 CRC was formed at PAF Kalar Kahar on 29 September 1979. Later, the unit moved to its peacetime location at PAF Base Mianwali on 5 April 1980 and started operations by deploying an MPDR-45 at Mianwali in the terminal role. The unit participated in all the major air defence exercises till 1983, and from then onward, the unit remained committed in western contingency operations with all its sensors deployed on hill tops along the western border. Round-the-clock operations were provided by the unit throughout the Afghan contingency. The unit has three controlled kills to its credit, one SU-22 on 17 May

1986, one AN-26 on 20 March 1987, and two SU-22s on 6 April 1987.

At the beginning of 1988, air space violations by Afghan/Russian aircraft heightened on the western border which required positioning of a radar at Laram top, at an altitude of 7520 feet above sea level. This task was accomplished on 26 June 1988 under the supervision of Squadron Leader Qazi Arif.

The activities of Afghan aircraft continued unabated and air space violations became a common phenomenon. The enemy then began night operations and Pakistan air space was also being violated frequently during the night. The CRC was, therefore, tasked to continue its operations at night. This arrangement resulted in a night engagement on 4 August 1988 at 1959 hours. Squadron Leader M. Taufique Raja was controlling a CAP of one F-16 (Shaheen-146) when two Afghan aircraft violated Pakistan's airspace by twelve nautical miles in Miran Shah area. One of the SU-25s was shot down and the pilot of the intruder aircraft managed to eject. The pilot was a Russian named Colonel

Alexander Rutskoi who later became the Vice President of Russia. This was the first night kill on the western border and Pakistan's first night kill after 1971.

The last kill took place on the western border on 12 September 1988. Squadron Leader Irfan-ul-Haq was controlling a formation of two F-16s when four Afghan aircraft violated eight nautical miles in the Northwest of Topsar. The encounter resulted in the shooting down of two Mig-23s. This was counted as the fifth kill of the unit.

After hostile activity had ceased on the western border, the CRC participated in five different air defence exercises in 1991, namely Tornado-V, Tornado-VI, Condor-I, Contrail-VI, and Sore Eyes-III. Later, the CRC participated in all the major air defence exercises which included High Mark-93, High Mark-95, Saffron Bandit-97, and Bedaar-98. The CRC was awarded the air defence excellence trophy, ADEX, in the year 1998.

No. 484 Control and Reporting Centre

No. 484 CRC is one of seven establishments of a similar kind, and was raised at PAF Base Chaklala in October 1978 as No. 484 CRC Cell. In July 1979 it was renamed the 484 Air Defence Wing with the shifting of its headquarters to PAF Base Masroor. In November 1979, the unit was shifted to its present peacetime location at PAF Base Malir. In July 1981, the unit was deployed with its full establishment at Chaklala for the defence of the Kahuta area. After the calibration of all the radars and the preparation of the sites, the unit handed over the complete equipment to No. 486 CRC in 1982. On 10 May 1986, the unit was renamed No. 484 CRC Wing and finally its present name, i.e. No. 484 CRC, was announced on 3 October 1987.

Since its inception, the CRC participated in a number of air defence exercises. The major exercises in which full contingents moved out from peacetime locations are Jetstream-80, 81, 83, 85, High Mark-87, Sea Spark-90 and High Mark-95. In the last decade, CRC participated in various DACT camps and its controllers were attached to CCS Sargodha for the conduct of exercise Saffron Bandit on a regular basis. Apart from accomplishing its own role and task, the CRC is regularly visited by officers and men of the Army Air Defence School, Malir, for training purposes.

been conducted at the wing. A total of 332 officers have graduated from these courses.

Apart from training activities, the unit has also participated in various routine, and major air defence exercises. It participated in Exercise High Mark-89 and Exercise Zarb-e-Momin, High Mark-93 and twice in Exercise Saffron Bandit.

The CRC was awarded the air defence excellence trophy, ADEX, on two occasions, i.e. in 1995 and 1996.

No. 485 CRC & OT Wing

No. 485 CRC was raised at PAF Base Rafiqui on 24 November 1980 under the command of Group Captain Farooq H. Khan. A year later, it was entrusted with the additional task of operational training of fresh ADWC graduates from air defence school and was, therefore, redesignated as 485 CRC & OT Wing.

Since 1988, eighteen operational training, five command and weapon employment, four pre-CCC and one advance GCI course have

No. 486 Control and Reporting Centre

No. 486 CRC was initially established at PAF Base Lahore in March 1981 under the command of Group Captain Ihsanullah Khan. At that time, one of the detachments of the CRC was deployed under the command of Group Captain Zubair at PAF Base Malir. It was finally redeployed at its present location at PAF Base Chaklala in November 1985.

The CRC has been entrusted with the honour of providing air defence to Pakistan's nuclear installations. Over the passage of

time, it has risen to the occasion and provided round-the-clock operations for the onerous task and has proved worthy of the trust reposed in it. The radar sites of the CRC are mostly located in difficult, hilly terrain. Under the adverse conditions of weather and terrain, the CRC has adequately been able to maintain its equipment and provide admin. support to its personnel round the year. The unit personnel have always remained geared up to take on the toughest of field deployments and severest of weather encountered in the northern areas of the country.

Between 1990 and 1998, the CRC participated in forty-five routine air defence exercises. In the wake of nuclear tests conducted by India, it participated fully in exercise Bedaar-98, and deployed an MPDR-90P at Pasni at very short notice. Later, another MPDR-90P was deployed in the Muzaffarabad area in August 1998, at a height of 9,967 feet. The area where the radar was deployed had toughest of weather and roughest of terrain. Considering the heavy

bulk of the specialist vehicles, and the steep gradients posed by the terrain, the deployment and safe retrieval of the radar in itself was considered a big achievement by the CRC.

The 'Certificate of Distinguished Performance' was conferred upon the unit by the CAS, PAF on 31 October 1995, as evaluated by the air defence evaluation team. The unit also received the air defence excellence trophy, ADEX, for the year 1997.

No. 487 Control and Reporting Centre

No. 487 CRC was established at PAF Base, Sargodha in July 1982 as a CRC Cell. It was redesignated as No. 487 CRC Wing in 1987. However, from 1982 to 1989, the CRC's specialist vehicles remained with 108 AED for use as test equipment. The CRC was shifted to PAC Kamra in October 1989 and placed under KARF (Kamra Avoinics and Radar Factory). It continued functioning as test equipment at PAC Kamra till June 1996.

On 20 June 1996, the CRC was relocated to PAF Base Sargodha under the command of Group Captain F. R. Kiyani. Since its relocation, the CRC is committed to CCS for training support and 24 CCC was the first course conducted by this CRC. Between 1996 and 1998, the CRC participated in two air defence exercises, namely Shikra-IV and Ray Rider. Saffron Bandit-97 was also conducted from this CRC in 1997.

No. 400 Squadron

The history of 400 Squadron dates back to early 1962 when it was formed and equipped with British Type 21 (a combination of T-13 and T-14) radars at PAF Walton, Lahore. The role assigned to the squadron was to act as GCI-cum-Receiving and Reporting Unit (RRU). Later, the squadron was deployed at Thatta during the Rann of Kutch operations

400 Squadron moved to PAF Base Samungli on 27 October 1982. The trials, at a designated site of 8000 feet, were successful, and the site was permanently selected. TPS-43G radar was switched on at 1300 hours on 1 November 1982.

During the Afghan war, this squadron actively participated by providing high-level air surveillance pictures from across the borders to higher echelons, and also controlled a number of hot CAP missions.

Between 1988 and 1998, the squadron participated in thirteen routine, medium and high-level air defence exercises. It also participated in five DACT camps from 1991 to 1995, in which controllers of various air defence units took part.

No. 401 Squadron

No. 401 Squadron was raised as an independent unit in June 1992 at PAF Base Sakesar. Prior to that, the FPS-20 high level radar of this squadron, which was commissioned at Sakesar in 1960, continued to function as an Early Warning cum GCI unit, and remained part of the operations wing of PAF Base Sakesar.

To improve the performance of this old vintage radar, Chinese engineers visited the site in 1988 to replace its analog receiver with a solid state digital receiver. The upgrade resulted in substantial improvement in the performance of the radar. Later, in 1992, another upgrade of the radar was successfully carried out by PAF engineers, when the radar was hooked up to the automation system, facilitating the passing of surveillance data to higher echelons in near real time. This upgrade marks an important event in the history of the squadron.

The location of this radar is ideally suited to cater to any high-level threat emanating from the east or the west. High-level

from 12 April 1965 to 7 July 1965. It participated in the India-Pakistan war of 1965 as an Early Warning cum GCI radar from Thatta in support of Master GCI station, Badin.

The squadron moved to PAF Base Malir in October 1970 where old vintage T-13 and T-14 radars were replaced with high powered British Condor radar S-330 (Surveillance) and S-404 (Height finder). This radar participated in the India-Pakistan war of 1971 from the same site. Soon after the war, it was moved to PAF Walton, Lahore, its permanent peacetime location. The squadron continued its operations in Early Warning cum GCI role till 1982 from Lahore.

After the acquisition of TPS-43G radars by the PAF, one of these was allotted to 400 Squadron in 1980. This period was the beginning of the Afghan war, and a high powered radar was essentially required to counter any high-level threat on the western border. No. 400 squadron was thus tasked to carry out Recce and select a suitable site in Quetta area. After the selection of a site, operations during the India-Pakistan wars of 1965 and 1971 were conducted from this radar. The role of the radar in the 1965 war was praise-worthy. The radar adequately met high-level GCI tasks allocated to the flying squadrons of PAF Base Sargodha, Rafiqui, Peshawar, and Mianwali. During peacetime, one of the major roles of the squadron is to provide live GCI training to the cadets of Air Defence Training School, Sakesar.

Between 1992 and 1994, 401 squadron participated in eleven air defence exercises including High Mark-93. During this exercise, the role of the squadron was restricted to provide recovery assistance to the strike aircraft. A total of fifty-four aircraft were provided recovery assistance by the squadron.

No. 402 Squadron

No. 402 Squadron was raised on an *ad hoc* basis in February 1988 and equipped with TPS-43G high-level surveillance radar. Prior

to that, the unit remained on care and maintenance status from August 1986 to February 1988. In 1986, field trials of this radar at Sakesar site did not produce satisfactory results due to mountainous terrain. Later the same year, the radar was shifted to PAF Base Lahore to its permanent peacetime location. The unit became fully operational in August 1988 under the command of Wing Commander Mushtaq A. Qureshi and started active participation in routine air defence activities. However, due to the imposition of a ban by the government on new establishments, the unit continued its functioning on an *ad hoc* basis until its establishment was formally approved in 1996.

Since its induction in the PAF, the squadron has undertaken thirteen field deployments, and has participated in twelve routine and major air defence exercises. Its role during Exercise High Mark-89/Zarb-e-Momin was commended with thirty-two successful interceptions achieving 92 per cent results.

The imposition of a ban on military hardware and spares by the US government under the Pressler Law forced the PAF to procure various components of the radar either locally, or through the open international market, to ensure continued operability of the radar. In this regard, heat exchanger, automatic voltage regulator, and air-conditioning plants were indigenously produced. Subsequently, these major components were used in other TPS-43G radars belonging to the PAF.

No. 403 Squadron

This squadron was initially commissioned in as 230 Squadron in early 1962 and equipped with a British Type-21 radar. In June 1962, the squadron was numberplated. However, prior to the India-Pakistan war of 1965, it was

In January 1980, the squadron was re-equipped with TPS-43G high-level surveillance radar. Being a mobile squadron, it made extensive field deployments from 1986 onwards, and moved to twenty-seven different field locations until 1998. Apart from participation in routine air defence exercises, it also participated in the exercise to counter Brass Tacks and in Exercise High Mark-86,-89,-95 and Bedaar-98.

No. 406 Squadron

No. 406 Squadron was established in August 1967 under the command of Squadron Leader Akhtar Khan. At that time, the unit was equipped with Type 13, Type 14, and Type 15 vintage British mobile radars. In January 1970, the squadron was re-equipped with Russian P-35 high-level, long-range radar and was deployed at Kurmitola near Dhaka to monitor high-level flying activity in the then East Pakistan. In June 1971, the squadron was shifted to PAF Base Malir under the command of Squadron Leader Javed S. Butt, where it

reactivated at Sargodha with the same Type-21 radar equipment. The squadron took part in the 1965 war from Rahwali, and was attacked by four Indian Air Force hunters on 6 September 1965 at about 1255 hours. Luckily, all rockets fell short of the radar, damaging an MODC tent only. Soon after the attack, the site of the radar was changed. This site could not be located by the enemy, and unhindered operations were provided by the squadron throughout the period of the war. After the war it was renamed 403 Squadron.

In 1970, the squadron was re-equipped with a British Condor S-330 high powered radar, and was deployed close to Muridke prior to the 1971 war, under the command of Squadron Leader Farooq H. Khan. It provided operations throughout the war from the same site and could not be located by the enemy due to its excellent camouflage.

In 1972, the squadron moved to PAF Malir and operated from 'Chota Malir' in an Early Warning cum GCI role until 1979. Later, it was numberplated and its equipment was shifted to PAF Base Lahore.

started its operations in the Early Warning cum GCI role. In April 1984, the squadron was re-equipped with a TPS-43G radar and was finally moved to its present peacetime location at PAF Sukkur in May 1984.

Since its deployment at Sukkur, the squadron has undertaken three major field deployments at designated sites. From 1995 onwards, the squadron has participated regularly in DACT camps of 1995, 1996, 1997, and 1998, and carried out 226 engagements. During Exercise High Mark-95, the unit was deployed in Rahimyar Khan area from 16 September 1995 to 17 October 1995. Besides carrying out high level interceptions, the radar also provided useful height information on those targets, which were allocated to the CRC deployed in close proximity to the radar.

The squadron was awarded the Air Defence Excellence trophy, ADEX in the year 1998.

No. 408 Squadron

No. 408 Squadron was established in 1960 at PAF Base Badin, and was equipped with FPS-20A high-level long-range static radar. This veteran of two wars, 1965 and 1971, was shifted from PAF Base Badin to PAF Base Malir in 1974. The purpose was to provide high-level surveillance and GCI support to the southern region of Pakistan, especially the Karachi complex. In 1984, under the PADS-77, this squadron was additionally equipped with a TPS-43G high-level radar. The operation room which housed the old, vintage FPS-20A console network was completely changed into a digital/synthetic display centre and was renamed Fixed Operation Communication Centre (FOCC). This network provided a real time air surveillance picture of the squadron to the Air Defence Command through Headquarters Sousec, PAF.

Until 1989, the surveillance data of FPS-20 radar was displayed on its own consoles and was passed to SOC manually. In 1989, Chinese engineers, in collaboration with PAF engineers, modified the Radar Data Extractor (RADEX) of the automation system, and connected the FPS-20 radar with the air defence automation network. In addition to conducting routine air defence activities, the squadron participated in various air defence exercises, specially in collaboration with the US Navy and Pakistan Navy. In 1992, 1995, and 1996 the squadron was actively involved in naval exercises, Sea Spark series, and its controllers were attached to the PN ships for conducting GCI missions. Between 1994 and 1997, the squadron participated in several joint PAF/USN exercises of the 'Inspired Alert' series in which USN aircraft carriers were also involved. During these exercises, PAF controllers got the opportunity to apply and learn different techniques to intercept raiders like F-14s and F-18s. The squadron also conducted a number of DACT camps in which controllers participated from all across the command.

In addition, this squadron had proudly participated in exercise Bedaar-98, after the Indian nuclear tests in May 1998. During this national contingency, the squadron controlled a number of hot CAP missions in the designated area, and successfully intercepted some of the US Navy aircraft flying close to our coastal boundaries.

No. 410 Squadron

No. 410 Squadron, PAF, was established in May 1960 at PAF Walton, Lahore, and was equipped with the British Type-21 radar. In 1967, the PAF acquired three British Condor high-level mobile radars, and one of these was allotted to this squadron. Throughout the 1970s, the radar was extensively deployed in the field and participated in a number of routine and major air defence exercises. The squadron was numberplated in March 1983

until it was re-equipped with TPS-43G radar in June 1983.

During the Afghan conflict, the squadron was deployed in the Hazro area in August 1988 to counter high level intrusions made by Soviet/Afghan aircraft. Extensive day and night CAP missions were flown by PAF fighter aircraft during that war. The squadron controlled a total of 127 CAP missions during 1988-89.

On 3 November 1988, Squadron Leader Saif-ur-Rahman was controlling a CAP mission of F-16s when two Afghan aircraft violated the Pak airspace. Both intruders were successfully intercepted and one SU-22 was shot down. The kill was awarded to the squadron and its performance was lauded at all levels.

Between 1988 and 1998, the squadron participated in thirty routine and major air defence exercises. It also participated in nine DACT camps in which 209 air defence weapon controllers of different units were exposed to advanced GCI techniques, and tactics. The squadron participated actively in Exercise Bedaar-98, by providing round-the-clock operations, and controlling twenty-six high level CAP missions.

The squadron was awarded the air defence excellence trophy, ADEX, in the year 1993.

No. 411 Squadron

No. 411 Squadron, PAF, was established at Cherat Hills in February 1971. The squadron consists of two flights: 4101 Flight, an Air Defence unit initially equipped with a British low-level Plessey AR-1 radar, and 213 Flight, vested with the responsibility of communication and coordination for all aircraft arriving and departing from Peshawar, Chaklala, and the northern areas since 1959. In 1983, 4101 Flight was re-equipped with a German MPDR-90 static radar.

command of Wing Commander Mahmood Jaffar. Since its deployment, the squadron's radars have been sharing watch and providing operations in the role of early warning.

In 1991, Chinese engineers visited the site, and carried out a few modifications in T-514A and the T-514B sets. The mechanical lifting system of both radar antennas was replaced with an electrical lifting system. Analog canceller/MTI system of both radar sets was replaced with digital canceller/ Digital MTI, and the older feed lines (transmission/reception) were replaced with new low-loss feed lines.

The squadron participated in the India-Pakistan war of 1971, and controlled various CAP missions operating from PAF Base, Peshawar. Also, during the Afghan war, this squadron directed a number of air defence missions operating from PAF Base Peshawar and PAF Base Minhas. Being located at an altitude of 5,000 feet above sea level, radar and radio performance of the squadron has always been excellent. It owes this advantage to the clear line of sight which is provided by the high altitude.

No. 412 Squadron
No. 412 Squadron was initially established as a detachment of 413 Squadron at PAF Base Malir, in August 1982. Later, it was raised to an independent squadron in June 1987, and numbered as 412 Squadron. The squadron was equipped with two sets of Chinese T-514 long-range surveillance radars namely T-514A, and T-514B. In June 1987, the squadron moved to its permanent peacetime location at PAF Sukkur, under the

No. 4071 Squadron
No. 4071 Squadron was established at PAF Base Korangi Creek in September 1972 under the command of Squadron Leader Shoukat A. Khan. It was equipped with a British Plessey AR-15 low-level surveillance radar. Being a mobile radar, it moved to various places throughout Pakistan in connection with routine and major air defence exercises. The

warning on enemy aircraft operating from the IAF bases of Jamnagar, Bhuj and Naliya. At that time, the area was not connected to WAPDA, and generators were the only source of electricity for the radar until 1984.

The unit actively participated in the India-Pakistan war of 1971 under the command of Squadron Leader S. Waheed Ahmed. A total of forty-three day/night raids were picked up. Out of these, fighters were allocated to eighteen hostile tracks, and interceptions were attempted.

After the induction of PADS-77, the role of the squadron was reduced to care and maintenance status in 1981. In June 1985, its role was again changed, and the unit was tasked to maintain operational status with varying watch timings as and when directed by Headquarters Air Defence Command through Headquarters Sousec.

Between 1988 and 1998, the squadron participated in various air defence exercises, namely Sea Spark, Blue Dolphin and the Sea Hawk series held in the area of responsibility of Headquarters Sousec.

radar of the squadron remained deployed at Karachi airport from 1982 to 1986, and functioned in the ATC role with the civil aviation authority. Later it moved to PAF Base Peshawar in September 1987, which is its permanent peacetime location.

Apart from its participation in the Afghan war between 1987 and 1989, the squadron also participated in exercise Bedaar-98 from PAF Murid. The squadron remained deployed at PAF Minhas from July 1998 to November 1998 in connection with DACT camp and conducted thirty-eight missions.

No. 4082 Squadron

No. 4082 Squadron was established in Makli (Thatta) in mid-1969 and was equipped with British Plessey AR-1 fixed low-level surveillance radar. In December 1969, the squadron was shifted to its permanent location of Pir Patho and was assigned the role of Early Warning cum GCI radar. The radar was suitably located to provide low-level early

Prior to 1998, the radar's surveillance data was manually conveyed upward to Headquarters Sousec. With the induction of Manual Entry Data Device (MEDD), the unit became semi-automated and its data can now be fed into the automation system of the PAF.

No. 4084 Squadron

No. 4084 Squadron was established in April 1974 at PAF Base Korangi Creek, under the command of Squadron Leader Muhammad Riaz. It was equipped with a British Plessey AR-15 mobile low-level surveillance radar. Being a mobile unit, it moved extensively during its early years. It moved to Sargodha in November 1980, and remained deployed at the Base until May 1984. Later, it moved to PAF Base Mianwali in June 1984, and provided operations as terminal radar until June 1986. It was finally shifted to its peacetime location at PAF Base Sargodha in July 1986.

Since its deployment at Sargodha, the squadron's peacetime role is to provide equipment support to CCS for the conduct of its training, like combat controllers courses, squadron upgradation programmes (SCUP) and Saffron Bandit exercises. Additionally, the squadron has been meeting *ad hoc* operational requirements in the role of Early Warning cum GCI station.

Apart from a busy peacetime role, the squadron also participated in exercises High Mark-93 and High Mark-95 from its designated field locations. The GCI results achieved during these exercises were 94 per cent and 100 per cent, respectively.

No. 4091 Squadron

No. 4091 Squadron was established at Kirana Hills in August 1970 under the command of Squadron Leader Tassaduq Hussain Malik. It was equipped with a British Plessey AR-1 fixed low-level surveillance radar. As a terminal radar, it played a vital role in defending PAF Base Sargodha during the

India-Pakistan war of 1971. A total of seventy-one raids were picked up by this radar, out of which five raids were successfully intercepted. Four SU-7s and one Canberra were shot down in these raids.

In March 1982, the squadron was re-equipped with a Siemens MPDR-90 low-level static radar. Being located at a height of 1,600 feet above sea level, it provides an excellent surveillance picture of low-level aircraft at extended ranges.

Between 1988 and 1998, the squadron actively participated in routine and major air defence exercises. This included exercises High Mark-89, Zarb-e-Momin, High Mark-93, 95 and Bedaar-98.

No. 4092 Squadron

No. 4092 Squadron was initially established as 4092 Flight at Rafiqui on 5 October 1968. Equipped with a British Plessey AR-1 fixed low-level surveillance radar, the unit became operational in August 1969 under the command of Squadron Leader H. Nur-ul-Islam.

The unit took active part in the India-Pakistan war of 1971. A total of fifty-three hostile tracks were picked up by the radar between 3 December 1971 and 16 December 1971. Out of these, eighteen hostile tracks, nine for day and nine for night, were allocated interceptors. Two SU-7s were shot down by the Ack Ack guns and one SU-7 was shot down by F-86s from Rafiqui, controlled by 4092 Squadron.

Between 1988 and 1998, apart from participation in routine air defence exercises, the unit also participated in exercise High Mark-89 and-93. During this period, a number of DACT camps were also held in which the controllers of various air defence units took part.

The squadron was awarded the air defence excellence trophy, ADEX, in the years 1996 and 1997.

No. 4093 Squadron

No. 4093 Squadron was established on 5 October 1968 at PAF Kallar Kahar and was equipped with a British Plessey AR-1 low-

level surveillance radar. The squadron was made operational in April 1969, and its operational control was vested in the Sakesar Sector Headquarters. It actively participated in the India-Pakistan war of 1971 by providing vital information on enemy aircraft picked up within its coverage. It continued functioning in the role of surveillance-cum-GCI radar till its status was changed to care and maintenance on 15 January 1981. After the shifting of 245 Squadron to Kallar Kahar, 4093 Squadron was placed on storage status on 15 December 1991.

No. 4094 Squadron

No. 4094 Squadron was established at PAF Base Chaklala on 9 March 1986 under the command of Squadron Leader Ishtiaq Ahmed. It was equipped with a British Plessey AR-1 fixed low-level surveillance radar. To augment the defence of the Kilo area, the squadron remained deployed at Chaklala as an Early Warning cum GCI radar until September 1993.

Through indigenous efforts, this radar was made semi-mobile by housing its operational equipment in a RVT in 1993. In October 1993, it was shifted to PAF Base Vehari, on its permanent peacetime location. The squadron actively participated in exercise High Mark-95 and provided recovery service to 242 strike and CAP aircraft.

No. 4102 Squadron

No. 4102 Squadron was raised at PAF Base Chaklala on 20 April 1974 and equipped with a British Plessey AR-15 mobile low-level surveillance radar. On 18 February 1975, it moved to PAF Base Mianwali, and became operational under the command of Squadron Leader M. Akram Khan. Besides looking after the flying activity of PAF Base Mianwali, it also performed the role of terminal radar for the Base. It moved to PAF Base Peshawar in December 1980 to meet the Afghan contingency. The squadron was again shifted to PAF Base Chaklala, in

August 1983, in connection with the defence of the Kilo area. It was finally shifted to its permanent peacetime location at PAF Base Samungli in January 1990.

Between 1988 and 1998, the squadron made a total of sixteen movements to different places, in connection with various tasks like EFM, site selection, calibration and DACT camps. During this period, it participated in thirteen routine air defence exercises and four DACT camps. The squadron actively participated during a western contingency by deploying its radar in Topsar, Inzari Kandao and Peshawar areas. A number of hot missions including CAP, air surveillance, and air space management over FEBA were conducted with the help of this radar.

No. 904 Squadron

In February 1982, MPDR-90S radar of 486 CRC was deployed in the Murree area under the command of Group Captain Muhammad Zubair. The *katcha* track leading to the site was in extremely bad shape and was made roadworthy with the help of the unit's manpower. In 1983, the establishment of the unit was formally approved and it was named 904 Squadron.

Since its deployment, the unit has provided round-the-clock operations either in independent or hooked-up mode with 486 CRC. The radar is suitably located to provide early warning on low and medium level ingressing aircraft towards the national VPs. During the mid-1980s, the unit defended sensitive installations by handling a number of CAP missions of F-6s and Mirages operating from PAF Base Chaklala.

No. 451 Squadron

No. 451 Squadron is one of the four surface-to-air missile squadrons initially raised at PAF Base Sargodha, in 1976. Equipped with a French made Crotale-2000 weapon system, the squadron's main role was to defend the PAF's main operating bases against enemy aerial attacks. The induction of this all-weather day/night weapon system represented a quantum leap in the overall air defence capability of the PAF in general, and the reinforcement of terminal weapons in particular. Soon after its formation, the squadron participated in the major air defence exercise Shahbaz-77 from PAF Base Sargodha. Subsequently, the squadron moved to PAF Base Rafiqui in 1978 and was tasked to conduct Familiarization and Induction courses for ADWC officers. In March 1980, one flight of the squadron was moved to PAF Base Peshawar in connection with the Afghan War. Later in 1981, the entire squadron along with its manpower, and equipment moved to Peshawar. During the 1980s, one flight of the squadron remained deployed at Peshawar whereas the other flight participated in various air defence activities from locations like Thal,

Miran Shah and Kahuta areas. In July 1991, 451 Squadron moved permanently to PAF Base Chaklala and all its assets including manpower were pooled up with 454 squadron. Since 1991, the squadron has been providing round the clock operations from its designated sites for the defence of the Kahuta area.

No. 452 Squadron

No. 452 Squadron was formed at PAF Base Sargodha in September 1976 under the command of Wing Commander Raja Aftab Iqbal. In 1977, the squadron moved to its permanent peacetime location at PAF Base Masroor, and was tasked to defend the VPs of the Karachi complex against aerial attacks. In early 1980, the squadron was assigned the additional task of conducting the training of officers and men from different branches and trades, and as such, was renamed 452 SAM Conversion Unit, PAF. Since its changed role, the unit has so far conducted 225 courses for officers, and airmen. A total of

686 officers and 1,943 airmen were trained on the system until December 1998.

Apart from participating in routine air defence exercises, the squadron has conducted live firing trials on three occasions, i.e. in 1984, 1986 and 1998. The first of these trials was conducted in February 1984 at the SUPARCO firing range on American BATs and French technical targets. These trials were witnessed by the then CAS, Air Chief Marshal M. Anwar Shamim, along with PSOs and AOCs. Out of four missiles fired, two achieved direct kills. The live trials of December 1986 were witnessed by the then CAS, Air Chief Marshal Jamal A. Khan, along with PSOs and AOCs. Out of three missiles fired, two achieved successful kill on their targets. In these trials, Chinese B2B drones were used as targets. The last trials of April 1998 were witnessed by CAS, Air Chief Marshal Parvaiz Mehdi Qureshi, along with PSOs, AOCs, and senior air defence officers. Out of the four missiles fired, two achieved direct kills on their targets.

The squadron was awarded the air defence excellence trophy, ADEX, in the terminal weapon group in the years 1994 and 1998.

No. 453 Squadron

No. 453 Squadron was formed at PAF Base Sargodha, in January 1977 under the command of Wing Commander Farooq H. Khan, and was equipped with two flights of the French-made Crotale Weapon System. In 1998, the squadron moved to PAF Base Masroor, on its peacetime location. However, after the Soviet invasion of Afghanistan, the squadron moved to PAF Base Samungli, in June 1980, and was deployed at the Base to counter aerial threats emanating from across the western borders. Subsequently, in 1981, the peacetime location of the squadron was also changed from Masroor to Samungli.

To augment the defence of the Kilo area, one flight of the squadron was despatched to PAF Chaklala in February 1987, and was deployed at its designated site. Since its deployment, the flight shares operational watch along with other SAM squadrons of the PAF.

In November 1987, the peacetime role of the squadron was changed to C & M status. The role is to observe operational watch as and when directed by Headquarters Air Defence Command through Headquarters Wessec.

Between 1988 and 1998, the squadron participated in exercises High Mark-89,-93 and-95. It also participated in exercise Saffron Bandit-92,-94 and-97.

The squadron was awarded the air defence excellence trophy, ADEX, in the year 1995.

No. 454 Squadron
No. 454 Squadron was formed at PAF Base Sargodha in June 1977 under the command of Wing Commander Ashraf Sami, and was equipped with the newly inducted Crotale

Weapon System. In the beginning, the squadron was tasked to conduct training courses for officers and airmen. By the end of 1979, this task was shifted to 452 SAM Conversion Unit.

In 1979, after the Soviet invasion of Afghanistan, the squadron was tasked to deploy one flight each at Mianwali and Chaklala, which subsequently moved to the Kilo area. The squadron formally moved from Sargodha to Chaklala on a permanent basis in October 1982. In addition to the Kilo area deployment, during the Afghan War, the squadron also deployed its flights at various sites in the Parachinar, Minhas, and Nilore areas. In October 1986, it shifted one of its flights, along with manpower, to Sonmiani and participated in live firing trials. During the last two decades, the squadron has had the honour of providing round-the-clock operations for the defence of national VPs.

The squadron was twice awarded the air defence excellence trophy ADEX in the years 1996 and 1997.

No. 455 Squadron

In 1985, two flights of the Crotale 4000 series (an advanced version of the Crotale 2000) were inducted in the PAF and a new Crotale squadron, 455 Squadron, was formed on an *ad hoc* basis. In June 1985, the squadron was deployed in the Kilo area and its complete manpower and equipment was pooled up with 454 Squadron. Since its deployment, the squadron has performed round-the-clock operations for the defence of our national VPs. In 1996, the *ad hoc* establishment of 455 Squadron was regularized into a permanent establishment, although its assets remained pooled up with 454 squadron.

While the main parameters of the Crotale 4000 are similar to those of the Crotale 2000 series, some additional facilities are incorporated in the new system which give it an edge over the older one. Crotale 4000 Firing Units can be hooked up with an Acquisition Unit without a cable link. This facility has enhanced the range between the Acquisition Unit and the Firing Unit from

300 meters to 3,500 meters. The other facility of TV tracking mode in the Firing Unit enables continued target tracking with the help of TV cameras even when the tracking radar is switched off.

No. 242 Squadron

No. 242 Squadron was raised as a Mobile Observer Squadron in September 1950 at PAF Base Lahore. Since the PAF did not possess mobile low-level radars during the India-Pakistan wars of 1965 and 1971, the MOUs deployed along the eastern border by this squadron provided early warning of enemy raider aircraft. Interceptions conducted on these raiders were through the lane control concept, where fighter aircraft were asked to fly at specified CAP points waiting for the raiders to cross them, at a pre-calculated time.

This squadron was numberplated on 3 June 1989, as the PAF decided to close down two of its MOU squadrons that year. After the acquisition of Mistral missiles from France, No. 242 Squadron was re-equipped and reactivated on 15 September 1991 and shifted from PAF Base Lahore to PAF Base Rafiqui. Since its re-equipment, the squadron has conducted twenty-two basic Mistral Operator Courses. Also, forty refresher courses of two weeks duration have been conducted in which training to 649 airmen has been imparted.

Between 1991 and 1998, the squadron has participated in sixteen routine and major air defence exercises. This includes Exercises High Mark-93, 95, Saffron Bandit-92, 94, 97 and Bedaar-98. Since May 1997, the squadron has actively participated in the defence of the national VPs by deploying its firing stations. This effort was augmented after the nuclear tests by India in May 1998. The squadron participated in the live firing camp held at Army Proof Range, Sonmiani in April 1998. The Mistral missile fired by the operators achieved 100 per cent result as it successfully hit the drone target.

An important event in the history of this squadron was the establishment of TWCC (Terminal Weapon Control Centre) in Exercise High Mark-93. The squadron provided terminal defence to PAF Base Rafiqui in conjunction with the air defence assets of the PAF and the Army Air Defence Units. The first-ever concept of TWCC was validated in this exercise. The main features of the TWCC were to prioritize the targets, with an allocation of appropriate SAMs or guns, thus making judicious use of surface-to-air weapons.

No. 249 Squadron

No. 249 Squadron was established as a Mobile Observer Squadron at PAF Base Badin in January 1973. With increased air activity on the western border, the squadron was shifted to PAF Base Samungli in April 1984 to deploy its MOUs along the border. It continued to perform its role of early warning till it was numberplated on 20 September 1989. After the procurement of Mistral surface-to-air missiles from France, the squadron was re-equipped and reactivated in February 1991 at PAF Base Masroor under the command of Wing Commander Zaheer Yousafzai. Its new role was to provide day/night point defence against low-level aerial attacks to the VPs of Southern Air Command.

Since it has been re-equipped, the squadron has conducted ten courses for officers and forty-eight courses for airmen. In these courses, 197 officers and 957 airmen have so far been trained.

The squadron also participated in a number of exercises like High Mark-93, 95, Sea Spark-92, 95, 96 and Saffron Bandit-95 and 97. It also participated in live firing at the Army Air Defence Range in Sonmiani in April 1998. One Mistral missile fired by the operators of the squadron achieved a kill on a drone target.

Nos. 471/472 Squadrons

The background of these squadrons can be traced to President General Ziaul Haq's visit to China in 1981, during which two squadrons of SA-II missile system were presented to Pakistan. The equipment reached Karachi on 25 March 1982. Meanwhile, a Chinese team visited Air Headquarters, and a building complex was designed and constructed at the present site to deploy the system. Apart from this, a fuel-testing laboratory was also established to test the liquid propellants used in the missile. Responsibility for training manpower was also given to the squadron, and training commenced on 27 April 1982 at PAF Base Chaklala. The equipment of the squadron was shifted and installed at the present site on 26 October 1983, and the unit was declared operational in March 1984.

The system is known as Red Flag-II in China and was renamed Black Arrow in Pakistan. It is an all-weather, day and night, medium range system capable of intercepting targets flying upto 80,000 feet. Between 1988 and 1998, the squadron took part in thirteen air defence exercises to evaluate its effectiveness as a terminal and area defence system. Since its deployment, the squadron has provided round the clock operations for the defence of the Kahuta area with different states of readiness.

No. 413 Squadron

No. 413 Squadron was formed at PAF Base Malir in August 1982, under the command of Wing Commander Raffatullah Shah. It was equipped with four sets of Chinese origin T-514 long-range radars. Two of these sets were moved to Pasni in 1987, whereas two other radar sets continued their operations from PAF Base Malir until May 1994.

In May 1994, the PAF inducted the indigenously produced Anza MK1 shoulder-mounted surface to air missiles. No. 413 Squadron was equipped with these missiles and its role was re-defined accordingly. PAF air defence assets, particularly forward radars close to the border areas, were increasingly vulnerable to enemy gunship aerial attacks. As such, forward-located radars were allocated a suitable number of Anza missiles for their defence.

The operational integration of the Anza weapons system has undergone various phases. In the last five years, the requisite number of officers and airmen have been trained on the system. Since June 1997, Anzas are regularly deployed in almost all air defence exercises thus acclimatizing the field air defence personnel with this new weapon system.

The versatility of the system has been proved in routine air defence exercises and particularly in exercises Shandur and Vigilance. The Anza weapon system has

completed one cycle of induction, and has greatly reduced the vulnerability of radars to low-flying aircraft and gunships.

Mobile Observer Units

The history of the PAF's Mobile Observer Units dates back to the year 1949 when the first MOU squadron was formed at Mauripur on 17 September 1949. In the later part of the year, two more MOU squadrons were formed. These squadrons were named Nos. 1,2 and 3 Observer Squadron with each squadron comprising two flights, and each flight having a strength of 20 MOUs. By 1959, these observer squadrons were transformed into eight wings, and renamed 210, 211, 212, 213, 214, 215, 216, and 217 Wireless Observer Wings. In January 1969, six of these wings were reverted to squadrons and were renamed 242, 243, 244, 245, 246, and 247 MOU squadrons. The last of the two wings were, however, reverted to 248 and No. 249 MOU squadrons in 1973.

All these squadrons actively participated in the India-Pakistan wars of 1965 and 1971. In the absence of low-level surveillance radar cover on Pakistan's long border with India, the MOU squadrons provided vital information to Sector Headquarters on low-level raids. In the 1965 war, most of the scrambles were ordered on reports made by these observer squadrons. The role of mobile observers was highly appreciated and lauded at all levels after the war.

Prior to the 1971 war, 246 Squadron was moved to East Pakistan. In February 1971, it was deployed along the Indian border to pass aircraft reports to the operations room of PAF Base Dhaka. In March 1971, with the escalation of political disturbance, the deployment of the squadron's personnel in remote field areas became untenable. Thirty-five airmen of the squadron were martyred before the unit personnel could be pulled back. The sacrifices made by the personnel of 246 Squadron are truly unmatched in the history of the PAF.

Soon after the Soviet invasion of Afghanistan in 1979, 22 MOUs of 243 Squadron were deployed on the western border in Miran Shah, Parachinar, Thal, and Waziristan areas. Most of the MOUs were deployed on mountain ridges and peaks overlooking the Pakistan-Afghanistan border. Considering the steep gradients and difficult mule tracks leading to the MOU sites, it was considered to be the toughest field deployment in the history of MOUs. After a prolonged deployment of more than six years, 243 Squadron was replaced with 245 Squadron in June 1986. This prolonged deployment necessitated a change in the war plan, and the sites of 245 Squadron were shifted from the eastern border to the western border.

In June 1989, the PAF decided to number plate two of its MOU squadrons, i.e. 242 and 249 Squadrons. These two squadrons were later equipped with Mistral missiles and were reactivated in 1991. Reduced to six squadrons, the MOU's role is to provide low-level early warning to VPs/VAs against aerial threats emanating from the eastern border.

Since their inception in the early-1950s, the MOUs have played a very useful and important role as far as early-warning is concerned. The MOUs are the only appropriate answer to fill gaps in radar surveillance, particularly in hilly terrains where ground-based radars are limited in their performance, and in plains, where radar coverage is lacking or insufficient.

Training Institutions

Transport Conversion School

On 21 October 1989, the TCS added a new dimension towards training of transport

aircrew, by conducting short familiarization courses for the pilots of 41 Light Communication Squadron. These courses greatly enhanced the capabilities of the aircrew operating light aircraft, about the latest navigational instruments, and air traffic procedures. A total of four such courses have been conducted so far.

In 1989, a Research and Development Cell (R&D Cell) was established in the TCS. This cell was tasked to review the existing procedures of air transport operations, and evolve new tactics to meet the challenges of modern warfare. It achieves these objectives by distributing handouts, brochures, pamphlets, and booklets as well as by arranging seminars, etc. This cell has also been playing a vital role in keeping aircrew abreast of the rapid advances in the air transport operations.

In July 1995, the TCS conducted a comprehensive one-week Low-Level Tactical Flying Course for the operational aircrew of 6 and 12 Squadrons. During the course, the latest concepts and techniques of

low-level tactical flying were taught and practised. At the end of the course, the aircrews of both the squadrons were awarded certificates of clearance to fly such missions independently.

The high operating cost of C-130s, and the inability to practise certain in-flight emergencies on the aircraft necessitated the introduction of simulator training for all the cockpit crew of C-130 aircraft in 1994. This training, which is conducted abroad, enables the trainees to practice all types of emergencies in the simulator. It has also cut down the syllabus of IF missions, thereby reducing the overall training cost on C-130 aircraft.

Because it has produced professionals of a high standard over a period of time, the TCS has earned a reputation for excellence, both nationally as well as internationally. Not only the Pakistan Navy, but also countries like the UAE, Nigeria, Jordan, and Sri Lanka get their transport aircrew trained at this prestigious institution. To date, the TCS has successfully conducted two captains' courses for the UAE and Sri Lanka, one Co-pilots' Course for Sri Lanka, three Navigation Courses for the UAE, Jordan, and Sri Lanka, two Flight Engineers' Courses for the UAE and Sri Lanka, and one Load Masters' Course for Sri Lanka.

In June 1995, the TCS was tasked to start conversion courses on F-27 aircraft also. The first F-27 Captains' and Co-pilots' Courses graduated on 19 October 1995. In May 1997, the TCS further expanded its role and task by undertaking conversion of aircrew on Boeing 707 and Y-12 aircraft. The TCS has so far conducted thirteen Captains', sixteen Co-pilots', twenty Navigation, thirteen Flight Engineers', eight Scanners', and seventeen Load Masters' Courses on C-130 aircraft. Besides, one Co-pilots' and one Flight Engineers' Courses on Boeing 707, two Captains' and three Co-pilots' Courses on

F-27, and one Captains' Course on Y-12 aircraft have also been conducted.

Flying Instructors' School

The PAF maintains a very prestigious flying training institution at Risalpur, namely Flying Instructors School (FIS). The FIS trains instructors, not only for the PAF but also for the Pakistan Army and Navy. Due to its high standards, the FIS has earned a good reputation outside the country as well. It is training instructors from friendly countries of the Middle East, Far East, and Africa. The FIS is also responsible for the maintenance of high standards of teaching in the College of Flying Training, and the Fighter Conversion units. The re-categorization of instructors in all the three services is an additional responsibility of the Flying Instructors School.

The FIS follows a three-dimensional training system including academic training, flying training, and instructional technique.

In academic training, students are taught different aviation-related subjects to increase their knowledge and conceptual know-how of the mechanics of all aspects of aviation. The flying syllabus is designed to develop, in the student instructor, the ability to execute a particular manoeuvre in the air, and at the same time to describe precisely how it is being executed. The focus is on the instructional technique. During the course, the FIS staff continuously guides the students in order to instill in them the qualities of an efficient instructor. These qualities include mental maturity, motivation, example, initiative, sense of duty and composure under stress.

During 1988-98, the FIS conducted courses on the T-37, K-8, and MFI-17 aircrafts. During this period, the school conducted twenty-two courses. It graduated a total of 468 instructor pilots that included 323 from the PAF, eighty-three from the Army, twenty-three from the Navy, and about forty students from foreign countries like the UAE, Saudi Arabia, Sri Lanka, Nigeria etc. Out of this number, 382 instructors were trained on MFI-17, eighty on T-37, and six on K-8 aircraft. A total of 105 instructors achieved 'C' category, whereas, thirty were withdrawn from the course for different reasons like slow progress, airsickness etc.

To enhance the training values, reciprocal visits were undertaken between the FIS and the Central Flying School (CFS), UK. A team of five officers from the CFS visited FIS in 1990 and 1997. Similarly, four PAF officers visited the CFS during the period.

Basic Staff School

The Basic Staff School (BSS) is a successor to a chain of developments aimed at providing training in the fundamentals of service. Previously, the

JC&SS used to provide officers with the training necessary to meet mid-career service needs. But this course was not mandatory for officers of all branches, and only a few selected officers could attend this course. A new in-service education scheme was launched for officers, which led to the establishment of the BSS at PAF Camp Badaber. Air Marshal Syed Masood Hatif, the then Vice Chief of the Air Staff, inaugurated the School on 28 July 1992. It is an independent unit and has been placed under the Training Branch for functional and administrative control.

The BSS course runs for nine weeks and is conducted for officers of all branches. Officers from some of the allied countries also attend this course. The faculty is responsible for imparting instruction in the disciplines of staff communication, management, administration, air force law and air operations. Instruction is given through lectures and discussion with the help of requisite multimedia training aids and oral, written, and practical exercises.

Educational visits are arranged for all officers. A one-week Pakistan study tour is exclusively organized for allied officers. Director-level guest speakers from almost all important directorates of the Air Headquarters, and from both the sister Services, are invited to acquaint officers with the role and task of these establishments. Additional lectures on Mass Media Awareness, Role and Task of the PAF, and Flight Safety have been recently included in the curriculum. Also, guest speakers from Peshawar University are invited to deliver lectures on morality and code of conduct to give student officers an opportunity to understand ethical values and their advantages to the individual, and to society.

The BSS has also introduced a new exercise, Vision, in an attempt to achieve the twin benefits of communication skills and awareness about current affairs. Student officers dedicate their evenings to games, working together on the computer and on learning the use of multimedia applications for their presentations.

To date, a total of thirty-three courses have been conducted at the Basic Staff School and more than 1,050 student officers have graduated, including eighty-seven foreign officers from allied countries.

Air Defence Training School

The Air Defence Training School (ADTS) was established in 1975. Since then, the school has graduated a total of seventy-eight Basic and Advanced Courses. The school conducts two basic courses for Air Defence Weapon Controllers in a year. The intake of this course is fifteen to twenty students and the duration is about twenty-four weeks. The trainees include aviation cadets, i.e. GD (P) or CAE students suspended from the PAF Academy, Risalpur. During the course, students are taught air defence, electronics,

and led to the establishment of a new training institution. It was envisaged that the PAF personnel would be trained at a faster pace on this newly inducted modern equipment. This school initiated its training at the Lahore Base under the name of Air Defence Modernization School (ADMS). In the beginning, the school initiated its training activity in a small hangar as a part of the 481 CRC Wing, and some classrooms and officers were made available to it. It was shifted to a new campus at PAF Walton in 1989 after a period of eleven years during which the school had already conducted about 200 courses and trained 3,000 personnel. At the same time, the school was renamed the Air Defence System School, commonly known as ADSS. The school's building comprises an auditorium, a library, a model room, nineteen offices and eleven classrooms.

The school is responsible for conducting basic and advanced training courses for operational and maintenance personnel on PADS-77 equipment.

and navigation in the theory phase. To those who qualify this phase, practical training is imparted which consists of simulator and live GCIs. After the successful completion of the course, aviation cadets are commissioned in the ADWC branch, given the rank of Flying Officer on the next day, and posted to 485 CRC & OT Wing, PAF. Before becoming operational, and being posted to their field units, the officers undergo a number of courses like the Balloon Barrage Course, the Mistral System Positional Qualification Course, the Anza Weapon System Course, the CRC/MPDR Positional Qualification Course, and the Operational Training Course at 485 CRC. The duration of these courses varies from one week in the case of the Balloon Barrage course to twenty-four weeks in the case of the Operational Training Course.

Air Defence System School
The induction of PADS-77 equipment changed the air defence training requirements,

Headquarters Air Defence Command exercises functional control over the ADSS through PAF Base Lahore, whereas PAF Base Lahore exercises administrative control, and provides necessary administrative and maintenance facilities to the ADSS.

The school not only trains PAF officers and airmen, but also provides training to personnel from friendly countries. Apart from training 1,769 officers and 6,977 airmen of the PAF, the school has also trained two foreign engineering officers, one each from Myanmar and the UAE.

Air War College

The changing conflict environment and geo-strategic compulsions, rapid diffusion of high technology in modern warfare, and the experience of the two wars (1965 & 1971) made the PAF realize the need for a higher institution, exclusively devoted to the study of war and related matters. As such, the Staff College was upgraded to Air War College.

The first Air War Course reported in July 1987 and graduated in June 1988. Till AWC Course No. 2, only officers from the three services were eligible for the course. Starting with course No. 3, however, a number of officers from friendly countries were also inducted. To date, officers from Bangladesh, Indonesia, Iran, Iraq, Jordan, Kenya, Malaysia, Nigeria, Qatar, Sri Lanka, Syria, Turkey, and the UAE have successfully completed their training at this institution. So far, eleven courses have been conducted, and 282 students, including forty-six foreigners, have completed the training in this prestigious institution.

The college is affiliated to the University of Karachi for the award of M.Sc. (Strategic Studies) and B.Sc. Hons. (War Studies) degrees to student officers, on the successful completion of the course. The total intake for this course is forty-five students. The college has modern facilities that include the Internet, close circuit TV, magnabite, and multimedia. The course has five different phases which include the study of Command, Leadership and Resource Management, Military Doctrine and Strategy, National Security Environment and Power Potential of Nations, besides individual and group research projects. The college shifted to the new building in January 1991. Mr Ghulam Ishaq Khan, the then President, officially inaugurated the new building on 8 December 1991.

College of Aeronautical Engineering

After the integration of flying and engineering training into one harmonious system, both the colleges, College of Aeronautical Engineering (CAE) and College of Flying Training (CFT), entered into a new era of progress and the CAE achieved some important milestones. Some of these were: affiliation to the National

University of Sciences and Technology (NUST), launching of the self-financing scheme, induction of paying cadets, the faculty progression programme through higher education abroad, the initiation of the MS programme, new avenues for provision of research and development, and consultancy for the college faculty in civilian or defence-related engineering projects.

The National University of Sciences and Technology (NUST) was established under the Presidential Ordinance 1/93 on 13 March 1993, and was assigned a major role in promoting defence-related research and development (R&D). Hence, the Air Staff felt that a formal relationship between CAE and NUST would suit the PAF's requirements.

The modalities to change the CAE's affiliation to NUST were worked out, and with the prior approval of the Air Staff, a formal request for affiliation was made to NUST in October 1994. On completion of the formalities, the CAE was granted the constituent college status by NUST on 5 January 1995. The regulations governing the academic policies and procedures of the CAE carried the approval of the NED University, Karachi. These policies and procedures provided an academically efficient relationship between the NED University and the CAE. It was considered appropriate to keep them in practice, while changing affiliation to NUST.

In the early nineties, the PAF conceived the idea of introducing the Paying Cadet Scheme at the CAE on the lines of other institutions of the armed forces, and self-supporting professional colleges like the Army Medical College, the Army College of Signals, and the EME College. A major stimulus behind this plan was the need to create a pool of civilian aeronautical engineers in view of the government's policy of encouraging the private aeronautical industry in the civilian sector. Moreover, the rapid expansion of PAC Kamra had already generated a pressing demand for aeronautical engineers, which the PAF was unable to satisfy. A body of civilian aeronautical engineers was, therefore, regarded essential to meet the national requirements. The self-financing scheme was finally adopted after carefully studying its pros and cons. The modalities of the scheme, academic and administrative arrangements at the Academy, and related actions were finally sorted out at Air Headquarters level and the scheme was launched, starting with the summer semester of 1994.

Candidates under the self-financing scheme are selected for the regular engineering courses after every six months, on open merit basis. The candidate's matriculation and F Sc. scores, and the academic entrance test decide the position of a candidate on the merit list.

The paying cadets are required to pay tuition fees, and other charges for one semester (six months) in advance, before the beginning of each semester. They abide by all the rules and regulations applicable to regular cadets in various fields of training, discipline, academics, honour code etc. They wear the same uniform and kit as the PAF cadets. The first batch of cadets under the scheme passed out in 1997. 'NUST Cadets' who are selected through the NUST selection process have also joined the CAE since 1998, and are gradually replacing the paying cadets.

The CAE faculty consists of officers who have had a distinguished academic career, and possess vision as well as a vast and valuable experience in their respective fields. A majority of the faculty is foreign qualified, with Ph.D and MS degrees from institutions of international repute. To benefit from their expertise, an active research and development programme has been embarked upon in various departments, which involves faculty members and research students. R&D activities at the CAE have entered a new era with the commencement of a post-graduate programme. The CAE has a vast potential for research and consultancy work in the related fields. As such, laboratories in the different departments have been modified to facilitate the goal of original research. At present these laboratories can cater for any original research by the students and faculty members. The capabilities of the CAE are evident from the fact that the CAS has granted it the status of an R&D institution.

The post-graduate programme was launched at the CAE in 1997. The programme aims at developing competence in selected areas of aeronautical engineering which are of interest to the aviation industry in general and military aviation in particular. These post-graduate courses in the fields of aerospace and avionics are a fine blend of theoretical and practical studies. Computer aided learning is being emphasized, and in

order to achieve this objective effectively, a sufficient number of computer laboratories have been set up. Thus maximum human and material resources are being utilized to keep pace with the modern educational trends.

The CAE established its credentials as a centre for excellence by meeting the international standards of quality management in education, in the recored time of just over four months. Recently the CAE has been awarded the ISO 9001 certification.

School of Aeronautics

The School of Aeronautics (SOA), PAF Base Korangi Creek, plays a vital role in imparting technical training and general service knowledge to the airmen of Engine, Airframe, Electrical, and Instrument trades. It is also a matter of pride for the Pakistan Air Force that this school, in addition to providing advanced trade training to PAF technicians, is also meeting the technical training requirements of the Pakistan Navy, and the armed forces of friendly countries. The laboratories in this institute are equipped with modern training facilities like Hydraulic Landing Gear System, Anti-Skid Brake System, etc. The trainees, initially trained at the PTTS Kohat, join the SOA as ACs and pass out as SACs. The School of Aeronautics lays emphasis on sports as well. These include Hockey, Football, Volleyball, Cross Country running, Cricket, Basketball, Kabadi, and Tug-of-War. There are TV viewing platforms in the SOA Trainees' Messes and a water filtration plant is provided to both the Messes of the school.

School of Electronics (SOE)

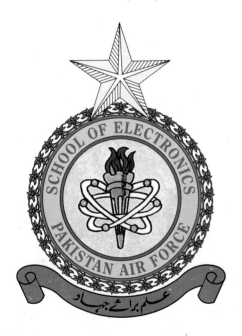

In 1990, the Advance Courses for the airmen of Radio and Radar (Air and Ground) trades in the School of Electronics, PAF Base Korangi Creek were discontinued and merged into the Initial Training. New training aids and models were in extensive

use. To cater for more space, the buildings of Mess No. 5, and the barracks were taken over by the SOE from the SOA in 1993, and a new building (No. 620) in the SOE trainees' camp was constructed in the year 1994. From 1988 to 1998, this school conducted 267 courses with a total strength of 8,861 airmen. To facilitate recreation, a TV viewing platform in the SOE Mess No. 5 was constructed in 1998.

Aero-Medical Institute

Developments in research and academic related activities necessitated the establishment of a biochemical laboratory in the Research Wing of the AMI in 1989. This also took up the role of a Drug Detection and Detoxification Centre. Courses in Aviation Medicine are regularly held for medical officers to qualify them as Flight Surgeons. These Flight Surgeons are also seconded to friendly countries in the Middle East to work with their Air Forces.

The ejection seat trainer procured from Polly Tech Inc. China had been installed in this unit in November 1998. The objective of this installation was to familiarize the pilots with the procedure to be followed, in sequence, prior to ejection from the aircraft. It proved to be extremely effective in dispelling apprehension and uncertainty among the PAF's younger pilots about ejecting from aircraft. Indoctrination courses on this trainer had been started in January 1989. The first Ejection Seat Trainer Course was conducted in 1999.

The Drug Detoxification and Rehabilitation Centre was established on 15 February 1989. The role of this centre was to carry out drug detoxification treatment and rehabilitation of drug addicts referred to this institute.

Pre-Trade Training School

In 1987, the Recruits Training School (RTS), Kohat was renamed the Pre-Trade Training School (PTTS) with the new role of training Aero Technician and Aero Support entries. The PTTS is presently imparting academic education and General Service Training (GST) to the young, newly inducted recruits arriving in the PAF from the civil sector. They join one of the two main training streams: the aero technicians stream (technical faculty), and the aero support stream (non-technical faculty). The overall training period for the aero technicians stream is spread over a period of two years and three months, and that of aero support is from one to two years, depending upon the trade allotted to the trainee. During the last decade, a lot of construction and renovation work was carried out at the PTTS. The unit mosque situated in the centre of the unit is under a comprehensive renovation. In all, eighteen trainees' barracks have been completely renovated. New notice boards, dressing mirrors, squadron nomenclature and colours, and peg sets provide the trainees a more conducive environment. A new mess building was constructed on the site of the old Recruits Mess which was renamed Khalid Bin Walid Mess in 1989. Full renovation of the Muhammad Bin Qasim Mess has also been completed. This effort has helped a great deal in inculcating healthy living habits among the trainees. Two staff rooms and a tea bar have been completely renovated and provided with new electric fittings, new furnishing, and other improvements.

An antique tower clock in the possession of the PAF, housed above the centre of the main building of the PTTS, had been unserviceable since long. It was repaired by two Radio Fitters of the unit, Senior Technician Ghazanfar and Senior Technician Bakht. These gentlemen completed the task at the cost of only four hundred rupees whereas a company based in Lahore had demanded Rs. 100,000 for its repair, without providing a guarantee. The clock was not only accurately set to Pakistan Standard Time, but also fitted with lights illuminating its arms and digits.

Motivation Boards and Slabs were affixed around the PTTS building to raise the faith and morale of the trainees. A calligraphic rendering of the *Kalema Tayyabah* was installed right beneath the clock tower in Headquarters building. Quranic verses and the Hadith of the Holy Prophet (Peace Be Upon Him) were displayed on the ground floor of the old academic block and more Quranic verses were displayed on cement slabs at the first floor of the old academic block. Slogan boards were affixed at the entrance of the PTTS campus and four thousand saplings were planted in the PTTS campus.

Administrative Trades Training School

To improve the spoken English of the trainees, a language laboratory, LLS-700, was installed in 1989. A total of 401 courses were conducted from 1988 to 1998 and 12,301 airmen trainees successfully passed out from this School in various disciplines. Three passing out parades were held every year, and reviewed by the Base Commander PAF Base Kohat. For the first time in the history of the Base, the passing out parade of ATTS and SOL trainees was scheduled from February 1999 onward.

School of Logistics

Prior to 1988, the Supply Training Squadron was responsible for training the Supply and Catering Assistants of the PAF, as well as the Cadets of the Maintenance Equipment Branch. It was later shifted to the College of Logistics, Risalpur which, as a result of the amalgamation of branches, was abolished in 1990. Direct induction of Supply Officers

was thus ceased, but short and refresher courses in Supply continued for the Engineering Officers at the CAE.

The acquisition of an Automated Logistics Maintenance System by the PAF in 1988 revealed that the existing force of supply personnel could not provide effective logistics support unless they were trained on the vastly sophisticated logistics system acquired by the PAF. Consequently, the CAS issued a directive to establish a physically and administratively independent School of Logistics at Kohat to modernize the training of supply personnel and also to centralize all logistics activities at a single point. The School of Logistics was thus established at Kohat, and started functioning in October 1992.

JCO's Academy

Located at PAF Base Korangi Creek, the JCO's Academy imparts training in English Language, Leadership, Management, Pakistan Studies, PAF Law, Organization and Administration, and Drill commands, to

prepare the SNCOs for higher appointments within the JCOs cadre. Starting from 1986, the Academy has conducted forty-six regular courses and has graduated over 5,800 SNCOs. Out of these graduates, over 401 SNCOs earned certificates of distinction by securing a score of 80 per cent and above.

Computer Training School

Established in 1974 as the Computer Training Centre (CTC), the unit was assigned to computerize the PAF records in collaboration with the International Business Management (IBM) who were also to provide the hardware and the training to selected personnel. Since 1980, there had been a rapid technological advancement in the field of computer science, resulting in rapid upgrades of computer hardware and software.

In order to keep abreast with these developments, the PAF began to update its own hardware and software facilities. This required a lot of training for the PAF personnel. In 1986, the CTC was established at PAF Camp Badaber, to fulfill the ever increasing requirements of computer training. During the mid-1980s, the role and influence of personal computers (PCs) in office management was at its peak. The PAF lost no time in switching over to this new field and, as such, the training on PCs proliferated. In a very short time span, the PAF trained thirty-five officers, sixty airmen and ninety civilians for PC operations, maintenance, and upgrades. At the start of the 1990s, Information Technology (IT) was assuming new dimensions due to the increasing popularity of the Internet and e-mail. Consequently, steps had to be taken to revise the role of the CTC. It was thus decided in 1997 that the status of the CTC be enhanced to Computer Training School (CTS) with the basic objective of training PAF personnel in

the field of computers, and to assist the Directorate of Data Automation (Dte of DA) by extending expert opinion on all computer related tasks and issues. The unit was thus tasked to train PAF officers, airmen, and civilians in different fields of computerization, to evaluate and categorize the latest developments in hardware and software technologies, and to help the Directorate of DA in formulating policies relating to IT.

The CTS conducts training for the newly commissioned officers of the Maintenance Data Automation (MDA) branch. In addition, it offers a general office automation course for all officers, and an Executive Course for managers, concerning middle and top level management. The airmen training for Data Processing Assistants (DP Assistant) consists of General Computer Operations and Computer Hardware Maintenance Courses which aim to make the trainees more effective in the use of the computer and its technology. All the planned courses keep a sharp focus on the best utility of PAF resources through the use of computers.

College of Education

The training of officers and men in different branches and phases is a continuous process in the PAF. One of the most important requirements in this regard is the standardization of the instructional technique which is fulfilled by the College of Education (COE), PAF Base Korangi Creek. The role of the COE is to impart general service and trade training to newly inducted education instructors and also to provide basic instructional training techniques to instructors of all trades throughout the PAF. In addition, it conducts refresher courses in Instruction Technique (IT), annually recategorizes education officer instructors at various training establishments, conducts IT cum

Training Supervisory (Trg. Sup.) Courses for education officers, and officers of other branches, and imparts professional training to newly commissioned Special Purposes Short Service Commission (SPSSC) Education officers in the PAF. It also provides English language training and technical teaching training to SNCOs of SOA and SOE.

After Dinner Literary Activities (ADLA) are regularly held at the COE to instill confidence in officers and airmen and also to improve their communication skills. In addition, educational visits are frequently arranged for students of both officer and airmen courses to provide them with practical knowledge, and to broaden their mental horizon. They are taken to different civil establishments like Madinatul-Hikmat, PIA Technical Training Center, the Oil Refinery, Thermal Power Station, Karachi University, Liaquat Memorial Library, DHA Libraries, etc. Besides these, PAF and Naval establishments are also visited, which include Naval Dockyard, PAF Museum, 102 AED, and the Air War College.

PAF College Sargodha

Prior to 1985, PAF College Sargodha was functioning as a Degree Science College imparting full military training to the GD (P) as well as Engineering Cadets of the PAF, followed by the flying training phase at PAF Academy Risalpur. However, in 1985, B.Sc. classes were shifted to Risalpur and once again only F.Sc. classes were conducted at the college. In 1990, a review of the PAF intake requirements was made, which highlighted the excellent contributions made by this college as a public school. It was, therefore, decided to revert the institution to its previous role of a public school imparting education from class VIII to F.Sc. to young men who would join the PAF and whose expenses would be borne by the PAF. Hence in 1990, the 94 GD (P) and 39 CAE became the last entries to pass through PAF College Sargodha, to join the PAF Academy, Risalpur for further training under the previous role of the PAF College.

On reopening of the College as a public school, all the eight student houses were renamed Attacker, Falcon, Fury, Halifax,

SARGODHA

Mirage, Sabre, Starfighter, and Tempest. Two entries of 100 students each were inducted in the eighth and ninth classes in January 1991 as the twenty-third and twenty-fourth entries. Later, the strength of the college was raised to 440. Air Commodore Fareed Ali Shah, a former Sargodhian, was appointed Commandant of this College to supervise the transition of PAF College Sargodha from a Degree Science College to a typical public school from December 1987 to April 1991. He was followed by Air Commodore Bilal A. Khan (April 1991 to January 1993), and later by Air Commodore (now Air Vice Marshal) Imtiaz Haider (January 1993 to November 1993) in the efforts to establish PAF College Sargodha as a typical public school.

To achieve the objective of running PAF College Sargodha on the lines of a public school, modified to meet the requirements of the PAF training doctrine, the Air Headquarters decided to appoint a retired Air Vice Marshal, and an old Sargodhian, as the Commandant of this College. Hence, Air Vice Marshal Raja Aftab Iqbal, (Retd.) took over as the Commandant of PAF College, Sargodha in November 1993. By December 1998, a number of projects were completed, providing this college with the most modern training aids and implements. These new additions included the latest WICOM language laboratory, a modern computer laboratory, construction of new buildings for two student houses, a well-maintained gymnasium, and a recreation room equipped with a multimedia projector.

Recently, a gymnasium has been developed in the Hobbies Club, for the students. The most striking feature of the Hobbies Club is the College History Room where achievements of young and old students of the college are highlighted. Souvenirs like Air Chief Marshal Farooq Feroze Khan's uniform are unique to this room. He is one of the distinguished Sargodhians who rose to a four-star rank and held appointments of the CAS and Chairman Joint Chiefs of Staff Committee. Air Marshal Masood Hatif, Air Marshal Shafique Haider, and Air Marshal Aliuddin, who rose to the prestigious appointment of VCAS, form yet another luminous chapter in the history of PAF College Sargodha. Their names decorate the walls of the College History Room.

There are nearly two dozen sports fields, and a swimming pool in the college. Sports and swimming are compulsory for all the students. Inter-House competitions are held throughout the year and prizes are awarded to winning houses for individual games as well as over all championship. The Quaid-i-Azam Trophy is the most coveted distinction, awarded to the House which emerges as the overall champion in sports, academics, and other spheres of training. Sports teams of other prestigious institutions like Cadet College Hasan Abdal, Military College Jhelum and Cadet College Petaro are also invited for sports competitions on reciprocal basis. Such friendly fixtures bring together the students of these institutions.

Engineering Depots and Logistic Centres

During the years 1989-90, the then 101 and 103 Air Logistics Depots (ALDs) were re-designated as Air Logistics Centres (ALC), and a common name, Air Engineering Depot, (AED) was allocated to all existing Air Maintenance Depots, Air Electronic Depots, and Air Ordnance Depots after the amalgamation of the engineering branches.

No. 101 Air Logistics Centre

There are three Air Logistics Depots (ALD) in 101 Air Logistic Centre (ALC), namely; 301 ALD, 302 ALD and 303 ALD. Among

these, 301 ALD looks after C-130, T-37, and light communication aircraft spares, 302 ALD deals with radar, electronic equipment and PME etc., and 303 ALD manages ground equipment and hardware. These depots are functioning under the weapon system management concept and are directly controlled by their respective weapon system management directorates at Air Headquarters.

In the year 1995, a facility for manufacturing packing boxes from corrugated paper sheets was established at this Centre. These boxes are used for packing and preservation of delicate, fragile and valuable items in order to ensure their safety and protection from dust. The ALC also provides cartons to other bases and units, on demand. In May 1996, the complete data of 101 ALC was transferred to IBM System 3090 from IBM system 36.

No. 102 Air Engineering Depot
In 1988, a testing facility for aircraft arresting barrier straps was established at 102

AED. This facility is used by all the flying bases to verify the required strength of aircraft arresting barrier straps.

The project for WP-7 type B engine overhaul (for F-7 aircraft) was initiated in 1991, and within one year an engine overhaul squadron was established which carries out the overhaul of WP-7 engines alongside the WP-6 engines (for F-6 aircraft). Also, in the year 1992, a Plasma spray facility was established through the efforts of the late Squadron Leader Sohail in 102 AED. Plasma spray is primarily used in the recovery of worn-out engine components during overhaul/EFM of WP-7 engines. This is the only facility of its kind in the PAF.

The General Engineering Squadron-II of the depot was renamed the Engineering Support Squadron in 1992. A new section, namely Machine Maintenance Flight, was added to this squadron to centralize the maintenance and repair activities of all the 750 machines of the depot. Experience gathered from the maintenance of these

machines and testers has also been put to use for recovering machines of other PAF bases. This activity facilitated the successful accomplishment of thirty-one tasks which resulted in the recovery of sixty-five unserviceable machines all over the command.

In 1996, WP-7 type E engines were inducted for overhaul, and the task was successfully accomplished in 1997. During the period 1996-98, the twin cell test-bed was upgraded, and its exhaust deflectors were modified to facilitate testing of engines after overhaul and EFM. It ensured the availability of serviceable WP-7 engines to support the PAF's F-7 fleet. In 1998, CATIC approved the skill level of the manpower of this depot as well as the quality of its production for WP-7 engines.

In 1997, for the first time in the PAF, a structural overhaul of the Allouette-III helicopter was launched in this unit. After successful accomplishment of the overhaul, the first helicopter rolled out in April 1998, followed by another in October 1998.

In 1997, the Ground Training School was revitalized and named, Technical Training Centre. This centre imparts training to all civilian technicians who are inducted into the Service. This is an exclusive set-up within the PAF, where civilian technicians are given formal training before they take up their technical assignments for jobs in the service. A revised and updated syllabus comprising a course of eight weeks' duration was prepared in line with the latest syllabus of the School of Aeronautics.

Various modifications have been completed on PAF aircraft by 102 AED during the period between 1988 and 1998. These include twenty-seven Structural Life Enhancement Programme (SLEP) modifications, twelve rewiring modifications on T-37 aircraft, seventeen modifications on MM-3 of A-5s, ten tow-banner modifications on F-6 and FT-6, and forty modifications pertaining to landing light, HUD, and bombs delay system of F-7 aircraft.

No. 103 Air Logistics Centre

In 1992, a batch of 61,000 line items of the Australian Mirages were added to the inventory of 103 ALC that was housed in 201 ALD. This inventory included mainly spares, ground support equipment, and tools.

The seventh Logistic Group was established at PAF Base Rafiqui to manage the inventory of F-7 and FT-7 aircraft. In 1994, it was shifted to PAF Base Chaklala and was made part of 103 ALC as 205 Air Logistics Depot. With the establishment of 205 ALD, 14,000 line items were added to the inventory of 103 ALC.

A detachment of 103 ALC is established at PAF Base Faisal to receive, store, and issue the spares of RD-9B, WP-6, and WP-7 engines to 102 AED for repair and overhaul.

PAF Base Faisal exercises both functional and administrative control over the detachment.

No. 104 Air Engineering Depot

No. 104 Air Engineering Depot was established in 1976. Its present role and task is repair, overhaul, inspection, and storage of specialist and common-user vehicles, aerospace ground equipment, and their engines.

In 1990-91, an area of 136,750 square feet belonging to 104 AED was handed over to Shaheen Bonded Warehouse (SBW). It included 20,276 square feet of covered area. This area was used earlier by auto repair, general engineering and component repair shops of the depot. Subsequently, two production hangars were constructed at the back of the depot to accommodate engine repair and vehicle repair shops.

In addition to its normal task, the depot was assigned two main projects in 1998 that comprised overhauling the power pack of Crotale vehicles and re-conditioning of staff cars of older models. The depot is committed to continuous improvement in the performance of its product and services.

In 1978, 104 MU (Detachment) was established at PAF Faisal to overhaul mechanical transport engines pertaining to the southern zone. It was redesignated as 112 MU in 1982 with the additional role of maintenance of air-conditioning and refrigeration units, generators, and all ground equipment of the south zone. The responsibility of receipt and despatch of new vehicles was also given to the detachment. However, in 1993, this unit was again redesignated as 104 AED (Dett) and the maintenance of air-conditioning and refrigeration units was deleted from its charter. The detachment works under the functional control of Air Headquarters and the administrative control of PAF Base Faisal.

No. 105 Air Engineering Depot
No. 105 AED was initially established in November 1947 as an ordnance storage unit. With the passage of time the complexity of high performance munitions increased, and it was considered necessary in the mid-1980s to assign only officers of the armament branch to command this depot. The unit's revised assignment included overhaul, modifications, major inspection and evaluation of combat stores, besides the provision of technical advice, and on-site recovery of stores.

A Munitions Training School (MTS) was established at the depot in June 1987 to promote better understanding of the latest system among senior armament supervisors, and to disseminate the knowledge gained through R&D at site.

No. 106 Air Engineering Depot

No. 106 Air Engineering Depot provides operational and training armament support to the bases under the Northern Air Command, and monitors and collects the indigenously produced armament stores from Pakistan Ordnance Factories, Air Weapon Complex, and other vendors in the region. These stores are then further distributed and despatched to other depots and bases. The depot also carries out tests and trials of the new and life expired stores.

The depot functioned under the command of Rear Air Headquarters (Directorate of Logistics) till 1998, and thereafter transferred to the engineering branch under the control of ACAS (Weapons). Over the period, the depot has provided excellent support to regional bases, its communication facilities have been improved, and its entire inventory has been computerized. Recently, a training centre for armament personnel, and an indent tracking cell have also been established. The depot constantly assists Air

Headquarters in planning future provisioning of operational and training armament support to the PAF.

Some of the buildings of the depot were damaged in 1991 due to an explosion in an adjacent Army Depot, and required reconstruction. Moreover, during 1991-94, two new explosive store houses were constructed, to meet the requirement of the unit.

No. 107 Air Engineering Depot

No. 107 Air Engineering Depot is responsible for providing prompt and effective inspection, installation, and calibration of the electronic equipment, in the PAF. With the induction of new electronic equipment, the task of 107 AED has also increased manifold. Accordingly, the Standards and Calibration (S&C) squadron of the AED, the only agency of its kind, was re-equipped and updated. A new Precision Measuring Equipment Laboratory (PMEL) was established to meet these challenges. Another new building was also commissioned in 1994 for the Avionics

Engineering and Electronics Engineering squadrons.

In 1996, two new concepts were introduced at the depot, namely the Self Reliance Cell and the Aircraft Modification Team. The Self Reliance Cell was established to undertake repair of airborne electronics equipment for which depot level repair did not exist either in the PAF or in the rest of the country. The Aircraft Modification Team was created to centralize the modification efforts on different types of aircraft in the PAF. With both cells functioning, the Depot's capability to support PAF operations was augmented.

No. 108 Air Engineering Depot

In the 1980s, the domain of 108 AED's responsibilities was expanded, and maintenance facilities for the Crotale weapon system and air defence automation system were established. In order to provide continued support to the aging air defence elements, an R&D cell was created on a self-help basis. Over the years, the role and task of 108 AED has increased manifold, and the need arose for reviewing the manpower and support facilities. Subsequently, in 1989, two more shops with a concomitant manpower were added to the automation facility.

Earlier, the depot could provide maintenance facilities only to the Crotale 2000 weapon system. However, in 1989, with the addition of the required equipment, repair capabilities were enhanced to support the Crotale 4000 system as well. A need was felt to establish overhauling facilities for Crotale 2000, which had been in service for some time. The Crotale overhaul project was launched in 1998, and an additional hangar was constructed for this purpose.

This unit also assisted in the interfacing of the Chinese Radar Data Extractor

(RADEX) with the SOC for automating manual radars. Moreover, shelterization of the AR-1 radar was started in 1998 in collaboration with MVRDE, and the project is making gradual progress.

No. 109 Air Engineering Depot

The present role of the 109 Air Engineering Depot is to upgrade Guidance and Control (G&C) units of the AIM-9B version to AIM-9P, provide third and fourth line maintenance to the G&C units of AIM-9P missiles, and to develop the facilities to cater for evaluation, analysis and repair of the G&C units.

The first of the three roles was time-dependent, hence, after the upgrade of all the G&C units, it ceased to be the objective. However, the sphere of the other two objectives became more complex, and demanding with the passage of time. The impact of the American embargo and the county's deteriorating economic conditions was felt by the depot also, and affected its output efficiency. As most of the electronic parts were not available through the normal supply route, an internal effort for exploring alternate methods began at the depot in order to keep the test stations serviceable and productive. Moreover, in the absence of any established third line maintenance depot for the test equipment and Alternate Mission Equipment (AME) of Armament specialty, an *ad hoc* section was established at 109 AED under the name of CARE (Central Armament Repair Establishment). Within a short span of time, this unit became so well-reputed within the PAF for its timely and efficient repair capabilities, that the influx of unserviceable electronic and electro-optical equipment from various PAF bases increased tremendously. 109 Air Engineering Depot took this on as a challenge and through the indefatigable efforts of its men and officers, it completed all its tasks including R&D jobs. The depot also carries out R&D for Armament specialty whenever tasked by Air Headquarters.

No. 110 Air Logistics Depot
Soon after the establishment of the PAF, there arose a need for a central store for items of clothing. For this purpose, a detachment of No. 103 MU Chaklala was established at Kohat, which continued to provide clothing for a long time. However, during the 1971 war, one of its major warehouses was damaged by the enemy. Thereafter, the PAF decided to shift this unit to some other place rather than re-constructing it. Eventually, in December 1973, the unit was shifted from Kohat to Badaber where storage facilities were already available. To improve upon the system of inventory management, its status was also upgraded from that of a detachment to a self-accounting unit. Accordingly, its organizational structure was also changed. Later, in December 1987, the unit was renamed No. 110 Air Logistics Depot.

Presently, the depot has thirteen warehouses of varying sizes that are used for storing thousands of line items of a multiple range.

The depot is under the functional control of AHQ (Dte of Log Support) while administrative control over it is exercised by RAHQ (U) Peshawar. It manages a sizeable inventory of clothing items, office equipment, barrack equipment, and fire-fighting equipment, etc.

No. 114 Air Engineering Depot
No. 114 Air Engineering Depot is a munition complex that was established on 27 March 1989 at Sargodha, and became functional in November 1990. The purpose of establishing this unit was to meet the requirements of PAF bases in the central region. Earlier, most such requirements were met by 105 AED, Karachi. The establishment of this unit has increased the dispersion of assets, heightened readiness, and simplified accessibility to munitions, when needed.

Some of the major responsibilities of the depot are to keep aircraft and ground defence munitions safe, secure, and serviceable. This unit has always endeavoured to come up to the expectations of the PAF.

No. 118 Software Engineering Depot
In 1986, the Centre for Air Defence Automation Management (CADAM) was formed on an *ad hoc* basis. The role of the Centre was to provide training and software maintenance support for the automation system. The basic establishment of CADAM did not cater for R&D projects. Due to various operational requirements, arising from time to time, CADAM initially started work on automation related projects on a limited scale. With the passage of time, this aspect of its work grew into a major activity involving projects related to automation,

CRC, the Crotale weapon system, radar/air defence simulators, and aircraft simulators.

To provide a suitable infrastructure, resources, and manpower for these software development tasks, the need was felt to revise the existing establishment to cater to R&D projects, in addition to its other roles. The establishment of 118 Software Engineering Depot (SED) at CADAM was, therefore, taken up in earnest.

The existing automation system has been in use for the last fifteen years. To ensure optimum performance, 118 SED has all along been carrying out modifications and debugging in the system software which is huge in size and complexity. In addition, the generation of load master tapes/cartridges, diagnostics, and simulation raid tapes for distribution to Operations Communication Centres (OCCs), Sector Operations Centres (SOCs), and Air Defence Operations Centre (ADOC) has been a continuous process.

The training conducted at 118 SED includes a wide variety of courses on the operations and maintenance aspects of the automation system's hardware and software. The nature and duration of the courses varies, from familiarization courses (one to two weeks) to software maintenance courses (nineteen weeks). The trainees include officers of GD (P), ADWC, Engineering, Data Automation, Army Air Defence, and airmen from Radar Operator, Radar Fitter and Radio Fitter trades.

The training courses to be conducted at CADAM were defined at the time of induction of the air defence automation system. With the passage of time, a better understanding of the automation system, coupled with the experience gained in conducting these courses, necessitated a major review of the training programme. This restructuring of training courses, was carried out in July 1995. It included new aspects such as an approach based on

integrating hardware and software diagnoses, for the purpose of detecting the fault at automation sites and in individual student software modification projects. The revised training programme incorporated this aspect in its software maintenance courses. Moreover, to cater for the smooth induction of R&D systems, developed at 118 SED, the preparation of operation, maintenance and training manuals and training of operation and maintenance officers and personnel for these systems was also included.

To effectively implement the restructured training programme and to enhance the quality of training, a simulator for HMD-22 console was developed and is being used for practical training of various automation system courses. A computer laboratory has been set up for simulator training, computer hardware and software training, and preparation of students' and instructors' presentations. In addition, a new comprehensive manual providing integrated treatment of hardware and software issues of the automation system has also been introduced. As a part of a study, 118 SED built a proof-of-concept system which could remotely extract and display CRC data so that the capability of displaying data from many MPDRs, with tracking facility, may be made available for enhancing the Forward Area Control Centre's role. The system was built and tested in November 1997.

No. 118 Software Engineering Depot made a humble start as training and programming centre for the automation system but has grown into a major software development centre for the PAF. It has a long list of challenging R&D projects that were successfully completed in a short period of time and with the limited available resources. TWCC, Crotale weapon simulators, air defence simulator, and Mirage-V simulator are just a few projects. These projects have not only contributed towards enhancing the operational efficiency of the PAF, but have also resulted in significant saving of foreign exchange. Indigenous development has resulted in evolution of infrastructure and expertise in the field of software engineering that is a unique capability with tremendous potential. After building of essential infrastructures, 118 SED is now embarking on a programme for acquiring ISO-9001 approval. Future plans include customizing existing systems, and developing new systems for the export market.

No. 120 Air Logistics Depot

No. 120 Air Logistics Depot (ALD) was established in 1984 at PAF Base Sargodha to provide logistics support to F-16 aircraft and related ground equipment. This depot has the distinction to be the first on-line logistics system in the PAF, based on an elaborate software completely interactive with the base-level supply operations on one end and the United States Air Force Logistics Command Supply Agencies on the other. The creation of this depot resulted later in the adoption of F-16 Logistics System by all other weapon systems of the PAF. The depot was established and organized on the pattern of the United States Air Force. The role and task of the depot includes requisition, collection, transportation, storage, and issue etc. of the items and equipment required for F-16 operations.

No. 130 Air Engineering Depot

Since the induction of the C-130 aircraft in the PAF, Inspection Required As Necessary (IRAN) was being carried out on these aircraft on the guidelines given by the manufacturers. In 1979, USAF changed over from IRAN to a highly comprehensive inspection of a forty-eight-month cycle known as Programme Depot Maintenance

(PDM). This programme not only included the requirement of earlier IRAN inspection but also mandated extensive Non-Destructive Inspection (NDI) of critical structural areas. In the beginning, the PAF could not establish a facility that could carry out these inspections, primarily owing to non-availability of skilled manpower, hangar space, NDI equipment, and shortage of spares.

As an alternative, the PAF started sending C-130 aircraft abroad for the PDM. Four aircraft were sent to Peru in 1989, 1990, and 1991. The PAF spent an average of US$ 537,500 per aircraft for the PDM of these four aircraft. The contracted production schedule was sixteen weeks per aircraft, whereas actual time taken varied from forty-one to fifty-two weeks. The PAF also sent three aircraft to Singapore for PDM in 1991-92 and 1994. The average cost on these PDM inspections in Singapore was US$ 750,253. The expenditure incurred on the last aircraft that was sent to Singapore for PDM was US$ 855,138. Keeping in view the exorbitant cost of PDM in foreign exchange and substantial delays in delivery of these aircraft, the PAF decided to establish a PDM facility in Pakistan. Thus, a wide hangar with all the requisite facilities was built at PAF Base Chaklala, and 130 Air Engineering Depot was set up with the following role and task:

a. To undertake PDM and other major structural repairs on two aircraft simultaneously.

b. To undertake all major modifications and TCTOs on C-130 aircraft.

No. 130 AED undertook in-country PDM of the first aircraft on 20 March 1993, and completed the inspection on 12 February 1994. A total of US$ 280,752 (excluding labour charges) were spent on the in-country PDM of this aircraft, thus saving foreign exchange amounting to US$ 480,391 as compared to the last PDM abroad. From late 1996 till early 1998, 130 AED remained suspended because the Canadian Aerospace Engineering-Shaheen joint venture had undertaken PDM of PAF C-130 aircraft at Chaklala. However, the project could not go ahead and 130 AED was reactivated in mid-1998. So far the depot has produced ten aircraft after PDM inspection. Approximately 4,900 man-hours are required for PDM of one C-130 aircraft. The main man-power comes from the airframe and metal-worker trades.

Central Technical Development Unit

In 1990, the Directorate of Technical Development was renamed the Directorate of Engineering Development (DED). In addition, the role of CTDU was enhanced to add 'rendering of scientific and engineering advice and assistance to flying and maintenance units on unusual and intricate technical problems'.

The unit also upgraded its design and development facility by computerizing the system through local area network. Presently, all engineering drawings are developed on computers, which not only saves man-hours, but also results in accuracy and precision. Designing of prototypes and their subsequent simulation through computers is also being implemented. Some of the significant achievements of this unit during 1988-98 are conversion of one Mirage-III EP to RP for reconnaissance, modification of F-6 and F-7P aircraft for carrying target tow banner, and development of lift computer (stall and recovery device) and fuselage jig for T-37 aircraft. Besides the indigenous development of a number of items for PASBAN vehicles used for the Crotale missile system, it also developed eighty-seven items for A-5, 109 items for F-7P, and forty-five items for the Mirage aircraft's Radar Warning Receiver, Chaff and Flare Dispenser and Radio transmitter/receiver modifications.

SUMMARY OF AIR VIOLATIONS BY AFGHANISTAN/RUSSIAN AIRCRAFT
FROM 01 JANUARY 1980 TO 15 FEBRUARY 1989

AREA	VIOLATIONS	AIRCRAFT INVOLVED	CASUALTIES INJURED	DEAD DUE TO ARMED ATTACK
Chaman	385	1,108	10	7
Chitral	355	1,231	60	22
Dir	17	41	06	08
Khyber	148	464	05	0
Kurram	795	2,125	448	225
Mohmand	185	669	32	11
North Waziristan	504	1,722	219	72
Qamaruddin Karez	35	71	0	0
South Waziristan	27	67	96	65
Wakhan	1	2	0	0
Zahidan	3	12	0	08
Zhob	2	4	0	0
Samungli	1	1	0	0
Not Available	15	53	0	0
Not Known	3	19	1	0
TOTAL	2,476	7,589	877	418

AFGHAN AND RUSSIAN AIRCRAFT THAT DEFECTED TO OR
LANDED IN PAKISTAN

S NO	TYPE	DATE	PILOT	REMARKS
AFGHAN AIRCRAFT				
1.	MI-8	26-04-81	Capt. Jamal	Landed at Samungli
2.	SU-7	20-11-83	Capt. M. Nabi	Landed at Dalbandin
3.	AN-26	22-11-84	Col. Haji Fakir	Landed at Miranshah
4.	MI-24	13-07-85	Capt. Hussain	Landed at Miranshah
5.	MI-24	16-07-85	Capt. Daud	Landed at Miranshah
6.	MI-24	23-10-86	Maj. Abdul Munir	Landed at Kohat
7.	MiG-21b	08-08-88	Capt. Waseh	Landed at Parachinar Strip
8.	MiG-21	08-12-88	Capt. Asadullah	Landed at Miranshah
9.	MI-24s	03-07-89	Capt. Sakhiullah	Landed at Qila Abdullah
10.	SU-22-M4	06-07-89	Capt. Jan Muhaddad	Landed at Peshawar
11.	MiG-21	29-09-89	Maj. Jalaluddin	Landed at Peshawar
12.	AN-12	07-03-90	Lt. Col. Ghulabdin	Landed at Peshawar
13.	MI-17	07-03-90	Pilot's Name Not known	Landed at Peshawar
SOVIET AIRCRAFT				
14.	MI-24	03-10-87	Capt. Nikolai Petrovich+2	Landed in Mastuj
15.	MI-24	03-10-87	Major Yevginin Koszminin+2	Landed in Mastuj

LIST OF THE PAF's CLAIMS AND AWARDS ON WESTERN BORDER

PILOT	SQN	A/C TYPE	RADAR CONTROLLER	CLAIM & DATE	AWARD	AREA
Sqn. Ldr. Hameed Qadri Pak/6113	9 Sqn	F-16	Flg Off Arshad Pak/8493	2 x SU-22 17.5.86	1 x SU-22 by missile 1 x SU-22 by gun	Parachinar
Wg. Cdr. Abdul Razzaq Pak/5837	9 Sqn	F-16	Sqn. Ldr. Pervaiz Pak/6625	1 x AN-26 30.3.87	1 x AN-26 by missile	Miranshah
Flt. Lt. Badar-ul-Islam Pak/7365	14 Sqn	F-16	Sqn. Ldr. Saif-ur-Rahman Pak/5319	1 x SU-22 16.4.87	1 x SU-22 by missile	Near Thal
Sqn. Ldr Athar Bokhari Pak/7238	14 Sqn	F-16	Sqn. Ldr. Taufeeq Raja Pak/5660	1 x SU-25 4.8.88	1 x SU-25 by missile	Miranshah (Boya)
Flt. Lt. Khalid Mehmood Pak/7952	14 Sqn	F-16	Sqn. Ldr. Irfan-ul-Haq Pak/6795	2 x Mig-23 12.9.88	2 x Mig-23 by missile	South Chitral (Nawagi)
Flt. Lt. Khalid Mehmood Pak/7952	14 Sqn	F-16	Sqn. Ldr. Saif-ur-Rahman Pak/6922	1 x SU-22 3.11.88	1 x SU-22 by missile	West of Thal

10 PRESERVING THE PROUD HERITAGE – THE PAF MUSEUM

The need to preserve the glorious heritage of the Pakistan Air Force had been felt for a long time, and found fulfillment in 1961 at Risalpur. In 1962, the basic material was shifted to Peshawar to be placed under the direct supervision and patronage of Air Headquarters. Years later, in 1986, a further addition to the history of PAF aviation was made by Air Chief Marshal Jamal A. Khan, when he established a Fighter Gallery at PAF Base Sargodha, which housed custom-made models of the top 100 fighter aircraft of the world, and former PAF aircraft. While both the old museum and the Fighter Gallery were impressive institutions, they could not take the form of a full-fledged museum. Too many aircraft and historically important exhibits remained outside the ambit of both these institutions. Equipment such as radar, vehicles and other pieces of hardware that had been prized assets of the Pakistan Air Force, lay neglected in varying stages of decay across the country.

In 1986, the then Base Commander of PAF Base Faisal, Air Commodore M. Abbas Khattak, conceived the idea of integrating the historical background of the PAF with all available exhibits. This was intended for educational purposes and for the benefit of posterity. PAF Base Faisal appeared most suitable for the project because of the availability of space, support of maintenance and logistic depots, and the large population of Karachi. Air Commodore Khattak continued to pursue this goal during his various appointments as AOC, SAC and DCAS (Trg). His elevation to the position of the Chief of Air Staff, in 1994, finally provided him with the opportunity to bring his vision to fruition. Air Chief Marshal

Khattak pursued the project with determination and vigour, and a series of presentations were held at the Air Board level at Air Headquarters to work out the modalities of establishing the Museum at PAF Base Faisal.

The Chief of Air Staff directed that the PAF Museum be completed by 14 August 1997, to mark Pakistan's Golden Jubilee year. This required meticulous planning and hard work. In order to remain within the modest financial budget, and simultaneously ensure quality work, it was decided to develop the museum in three phases:

a. Basic display of aircraft and various exhibits in the park or around the Museum hangar.
b. Construction of the main building.
c. Establishment of a theme park for the general entertainment of the public.

To complete all the foregoing phases, it was calculated that the project would cost approximately Rs. 250 million. The Chief of Air Staff, with the help of the Air Board, finalized a scaled down version of the entire project and reduced the overall cost of the project to approximately 10 per cent of the original estimate. The CAS allocated only Rs. 25 million after the first major phase of the project was completed, and directed that all local resources of the Southern Air Command be utilized to complete this task. After considering the financial and time constraints, PAF Base Faisal accepted this challenge, and a dedicated group of officers, men, and civilians prepared a master plan which catered for the future development of different phases. This master plan was made on the proposed site approved by the Chief of the Air Staff. The Air Officer Commanding, Southern Air Command was designated as the Chairman of the Museum Committee and the prime responsibility at the field level was allocated to the Base Commander PAF Base Faisal. Fortunately, the PAF has a tremendous resource in the form of its competent and highly motivated manpower, and PAF Faisal had its proportionate share of this enviable asset. Each and every individual of the Base contributed his best effort towards the completion of the project.

Once it was decided that the PAF Museum would be housed at PAF Faisal, the selection of an appropriate site was another important decision to be made. Different areas of the Base were considered and studied against the main criteria established for the Museum. The present site met most of the criteria. This entire area had traditionally been the backyard of the Base and very little construction or development work had taken place here, largely because it was remote and lacked infrastructure. The area is situated in the southwest corner of the Base where an old abandoned hangar, built in 1917, is located. The only buildings nearby were of pre-Independence vintage, at which time it formed the large dispersal area of an active airfield. The chosen hangar and area around it were in a state of disrepair and needed to be made presentable. A huge clean-up operation was launched: the area was levelled, pot holes filled, wild shrubs cleared and the environment made habitable. The contribution of the personnel of the Defence Service Group (the MODC, as they were known previously), must be acknowledged gratefully.

Having cleared the ground, it was necessary to plant afresh, develop lawns, prepare flowerbeds and landscape the area.

A view of the PAF Museum

ACM Muhammad Abbas Khattak inaugurating the PAF Museum at the PAF Base Faisal on 14 August 1997

For this, water was necessary and it was at this stage that the Base ventured into the mystic and paranormal. Water diviners were found and they walked with forked branches in search of water. The branches dipped earthwards; eager crews dug feverishly, but unfortunately nothing transpired. The diviners were eventually dispensed with and more practical and reliable methods adopted. Pipes were laid and water carried over 2.5 km to bring this precious commodity to the location. The involvement of people in this project was not limited to uniformed personnel; many civilian well-wishers willingly devoted their time and effort. Wherever possible, families of PAF personnel also made a significant contribution. Above all, the Committee regularly deliberated upon each and every detail of the Museum with professional precision.

In another important area of activity, teams were set up to locate aircraft all over the country, and identify the nature of work needed on each frame to enable it to make the journey to Faisal. The transportation of all these aircraft to Faisal through different means, depending upon size, physical condition, and mode of conveyance, was achieved by the careful planning of team members. The extent of meticulous planning required for the transportation of thirty-three aircraft finally selected for the Museum can be gauged from the example of the transportation of the Quaid's aircraft. The Vickers Viking was parked in a corner of a hangar at PAF Peshawar. In its prime, it had been the personal aircraft of Quaid-i-Azam Mohammad Ali Jinnah, the founder of Pakistan. This aircraft qualified as one of the prime exhibits of our heritage. To move it over 1,000 miles was a monumental

ACM Muhammad Abbas Khattak unveiling the plaque of the PAF Museum on 14 August 1997

task. The risk of not being able to reconstruct this priceless asset also hung heavily on the minds of those involved, as they started to dismantle this huge aircraft. Each panel, each nut, each bolt and each and every item was photographed, tagged and made fit for surface transportation. The entire aircraft was dismantled and moved by specially modified flatbed trailers through the tortuous road network of Pakistan, from the very north of the country to its southern most point. The aircraft was put together on the main tarmac of the Base and reconstructed. Incidentally, the final move from the tarmac to the Museum hangar was as problematic as the long haul from Peshawar: walls, electric poles, guard rooms etc. had to be negotiated, and the aircraft had to be towed over some very rough surfaces before finally arriving at its resting place.

While dedicated personnel moved aircraft and models to Faisal, the Logistics Branch was busy digging into their records and their cavernous hangars at various depots to identify and select items for display. Every now and then someone would heave a sigh of sorrow, especially as he realized how careless we had been with our heritage. Nonetheless, artefacts were traced, identified, recovered and in most cases, rehabilitated to make them fit for display purposes. The Logistics Branch also conducted research and provided finished items for the section of the museum which records and displays the uniforms the PAF donned over its fifty-year history.

It has always been the PAF's hallmark to keep in step with emerging technologies and trends. The Multimedia Kiosk at the PAF Museum is yet another manifestation of this tradition. The PAF kiosk harnesses the power of the multimedia computer to preserve and present the PAF's glorious history in a captivating manner. The interactive presentation allows the viewer to navigate through the presentation at will and explore audio and video text images, on the subject of his choice. The flexibility and ease of use make the Multimedia Kiosk an ideal platform for presenting information.

The software for the Kiosk was developed by a team of PAF professionals, who surfed through all available information sources on the subject. They selected the very best for the presentation. The team, comprising five officers, a fighter pilot and four aeronautical engineers, completed the presentation in a limited time of eight weeks. It is worth mentioning that this was their very first venture into the area of multimedia presentation.

The information is presented under six broad categories, each having further sub-components. The subjects dealt within the presentation include information on all PAF weapon systems, aircraft and air defence weapons, significant operations of the 1965 and 1971 wars, operational exercises, and other events of significance in the PAF's history. The presentation also covers the organization of the PAF with reference to its branches and trades, the history of the PAF Museum and PAF's contribution in the area of sports. A separate category pays tribute to our heroes, the 'Shuhada', and award winners of the 1965 and 1971 wars.

While all those involved with the project worked ceaselessly, and struggled with problems of logistics and deadlines, the Air Officer Commanding, Southern Air Command and Base Commander, PAF Base Faisal, had to deal with the scarcity of funds. The funding position of the Museum was indeed critical. The dilemma was that while there had to be a very frugal approach to the development, the Museum simply could not be allowed to become 'cheap',

either in appearance or in character. This was the laying of the foundation for something permanent and enduring; this was to become the window to the history of the PAF, and it was here that future generations would seek, and indeed find, the motivation to become part of the PAF. It was hoped that in this environment, both young and old would be taken on an emotional journey into the past. Veterans could walk up to the machines and equipment they had operated; in and around which they had grown from raw teenagers to seasoned professionals.

Lawns and flower beds appeared, systematic pathways were made, tastefully designed fountains were installed, lights blazed where it had once been considered imprudent to venture after sunset. It must be admitted that in their hurry to accomplish the task, the team members were not permitted the luxury of detailed and meticulous planning. Hence, there were a few hiccups. Certain activities were repeated, much to the distress of those who were involved in this twenty-four-hour vigil. Often this meant the laborious re-doing of what had been undone. But the perseverance of the team members paid off, and in the end, the directive of the Chief of Air Staff was complied with successfully.

The well coordinated effort, continuous hardwork, sense of responsibility and solid determination of the PAF uniformed and civilian personnel bore fruit when, on 14 August 1997, the then Chief of the Air Staff, Air Chief Marshal M. Abbas Khattak, inaugurated the Museum in a colourful ceremony. It was eventually opened to the general public on 24 November 1997 by the then Governor Sindh, Lt. General (Retd.) Moinuddin Haider.

11 AT THE HELM

God give us men, a time like this demands,
Strong-minds, great hearts, true faith and
ready hands!
Men whom the lust of office does not kill,
Men whom the spoils of office cannot buy,
Men who possess opinions and a will,
Men who love honour, men who cannot lie.

J.G. Holland

The PAF, during the last decade, has had five Chiefs of Air Staff, the current one being Air Chief Marshal Parvaiz Mehdi Qureshi. Air Chief Marshal Jamal A. Khan handed over to his successor, Air Chief Marshal Hakimullah in March 1988. It is noteworthy that Air Chief Marshal Jamal was the first head of the PAF who was over fifty years old when he assumed command. It was an indication of the maturity that the Service had reached considering that its first Pakistani Chief, Air Marshal M. Asghar Khan, was barely thirty-six years of age when he took over the command of the then RPAF in 1957.

PAF commanders have always been the pick of the professionals. They have provided effective leadership, and have been able to maintain the reputation of the PAF as a small, but well trained and hard-hitting force. Leadership at the top calls for rare intellectual, moral, managerial, and professional qualities. The Service chief has to both meet challenges as they come and interact meaningfully with the other Services and government of the time.

The last decade has seen many ups and downs. The Chiefs of Air Staff had to successfully tackle issues related to the PAF's unconventional role in the Afghan war, the devastating effects of the Pressler Amendment, maintaining a force equilibrium through additions to the fleet from French and Chinese sources, upgrading and modernizing the fleet etc. These responsibilities were complicated by the political scene, which saw four interim and four regular governments. It goes to the credit of the PAF Chiefs that they were able to steer the Service through these difficult times and maintain its image as a thoroughly dedicated and professional service.

The Crusade against the Erosion of Ethics (6 March 1985–9 March 1988)

During a career spanning over thirty-five years, Air Chief Marshal Jamal A. Khan achieved numerous unique distinctions. He was the first Vice Chief of Air Staff in the history of the PAF to have eventually been appointed its Chief . He is also the only PAF officer to have commanded two Air Forces—those of the UAE and Pakistan. A distinguished fighter pilot, he was the first Pakistani to fly the F-16 aircraft.

Born in 1934 and commissioned in 1953, he was selected to join the first PAF jet squadron of Supermarine Attackers. He later served in different fighter squadrons for six years before becoming instructor-cum-member of the prestigious newly formed Fighter Leaders' School. Subsequently, he commanded an F-104 fighter squadron from 1962 to 1965. He also commanded a fighter wing for two years. During the 1965 war, he flew thirty operational missions and was awarded the Sitara-e-Jurat for his courage and aggressive leadership in the air. During the 1971 war, he held a senior staff appointment at the Command Operations Centre (COC).

His various command and staff appointments include Director of Flight

Air Chief Marshal Jamal A. Khan, the eleventh Chief of the PAF

Safety and Director of Plans at Air Headquarters before he was appointed Base Commander, PAF Sargodha, in 1973. Two years later, he returned to Air Headquarters to become the Chief Inspector and later the Assistant Chief of the Air Staff (Plans). Seconded to the UAE in 1977, he commanded the UAE Air Force for three years. On completion of his assignment, he was appointed Assistant Chief of Air Staff (Operations) for a short period before taking charge as Deputy Chief of Air Staff (Operations). He took over as Vice Chief of Air Staff in April 1984 and as the CAS on 6 March 1985.

Air Chief Marshal Jamal A. Khan was closely associated with the first volume of 'The Story of the Pakistan Air Force'. He contributed one chapter to the book and his efforts culminated in the publication of the volume in 1988, under the supervision of Air Commodore M. Zafar Masud.

After taking over as the CAS, he gave first priority to what he felt was the erosion of ethics amongst PAF personnel. By setting a personal example, he endeavoured to portray the PAF as the highly professional and serious-minded service that it truly was. He issued Command Doctrine AFM-1, which outlined his ideas as a Commander, of the duties and responsibilities of all ranks of the PAF. He went around various bases and addressed Airmen, JCOs and Officers separately. He tried to instill in them a sense of honesty, work ethics, loyalty, and the need to subordinate their personal interests to the Air Force. Another matter that disturbed him concerned the unethical role played by middle men and agents in the procurement of equipment in the defence forces in general, and the PAF in particular. He was engaged in a constant battle against influence peddling and kickbacks, especially from retired servicemen, and focused on eliminating the temptations which those in the decision-making chain were exposed to. He also focused his attention on another issue, which had become contentious: the Pakistan Air Force Women's Association (PAFWA). The Air Chief Marshal issued an Air Force Order (AFO) to reorganize the PAFWA, and ensured that it was implemented in letter and spirit.

Air Chief Marshal Jamal's tenure was also significant because some epoch-making events took place in the country during that period. The Afghan war was at its zenith and the PAF was tasked to stop Russian and Afghan intrusions into Pakistan's airspace, but under very restrictive Rules of Engagement (ROEs). The aggressive Indian Army exercise, Brass Tacks, was also held during this period and it had to be responded to. All this occurred while the country was transitioning from a long period of martial law to democracy. It stands to the credit of Air Chief Marshal Jamal that he handled all these issues with great dexterity, and was able to project the PAF's vital position in the country's security, at all the inter-Services and national forums.

ACM Jamal was known for being meticulous in his work and he expected the same from those who worked with him—a task that proved too demanding for some. He was also known for his reserved and reticent nature. He abhorred self-projection and undue publicity, an uncommon quality among those who hold important positions. But Jamal was quite assertive and forthright when required, and ensured that the PAF point of view was clearly registered in all decision making forums. He enjoyed the confidence and respect of the highest echelons in both the armed forces and the government.

The Difficult Years
(9 March 1988–9 March 1991)

Born in 1935, Air Chief Marshal Hakimullah was commissioned in 1957 as a fighter pilot.

Air Chief Marshal Hakimullah, the twelfth Chief of the PAF

During a distinguished career of more than thirty-four years, he gained extensive command experience at various levels, and also held senior staff appointments at Air Headquarters. He is a graduate of the Air Command and Staff College, USA and the Royal College of Defence Studies, UK.

After serving as a squadron pilot and flight commander in different squadrons, he qualified as a fighter leader and commanded a number of fighter squadrons. He was appointed Project Officer for the induction of Mirage aircraft in 1966. Thereafter he commanded a Mirage squadron. He was awarded the Sitara-e-Jurat for his valour and leadership in the air during the 1971 war. Subsequently, he commanded a fighter wing. He also had the distinction of commanding the PAF's prestigious Combat Commanders School, and PAF Base Rafiqui—one of the major operational bases of the Pakistan Air Force.

His staff appointments at Air Headquarters included Director of Operations, Assistant Chief of Air Staff (Operations), Chief Project Director Falcon—the project related to the induction of F-16 aircraft—and Deputy Chief of the Air Staff (Operations). He was Deputy Chief of Air Staff (Admin.) prior to taking over command of the PAF.

He played a major role in the smooth induction of the Mirage and the F-16 aircraft in the PAF. As head of Project Falcon, he overcame several obstacles to ensure that the F-16s, in the required configuration, were made available to the PAF in the shortest possible time. The timely induction of these aircraft proved to be particularly useful when the Afghan air violations increased, and reached their crescendo during the earlier part of his tenure as CAS. He was also responsible for placing orders for an additional sixty F-16s, which could not be delivered because of the Pressler Amendment.

The credit of inducting ex-Australian Mirages goes to Air Chief Marshal Hakimullah. This was a contract that was more beneficial to the PAF than had been expected. The PAF was not only able to recover forty-five Mirages for its fleet, but also recovered spares, jigs and fixtures which were to prove handy in the difficult times ahead. He was also responsible for the acquisition of the Mistrals. Although this procurement elicited some concern at the time, the vision and farsightedness of his decision was vindicated later. One of the most important milestones of his tenure as the CAS was the decision to amalgamate the Engineering Branches of the PAF. The Air Chief formed a high-powered team to study the problem. The team, after studying the system used by the leading air forces of the world, finally presented their recommendations. The decision to amalgamate the engineering branches was made after thorough deliberation at the Air Board level, and consultation with the subordinate commanders. In the short term there were some problems, yet in the long term the PAF gained substantially, even though the recommendations had to be implemented with some modifications due to certain practical difficulties. Under ACM Hakimullah's command, the PAF conducted Exercise High Mark-89, including a large-scale army exercise entitled Zarb-e-Momin, and a very large-scale Fire Power Demonstration in 1989.

During his tenure as CAS, schools for Grades 1 and 2 employees were established at Sargodha, Karachi and Chaklala. The services of the teachers at the PAF Schools/ Colleges were made pensionable. PAFWA's role was carefully defined and its efforts were directed to the areas where these could best be productive.

Hakim had an eventful career. He always held the best professional appointments that the service could offer, and gave a good

Air Chief Marshal Farooq F. Khan, the thirteenth Chief of the PAF

account of himself. Intelligent, aggressive, and articulate, he projected the Air Force point of view effectively. He is also a family man, and his hobbies include fishing and playing Bridge.

The Period of Stabilization
(9 March 1991–8 November 1994)

Born on 17 August 1939, Air Chief Marshal Farooq Feroze Khan joined the PAF after completing his Senior Cambridge from PAF Public School, Sargodha. He was selected for training in the USA and on return, was commissioned in January 1959. He has had a distinguished Air Force career, spread over nearly forty years—the only PAF officer perhaps to serve that long. He was a fighter pilot of distinction, and had flown almost all the fighter airplanes in the PAF inventory, in addition to Hunters, which he flew while on attachment to the RAF. A graduate of the Fighter Leaders' School, PAF, he has been a Flight Commander of the F-86 and Mirage squadrons, Chief Instructor in an Operational Conversion Unit, Squadron Commander of a Mirage squadron, and Officer Commanding of an Air Superiority Wing. He also commanded two important fighter bases: Sargodha and Masroor. Air Chief Marshal Farooq also had the distinction of commanding a Fighter Wing in the UAE Air Force for three years.

Some of his staff appointments included Personal Staff Officer to the Chief of Air Staff, Assistant Commandant of Air War College, Senior Air Staff Officer at the Southern Air Command, Assistant Chief of Air Staff (Plans.), Deputy Chief of Air Staff (Operations), and Vice Chief of the Air Staff. He was on secondment to the PIAC as Chairman/MD before assuming the command of the PAF in 1991. He was decorated with Nishan-e-Imtiaz (Military), Hilal-i-Imtiaz (Military), Sitara-e-Imtiaz (Military), and Sitara-e-Basalat for his meritorious services to the PAF.

He was the CAS, PAF for three years and eight months, and then became the first PAF officer to be appointed as Chairman, Joint Chiefs of Staff Committee. This was an appointment that he held for three years until his retirement in November 1997.

Farooq, a family man who took a keen interest in welfare activities, was also a versatile sportsman. He concentrated on golf in the later years of his career.

Air Chief Marshal Farooq assumed command of the PAF at a difficult time in its history. The Pressler Amendment had just been enforced and all the plans made for restructuring the Force had to be changed. He undertook a review and oversaw the induction of the Australian Mirages, their upgrade, and the induction of the F-7s. He also launched a search for a hi-tech weapon system in lieu of the F-16s that had been denied. He ensured a smooth amalgamation of the engineering branches, reorganized the Personnel Branch, and injected new life into the Inspectorate system by creating the post of an Inspector General with wide ranging powers. He believed in a policy of delegation of authority to subordinate commanders and staff, to inculcate a sense of responsibility amongst them, a measure which was not appreciated by some. Farooq's experience, (having held almost all the important assignments during his career), his quick-wittedness, and tactfulness helped him to hold his own in meetings at the inter-Services and Government levels.

New Challenges
(8 November 1994–7 November 1997)

Air Chief Marshal Muhammad Abbas Khattak was born on 16 July 1943 at Peshawar. After his initial education at Cadet College Hasanabdal, he joined the PAF and

Air Chief Marshal M. Abbas Khattak, the fourteenth Chief of the PAF was commissioned on 20 January 1963. In a career spanning more than thirty-four years, Air Chief Marshal Khattak has had a challenging tenure. A fighter pilot of distinction, he held choice appointments as Squadron Commander, Officer Commanding a Fighter Wing, and command of a fighter base. He has the distinction of having attended the Air Command and Staff College, USA, the Armed Forces War Course at the National Defence College, and the Royal College of Defence Studies, UK.

The important appointments held by him include Officer Commanding 33 Air Superiority Wing, Director of Flight Safety, Officer Commanding Combat Commanders' School, Base Commander, PAF Base Masroor, Base Commander, PAF Base Faisal, Assistant Chief of the Air Staff (Plans), Air Officer Commanding, Southern Air Command, and Deputy Chief of Air Staff (Training). He was serving as DCAS (O) when appointed as the Chief of Air Staff, in November 1994.

Air Chief Marshal Khattak participated in both the 1965 and 1971 India-Pakistan wars. He also spent over two years on deputation with the Syrian Air Force. He is a recipient of the Nishan-e-Imtiaz (Military), Hilal-e-Imtiaz (Military) and Sitara-e-Basalat. He is married and has two sons.

Air Chief Marshal Khattak was the Chief of the Air Staff, PAF during a period that can best be described as traumatic. Pakistan's economy had continued its downslide. The adverse effects of the Pressler Amendment had become accentuated. The decline in public morality was adversely affecting the morale and motivation of PAF personnel. There was increased political interference in Service affairs. There were as many as three changes of government during his tenure, which compounded his problems as head of the Service.

Air Chief Marshal Khattak relied heavily on the collective wisdom of his deputies at the Air Board when tackling important issues. He was known for keeping his fingers on the pulse of all ranks of Service. From 1991-93, as DCAS (T), he had played a pivotal role in introducing a new in-Service education scheme for the officers in the PAF. As a result, the Basic Staff School and the Senior Command and Staff School were established. The Air Chief also took a strategic decision by reviving the PAF Public School, Lower Topa to ensure quality admissions in the Academy. Preserving the PAF heritage was an obsession with him. This is how the idea of setting up the PAF Museum was conceived, and he took a keen personal interest in the project until it was completed in 1997, during his tenure as CAS.

He strived hard to provide a hi-tech component to the PAF fleet, and set up two elaborate projects—one for the induction of the Mirage 2000-V, and the other for the Super-7, a joint collaboration project between Pakistan and China. His efforts to acquire the Mirage 2000-V almost succeeded. The then government had agreed to fund the programme, but unfortunately this project became the victim of a vicious media campaign, and within a few months, due to the change in government, the project went into limbo. Another landmark decision during his tenure was the contract for the purchase of forty ex-French Mirages, which survived despite some skepticism in the press and influential lobbies. This was a unique contract that brought night attack capability to the PAF.

Eloquent, forceful and somewhat flamboyant, ACM Khattak was a thorough professional who excelled in various assignments, as he climbed the Air Force hierarchy, reaching its pinnacle as the Chief of the Air Staff.

Air Chief Marshal Farooq Feroze Khan, Chairman Joint Chiefs of Staff Committee called on Air Chief Marshal Muhammad Abbas Khattak, Chief of the Air Staff, on a farewell visit to AHQ Chaklala on 6 November 1997

President Muhammad Rafiq Tarar awarding the Nishan-e-Imtiaz (Military) to Air Chief Marshal Parvaiz Mehdi Qureshi, Chief of the Air Staff, at an Investiture Ceremony held at Aiwan-e-Sadar, Islamabad on 10 January 1998

The former Air Chiefs on the occasion of the Golden Jubilee of the Quaid's visit to the PAF Academy

Air Chief Marshal Muhammad Abbas Khattak, the outgoing Chief of the Air Staff invests the badges of rank of Air Chief Marshal on Air Marshal Parvaiz Mehdi Qureshi, the new Chief of the Pakistan Air Force at the Relinquishment and Assumption of Command Ceremony, held at AHQ Chaklala on 7 November 1997

The Right Hand Men

Air Marshal Shabbir Hussain Syed, Vice Chief of Air Staff (December 1985-March 1988) giving away the Chief of the Air Staff Trophy for best overall performance to Flying Officer Akmal Abbas Khan at the graduation ceremony held at the Transport Conversion School, Chaklala on 25 January 1987

Air Marshal Farooq Feroze Khan, Vice Chief of Air Staff (August 1988-December 1989) awarding the Sarfraz Rafiqui Leadership Trophy to Warrant Officer Iftikhar Ahmed at JCO's Academy, Korangi Creek on 18 December 1988

Air Marshal Syed Masood Hatif, Vice Chief of Air Staff (February 1990-July 1993) presenting the office crest to General Fikret Kupely, Deputy Chief of Turkish General Staff on 24 February 1992

Air Marshal Shafique Haider, Vice Chief of Air Staff (July 1993-November 1994) with Robert G. Joseph of US National War College, at Air Headquarters, Chaklala on 9 May 1994

Air Marshal Muhammad Arshad Chaudhry, Vice Chief of Air Staff (December 1994-January 1997) with Mr. Larry Prokop, President CAE Aviation Ltd. Canada, at Air Headquarters, Chaklala on 26 May 1996

Air Marshal Parvaiz Mehdi Qureshi, Vice Chief of Air Staff (May 1997-November 1997) presenting the office crest to Lt. Col. Hamad Abdullah Al Khalifa of Bahrain Armed Forces at Air Headquarters, Chaklala on 10 May 1997

Air Marshal Aliuddin, Vice Chief of Air Staff (December 1997-November 1999) with Major General Turki Bin Nasser, Deputy Commander, Royal Saudi Air Force at Air Headquarters, Chaklala on 16 October 1998

APPENDIX 1

Key Appointments—High Command

Operations

Deputy Chief of Air Staff (Operations)

AVM	Farooq Feroze Khan	Dec 86
AVM	Dilawar Hussain	Aug 88
AVM	Bahar-Ul-Haque	Aug 89
AVM	Shafique Haider	May 91
AM	M. Abbas Khattak	Jul 93
AM	S. Shahid Zulfiqar Ali	Nov 94
AM	Parvaiz Mehdi Qureshi	Nov 96
AM	Aliuddin	Jun 97
AM	Zahid Anis	Jan 98

ACAS (Operations)

Air Cdre	M. Amanullah	Dec 87
Air Cdre	Shafique Haider	Apr 89
Air Cdre	Parvaiz Mehdi Qureshi	Feb 90
Air Cdre	M. Saleem-Ud-Din	Jul 90
Air Cdre	Zahid Anis	Jun 91
Air Cdre	Najib Akhtar	Apr 92
Air Cdre	Qazi Javed Ahmed	Nov 93
Air Cdre	Pervez Iqbal Mirza	Jan 95
Air Cdre	Riffat Munir	Jan 96
Air Cdre	Sarfraz Arshad Toor	Jul 97
Air Cdre	Riffat Munir	Nov 97
AVM	Muhammad Abid	Jun 98

ACAS (Air Defence)

Air Cdre	Farooq Haider Khan	Jan 88
Air Cdre	Ijaz Ahmad Khan	Feb 90
Air Cdre	Jahangir Akhtar	Apr 92
Air Cdre	S. M. Ershad Ahsan	Jul 93
Air Cdre	Mansoob Ahmad	Jul 95
Air Cdre	Ishtiaque Hussain	Jan 97

Engineering

Deputy Chief of Air Staff (Engg)

AVM	Sardar Khan	Jul 87
AVM	M. Yusaf Khan	Jan 91
AVM	Mozammil Saeed	Jan 91
AVM	Muhammad Afzal	Sep 93
AVM	Niaz Hussain	Dec 96

ACAS (Log)

Air Cdre	Tahir Ahmad	Feb 88
Air Cdre	Syed Aley Raza	Sep 90
Air Cdre	Abdul Ghafoor Tahir	May 93
Air Cdre	Muhammad Tufail	Mar 96
Air Cdre	M. Sabir Piracha	Jun 97

ACAS (Aircraft Engg)

Air Cdre	Ijaz Rasul	Nov 87
Air Cdre	Mozammil Saeed	May 90
Air Cdre	Ikramullah	Feb 91
Air Cdre	Nihal-e-Abid	Mar 91
Air Cdre	Muhammad Afzal	Aug 91
Air Cdre	Nihal-e-Abid	Sep 93
Air Cdre	Niaz Hussain	Feb 96
Air Cdre	Javed Zafar Pasha	Jan 97

ACAS (Air Defence Weapon System)

Air Cdre	M. Yusaf Khan	Mar 90
Gp Capt	S. Akhtar Reza	Jan 91

ACAS (Radar Engg)

Gp Capt	S. Akhtar Reza	Apr 91

AVM	Muhammad Ikramullah	Jul 92		AVM	Javed Hayat Malik	May 91
Gp Capt	Saeed Nawaz Khan	Mar 95		AVM	Mushtaq A Laghari	Mar 93
Air Cdre	Azfar Ali Khan	Jul 95		AVM	M Farooq Qari	Jan 95
Air Cdre	Maqbool Nisar Ali Beg	Aug 96		AM	Aliuddin	Nov 96
Air Cdre	Azhar Maud	Jul 97		AVM	A. Rahim Yousefzai	Jun 97
				AM	Riazuddin Shaikh	Nov 97

ACAS (Elect)

Air Cdre	Syed Hashim Jafri	Mar 87
Air Cdre	M. Hussain Khattak	Aug 89
Air Cdre	Muhammad Ikramullah	Jan 91
Air Cdre	M. Rasheed Pervez	Apr 93
Gp Capt	Saleem Rehman	Sep 93
Air Cdre	Azhar Hussain	Dec 93
Air Cdre	Saleem Rahman	Apr 96

ACAS (Weapons)

Gp Capt	M. Anwar Khokhar	Jul 87
Air Cdre	M. Afzal Choudhry	Aug 90
Gp Capt	M. Anwar Khokhar	Sep 91
Air Cdre	M. Anwar Khokhar	Jul 93
Air Cdre	Anwar Saeed	Jul 97
Air Cdre	S. Sohail Habib Sadiq	Dec 98

ACAS (Support)

Air Cdre	M. Afzal Choudhry	Jul 90
Air Cdre	Tariq Hamid	Aug 90
Gp Capt	Omar Mazhar	May 92
Air Cdre	Mahmood S. Bajwa	Aug 92
Air Cdre	Mukhtar Ahmad Khan	Dec 93
Air Cdre	M Khalid Hussain	Jun 97
Air Cdre	Khalid Javed Durrani	Sep 98

Administration

Deputy Chief of Air Staff (Admin)

AVM	Hakimullah	Dec 86
AVM	Sardar Muhammad Asif	Apr 88
AVM	Shafique Haider	Jan 90

ACAS (Admin)

Air Cdre	M. Ehtisham Akram	Jan 87
Air Cdre	Anwar Ali	Jul 88
Air Cdre	Aamer Ali Sharieff	Jun 90
Air Cdre	Mirza Ilyas Baig	Apr 91
Air Cdre	Aurangzeb Latif	Jul 94
Air Cdre	Syed Ata-ur-Rahman	Jan 96
Air Cdre	Nayyar Qayum Khawja	Jan 97
Air Cdre	Sabahat Ali	Dec 98

ACAS (Housing & Project)

Air Cdre	Azmat Ullah	Jul 98

ACAS (Works)

Air Cdre	M. Habib-ur-Rehman	Apr 87
Air Cdre	Taimoor M. Qureshi	Aug 89
Air Cdre	Daud Khan	Apr 91
Air Cdre	Shabbir Ahmad Khan	Jul 92
Air Cdre	Naseem Gul	Jul 94
Air Cdre	M. Arif Pervaiz	Jul 98

Training

Deputy Chief of Air Staff (Training)

AVM	Anwar Mahmood Khan	Jul 89
AVM	Dilwar Hussain	Jul 90
AVM	M. Abbas Khattak	Apr 91
AVM	Aliuddin	Jul 93
AVM	Aamer Ali Sharieff	Jan 95
AVM	M. Hamid Akhtar Malik	Feb 97

AVM	Pervez Akhtar Nawaz	Dec 97

ACAS (Training)

Air Cdre	Muhammad Saleem	Jun 83
Air Cdre	Abdul Rahim Yousefzai	Jun 88
Air Cdre	Khalid Iqbal	Mar 89
Air Cdre	Naseem Gul	Sep 91
Air Cdre	Tayyab Naeem Akhtar	Jul 93
Air Cdre	Azmat Kazi	Aug 95
Air Cdre	Zubair Alam	Jul 96
Air Cdre	Abdul Ghaffar	Jul 97

ACAS (Education)

Gp Capt	Muhammad Nasim	Oct 89
Gp Capt	Muhammad Razzaq	Aug 93
Air Cdre	Pervez Aslam Niazi	Oct 94
Air Cdre	Farooq Hussain Kiyani	Jan 97
Air Cdre	Khayyam Durrani	Jul 98

Personnel

Deputy Chief of Air Staff (Personnel)

AM	M. Arshad Chaudhry	Jun 94
AM	Aliuddin	Dec 94
AM	S. Shahid Zulfiqar Ali	Nov 96
AM	Qazi Javed Ahmed	Sep 98

ACAS (Personnel - Officers)

Air Cdre	Khalid Saeed Haroon	Jan 94
Air Cdre	Muhammad Bilal Khan	Jun 95
Air Cdre	Pervez Akhtar Khan	Nov 96
Air Cdre	M. Tariq Shahab	Jul 98

ACAS (Personnel Airmen/Civilians)

Air Cdre	Muhammad Sharif	Jun 94
Air Cdre	Sardar Allahyar Khan	Sep 94
Air Cdre	Zulfiqar Haider	Oct 96

OC Record Office

Air Cdre	Javaid Amjad Endrabi	Aug 86
Gp Capt	S. L. B. Bokhari	Jun 89
Air Cdre	Farooq Haider Khan	Feb 90
Air Cdre	M. Qamar Sultan Kiani	Jul 91
Air Cdre	Naeem A. Siddiqui	Jan 94
Air Cdre	Mirza Ilyas Baig	Jul 94
Air Cdre	Ishtiaq Ahmad Khan	Mar 95
Air Cdre	Jameel Kayani	Jun 96
Air Cdre	Mahmood Gul	Jul 97
Air Cdre	Zafar Ahmed	Mar 98

IG's Branch

Inspector General

AVM	Abbas Hussain Mirza	Apr 91
AVM	Najib Akhtar	Dec 93
AVM	Syed Imtiaz Hyder	Jan 95
AVM	Pervez Iqbal Mirza	Mar 97
AVM	Syed Qaiser Hussain	Dec 97

Deputy Inspector General

Air Cdre	Zulfiqar Ahmad Shah	Jul 91
Air Cdre	Aurangzeb Latif	Jun 92
Air Cdre	Riazuddin Shaikh	Jun 94
Air Cdre	Salim Arshad	Jul 97
Air Cdre	Javed Ishaq Khan	Dec 97

Flight Safety

ACAS (Flight Safety)

Air Cdre	Momin Arif	Apr 87
Air Cdre	Abbas Hussain Mirza	Jun 88
Air Cdre	S. Shahid Zulfiqar Ali	Oct 89
Air Cdre	Khalid Saeed Haroon	Jul 90
Air Cdre	Abdul Rahim Yousefzai	Apr 91
Air Cdre	Jamal Hussain	Jul 93
Air Cdre	Muhammad Farooq Qari	Aug 94

Air Cdre	Arshad Rashid Sethi	Jan 95
Air Cdre	Aurangzeb Khan	Aug 96
Air Cdre	Jamshed Afzal	Jul 97

Command Warrant Officers

C W O	Abdul Qayyum Durrani	Jan 87
C W O	Muhammad Riaz Abbasi	Jul 89
C W O	M. Zahoor Malik	Oct 92
C W O	Muhammad Akram	Nov 98

Air Commands

Air Officers Commanding (ADC)

AVM	Saeed Kamal Khan	Aug 85
AVM	Raja Aftab Iqbal	Jul 88
AVM	Dilawar Hussain	Aug 89
AVM	Anwar Mahmood Khan	Jul 90
AVM	Anwar-ul-Haq Malik	May 91
AM	Parvaiz Mehdi Qureshi	May 93
AM	Najib Akhtar	Nov 96

Air Officers Commanding (NAC)

AVM	Bahar-ul-Haq	Jun 87
AVM	Abbas Hussain Mirza	Aug 89
AVM	Aliuddin	Apr 91
AVM	Abdul Rahim Yousefzai	Jul 93
AVM	Mushtaq Ahmad Laghari	Jan 95
AVM	Riazuddin Shaikh	Mar 97
AVM	Pervez Iqbal Mirza	Dec 97

Air Officers Commanding (CAC)

AVM	Syed Masood Hatif	Jun 86
AVM	Anwar-ul-Haque Malik	Jun 89
AVM	M. Arshad Chaudhry	May 91
AVM	S. Shahid Zulfiqar Ali	May 93
AVM	Najib Akhtar	Dec 94
AM	Muhammad Farooq Qari	Nov 96

Air Officers Commanding (SAC)

AVM	Amjad Hussain Khan	May 86
AVM	Syed Masood Hatif	Jan 89
AVM	M. Abbas Khattak	Mar 90
AVM	Parvaiz Mehdi Qureshi	Jun 91
AVM	Saeed Anwar	Mar 93
AVM	Zahid Anis	Jan 95
AVM	Mushaf Ali Mir	Jun 97

Air Officers Commanding PAF Academy

AVM	Anwar Mehmood Khan	Aug 87
AVM	Raja Aftab Iqbal	Aug 89
AVM	Aamir Ali Sharieff	Mar 93
AVM	M. Hamid Akhtar Malik	Jan 95
AVM	Syed Imtiaz Hyder	Feb 97
AVM	Qazi Javed Ahmed	Jul 97
AVM	Syed Ata-ur-Rahman	Aug 98

Bases

Sargodha

Air Cdre	Parvaiz Mehdi Qureshi	Jun 88
Air Cdre	Najib Akhtar	Feb 90
Air Cdre	Zahid Anis	Apr 92
Air Cdre	Mushaf Ali Mir	Dec 93
Air Cdre	Hamid Abbas Khawaja	Dec 95
Air Cdre	Tanveer M. Ahmad	Dec 97

Masroor

Air Cdre	S. Shahid Zulfiqar Ali	Dec 87
Air Cdre	Saeed Anwar	Oct 89
Air Cdre	Aurangzeb Latif	Oct 90
Air Cdre	Zulfiqar Ali Shah	Jun 92
Air Cdre	Riffat Munir	Dec 93
Air Cdre	Kamran Qureshi	Jul 95
Air Cdre	M. Arif Pervaiz	May 96
Air Cdre	Abdul Razzaq	Jul 98

Rafiqui

Air Cdre	M. Arshad Chaudhry	Jul 87
Air Cdre	A. Sattar Alvi	Jul 89
Air Cdre	Mushtaq Ahmad Laghari	Nov 90
Air Cdre	Pervez Iqbal Mirza	Mar 93
Air Cdre	Syed Qaiser Hussain	Jan 95
Air Cdre	Iqbal Haider	Dec 96
Air Cdre	Raashid Kalim	Sep 98

Samungli

Air Cdre	Khalid Iqbal	Jun 87
Air Cdre	M. Hamid Akhtar Malik	Mar 89
Air Cdre	S. Shahid Zulfiqar Ali	Jul 91
Air Cdre	Riazuddin Shaikh	Jun 92
Air Cdre	Salim Arshad	Jun 94
Air Cdre	Arshad Rashid Sethi	Jul 96
Air Cdre	Shahid Nisar Khan	Jul 98

Minhas

Air Cdre	Shafique Haider	Jan 87
Air Cdre	Abdul Rahim Yousefzai	Apr 89
Air Cdre	Shahid Kamal Khan	Apr 91
Air Cdre	Qazi Javed Ahmed	Mar 92
Air Cdre	Syed Ata-ur-Rehman	Nov 93
Air Cdre	Javed Ishaq Khan	Jan 96
Air Cdre	Masood Akhtar	Dec 97

Peshawar

Air Cdre	Aamer Ali Sharieff	Dec 87
Air Cdre	Jamal Hussain	Jul 89
Air Cdre	Syed Imtiaz Hyder	May 91
Air Cdre	Muhammad Bilal Khan	Jan 93
Air Cdre	Pervez Akhtar Nawaz	Jul 94
Air Cdre	Azmat Kazi	Jun 96
Air Cdre	Kaleem Saadat	Jul 97

Mianwali

Air Cdre	Taimur M. Qureshi	Jun 87
Air Cdre	Mirza Ilyas Baig	Aug 89
Air Cdre	Aamir Ali Sharieff	Apr 91
Air Cdre	Muhammad Farooq Qari	Mar 93
Air Cdre	Sarfraz Arshad Toor	Aug 94
Air Cdre	Muhammad Abid Rao	Jul 96
Air Cdre	Shaukat Haider	May 98

Chaklala

Air Cdre	Javed Hayat Malik	Jul 86
Air Cdre	Mir Alam Khan	Apr 88
Air Cdre	Nafees Ahmad Najmi	Jul 89
Air Cdre	Fareed Ali Shah	Apr 91
Air Cdre	Zubair Alam	Jul 93
Air Cdre	Abdul Ghafoor	Aug 95
Air Cdre	Sabahat Ali	Dec 96
Air Cdre	Nayyar Qayum Khawja	Dec 98

Faisal

Air Cdre	M. Saleem-ud-Din	Dec 87
Air Cdre	Syed Imtiaz Hyder	Jul 89
Air Cdre	Muhammad Farooq Qari	May 91
Air Cdre	Naseem Gul	May 93
Air Cdre	Shabbir Ahmad Khan	Jul 94
Air Cdre	M. Tariq Shahab	Aug 96
Air Cdre	Muhammad Tauqeer	Aug 98

Malir

Air Cdre	Javaid Sultan Butt	Oct 87
Air Cdre	Nisar-Ud-Din Qureshi	Jul 89
Air Cdre	Abdul Waheed	Jan 91
Air Cdre	Muhammad Zafar Iqbal	Oct 92
Air Cdre	M. Yaqoob Khan	Aug 94
Air Cdre	Tausif Azmat	Sep 96

Lahore

Air Cdre	Altaf Sheikh	Jul 86
Air Cdre	Anwar-Ul-Haque Malik	Jun 88
Air Cdre	Javaid Amjad Endrabi	Jun 89
Air Cdre	Khalid Saeed Haroon	Jan 92
Air Cdre	Kamran Qureshi	Jan 94
Air Cdre	Mahmood Gul	Jul 95
Air Cdre	Hameedullah Khan	Jun 97

Korangi Creek

Air Cdre	M. Ilyas Majid	Jan 87
Air Cdre	Shaukat Ali Khan	Feb 90
Air Cdre	S. N. A. Rizvi	Aug 91
Air Cdre	M. Rasheed Pervez	Sep 93
Air Cdre	Anwar Saeed	May 96
Air Cdre	M. Abdul Qadir Sargana	Jul 97

Kohat

Air Cdre	Khalil-Ullah Khan Ghauri	Apr 88
Air Cdre	Khudadad Khan	May 89
Air Cdre	Iftikhar Akbar Naqvi	May 90
Air Cdre	Syed Tanveer Hussain	Aug 92
Air Cdre	Abdul Ghafoor	Jul 93
Air Cdre	Tayyab Naeem Akhtar	Aug 95
Air Cdre	Muhammad Ashraf Gill	Aug 96
Air Cdre	Mustansar Sohail Toor	Jul 98

Sakesar

Gp Capt	M. Akbar Shahzada	May 88
Gp Capt	Mahboobullah	Aug 89
Gp Capt	Saleem Rahman	Jul 90
Air Cdre	Ikram-ul-Haq	Apr 93
Gp Capt	Shabeer Ahmed Sheikh	Jun 95
Air Cdre	Athar Mahmood Qureshi	Aug 97
Gp Capt	Sadoon Pervaiz Memon	Jun 98

Lower Topa

Gp Capt	Niaz A. Nabi	Jul 87
Gp Capt	Zaheer H. Zaidi	Jan 89
Gp Capt	M. Anwar Khokhar	Aug 90
Gp Capt	Muhammad Rashid	Sep 91
Air Cdre	Mansoob Ahmad	Feb 94
Air Cdre	Rehmatullah Khan	Jul 95
Air Cdre	Shaukat Haider	Jul 97
Air Cdre	Mirza Zafar Hussain	May 98

Kalabagh

Gp Capt	Saeed Akhtar Malik	Jun 88
Gp Capt	Naunehal Shah	Dec 89
Gp Capt	Aijaz S. Bhatti	Aug 92
Air Cdre	Naunehal Shah	Oct 93
Gp Capt	Mirza Kamran Ali Khan	Jul 95
Gp Capt	Shahed Ghani	Jul 97

Flying Wings

No. 31 Wing

Gp Capt	Riffat Munir	Oct 87
Gp Capt	Nusrat Ullah Khan	Aug 89
Gp Capt	Javed Ishaq Khan	Jul 91
Gp Capt	Raashid Kalim	Jul 92
Gp Capt	Khalid Mahmood	Jul 93
Gp Capt	Shaukat Haider	Apr 94
Gp Capt	Rao Qamar Suleman	Jun 95
Gp Capt	Asif ur Rehman	Jul 96
Gp Capt	S. Rashid Hasan Bukhari	Jun 97
Gp Capt	Naeem Ashraf	Jul 98

No. 32 Wing

Gp Capt	Syed Imtiaz Hyder	Jun 87
Gp Capt	Syed Ata-ur-Rehman	Jul 89

Gp Capt	Kaleem Saadat	Feb 91
Gp Capt	Shaheen Mazhar	Jun 92
Gp Capt	Arshad Hussain Siraj	Oct 93
Gp Capt	M Ateeb Siddiqui	May 94
Gp Capt	Khalid Bashir Cheema	Jul 95
Gp Capt	Faisal Tariq	Jul 96
Gp Capt	S. Adeeb Niazi	Jul 97
Gp Capt	Inamullah Khan	Jul 98

No. 33 Wing

Gp Capt	Zulfiqar Ali Shah	Jun 88
Gp Capt	Mahmood Gul	Jul 89
Gp Capt	Tayyab Naeem Akhtar	Jun 91
Gp Capt	Muhammad Tariq Shahab	Jul 92
Gp Capt	Aurangzeb Khan	Jul 93
Gp Capt	Hifazatullah Khan	Jul 94
Gp Capt ·	Arif Moinuddin	Jun 95
Gp Capt	M. Ikram-ullah Bhatti	Jun 96
Gp Capt	Muhammad Safdar Khan	Jul 97
Gp Capt	Tariq Mahmud Ashraf	Aug 98

No. 34 Wing

Gp Capt	Pervez Iqbal Mirza	Jul 87
Gp Capt	Aurangzeb Latif	Jul 88
Gp Capt	Sarfraz Arshad Toor	Sep 89
Gp Capt	M. Abdul Qadir Sargana	Oct 90
Gp Capt	Kamran Qureshi	Sep 91
Gp Capt	Syed Qaiser Hussain	May 92
Gp Capt	Iqbal Haider	Jul 93
Gp Capt	Shahid Lateef	Jul 94
Gp Capt	Saleem Akhtar Nawaz	Jul 95
Gp Capt	M. Kaiser Tufail	Jun 96
Gp Capt	Shahid Shigri	Jun 97
Gp Capt	Shaheen Hamid Butt	Jul 98

No. 35 Wing

Gp Capt	Mian Maqsood Qadir	Aug 87
Gp Capt	Zubair Alam	Mar 89
Gp Capt	Zakir A. Khan	Jul 91

Gp Capt	Sabahat Ali	May 93
Gp Capt	Munawar Alam Siddiqui	Jun 94
Gp Capt	Nayyar Qayum Khawja	Jul 95
Gp Capt	Mustansar Sohail Toor	Jul 96
Gp Capt	M. Arshad Javed	Sep 97

No. 36 Wing

Gp Capt	Hamid Saeed Khan	Jun 87
Gp Capt	Naseem Gul	Mar 88
Gp Capt	Wali Mughni	Jul 89
Gp Capt	Muhammad Abid	Jul 90
Gp Capt	Hameedullah Khan	Mar 91
Gp Capt	Azmat Kazi	Jul 92
Gp Capt	Shahid Nisar Khan	Jul 93
Gp Capt	Abdus Sami Toor	Jul 94
Gp Capt	Masroor ul Hassan	Jun 95
Gp Capt	M. Suhaib Afzal	May 96
Gp Capt	Salman Hussain Tirmzey	Apr 97
Gp Capt	Nauman Farrukh	Jun 98

No. 37 Wing

Gp Capt	Aurangzeb Khan	Sep 88
Gp Capt	Pervez Akhtar Nawaz	Sep 89
Gp Capt	Zaka-ullah Khan	Jul 90
Gp Capt	Azmat Kazi	Jul 91
Gp Capt	Fahmid Iqbal Chowdhry	Feb 92
Gp Capt	Masood Akhtar	Jul 93
Gp Capt	Mirza Zafar Hussain	Jul 94
Gp Capt	Tanveer M. Sheikh	Jun 95
Gp Capt	M. Azam-Uddin	May 96
Gp Capt	Inamullah	Jul 97
Gp Capt	Qadeer Ahmad Hashmi	Jun 98

No. 38 Wing

Gp Capt	M. Hamid Akhtar Malik	Dec 87
Gp Capt	Imtiaz A. Khan	Mar 89
Gp Capt	Tanveer M. Ahmad	Feb 91
Gp Capt	Hamid Abbas Khawaja	Jul 92
Gp Capt	Khalid Choudhry	Jul 93

Gp Capt	Jamshed Afzal	Mar 94
Gp Capt	Muhammad Avais	Jul 95
Gp Capt	Shahzad A. Chaudhry	May 96
Gp Capt	Muhammad Yousaf	Jun 97
Gp Capt	Wasim-ud-Din	Jul 98

Combat Commanders' School

Gp Capt	Zahid Anis	Dec 87
Gp Capt	Shahid Javed	Jul 89
Gp Capt	Riffat Munir	Jul 91
Gp Capt	Abdul Razzaq	Aug 92
Gp Capt	Khalid Choudhry	Mar 94
Gp Capt	Abdul Hameed Qadri	Jul 95
Gp Capt	Sabeeh Hussain	Jul 96
Gp Capt	Faaiz Amir	Oct 97

Flying Squadrons

No. 1 Fighter Conversion Unit

Wg Cdr	Abid Pervez Chaudhry	Jun 86
Wg Cdr	Fahmid Iqbal Chowdhry	Jul 88
Wg Cdr	Pervez Akhtar Khan	Jul 89
Wg Cdr	Syed Riaz Ali	Mar 91
Wg Cdr	Qadeer Ahmad Hashmi	Jul 93
Wg Cdr	Muhammad Ashraf	Dec 94
Wg Cdr	Gulzar Ahmed Janjua	Jun 96
Wg Cdr	Tanvir Anwar	Feb 98

No. 2 Squadron

Wg Cdr	Muhammad Tayyab	Apr 87
Wg Cdr	Abid Pervez	Jun 89
Wg Cdr	Nauman Farrukh	Sep 90
Wg Cdr	Junaid Ameen	Jul 91
Wg Cdr	Awal Nawaz Khattak	Jul 93
Wg Cdr	Khalil-Ullah Khan	Dec 94
Wg Cdr	Muhammad Hanif	Jul 96
Wg Cdr	Muhammad Arif	Feb 98

No. 5 Squadron

Wg Cdr	M. Abdul Qadir Sargana	Jul 87
Wg Cdr	Hifazatullah Khan	Jul 89
Wg Cdr	Iqbal Khan	Aug 90
Wg Cdr	Zia-ul-Hassan	Dec 90
Wg Cdr	Faisal Tariq	Sep 91
Wg Cdr	M. Ehtesham-uddin	Aug 93
Wg Cdr	Ghulam Mujaddid	Sep 94
Wg Cdr	Khalid Parvez Marwat	Mar 96
Wg Cdr	Farrukh Nazir	Oct 97

No. 6 Squadron

Wg Cdr	Mashood F. Hassan	Jun 87
Wg Cdr	Munawar Alam Siddiqui	Aug 88
Wg Cdr	Nayyar Qayum Khawja	Jul 90
Wg Cdr	Mustansar Sohail Toor	Jul 91
Wg Cdr	Imtiaz Aziz	Jun 93
Wg Cdr	Malik Hakim Khan	Dec 94
Wg Cdr	Alamgir Akhter	Aug 96
Gp Capt	Sarfraz Ahmad Khan	Aug 97

No. 7 Squadron

Wg Cdr	Hashim Yamin	Jul 87
Wg Cdr	Shaheen Hamid	Oct 88
Wg Cdr	Babar Hassain	Feb 91
Wg Cdr	Shoukat Mehmood	Jul 93
Wg Cdr	Muhammad Saleem	Jan 95
Wg Cdr	Hafeezullah	Jul 96
Wg Cdr	Shahid Mahmood	Feb 98

No. 8 Squadron

Wg Cdr	Irfan Musum	Jul 87
Wg Cdr	Saleem Akhtar Nawaz	Jul 89
Wg Cdr	Shahid Lateef	Jul 91
Wg Cdr	Kaisar Tufail	Jul 93
Wg Cdr	Asim Suleman	Feb 95

| Wg Cdr | Wasim Ahmed | Jun 96 |
| Wg Cdr | Khawaja A. Majeed | Jan 98 |

No. 9 Squadron

Wg Cdr	Shahzad A. Chaudhry	Jul 87
Wg Cdr	Tariq M. Ashraf	Feb 89
Wg Cdr	Farhat Hussain Khan	Feb 91
Wg Cdr	Shahid Dad	Feb 93
Wg Cdr	Waseem-ud-Din	Aug 94
Wg Cdr	Zahid Qadeer	Jan 96
Wg Cdr	Azher Hasan	Jul 97

No. 11 Squadron

Wg Cdr	Khalid Choudhry	Sep 86
Wg Cdr	Muhammad Avais	Apr 88
Wg Cdr	Javed Anwar	Sep 90
Wg Cdr	Muhammad Yousaf	Mar 92
Wg Cdr	Ali Asad Khan	Mar 94
Wg Cdr	Rizwan-Ullah Khan	Jul 95
Gp Capt	Akhtar H. Bukhari	Apr 97

No. 12 Squadron

Wg Cdr	Sabahat Ali Mufti	Jul 86
Wg Cdr	Munawar Alam Siddiqui	Jul 88
Wg Cdr	Mashood F. Hassan	Aug 88
Wg Cdr	Sabahat Ali Mufti	Aug 88
Wg Cdr	Tahir H. Siddiqui	Jul 89
Wg Cdr	M. Arshad Javed	Jun 91
Wg Cdr	S. Jamal Uddin	Jul 93
Wg Cdr	Ahmed Saeed Anjum	Dec 94
Wg Cdr	Rizwan Yusuf	Jul 96
Wg Cdr	M. Khalid Kamal Khan	Jul 98

No. 14 Squadron

Wg Cdr	Abdus Sami Toor	Jun 87
Wg Cdr	Abdul Razzaq	Jul 88
Wg Cdr	S. Muzaffar Ali	Feb 89

Wg Cdr	Sabeeh Hussain	Jan 91
Wg Cdr	Gul Abbas Mela	Feb 93
Wg Cdr	Abbas Mohsin Petiwala	Oct 93
Wg Cdr	Abid Hussain Khawaja	May 95
Wg Cdr	M. Jamshaid Khan	Jan 97
Wg Cdr	Khaleel Ahmad	Jun 98

No. 15 Squadron

Wg Cdr	Tariq K. R. Awan	Jul 87
Wg Cdr	M. Ateeb Siddiqui	Dec 88
Wg Cdr	S. A. Muddasir	Dec 90
Wg Cdr	Rao Qamar Suleman	Jan 92
Wg Cdr	M. Hassan	Dec 93
Wg Cdr	Hamayun Khurshid	Jun 95
Wg Cdr	M. Altaf Saleemi	Jan 97
Sqn Ldr	Malik M. Rafiq	Jul 98

No. 16 Squadron

Wg Cdr	Ashfaq Ahmed Shaikh	Sep 87
Wg Cdr	Mirza Zafar Hussain	Jul 89
Wg Cdr	Muhammad Younas	Aug 91
Wg Cdr	Shadab Husnain	Feb 93
Wg Cdr	Zafar Iqbal Haider	Jul 94
Wg Cdr	M. Shahid Khan	Jul 95
Wg Cdr	Sajid Habib	Jan 97
Wg Cdr	Razi Nawab	Jun 98

No. 17 Squadron

Wg Cdr	Shaukat Haider	Feb 87
Wg Cdr	S. Rashid Hasan Bukhari	Jul 89
Wg Cdr	Zahoor A. Shaikh	Jul 91
Wg Cdr	M. Suhaib Afzal	Jul 93
Wg Cdr	Arshad Quddus	Jan 95
Wg Cdr	Khalid Farooq Chishti	Jul 96
Wg Cdr	Muhammad Jamil	Feb 98

No. 18 Squadron

| Wg Cdr | Abdul Ghaffar | Aug 86 |
| Wg Cdr | Shaheen Mazhar | Jun 88 |

Wg Cdr	Asif Rehman	Sep 89
Wg Cdr	Shahid Hamid Shigri	Jul 91
Wg Cdr	Azam Uddin Khan	Jun 93
Wg Cdr	Sohail Asghar	Jul 94
Wg Cdr	Mehboob A. Khalid	Jan 96
Wg Cdr	Zaheer Ahmad Khan	Jul 97

No. 19 Squadron

Wg Cdr	Javed Ishaque	Jul 87
Wg Cdr	Nauman Farrukh	Jul 89
Wg Cdr	Gulrez Akhtar	Aug 90
Wg Cdr	Tahir Rafiqui Butt	Jul 91
Wg Cdr	M. Usman	Oct 93
Wg Cdr	Rahim Bakhsh	Apr 95
Wg Cdr	Khawaja Abdul Latif	Sep 96
Wg Cdr	Tanweer Nazim Siddiqui	Feb 98

No. 20 Squadron

Wg Cdr	Shahid Aslam	Apr 86
Wg Cdr	Ghazanfar Hussain	Mar 88
Wg Cdr	Aurangzeb Khan	May 89
Wg Cdr	Adeeb Niazi	Jul 90
Wg Cdr	Masroor-ul-Hassan	Jun 92
Wg Cdr	Nadeem Anjum	Mar 94
Wg Cdr	Gul Abbas Mela	Oct 95
Wg Cdr	Junaid Ahmed	Jan 97
Wg Cdr	Sohail Aman	Jul 98

No. 22 Squadron

Wg Cdr	Iqbal Haider	Jun 87
Wg Cdr	M. Ikram-ullah Bhatti	Jan 89
Wg Cdr	Khalid Cheema	Feb 91
Wg Cdr	Inamullah Khan	Feb 93
Wg Cdr	Nadeem Hanif	Jun 95
Wg Cdr	Khalid Banuri	Nov 96
Wg Cdr	M. Laeeque Khan	Jun 98

No. 23 Squadron

Wg Cdr	Rehmat Ullah Khan	Dec 86
Wg Cdr	Syed Javid Sabir	Mar 89
Wg Cdr	Sikandar Siddique Khan	Dec 90
Wg Cdr	M. Safdar Khan	Jun 93
Wg Cdr	Amjad Bashir	Jun 94
Wg Cdr	Syed Najam-ul-Asar	Jun 96
Wg Cdr	Ghulam Mustafa Abbasi	Jul 97

No. 24 Squadron

Wg Cdr	Masood Akhtar	Dec 86
Wg Cdr	Tanveer M. Shiekh	May 90
Wg Cdr	Aftab Iqbal	Jul 92
Wg Cdr	Ayaz Ul Haq	Jul 94
Wg Cdr	Tanzeem A. Khan	Jun 96
Wg Cdr	M. Nisar Raja	Jun 98

No. 25 Squadron

Wg Cdr	Khalid Mehmood	Aug 86
Wg Cdr	Malik Nazar Hussain	Jul 88
Wg Cdr	Yalmas S. Arshi	Oct 88
Wg Cdr	Shahid Nisar Khan	Jan 90
Wg Cdr	Naeem Ashraf	Jul 91
Wg Cdr	Tahir Ehsan Malik	Jul 93
Wg Cdr	Zafar Yasin	Dec 94
Wg Cdr	Waqar Haider	Jun 97

No. 26 Squadron

Wg Cdr	Hameedullah Khan	Feb 87
Wg Cdr	Wali Mughni	Nov 88
Wg Cdr	M. Tariq Shahab	Jul 89
Wg Cdr	Salman H. Tirmzey	Jul 91
Wg Cdr	Tahir R. Sajid	Jul 93
Wg Cdr	Nadeem Ahmad Khan	Feb 95
Wg Cdr	Imran ul Hassan	Jul 96
Wg Cdr	Nadeem Ahmad Khan	Feb 98

CCS Mirage

Wg Cdr	Maqbool Ali Shah	Dec 87
Wg Cdr	Zia Ul Hassan	Jul 90
Wg Cdr	Muhammad Ateeb	Dec 90
Wg Cdr	Faisal Tariq	Jul 91
Wg Cdr	Arif Moin	Sep 91
Wg Cdr	Faaiz Amir	Jul 93
Wg Cdr	Aslam Pervaiz	Dec 94
Wg Cdr	Sohail Gul	Jul 96
Wg Cdr	Hassan Raza	Jan 98

CCS F-7

Wg Cdr	Hameed Qadri	Jan 93
Wg Cdr	Riaz Ul Haque	Jun 94
Wg Cdr	Atique Rafique	Nov 95
Wg Cdr	Saeed M. Khan	Jul 97

CCS F-6

Wg Cdr	Jamshed Afzal	Jul 87
Wg Cdr	Inamullah Khan	Dec 89
Wg Cdr	Hameed Qadri	Jul 92

No. 41 Squadron

Wg Cdr	Nayyar Qayum Khawaja	Aug 87
Wg Cdr	Fateh Sher Bhatti	Aug 89
Wg Cdr	Nazar Muhammad	Jul 91
Wg Cdr	Zahid Latif	Sep 93
Wg Cdr	Muhammad Ali	Aug 94
Wg Cdr	Mujahid Islam Khan	Jul 96
Wg Cdr	Shamim Akhtar	Jul 97

No. 81 Squadron

Sqn Ldr	Fazl-I-Akbar	Jun 86
Sqn Ldr	Abid Hameed	Oct 88
Wg Cdr	Saqib Qazi	Jan 91

Wg Cdr	Farooq Azam	Aug 93
Wg Cdr	Fazl-I-Akbar	Oct 94
Wg Cdr	Asad Rasheed	Jul 96

No. 82 Squadron

Sqn Ldr	Ahmed Ali	Jan 86
Wg Cdr	Shaharyar	Jun 89
Wg Cdr	Ikramullah	Jul 92
Wg Cdr	Asad Rasheed	Sep 93
Wg Cdr	Khalid Ismail	Jul 95
Wg Cdr	Abrar Ahmad	Jul 97

No. 83 Squadron

Sqn Ldr	Iftikhar Ahmed Bhatti	Oct 88
Sqn Ldr	Saeed A. Butt	Oct 90
Wg Cdr	Khalid Ismail	May 91
Sqn Ldr	Saqib Shafi	Sep 93
Wg Cdr	Shahid Tufail	Jan 94
Wg Cdr	Nasir Majeed	Jul 95

No. 84 Squadron

Wg Cdr	Pervez	Jul 87
Wg Cdr	M. Azam	Jan 92
Wg Cdr	Khalid	Apr 94
Wg Cdr	Saqib	Jan 96
Wg Cdr	M. Rizwan	Jul 96

No. 85 Squadron

Sqn Ldr	Muhammad Azam	Dec 87
Wg Cdr	M. Farooq Azam	Feb 91
Wg Cdr	Khalid Niazi	Nov 91
Wg Cdr	Syed Asif Masood	Sep 93
Wg Cdr	M. Farooq Azam	Oct 94
Wg Cdr	Mussarat Ali	Apr 96
Wg Cdr	M. Usman Ghani	Apr 98

No. 86 Squadron

Sqn Ldr	S. J. Maula	Dec 86
Sqn Ldr	Asad Rashid	Jan 89
Wg Cdr	Fazal-i-Akbar	Jan 90
Sqn Ldr	Raja Zafar Abbas	Oct 91
Wg Cdr	Muhammad Azam	Feb 93
Wg Cdr	Ikram Ullah Khan	Apr 94
Sqn Ldr	Tanvir Hussain	Jan 96
Wg Cdr	Khurram Naseem	Jun 98

Engineering Units

No. 101 Air Logistics Centre

Gp Capt	Syed Aley Raza	May 86
Gp Capt	M. Ashraf Javed	May 88
Gp Capt	S. Zeeshan Hasnain	Apr 91
Gp Capt	Asif Mahmood Malik	May 93
Gp Capt	Maqbool Ahmad Ranjha	Dec 96

No. 102 Air Engineering Depot

Gp Capt	Khalid Sarfraz	Aug 86
Air Cdre	Imtiaz Rasool Khan	Aug 88
Gp Capt	Mehmood Sultan Bajwa	Oct 89
Gp Capt	M. Aslam Ansari	Mar 91
Gp Capt	Syed Javed Raza	Mar 96
Gp Capt	M. Arshad Ali Khan	Aug 97

No. 103 Air Logistics Centre

Gp Capt	S. Shabbir	Jun 87
Gp Capt	Abdul Ghafoor Tahir	Sep 89
Air Cdre	Muhammad Masud	Jan 92
Gp Capt	Muhammad Tufail	Dec 94
Gp Capt	Ikramullah Shad	Mar 96

No. 104 Air Engineering Depot

Gp Capt	Muhammad Saleem	Jun 86
Wg Cdr	Muhammad Irshad	Mar 89

Wg Cdr	Iftikhar Ahmad	Feb 92
Gp Capt	Ejaz Yaqub	Jul 94
Gp Capt	Shoaib Ahmed	Aug 96
Gp Capt	Naveed Arshad	Jun 98

No. 105 Air Engineering Depot

Wg Cdr	Anwar Saeed	Nov 87
Wg Cdr	Zulfiqar H. Shirazi	Jul 90
Sqn Ldr	Aurangzeb Khan	Sep 92
Gp Capt	Mujahid Sadiq	Aug 93
Gp Capt	Ghazanfar Ali Chaudhry	Apr 97

No. 106 Air Engineering Depot

Gp Capt	James Luke	Aug 88
Sqn Ldr	Inayat Ullah	Sep 90
Sqn Ldr	Farooq M. Hayat	May 94
Sqn Ldr	Zaki Ullah	Oct 95
Sqn Ldr	Aurangzeb Khan	Jul 97

No. 107 Air Engineering Depot

Gp Capt	N. A. Khawaja	Oct 87
Gp Capt	Ramzan A. Sayani	Jun 89
Gp Capt	Bashir A. Mohsin	Jun 91
Gp Capt	Naeem A. Siddiqui	Dec 92
Gp Capt	Jamil A. Sharif	Feb 95
Gp Capt	Nasir A. Hamadani	Apr 97

No. 108 Air Engineering Depot

Gp Capt	M. Irshad Malik	Dec 87
Air Cdre	Azfar A. Khan	Jul 90
Gp Capt	Saeed Nawaz Khan	Jul 92
Gp Capt	Javaid Iqbal Ahmed	Jun 94
Gp Capt	M. Abdul Rauf	Apr 96
Gp Capt	Mansoor Shaukat	Jun 98

No. 109 Air Engineering Depot

Sqn Ldr	Akeel H. Kizilbash	Mar 88

Sqn Ldr	Muhammad Munir	Aug 89
Flt Lt	Altaf H. Jadoon	Jan 90
Wg Cdr	Akeel H. Kizilbash	Jun 92
Gp Capt	Asif Mahmood	Jul 94
Sqn Ldr	Muhammad Munir	Aug 95
Wg Cdr	Ahmed Ali	Jul 96
Wg Cdr	Zakiullah	Jul 97

No. 110 Air Logistics Depot

Wg Cdr	M. R. Qureshi	Dce 87
Wg Cdr	M. Younas Kashmiri	May 90
Wg Cdr	I. U. Shad	May 91
Wg Cdr	Nizam uddin Khattak	Apr 93
Wg Cdr	Javed Iqbal Chaudhry	Mar 96
Wg Cdr	Siraj-ul-Munir	Sep 98

No. 114 Air Engineering Depot

Wg Cdr	M. H. Khalil	Jun 89
Wg Cdr	Ghazanfar Ali Chaudhry	Sep 90
Gp Capt	M. H. Khalil	May 94
Sqn Ldr	Syed Rahat Ashfaq	Jan 96
Wg Cdr	Muhammad Rashid	Mar 96

No. 118 Software Engineering Depot

Air Cdre	Rafi-ul-Qadir	Nov 86
Gp Capt	Azfar Ali Khan	Apr 89
Gp Capt	Azhar Maud	Jul 90
Gp Capt	Agha Saifullah Khan	Oct 92
Gp Capt	M. Shahim Baig	Dec 94

No. 120 Air Logistics Depot

Sqn Ldr	Naeem Malik	Jun 86
Sqn Ldr	Walayat Hussain	Jun 88
Gp Capt	Zeeshan Hasnain	Nov 88
Wg Cdr	M. S. Piracha	Mar 91
Gp Capt	Zaka-ud-Din	Jul 91
Gp Capt	Mehboob Ali Khan	Feb 92

Gp Capt	M. S. Piracha	Dec 93
Wg Cdr	Khalil-ur-Rehmani	Sep 96
Gp Capt	Mushtaq Ahmed Alvi	Apr 98

No. 130 Air Engineering Depot

Gp Capt	Basit R. Abbasi	Jan 93
Wg Cdr	Akhtar Ali	Dec 95
Wg Cdr	Kamal Alam	Feb 98

Central Technical Development Unit

Sqn Ldr	Sharafat Pirzada	Jan 88
Wg Cdr	Abdul Sattar	Jun 89
Wg Cdr	Insha Hamid	Mar 90
Wg Cdr	S. J. Raza	Aug 91
Gp Capt	M. T. Saleem	Jul 93
Wg Cdr	Sharafat Pirzada	Nov 94
Gp Capt	Azhar H. Jawed	Apr 96
Wg Cdr	Ahmed Safi Qudsi	Oct 98

Air Defence Units

Headquarters Norsec, PAF

Gp Capt	Abdul Waheed	May 88
Gp Capt	Ijaz A. Khan	Jun 89
Gp Capt	M. Zafar Iqbal	Feb 90
Gp Capt	Jahangir Akhtar	Jan 91
Gp Capt	Mansoob Ahmed	Jun 91
Air Cdre	S. Arshad Toor	Apr 92
Air Cdre	M. Yaqoob Khan	Aug 93
Air Cdre	Amjad Mahmood Ali	Aug 94
Air Cdre	K. U. Durrani	Sep 96
Air Cdre	Saif-ur-Rehman	Jun 98

Headquarters Censec, PAF

Gp Capt	Ijaz A. Khan	Jan 98
Gp Capt	Qamar S. Kiani	Jun 89
Air Cdre	Javed Akbar Khan	Jul 91
Gp Capt	M. Arif Pervaiz	Jun 93

Air Cdre	M. Abid Rao	Jul 94
Air Cdre	Abdul Ghaffar	Jul 96
Air Cdre	Khalid B. Cheema	Jul 97

Headquarters Sousec, PAF

Air Cdre	N. D. Qureshi	Nov 88
Gp Capt	Abdul Waheed	Jun 89
Gp Capt	S. M. Ershad Ehsan	Jan 91
Gp Capt	Mansoob Ahmed	May 92
Air Cdre	M. Tanveer	Feb 94
Air Cdre	Zafar A. Khan	Dec 95
Air Cdre	Kamran Ali Khan	Jul 97

Headquarters Wessec, PAF

Gp Capt	Qamar S. Kayani	Mar 88
Gp Capt	Bakht Bedar	May 89
Gp Capt	Ghazanfar Butt	Jun 91
Sector on C & M Status Mar 92 – Aug 97		
Air Cdre	Mahmood Jafar	Aug 97
Gp Capt	Shamher Ali	Nov 98

No. 481 CRC

Gp Capt	Saeed M. Khan	Feb 88
Gp Capt	Ijaz Bhatti	Jun 90
Gp Capt	Zafar A. Khan	Aug 92
Gp Capt	Ishtiaq A. Khan	Aug 93
Gp Capt	Mahmood Jafar	Mar 95
Gp Capt	Shamsher Ali	Sep 96
Gp Capt	F. R. Kiyani	Aug 97
Gp Capt	M. Malik Hijazi	Jun 98

No. 482 CRC

Gp Capt	S. Tasneem Ali	Apr 88
Wg Cdr	Imtiaz Ullah Siddiqui	Jul 89
Gp Capt	Khalid H. Durrani	Jul 93
Gp Capt	Khalid M. Kirmani	Jun 94
Gp Capt	Sikander Hussain	Jun 96
Gp Capt	Saleem Ahmed	Jul 98

No. 483 CRC

Gp Capt	Mansoob Ahmed	Jul 87
Gp Capt	Amjad Mahmood Ali	Jun 89
Gp Capt	Tausif Azmat	May 91
Gp Capt	Ajmal Shah	Jul 93
Gp Capt	Inam-ul-Haq Farrukh	Jul 95
Gp Capt	S. P. Memon	Jun 97
Wg Cdr	Asif Bashir	Jul 98

No. 484 CRC

Gp Capt	S. M. Ershad Ahsan	Oct 88
Gp Capt	Amjad Mahmood Ali	May 91
Gp Capt	Ghulam Nabi Khan	Jul 93
Gp Capt	Ziaur Rahman	Jun 95
Gp Capt	Talat Manzoor	Jan 97
Gp Capt	Rizwan Ullah Sanai	Jun 98

No. 485 CRC & OT Wing

Wg Cdr	M. Yaqoob Khan	May 88
Wg Cdr	Jameel Kiyani	Apr 89
Gp Capt	Muhammad Tanveer	Jul 91
Gp Capt	Yousaf Haroon Aziz	Nov 92
Gp Capt	M. Kamran Ali Khan	Feb 94
Gp Capt	M. Taufique Raja	Jun 95
Gp Capt	Waqar Ahmed Satti	Sep 96
Gp Capt	S. Hussain Wajih Jafri	Jul 98

No. 486 CRC

Gp Capt	Bakht Bedar	Jun 88
Gp Capt	Ijaz Ahmed	May 89
Gp Capt	Ghazanfar Ali Butt	May 90
Gp Capt	Yousaf Haroon	Jun 91
Gp Capt	K. H. Durrani	Jun 94
Gp Capt	Saif-ur-Rahman	Jul 95
Gp Capt	Ayaz Mahmood	Jul 97
Gp Capt	Anjum Shehzad	Jul 98

No. 487 CRC

Gp Capt	F. R. Kayani	May 97
Gp Capt	Ajab Khan Khattak	Aug 97

Training Units

Transport Conversion School

Wg Cdr	Tahir H. Siddiqui	Dec 86
Gp Capt	Zakir A. Khan	Aug 89
Gp Capt	Sabahat Ali	Jul 91
Gp Capt	Zulqarnain	May 93
Wg Cdr	Kazim Ali Awan	Dec 94
Wg Cdr	Ashiq Ali Virk	Aug 96
Wg Cdr	Syed Rameez Gilani	Jul 98

Flying Instructors School

Wg Cdr	Shahzad M. Bakhshi	Jun 87
Wg Cdr	Khalid Mahmood	Jul 89
Wg Cdr	Hameed Qadri	Jun 90
Wg Cdr	Imtiaz A. Shaikh	Jul 91
Wg Cdr	Zafar Iqbal Mir	Jan 92
Wg Cdr	Jamshed Ahmed	Jul 93
Wg Cdr	Muhammad Farooq	Jan 95
Wg Cdr	Tubrez Asif	May 96
Wg Cdr	Bilal Ahmed	Jul 97

Basic Staff School

Gp Capt	Inam-ur-Rehman	Jul 92
Wg Cdr	Tabassam Pervez Khan	Oct 93
Wg Cdr	Bahre Kamal Khan	Jan 94
Gp Capt	M. R. Zia	Oct 94
Wg Cdr	S. Asif Masood	Jun 95
Gp Capt	Najam Salam Butt	Jul 96
Gp Capt	Muhammad Younus	Jan 97

Air Defence Training School

Wg Cdr	Tasnim R. Rizvi	Jul 87
Wg Cdr	Zafar A. Khan	May 89
Wg Cdr	Ishtiaq A. Khan	Aug 90
Wg Cdr	Shamsher Ali	Sep 91
Wg Cdr	Imran Hassan Malik	Jul 93
Wg Cdr	Qazi Muhammad Arif	Aug 94
Wg Cdr	Muhammad Asghar	Jul 96
Wg Cdr	Ashfaq Ahmed	Oct 97
Wg Cdr	Sadiq Hussain	Nov 98

Air War College

Air Cdre	Nasir Ali	Jun 86
Air Cdre	Aliuddin	Jul 88
Air Cdre	Pervez Iqbal Mirza	Dec 89
AVM	Shahid Zulfiqar	Jun 92
Air Cdre	Riffat Munir	Apr 93
Air Cdre	Zulfiqar A. Shah	Dec 93
AVM	Qazi Javed Ahmed	Jan 96
AVM	Saleem Arshad	Jul 97

College of Flying Training

Air Cdre	M. Javeed Ahsan	Feb 87
Air Cdre	Momin Arif	Apr 88
Air Cdre	Qazi Javed Ahmed	Oct 89
Air Cdre	Shabbir A. Khan	Sep 91
Air Cdre	Tayyab N. Akhtar	Jul 92
Air Cdre	Pervez A. Nawaz	Jul 93
Air Cdre	Kaleem Saadat	Jul 94
Air Cdre	M. A. Qadir Sargana	Aug 96
Air Cdre	Abdus Sami Toor	Jul 97

College of Aeronautical Engineering

Air Cdre	Shaukat A. Khan	Mar 87

Air Cdre	Mozammil Saeed	Jul 88	Wg Cdr	Razaullah Khan	Nov 91
Air Cdre	Khalid Sarfraz	May 90	Wg Cdr	Muhammad Yunus	Jul 92
Air Cdre	Naeem A. Siddiqui	Apr 92	Wg Cdr	M. Anwar Hamid	Nov 94
Air Cdre	N. B. Paracha	Jan 94	Wg Cdr	Gohar Javed	Aug 95
Air Cdre	Ijaz A. Malik	May 96	Wg Cdr	M. Zamurrad Choudhry	Aug 96
Air Cdre	Sajid Hussain	Jun 98			

School of Aeronautics

Administrative Trade Training School

Gp Capt	Riaz H. Zaidi	Jan 87
Gp Capt	Muzaffar Islam	Jul 89
Gp Capt	Azhar H. Jawed	Nov 92
Wg Cdr	Ch. Jawed Iqbal	Mar 95
Gp Capt	Bakhtiar A. Malik	Oct 97

Wg Cdr	Malik Khuda Baksh	Sep 87
Wg Cdr	M. Iqbal Khattak	Jul 89
Wg Cdr	Razaullah Khan	Sep 91
Wg Cdr	M. Iqbal Khattak	Nov 91
Wg Cdr	Muhammad Khan	Jul 92
Wg Cdr	M. Anwar Hamid	Apr 94
Wg Cdr	A. Rehman Faiz	Nov 94
Wg Cdr	R. U. Javed	Nov 96
Wg Cdr	M. Saleem	Jun 98

School of Electronics

Gp Capt	Naeem A. Siddiqui	Jan 88
Wg Cdr	M. Majid Baig	Apr 89
Gp Capt	M. A. Pasha	Apr 90
Wg Cdr	Hamayun Mirza	Sep 92
Gp Capt	Muhammad Hafeez	Dec 93
Gp Capt	Aftab Ahmed Khan	May 97

School of Logistics

Wg Cdr	Abdul Rashid Awan	Feb 92
Wg Cdr	Habib ur Rehman	Nov 92
Wg Cdr	Zia Hussain Kazmi	Jan 94
Wg Cdr	M. Afzal Chatha	Oct 96
Wg Cdr	Allen Robson	Aug 98

Aero Medical Institute

Air Cdre	M. Arif Khan	Mar 86
Wg Cdr	M. Yousaf	Oct 89
Gp Capt	M. Yousaf	Mar 91
Gp Capt	Izhar Chaudhri	Nov 93
Gp Capt	Ashfaq Elahi	Oct 94
Wg Cdr	Ghulam Hussain	Mar 95
Wg Cdr	Abdul Samad Shaikh	Oct 98

JCO's Academy

Gp Capt	Tanveer Afghan	Jul 88
Gp Capt	Qazi Mahboobul Haq	Jun 89
Gp Capt	M. Abdul Hameed	Mar 90
Gp Capt	Najam Salam Butt	Jul 94
Wg Cdr	Imtiaz Aziz	Jul 96

Pre-Trade Training School

Wg Cdr	I. R. Pirzada	Dec 87
Wg Cdr	Ikram H. Ramay	Oct 89
Wg Cdr	M. Iqbal Khattak	Sep 91

College of Education

Wg Cdr	Aijazul Haq Aijaz	Oct 86
Wg Cdr	Khayyam Durrani	May 91
Wg Cdr	Afaq Ahmed Zaidi	Nov 91

Gp Capt	Aijazul Haq Aijaz	Oct 93
Wg Cdr	Syed Farooq	Aug 95
Gp Capt	S. Viqar Ali	Feb 97

Sea Survival School

Flt Lt	Shahid Jamil Baig	Oct 86
Sqn Ldr	S. M. Nasir	Jan 94
Sqn Ldr	Tariq Mahmood	Nov 95

FLIGHT SAFETY TROPHIES

Inter Base Flight Safety Trophy

Sarfraz Rafiqui Trophy

Inter Base Maintenance Efficiency Trophy

Masroor Hussain Flight Safety Trophy

Iqbal Ahmed Flight Safety Trophy

Best FSO of the year Trophy

Inter Squadron Maintenance Efficiency Trophy

APPENDIX 2

Professional Trophies

Sher Afgan Trophy

Sqn Ldr	Gul Abbas Mela	1989
Sqn Ldr	Asim Zaheer	1996

No. 17 Squadron 1998

Inter Squadron Armament Trophy

No. 11 Sqn	1989
No. 9 Sqn	1996

Inter Base Flight Safety Trophy

Sargodha	1988
Mianwali	1989
Sargodha	1990
Sargodha	1991
Mianwali, Minhas	1992
Rafiqui	1993
Samungli	1994
Peshawar	1995
Risalpur	1996
Minhas	1997
Sargodha	1998

Sarfraz Rafiqui Flight Safety Trophy

No. 23 Squadron	1988
No. 25 Squadron	1989
No. 23 Squadron	1990
No. 23 Squadron	1991
No. 26 Squadron	1992
No. 23 Squadron	1993
No. 26 Squadron	1994
No. 26 Squadron	1995
No. 26 Squadron	1996
No. 8 Squadron	1997

Masroor Hussain Flight Safety Trophy

No. 1 BFT	1988
No. 1 PFT	1989
No. 1 BFT	1990
No. 2 BFT	1991
No. 1 FCU	1992
No. 2 BFT	1993
No. 2 BFT	1994
No. 1 FCU	1995
No. 1 PFT	1996
No. 1 PFT	1997
No. 1 FCU	1998

Iqbal Ahmed Flight Safety Trophy

No. 6 Squadron	1988
No. 6 Squadron	1989
No. 6 Squadron	1990
No. 12 VIP Squadron	1991
No. 41 Squadron	1992
No. 41 Squadron	1993
No. 41 Squadron	1994
No. 6 Squadron	1995
No. 6 Squadron	1996
No. 41 Squadron	1997
No. 41 Squadron	1998

Flight Safety Officer Trophy

Sqn Ldr Rahat (PAF Sargodha)	1987

Flt Lt Andleeb		Combat Flying Training	No. 11 MR Sqn
(PAF Rafiqui)	1988	Maintenance Efficiency	No. 11 MR Sqn
Sqn Ldr Imran			
(PAF Mianwali)	1989		
Sqn Ldr Paracha		**1995**	
(PAF Rafiqui)	1990		
Sqn Ldr Paracha		Top Gun Squadron	No. 11 MR Sqn
(PAF Rafiqui)	1991	Multi Role Squadron	No. 11 MR Sqn
Sqn Ldr M Ishfaq Arain		Tactical Attack Squadron	No. 26 TA Sqn
(PAF Sargodha)	1992	Air Superiority Squadron	No. 18 AS Sqn
Sqn Ldr Pirzada			
(PAF Rafiqui)	1993	**1996**	
Sqn Ldr Ahsan			
(PAF Samungli)	1994	Top Gun Squadron	No. 18 AS Sqn
Wg Cdr Shahid		Multi Role Squadron	No. 9 MR Sqn
(PAF Sargodha)	1995	Tactical Attack Squadron	No. 8 TA Sqn
Sqn Ldr Tariq Nazir		Air Superiority Squadron	No. 18 AS Sqn
(PAF Samungli)	1996		
Wg Cdr Tariq Nafees		**1997**	
(PAF Samungli)	1997		
Wg Cdr Habib ul Haq		Top Gun Squadron	No. 9 MR Sqn
(PAF Minhas)	1998	Multi Role Squadron	No. 9 MR Sqn
		Tactical Attack Squadron	No. 16 TA Sqn
		Air Superiority Squadron	No. 2 AS Sqn

Inter Base Maint. Efficiency Trophy

1998

PAF Academy, Risalpur	1988		
Rafiqui	1989	Top Gun Squadron	No. 9 MR Sqn
Minhas	1990	Multi Role Squadron	No. 9 MR Sqn
Chaklala	1991	Tactical Attack Squadron	No. 7 TA Sqn
Minhas	1992	Air Superiority Sqn	No. 2 AS Sqn
Sargodha	1993		
Peshawar	1994		
Sargodha	1995	## ADET/ADEX Trophies	
Chaklala	1996		
Chaklala	1997	**1993**	
PAF Academy, Risalpur	1998		
		CRC Group	481 CRC
		Tact Radar Group	410 Squadron
## ACES Trophies		Terminal Weapon Group	452 Squadron
		Sector Group	HQ Norsec
1994			
		1994	
War Readiness	No. 9 MR Sqn		
Best Combat Readiness	No. 11 MR Sqn	CRC Group	486 CRC

Tact Radar Group	408 Squadron
Terminal Weapon Group	452 Squadron
Sector Group	HQ Norsec

1995

CRC Group	485 CRC
Tact Radar Group	400 Squadron
Terminal Weapon Group	453 Squadron
Sector Group	HQ Censec

1996

CRC Group	485 CRC
Tact Radar Group	408 Squadron
Terminal Weapon Group	454 Squadron
Sector Group	HQ Sousec
Composite Group	4092 Squadron
MOUs Group	245 Squadron

1997

CRC Group	486 CRC
Tact Radar Group	406 Squadron
Terminal Weapon Group	454 Squadron
Sector Group	HQ Censec
Composite Group	4092 Squadron
MOUs Group	243 Squadron

1998

CRC Group	483 CRC
Tact Radar Group	410 Squadron
Terminal Weapon Group	452 Squadron
Sector Group	HQ Censec
Composite Group	4092 Squadron
MOUs Group	244 Squadron

APPENDIX 3

Training Trophies / Awards (Officer's Training)

College of Flying Training (CFT)

Winners of All Three Trophies

Rank	Name	Course	Date
Avn Cdt AUO	Ghazanfar Latif	93 GD (P)	29 May 93
Avn Cdt SUO	Azkar ul Hasnain	102 GD (P)	16 May 98

Sword of Honour
(Best All Round Performance)

Rank	Name	Course	Date
Avn Cdt Sgt	Hamid Ali Khan	83 GD (P)	23 Jun 88
Avn Cdt WUO	Nadeem Sabir	84 GD (P)	29 Dec 88
Avn Cdt WUO	Jawad Zafar Ch	85 GD (P)	22 Jun 89
Avn Cdt	M. Nadeem	86 GD (P)	28 Dec 89
Avn Cdt	Mehmood Faizi	87 GD (P)	11 Jun 90
Avn Cdt	Nasir Iqbal	88 GD (P)	19 Dec 90
Avn Cdt AUO	M. Athar	89 GD (P)	30 May 91
Avn Cdt	M. Akram	90 GD (P)	16 Dec 91
Avn Cdt WUO	Imran Qadir	91 GD (P)	04 Jun 92
Avn Cdt SUO	Bilal Khan Niazi	92 GD (P)	23 Dec 92
Avn Cdt AUO	Ghazanfar Latif	93 GD (P)	29 May 93
Avn Cdt SUO	Ali Nadeem Zahoor	94 GD (P)	22 Dec 93
Avn Cdt WUO	Arif Salam Qazi	95 GD (P)	09 Jun 94
Avn Cdt	Raza ul Haq Qudsi	96 GD (P)	17 Dec 94
Avn Cdt	Yamin Iqbal	97 GD (P)	30 May 95
Avn Cdt Sgt	Rizwan Ahmed	98 GD (P)	21 Dec 95
Avn Cdt AUO	Farooq Haider	99 GD (P)	06 Jun 96
Avn Cdt SUO	Ghazi Salahuddin	100 GD (P)	12 Dec 96
Avn Cdt SUO	Tariq	101 GD (P)	22 Nov 97
Avn Cdt SUO	Azkar ul Hasnain	102 GD (P)	16 May 98
Avn Cdt Sgt	Tabarak Hussain	103 GD (P)	21 Nov 98

Best Pilot Trophy

Rank	Name	Course	Date
Avn Cdt	Iftikhar Rahim	83 GD (P)	23 Jun 88
Avn Cdt WUO	Nadeem Sabir	84 GD (P)	29 Dec 88
Avn Cdt	Amir Bashir	85 GD (P)	22 Jun 89
Avn Cdt	Abdul Moin Khan	86 GD (P)	28 Dec 89
Avn Cdt	Faisal Azmat	87 GD (P)	11 Jun 90
Avn Cdt	Fawad Masood Khatmi	88 GD (P)	19 Dec 90
Avn Cdt SUO	S. Sibte Hassan	89 GD (P)	30 May 91
Avn Cdt	Zaeem Azal	90 GD (P)	16 Dec 91
Avn Cdt	Amir Altaf	91 GD (P)	04 Jun 92
Avn Cdt	Gohar Rabbani	92 GD (P)	23 Dec 92
Avn Cdt AUO	Ghazanfar Latif	93 GD (P)	29 May 93
Avn Cdt WUO	Ronald Afzal	94 GD (P)	22 Dec 93
Avn Cdt	M. Sharjeel Riaz	95 GD (P)	09 Jun 94
Avn Cdt	Zeeshan Saeed	96 GD (P)	17 Dec 94
Avn Cdt	Abrar Butt	97 GD (P)	30 May 95
Avn Cdt	Waqar Ahmed	98 GD (P)	21 Dec 95
Avn Cdt	Fawad Waheed	99 GD (P)	06 Jun 96
Avn Cdt Sgt	M. Asim	100 GD (P)	12 Dec 96
Avn Cdt AUO	Omer Rasheed	101 GD (P)	22 Nov 97
Avn Cdt SUO	Azkar ul Hasnain	102 GD (P)	16 May 98
Avn Cdt Sgt	Tabarak Hussain	103 GD (P)	21 Nov 98

Trophy for Best Performance in Ground Subjects

Rank	Name	Course	Date
Avn Cdt	S. Hamid Ali	83 GD (P)	23 Jun 88
Avn Cdt	Ahmed Shuja	84 GD (P)	29 Dec 88
Avn Cdt	Ahsan Rafique	85 GD (P)	22 Jun 89
Avn Cdt	M. Nadeem	86 GD (P)	28 Dec 89
Avn Cdt	Tariq Zia	87 GD (P)	11 Jun 90
Avn Cdt	Amir Rashid	88 GD (P)	19 Dec 90
Avn Cdt	Hasanat Ikram	89 GD (P)	30 May 91
Avn Cdt	M. Akram	90 GD (P)	16 Dec 91
Avn Cdt	Imran Qadir	91 GD (P)	04 Jun 92
Avn Cdt	Farooq Zamir	92 GD (P)	23 Dec 92
Avn Cdt	Ghazanfar Latif	93 GD (P)	29 May 93
Avn Cdt	Asghar Abbas	94 GD (P)	22 Dec 93
Avn Cdt	Arif Salam Qazi	95 GD (P)	09 Jun 94
Avn Cdt	Raza ul Haq	96 GD (P)	17 Dec 94

Avn Cdt	M. Yamin Iqbal	97 GD (P)	30 May 95
Avn Cdt	Rizwan Ahmed	98 GD (P)	21 Dec 95
Avn Cdt	Amjad Mehmood	99 GD (P)	06 Jun 96
Avn Cdt	Ghazi Salahuddin	100 GD (P)	12 Dec 96
Avn Cdt	Faisal Nawaz	101 GD (P)	22 Nov 97
Avn Cdt	Azkar ul Hasnain	102 GD (P)	16 May 98
Avn Cdt	Ahmer Zia	103 GD (P)	21 Nov 98

Joint Chiefs of Staff Gold Medal
(Best in General Service Training)

Rank	Name	Course	Date
Flt Cdt (AUO)	Abdul Jalil Khattak	83 GD (P)	23 Jun 88
Avn Cdt	Muhammad Nadeem Sabir	84 GD (P)	29 Dec 88
Avn Cdt (AUO)	Waqar Ahmed	85 GD (P)	22 Jun 89
Avn Cdt (WUO)	Aamir Hussain	86 GD (P)	28 Dec 89

College of Aeronautical Engineering (CAE)

Sword of Honour
(Best All Round Performance)

Rank	Name	Course	Service	Date
Avn Cdt	Asad Ikram	27th Engg	PAF	23 Jun 88
Avn Cdt	Rizwan Ahmed	28th Engg	PAF	29 Dec 88
G Cdt	Sohaib Ahmed	29th Engg	Pak Army	22 Jun 89
Avn Cdt	Arjumand Micheal	30th Engg	PAF	28 Dec 89
Avn Cdt	Usman Gul	31st Engg	PAF	11 Jun 90
Avn Cdt	Munir Hassan Farihat	32nd Engg	RJAF	19 Dec 90
Avn Cdt	M. Nadeem Akhtar	33rd & 34th Engg	PAF	30 May 91
Avn Cdt	Muhammad Ajmal Khan	35th Engg	PAF	16 Dec 91
Avn Cdt	Imran Rauf	36th Engg	PAF	04 Jun 92
Avn Cdt	Ahmed Shakil	37th Engg	PAF	23 Dec 92
Avn Cdt	Messam Abbas	38th Engg	PAF	29 May 93
Avn Cdt	Jehanzeb Burki	39th Engg	PAF	22 Dec 93
Avn Cdt	Khalid Usman	40th Engg	PIA	09 Jun 94
G Cdt	Zahid Mahmood	41st Engg	Pak Army	17 Dec 94
Avn Cdt	Azmat Ahmad	42nd Engg	PIA	30 May 95
Avn Cdt	Stanley Reginald Paul	43rd Engg	PIA	21 Dec 95
Avn Cdt	Syed Adeem Usman	44th Engg	PIA	06 Jun 96

Avn Cdt	Athar Osama	45th Engg	PIA	12 Dec 96
Avn Cdt	M. Nauman Qureshi	46th Engg	PAF	24 May 97
Avn Cdt	M. Akhtar Jamil	47th Engg	BDAF	22 Nov 97
G Cdt	Syed Ibrar Hussain	48th Engg	Pak Army	16 May 98
Avn Cdt	Shuaib Salamat	49th Engg	PAF	21 Nov 98

CAS Trophy
(Best in Academics)

Rank	Name	Course	Service	Date
Avn Cdt	Asad Ikram	27th Engg	PAF	23 Jun 88
Avn Cdt	Rizwan Ahmed	28th Engg	PAF	29 Dec 88
G Cdt	Sohaib Ahmed	29th Engg	Pak Army	22 Jun 89
Avn Cdt	Umar Bashir	30th Engg	PAF	28 Dec 89
G Cdt	S. M. Tahir	31st Engg	Pak Army	11 Jun 90
Avn Cdt	Muhammad Abdullah	32nd Engg	PAF	19 Dec 90
Avn Cdt	M. Nadeem Akhtar	33rd & 34th Engg	PAF	30 May 91
	Muhammad Ajmal Khan	35th Engg	PAF	16 Dec 91
Avn Cdt	Imran Rauf	36th Engg	PAF	04 Jun 92
Avn Cdt	Ahmed Shakil	37th Engg	PAF	23 Dec 92
Avn Cdt	Messam Abbas	38th Engg	PAF	29 May 93
Avn Cdt	Jehanzeb Burki	39th Engg	PAF	22 Dec 93
Avn Cdt	Khalid Usman	40th Engg	PIA	09 Jun 94
Avn Cdt	Rana Kashif Altaf	41st Engg	PIA	17 Dec 94
Avn Cdt	Azmat Ahmad	42nd Engg	PIA	30 May 95
Avn Cdt	Stanley Reginald Paul	43rd Engg	PIA	21 Dec 95
Avn Cdt	Syed Adeem Usman	44th Engg	PIA	06 Jun 96
Avn Cdt	Athar Osama	45th Engg	PIA	12 Dec 96
Avn Cdt	M. Nauman Qureshi	46th Engg	PAF	24 May 97
BDAF Cdt	M. Akhtar Jamil	47th Engg	BDAF	22 Nov 97
G Cdt	Nauman Ahmed	48th Engg	PIA	16 May 98
Avn Cdt	Shuaib Salamat	49th Engg	PAF	21 Nov 98

Joint Chiefs of Staff Trophy
(Best in General Service Training)

Rank	Name	Course	Date
Avn Cdt (AUO)	Soban Nazir Syed	28th Engg	29 Dec 88
Avn Cdt (SUO)	Muizuddin	29th Engg	22 Jun 89
Avn Cdt (AUO)	Tariq Yasin	30th Engg	28 Dec 89

Joint Chiefs of Staff Trophy
(Best in General Service Training)

(Combined for CFT & CAE)

Rank	Name	Course	Date
Avn Cdt (AUO)	Haider Ali Shah	87 GD (P)	11 Jun 90
RJAF Cdt (AUO)	Munir Hassan	32nd Engg	19 Dec 90
Avn Cdt (WUO)	Syed Hossein Raza	33rd Engg	30 May 91
Avn Cdt (AUO)	Asim Rasheed	90 GD (P)	16 Dec 91
Avn Cdt (AUO)	Shahab Nawaz	91 GD (P)	04 Dec 92
Avn Cdt (AUO)	Liaqat Ali Khan	37th Engg	23 Dec 92
Avn Cdt (AUO)	Ghazanfar Latif	93 GD (P)	29 May 93
Avn Cdt (AUO)	Jehanzeb Burki	39th Engg	22 Dec 93
Avn Cdt (AUO)	Sajjad Noori	95 GD (P)	09 Jun 94
G Cdt	Shahid Rafique	41st Engg	17 Dec 94
Avn Cdt (AUO)	Sohail Akbar	97 GD (P)	30 May 95
G Cdt	Asif Sultan	43rd Engg	21 Dec 95
RJAF Cdt	Ra'aid Abdul Razzaq	44th Engg	06 Jun 96
Avn Cdt	Kashif Amjad Butt	45th Engg	12 Dec 96
G Cdt (SUO)	Aqueel Ahmad Awan	46th Engg	24 May 97
Avn Cdt (AUO)	Omer Rasheed	101 GD (P)	22 Nov 97
Avn Cdt Sgt	Noman Imran	48th Engg	18 May 98
Avn Cdt (WUO)	M. Aamir Bashir	49th Engg	21 Nov 98

Role of Honour
Aerospace Engineering

Year	Course	Rank	Name	Cum GPA	Service
1988	27th Engg	Avn Cdt	Ejaz Mazhar	3.27	PAF
1988	28th Engg	Avn Cdt	Obaidullah Soomro	3.42	PIA
1989	29th Engg	Avn Cdt	Zubair Islam	3.55	PAF
1989	30th Engg	Avn Cdt	Azfar Sameen	3.29	PAF
1990	31st Engg	G Cdt	Salman Naeem	3.53	Pak Army
1990	32nd Engg	Avn Cdt	Munir Hassan Farihat	3.75	RJAF
1991	33rd Engg	Avn Cdt	Mudassar Tufail	3.93	PIA
1991	34th Engg	Plt Off	Gohar Majeed	3.49	PAF
1991	35th Engg	Avn Cdt	Izhar Hussain Kazmi	3.35	PAF
1992	36th Engg	Avn Cdt	Sartaj Alam	3.56	PAF
1992	37th Engg	Avn Cdt	Ahmed Shakil	3.95	PAF
1993	38th Engg	Avn Cdt	Messam Abbas	3.94	PAF
1993	39th Engg	Avn Cdt	Syed Irtiza Ali Shah	3.81	PAF

1994	40th Engg	Avn Cdt	Muhammad Hamood Alam	3.68	PIA
1994	41st Engg	Avn Cdt	Farooq Ahmad	3.56	Pak Army
1995	42nd Engg	Avn Cdt	Azmat Ahmad	3.60	PIA
1995	43rd Engg	Avn Cdt	Muhammad Ali Jaffery	3.58	PIA
1996	44th Engg	G Cdt	Imran Akhtar	3.36	Pak Army
1996	45th Engg	Avn Cdt	Muhammad Shakeel	3.14	PAF
1997	46th Engg	G Cdt	Muhammad Sohail Arshad	3.54	Pak Army
1997	47th Engg	Avn Cdt	Syed Salman Jafri	3.51	PAF
1998	48th Engg	G Cdt	Syed Ibrar Hussain	3.72	Pak Army
1998	49th Engg	Avn Cdt	Shuaib Salamat	3.89	PAF

Avionics Engineering

Year	Course	Rank	Name	Cum GPA	Service
1988	27th Engg	Avn Cdt	Asad Ikram	3.56	PAF
1988	28th Engg	Avn Cdt	Iqbal Mehmood Dar	3.90	PIA
1989	29th Engg	G Cdt	Sohaib Ahmed	3.78	Pak Army
1989	30th Engg	Avn Cdt	Umer Bashir	3.85	PAF
1990	31st Engg	G Cdt	S. M. Tahir	3.75	Pak Army
1990	32nd Engg	Avn Cdt	Muhammad Abdullah	3.82	PAF
1991	33rd Engg	Avn Cdt	M. Nadeem Akhtar	3.88	PAF
1991	34th Engg	Avn Cdt	Fraz Ahmed	3.68	PAF
1991	35th Engg	Avn Cdt	Muhammad Ajmal Khan	4.00	PAF
1992	36th Engg	Avn Cdt	Imran Rauf	4.00	PAF
1992	37th Engg	Avn Cdt	S. Zafar Ali Shah	3.74	PAF
1993	38th Engg	Avn Cdt	Usman Riaz	3.73	PAF
1993	39th Engg	Avn Cdt	Jehanzeb Burki	3.97	PAF
1994	40th Engg	Avn Cdt	Khalid Usman	3.78	PIA
1994	41st Engg	Avn Cdt	Rana Kashif Altaf	3.72	PIA
1995	42nd Engg	Avn Cdt	Omer Majeed Tareen	3.59	PIA
1995	43rd Engg	Avn Cdt	Stanley Reginald Paul	3.92	PIA
1996	44th Engg	Avn Cdt	Syed Adeem Usman	3.57	PIA
1996	45th Engg	Avn Cdt	Athar Osama	3.84	PIA
1997	46th Engg	Avn Cdt	M. Nowman Qureshi	3.55	PAF
1997	47th Engg	Avn Cdt	M. Akhtar Jamil	3.77	BDAF
1998	48th Engg	Avn Cdt	Noman Ahmed	3.87	PIA
1998	49th Engg	Avn Cdt	Fahad Riaz	3.88	PAF

APPENDIX 4

Training Trophies / Awards (Airmen Training)

Pre-Trades Training School

Best All Round Trophy

Entry	Rank	Name	Pak No.
AS-8808	AS Cpl	Islam Lodhi	424
AS-8902	AS Cpl	Muslim	537
AS-8909	AS Cpl	Mazhar	729
AS-9002	AS W Sgt	Ejaz Ali	1102
AS-9009	AS CpI	Ejaz Khan	1658
AS-9102	AS CpI	A. Waheed	2225
AS-9108	AS W Sgt	M. Zia	2632
AS-9111	AS Sgt	Sattar Khan	2939
AS-9205	AS Cpl	Sohail	3532
AT-9209	AT Sgt	Ehsanullah	3837
AS-9302	AS Sgt	Shiraz	4020
AS-9306	AS Sgt	A. Ghaffar	4586
AT-9312	AT Sgt	Tanveer	5390
AS-9403	AS Sgt	Salahuddin	5220
AS-9407	AS Sgt	Shahid	5951
AT-9411	AT Sgt	M. Kamal	6411
AS-9503	AS Sgt	M. Tahir	7111
AT-9507	AT Sgt	Saeed Zafar	37734
AS-9511	AS Sgt	Saeed Ur Rehman	86173
AT-9603	AT Sgt	Urangzeb	38656
AT-9607	AT Sgt	Pervez Mehdi	39075
AT-9611	AC2 Cpl	Tahir Shafique	39856
AT-9703	AC Sgt	Zahid Ali	3105517
AT-9707	AC W Sgt	M. Yaseen	311041
AS-9711	AC Cpl	Adnan Zafar	610567
AS-9803	AC Sgt	Syed Farhan Shah	611027

Administrative Trade Training School

Best All Round Trophy

Rank	Name	Pak No.	Trade	Date
AC	Sajjad	486739	MTM	02 Apr 96
AC	Ali Raza	487143	GC	02 Jun 96
AC	Khalid	487654	MTM	03 Nov 96
AC	Irfan	487964	MTM	14 Feb 97
AC	Rab Nawaz	488534	GC	29 May 97
AC	Bashir	488913	GC	20 Nov 97
AC	Zahid	489163	MTM	14 Feb 98
AC	Sharifuddin	489980	ACCTS	20 Oct 98

School of Aeronautics

CAS Trophy
(Best in Aerospace Technology)

Rank	Name	Pak No.	Trade	Date
Jnr Tech	Muhammad Saleem	851725	Afr	Feb 88
Jnr Tech	Noor Khan	852163	Armt	Mar 89
Jnr Tech	Niaz Ghous	852487	Inst	Mar 90
Jnr Tech	Karnal Sher	853149	Elect	Jan 91
AC2	Ansar Iqbal	853330	Armt	Aug 91
AC2	Muhammad Ishaq	853457	Armt	Feb 92
AC2	Muhammad Inam	853566	Armt	Feb 92
AC2	Ghulam Akbar	853929	Eng	May 92
AC2	Muhammad Ashraf	854281	Eng	Nov 92
AC2	Muhammad Rafqat	854631	Armt	May 93
AC2	Mir M. Tipu Sultan (BDAF)	459592	Elect	Oct 93
AC2	Muhammad Arshad	855388	Afr	Feb 94
AC2	Tanveer Nawaz	857843	Eng	May 96
AC2	Altaf Hussain	858272	Eng	Oct 96
AC2	Shahid Shah	858565	Afr	Feb 97
AC2	Zulqarnain Khan	859005	Afr	Jun 97
AC2	Ghulam Abbas	859489	Eng	Oct 97
AC2	Asif Mehmood	859840	Afr	Feb 98
AC2	Muhammad Khalil	860291	Afr	Oct 98
AC2	Nasir Mehmood	860675	Afr	Oct 98

School of Electronics

CAS Trophy
(Best in Avionics Technology)

Rank	Name	Pak No.	Trade	Date
Aero Tech.	Jaffar	851356	Radar	Feb 88
Aero Tech.	Akhtar	852092	Radio	Mar 89
Aero Tech.	M. Asghar	852304	Radio	Jun 89
Aero Tech.	Imran	852615	Radar	Feb 90
Aero Tech.	Arif	852796	Radar	Jan 91
Aero Tech.	A. Munaf	853300	Radar	Aug 91
Aero Tech.	Amjad	853763	Radio	Feb 92
Aero Tech.	Javaid	853822	Radio	Mar 92
Aero Tech.	Maqbool	853905	Radar	May 92
Aero Tech.	Zafar Iqbal	854284	Radar	Nov 92
Aero Tech.	Irfan Sohail	854633	Radio	May 93
Aero Tech.	M. Afzal	855075	Radio	Oct 93
Aero Tech.	M. Ali	855385	Radio	Feb 94
Aero Tech.	Azhar	855748	Radar	Jul 94
Aero Tech.	Sultan Mehmood	858122	Radar	Oct 94
Aero Tech.	M. Ismail	856473	Radio	Feb 95
Aero Tech.	Sharafat Ali	856961	Radar	Oct 95
Aero Tech.	Mazhar	857498	Radar	Jan 96
Aero Tech.	Shakeel Ahmed	857846	Radio	May 96
Aero Tech.	Umer Mushtaq	858273	Radio	Oct 96
Aero Tech.	Abid	858564	Radar	Feb 97
Aero Tech.	Shakeel	859007	Radio	Jun 97
Aero Tech.	Safeer	859494	Radar	Oct 97
Aero Tech.	Asif	859838	Radio	Feb 98
Aero Tech.	Fateh	860292	Radio	Jun 98
ART-I	Riasat (Pak Navy)	O No-950870	Radar	Oct 98

JCO's Academy

Sarfaraz Rafiqui Shaheed Trophy

Rank	Name	Pak No.	Trade	Date
Wrt Off	Amanat	79934	Radar Fitt	28 Feb 88
Wrt Off	Iftikhar	84545	Sect Asstt	26 Jun 88
Wrt Off	Iftikhar	78306	Radio Fitt	18 Dec 88
Chf Tech	Riaz	441088	Sect Asstt	30 Apr 89

Wrt Off	Liaquat	84119	Radar Fitt	19 Sep 89
Wrt Off	Saeed	87068	Radar Fitt	14 Dec 89
Chf Tech	Manzoor	81068	Radio Fitt	07 Mar 90
Chf Tech	Wadud	80313	Radio Fitt	31 May 90
Chf Tech	Rafique	444075	Gen Fitt	30 Aug 90
Chf Tech	Asghar	442765	Gen Fitt	22 Nov 90
Chf Tech	M. Shafi	442644	Eng Fitt	18 Feb 90
Wrt Off	Zafar	86911	Radar Fitt	16 May 91
Chf Tech	M. Javed	443724	Sect Asstt	22 Aug 91
Chf Tech	M. Ilyas	87390	Radio Fitt	14 Nov 91
Chf Tech	Rasul-ul-Rehman	87342	Radio Fitt	06 Feb 92
Chf Tech	Siddique	440410	Radar Fitt	30 Apr 92
Chf Tech	Iftikhar	440962	Elect Fitt	23 Jul 92
Chf Tech	Shafqat	451118	Radar Opt	22 Nov 92
Chf Tech	Jabbar	445801	Eng Fitt	07 Nov 93
Chf Tech	Akmal	440376	Inst Fitt	21 Mar 93
Chf Tech	Khurshid	447847	Eng Fitt	27 Jun 93
Chf Tech	Mahmood	490205	Sect Asstt	22 Sep 93
Chf Tech	Yousaf	442539	Supp Asst	22 Dec 93
Chf Tech	Akram	444172	Radar Fitt	02 Mar 94
Chf Tech	Khalid	441722	Armt Fitt	29 Jun 94
Chf Tech	A. Qadir	443826	Eng Fitt	14 Sep 94
Chf Tech	M. Khalid	490290	Sect Asstt	07 Dec 94
Chf Tech	Sahib Zaman	451147	Eng Fitt	22 Feb 95
Chf Tech	Afsar Shah	459360	Edu Inst	14 Jun 95
Chf Tech	M. Ayub	87346	Inst Fitt	05 Sep 95
Chf Tech	Sultan	481542	Edu Inst	29 Nov 95
Chf Tech	Mumtaz	447937	Supp Asstt	14 Feb 96
Chf Tech	M. Waris	446931	Afr Fitt	18 Jul 96
Chf Tech	Anwar	491326	Sect Asstt	03 Oct 96
Chf Tech	A. Sattar	465826	Flt Engg	24 Dec 96
Chf Tech	Nazar	89664	Radar Fitt	20 Mar 97
Chf Tech	Yar	459061	Radio Fitt	14 Jun 97
Chf Tech	Munawar	481963	Edu Inst	27 Dec 97
Chf Tech	Razzaq Ahmed	90658	Edu Inst	27 Dec 97
Chf Tech	Nasir Shah	491200	PF & DI	23 Apr 98
Chf Tech	Sanaullah	451527	Afr Fitt	17 Jul 98
Chf Tech	Muhammad Iqbal	462247	Eng Fitt	02 Sep 98
Chf Tech	Ali Ahmed	457175	Sect Asstt	24 Dec 98

APPENDIX 5

Achievements in Sports

Inter Services Golf Championships

1988	Silver Medal
1989	Gold Medal
1990	Silver Medal
	Silver Medal
1991	Gold Medal
1992	Gold Medal
1993	Gold Medal
1994	Silver Medal
1995	Silver Medal
1996	Gold Medal

Inter Base Golf Championships

1998	Gold Medal (Individual)

National / Provincial

1989	COAS Golf Championship, River view Golf Club Jhelum
1989	Habib Bank Golf Trophy, River view Golf Club Jhelum
1997	Rehmatullah Golf Championship, Golf Club, Karachi

Renowned Sportsmen of PAF

Athletics

Cpl Tech	Sarfraz	Service Colour Holder	1995

Football

Snr Tech	Muhammad Tahir	Pakistan Colour Holder	1992
Snr Tech	Muhammad Arshad	Pakistan Colour Holder	1995
Snr Tech	Ghias	Pakistan Colour Holder	1995
Cpl Tech	Shaheen	Pakistan Colour Holder	1995
Cpl Tech	Ibrarullah	Pakistan Colour Holder	1995
Snr Tech	Fazal	Service Colour Holder	1995

Basketball

Snr Tech	Akram	Pakistan Colour Holder	1992

Squash

WO	Omer Zaman	Pakistan Colour Holder	1992
WO	Fakhar Zaman	Pakistan Colour Holder	1992

Shooting

Snr Tech	Muhammad Asghar	Pakistan Colour Holder	1996

Sailing

Snr Tech	Ismail	Pakistan Colour Holder	1998

BIBLIOGRAPHICAL NOTE

Material for this book came from a variety of sources. Documents provided by the air force, interviews conducted with a large number of serving and retired officers, impressions gathered during visits to various formations and bases and a certain amount of library research, have all helped in writing of this book.

GLOSSARY OF TERMS

A&SD	Admin & Special Duties	AM	Air Marshal
A/C	Aircraft	AME	Alternate Mission Equipment
AAA	Anti Aircraft Artillery	AMF	Aircraft Manufacturing
AC	Aircraftman		Factory
ACAS	Assistant Chief of Air Staff	AMI	Aero Medical Institute
ACES	Assessment of Combat	AMSL	Above Mean Sea Level
	Efficiency of Squadrons	AOC	Air Officer Commanding
ADA	Air Defence Alert	ASR	Air Staff Requirement
ADC	Air Defence Command	ATC	Air Traffic Control
ADET	Air Defence Excellence	ATLIS	Automatic Tracking and
	Trophy		Laser Illumination System
ADEX	Air Defence Excellence	ATTS	Administrative Trade
	Competition		Training School
ADGE	Air Defence Ground	AVM	Air Vice Marshal
	Environment	AUO	Academy Under Officer
ADLA	After Dinner Literary	AVTR	Airborne Video Tape
	Activity		Recorder
ADOC	Air Defence Operation	AWACS	Airborne Warning and
	Centre		Control System
ADTS	Air Defence Training School	AWC	Air Weapon Complex/Air
ADWC	Air Defence Weapon		War College
	Controller	AWO	Assistant Warrant Officer
AED	Air Engineering Depot	BAI	Battlefield Air Interdiction
Aero Supp	Aero Support	BBC	British Broadcasting
Aero Tech	Aero Technician		Corporation
AFA	Assistant Financial Advisor	BCCP	Board of Control for Cricket
AFI	Air Force Instructions		in Pakistan
AFL	Air Force Letter	BCR	Beyond Country Repair
AFM	Air Force Manual	BDAF	Bangladesh Air Force
AFO	Air Force Order	BFT	Basic Flying Training
AFOHS	Air Force Officers Housing	BHQ	Base Headquarters
	Scheme	BSS	Basic Staff School
AGL	Above Ground Level	BVR	Beyond Visual Range
AHQ	Air Headquarters	C^3I	Command, Control,
AI & AS	Anti Infiltration and Anti		Communication and
	Sabotage		Intelligence
AI	Air Intercept/Air Intelligence	C^3 CM	Command, Control,
AIB	Accident Investigation Board		Communication Counter
ALC	Air Logistics Centre		Measures
ALD	Air Logistics Depot	CAA	Civil Aviation Authority
ALMS	Automated Logistics	CAC	Central Air Command
	Management System	CAD	Computer Aided Design

CADAM	Centre for Air Defence Automation Management	D of P	Director of Personnel
CADI	Chengdu Aircraft Design Institute	DACT	Dissimilar Air Combat Training
CAE	College of Aeronautical Engineering	DAIMS	Depot Automated Inventory Management System
CAO	Central Account Office	DCAS	Deputy Chief of Air Staff
CAP	Combat Air Patrol	DCC	Defence Committee of the Cabinet
CAS	Chief of the Air Staff	DCP	Director Civilian Personnel
CATIC	China Aero-Technology Import and Export Corporation	DDG	Deputy Director General
		DG	Director General
CBT	Computer Based Training	DGDP	Director General Defence Procurement
CCC	Combat Commander Course	DGMP	Director General Munitions Production
CCR	Constant Current Regulator		
CCS	Combat Commanders' School	DIAC	Defect Investigation and Analysis Cell
CEIEC	China Electronics Import and Export Corporation	DIT	Directorate of Information Technology
CETS	Contractor Engineering Technical Services	DLZ	Dynamic Launch Zone
		DMIS	Depot Management Information System
CFD	Chaff and Flare Dispensers	DP	Data Processing / Defence Production
CFOS	Contract Follow on Support		
CFT	College of Flying Training	DS	Directing Staff
CKD	Completely Knocked Down	ECG	Electro Cardiograph
CLO	Chief Liaison Officer	ECM	Electronic Counter Measures
CMB	Central Medical Board	EDM	Electronic Database Management
CNC	Computer Numerically Controlled		
COC	Command Operations Centre	EFM	Extended Field Maintenance
COE	College of Education	ELINT	Electronic Intelligence
COMINT	Communication Intelligence	ENT	Ear Nose Throat
COMO	Combat Oriented Maintenance Operations	ESM	Electronic Support Measures
		ETS	Engineering Technical Service
CPD	Chief Project Director		
Cpl Tech	Corporal Technician	EW	Electronic Warfare
CPRE	Cardio Pulmonary Resuscitating Equipment	F-6 RF	F-6 Rebuild Factory
		FA	Financial Advisor
CRC	Control and Reporting Centre	FBISE	Federal Board of Intermediate and Secondary Education
CTC	Computer Training Centre		
CTDU	Central Technical Development Unit		
		FC	Frontier Constabulary
CTO	Chief Technical Officer	FCF	Functional Check Flight
CTS	Computer Training School	FCU	Fighter Conversion Unit
CTTB	Central Trade Test Board	FEBA	Forward Edge of Battle Area

402

FLIR	Forward Looking Infrared Radar	ISSB	Inter Services Selection Board
FM	Frequency Modulation	IT	Information Technology / Instructional Techniques
FMS	Foreign Military Sales		
FMU	Field Maintenance Unit	ITC	Intensive Treatment & Care
FOB	Forward Operating Base	JC & SS	Junior Command & Staff School
FOD	Foreign Object Damage		
FSO	Flight Safety Officer	JCO	Junior Commissioned Officer
FTD	Field Training Detachment	JCSC	Joints Chiefs of Staff Committee
FWIC	Fighter Weapon Instructor Course		
		JEIM	Jet Engine Intermediate Maintenance
GC	Ground Combateer		
GCI	Ground Controlled Interception	JFS	Jet Fuel Starter
		KARF	Kamra Avionics and Radar Factory
GD (P)	General Duty (Pilot)		
GEC	General Electric Company	LAF	Lebanese Air Force
GOH	General Overhaul	LAN	Local Area Network
GPS	Global Positioning System	LC	Letter of Credit
GSE	Ground Support Equipment	LCA	Light Communication Aircraft
GSK	General Service Knowledge		
GSO	Ground Signals Operator	LEFRA	Leading Edge Flap Rotary Actuator
GST	General Service Training		
GTC	Gas Turbine Compressor	LGB	Laser Guided Bomb
HQ	Headquarters	LL	Low Level
HRL	Human Resource Laboratory	LLO	Local Liaison Officer
HS	Hand Shake	LLR	Low Looking Radar
HSSC	Higher Secondary School Certificate	LMTAS	Lockheed Martin Tactical Aircraft Systems
HUD	Heads Up Display	LOA	Letter of Offer and Acceptance
I & SC	Information & Selection Centre		
		LORAP	Long Range Aerial Photography
IAS	Institute of Air Safety		
IFF	Identification Friend or Foe	LRU	Line Replaceable Unit
IG	Inspector General	M Ed	Masters in Education
ILC	Increased Life Cycle	MDA	Maintenance Data Automation
ILS	Integrated Logistics Support / Instrument Landing System		
		Mirage III EA	Ex-Australian Mirage III aircraft
IMET	International Military Education Programme		
		MIS	Management Information System
IOD	Internal Object Damage		
IR	Infra Red	MOB	Main Operating Base
ISAC	Inter Squadron Armament Competition	MODC	Ministry of Defence Constabulary
ISF	International Ski Federation	MOST	Ministry of Science and Technology
ISS	Individual Study Scheme		

MoU	Memorandum of Understanding	OT	Operation Theatre
MOU	Mobile Observer Unit	OTI	One Time Inspection
MPDR	Mobile Pulse Doppler Radar	OWIP	Outer Wing Improvement Programme
MR	Multi Role	PAC	Pakistan Aeronautical Complex
MRAAM	Medium Range Air to Air Missile	PAF	Pakistan Air Force
MRF	Mirage Rebuild Factory	PAFROA	Pakistan Air Force Retired Officers Association
MTD	Mechanical Transport Driver	PAFWA	Pakistan Air force Women Association
MTM	Mechanical Transport Mechanic	PC	Permanent Commission / Personal Computer
MU	Maintenance Unit	PDM	Programme Depot Maintenance
MUCO	Material Control Utilization Office	PFT	Primary Flying Training
MVRDE	Motor Vehicle Research and Development Establishment	PIA	Pakistan International Airlines
MWS	Medical Welfare Scheme	PLUS	PAF Logistics Update System
NAC	Northern Air Command	PME	Precision Measuring Equipment
NAU	Navigation and Attack Unit		
NDFC	National Development Finance Corporation	PMEL	Precision Measuring Equipment Laboratory
NDI	Non Destructive Inspection	PMO	Project Management Officer
NI (M)	Nishan-i-Imtiaz (Military)	PNS	Pakistan Naval Ship
NORS	Not Operationally Ready-Supply	POR	Personnel Occurrence Report
NOK	Next of Kin	PSO	Principal Staff Officer/ Personal Staff Officer
NUST	National University of Sciences and Technology	PTCL	Pakistan Telecommunication Corporation Limited
O&M	Operation and Maintenance	PTTS	Primary Trade Training School
OC	Officer Commanding		
OCC	Operations Communication Centre	QA	Quality Assurance
OCU	Operational Capabilities Upgrade / Operational Conversion Unit	QAP	Quality Assurance Programme
		QC	Quality Control
OEMs	Original Equipment Manufacturers	QE	Qualifying Examination
OER	Officers Evaluation Report	QFI	Qualified Flying Instructor
OJT	On-the-Job Training	QHI	Qualified Helicopter Instructor
OLTP	On Line Transaction Processing	R&D	Research and Development
OPE	Officers Promotion Examination	RAAF	Royal Australian Air Force
ORI	Operations Readiness Inspection	RADEX	Radar Data Extractor
		RAF	Royal Air Force

404

RAHQ	Rear Air Headquarters	SOE	School of Electronics
RAM	Random Access Memory	SOI	School of Intelligence
REO	Radar Electro Optics	SOL	School of Logistics
Retd	Retired	SOS	Struck off Strength
RJAF	Royal Jordanian Air Force	SPSSC	Special Purposes Short
RJMA	Rehana Jamal Mujahida		Service Commission
	Academy	SRAAM	Short Range Air to Air
RMC	Radar Maintenance Centre		Missile
ROD	Report of Discrepancy	SRC	Self Reliance Cell
ROE	Rules of Engagement	SSG	Special Services Group
ROSE	Retrofit of Strike Element	STA	Surveillance, Targeting and
RRR	Rapid Runway Repair		Analysis
RSAF	Royal Saudi Air Force	STG	Special Task Group
RTA	Royal Thai Army	SUO	Squadron Under Officer
RTV	Refugee Tented Village	SWF	Shaheen Welfare Fund
RWR	Radar Warning Receiver	TA & R	Tactical Attack and
S&C	Standards and Calibration		Reconnaissance
S&R	Search and Rescue	TA	Tactical Attack
SAC	Southern Air Command /	TAF	Turkish Air Force
	Senior Aircraftman	TASC	Tactical Air Support Centre
SAI	Shaheen Air International	TCM	Teledyne Continental Motors
SAM	Surface to Air Missile	TCTO	Time Compliance Technical
SAPS	Shaheen Airport Services		Order
SASO	Senior Air Staff Officer	TD Box	Target Designator Box
SBP	Small Batch Production	TO	Technical Order
SBt	Sitara-i-Basalat	TOT	Time Over Target
SC & SS	Senior Command and Staff	ToT	Transfer of Technology
	School	TPC	Technical Publications
SCUP	Squadron Combat		Centre
	Upgradation Programme	TTS	Technical Trade Squadron
SED	Software Engineering Depot	UAE	United Arab Emirates
SILLACS	Siemens Low Level Air	UK	United Kingdom
	Control System	UR	Unsatisfactory Report
SKD	Semi Knocked Down	US	United States
SLAF	Sri Lankan Air Force	USAF	United States Air Force
SLEP	Structural Life Enhancement	USG	United States Government
	Programme	VCAS	Vice Chief of Air Staff
SNCO	Senior Non Commissioned	VIP	Very Important Person
	Officer	VP	Vulnerable Point
SOA	School of Aeronautics	WAN	Wide Area Network
SOC	Sector Operation Centre	WUO	Wing Under Officer
SOD	Struck off Duty		

INDEX